DISMAL SWAMP CANAL   South Mills
Currituck
Currituck C H
Indian Town
Camden C H
Shiloh

Gates
Gatesville
Camden

Granville
Person
Warren
Weldon
Winton
Hertford
Elizabeth City
Perquimans
ALBEMARLE & CHESAPEAKE CANAL
Pasquotank
Powells Pt
Ft Huger
Nags Head
Ft Forrest
Ballast Pt
Ft Bartow
Ashby Harbor
Ft Oregon

swell
Northampton
Halifax
Edward's Ferry
Bertie
Chowan
Edenton

Orange
Franklin
Nash
Edgecombe
Windsor
Hamilton
ALBEMARLE SOUND
Columbia

ance
Hillsboro
Durham
Bennett Farmhouse
Tarboro
Martin
Williamston
Plymouth
Washington
Tyrrell

Raleigh
Wake
Johnston
Wilson
Beaufort
Washington
Hyde
CHICAMACOMICO

Chatham
Smithfield
Wayne
Greene
Pitt
Hill's Point
PAMLICO R
Ft Hatteras
Ft Clark

ere
Harnett
Averasboro
Bentonville
Everittsville
Dudley
Goldsboro
Kinston
Whitehall
Craven
Batchelder's Creek
Ft Anderson
New Bern
Ft Thompson
PAMLICO SOUND
Ft Ocracoke
Portsmouth

Monroe's Cross Roads
Fayetteville
Cumberland
Lenoir
Trenton
Deep Gully
Havelock

iam
Sampson
Duplin
Magnolia
Jones
Pollocksville
Onslow
Jacksonville
Carolina City
Beaufort

Robeson
Bladen
Lumberton
New Hanover
Morehead City
Ft Macon
Swansboro

Columbus
Brunswick
Ft Anderson
Old Brunswick
Smithville
Ft Johnston
Sugar Loaf
Ft Fisher
SMITH'S ISLAND
Ft Campbell
Ft Caswell
Ft Holmes
Wilmington

ROANOKE R
CASHIE R
ALIGATOR R
TAR R
NEUSE R
ATLANTIC
NEUSE R
NEW R
GASTON &
RALEIGH
WELDON
N C
WILMINGTON
CAPE FEAR R
N E CAPE FEAR R
RUTHERFORD

NORTH CAROLINA 1861–1865

*************************** Kirk's Raid on Morganton
◄◄◄◄◄◄◄◄◄◄◄◄ Stoneman's Raid
● ● ● ● ● ● ● ● ● Sherman's March
××××××××××××××× Wild's Raid
– · – · – · – · – · Foster's Raid on Tarboro
————————— Foster's Raid on Goldsboro

NORTH CAROLINA CIVIL WAR DOCUMENTARY

NORTH CAROLINA
CIVIL WAR
DOCUMENTARY

EDITED BY W. BUCK YEARNS AND JOHN G. BARRETT

The University of North Carolina Press Chapel Hill

© 1980 The University of North Carolina Press

All rights reserved

Manufactured in the United States of America

ISBN 0-8078-1407-5

Library of Congress Catalog Card Number 79-17604

Library of Congress Cataloging in Publication Data
Main entry under title:

North Carolina Civil War documentary.

Bibliography: p.
Includes index.
1. North Carolina—History—Civil War, 1861–1865—
Sources. I. Yearns, Wilfred Buck, 1918–   II. Bar-
rett, John Gilchrist, 1921–
E573.9.N67   973.7'09756   79-17604
ISBN 0-8078-1407-5

Dedicated to the Memory of

Fletcher Green

CONTENTS

ILLUSTRATIONS

PREFACE

In 1860 Union sentiment was still strong in North Carolina. Despite the sectional crisis then approaching, a majority of her people was opposed to secession. The Fort Sumter confrontation of April 1861, however, changed this picture drastically. When President Lincoln called on North Carolina to furnish two militia regiments to help restore order in the South, Governor John W. Ellis, a strong secessionist, replied immediately that the state would furnish no troops for a "war upon the liberties of a free people."[1]

Most North Carolinians looked upon Lincoln's move as an attempt at coercion. Even staunch Unionists now became reconciled to secession and conflict. The state prepared for war. Governor Ellis ordered the seizure of Forts Caswell, Macon, and Johnston along with the United States Arsenal at Fayetteville and the Branch Mint at Charlotte. He then hurried the General Assembly into special session, and it wasted little time in setting the date for a convention to meet in Raleigh. On 20 May the convention unanimously adopted an ordinance of secession. According to a local newspaper "the good old North State" left the Union "amid the ringing of bells and the booming [of] cannon mingled with the deafening shouts of thousands of loyal voices."[2] Meanwhile the General Assembly was organizing the state for war.

Though North Carolina's interior position in the Confederacy made her only a secondary battlefield, it was not unimportant in the grand strategy of the war. Occupation of the state's coastal region would pose a constant threat to the Confederate communication lines running south from Richmond, while the state itself was an important source of supply for the Army of Northern Virginia. Attacks along the coast, therefore, were not long in coming.

As early as 29 August a Union squadron captured Hatteras, and attacks along the coast continued unrelentingly. By the summer of 1862

1. John W. Ellis to Simon Cameron, 15 Apr. 1861, Noble J. Tolbert, ed., *The Papers of John Willis Ellis*, 2:612.
2. Raleigh *State Journal*, 22 May 1861.

Roanoke Island, New Bern, and much of the coastal region of the state were under Federal control. In the eyes of most North Carolinians they were sacrificed by the Confederate high command for the defense of Virginia. Residents of the occupied region pressed officials in Raleigh for relief, and both Governors Clark and Vance maintained a vigorous correspondence with Richmond, demanding that more troops be committed to eastern North Carolina. But when Lee and Davis released units for duty in the state, which was seldom, the results were usually far from satisfactory. In 1863 General D. H. Hill was sent from Virginia and the next year George Pickett was detached by Lee for duty in North Carolina. Both officers, however, failed to capture New Bern, their primary objective, and returned to the Army of Northern Virginia. General Robert F. Hoke, Pickett's able subordinate, did manage in May 1864 to capture Plymouth, but by autumn the sound region was once again firmly under Union control.

Although North Carolina had left the Union reluctantly—the last state to secede—and had suffered relatively few of the pains of invasion, her contributions to the Confederacy were tremendous, especially in manpower and war supplies. Actually her distance from the major battle lines was a mixed blessing, for Confederate laws could best be applied when no distracting enemy forces were nearby. And the civilian population, which was subjected to increasingly severe demands upon its resources by the Confederate government, did not have the threat of imminent invasion to make sacrifice more palatable.

North Carolina's chief contribution to the Confederacy was in manpower. One hundred twenty-five thousand North Carolina troops served the South. With one-ninth of the population of the Confederacy, North Carolina still furnished between one-sixth and one-seventh of all Confederate soldiers. In fact, early in the war the state's youth volunteered in such large numbers that they could not be properly equipped. Arms, ammunition, and uniforms were all very scarce at the time.

North Carolina was the only southern state to monopolize the entire output of its textile factories throughout the war, a policy most disturbing to the Confederate quartermaster general. Forced to strain itself to the limits, the state even turned to bringing in supplies through the blockade at Wilmington. It has been estimated that cargoes valued in excess of $65 million in gold were brought into this port city alone during the war, much of it on order from the North Carolina government. In the fall of 1862 Governor Vance put the state into the important and highly profitable business of blockade-running. He authorized, with legislative approval, the purchase of a blockade-runner in England. Soon North Carolina owned the *Advance* and had part interest in three other vessels.

In the process of raising and equipping troops for the Confederacy, state officials encountered serious problems with Richmond. Vance in particular attempted to monitor every Confederate policy that might infringe on the rights of the state or its citizens. He criticized President Davis for discriminating against North Carolina in civil and military appointments. He complained about outsiders, Virginians in particular, being appointed to nonmilitary posts in the state. He was disturbed further by the outrageous conduct of certain Confederate forces operating in North Carolina, threatening on one occasion "to call out the militia and shoot the first man who attempts to perpetrate a similar outrage."[3] Also, Vance was angered by the arbitrary arrest of local citizens suspected of being disloyal. They were usually imprisoned without being charged and later released without trial. He declared it was his duty to protect the rights of his people to a fair hearing and to maintain civil law. Then in the spring of 1863 Richmond, much to the governor's displeasure, began to ignore adverse decisions of state judges. Vance made it clear to the secretary of war that he could not allow the substitution of martial law for civil law.

The proper enforcement of the legal process was but one way in which Governor Vance attempted to maintain the sovereignty of his state while still supporting the southern cause. Throughout his administration he insisted upon the right to exempt from military service all persons whom he considered to be "necessary to the operation of this government."[4] He even feared that the Danville connection, the most significant improvement to be made in the entire Confederate railroad system during the war, would be injurious to North Carolina's best interests. Governor Vance strongly objected to the Confederate policy instituted late in the war of commandeering cargo space on blockade-runners, including those partially owned by the state. The port of Wilmington, he declared, "is now more effectively blockaded from within than from without."[5] The universally unpopular Confederate impressment policy also drew the governor's ire. He denounced in no uncertain terms the illegal seizures of produce in those areas where food was already scarce. Furthermore, he was fully aware that impressment fell heaviest upon those who could least cope with it—the poor, the rural yeoman families of the state.

Vance, hand in hand with the General Assembly, worked hard to relieve the economic distress of the people burdened by shortages, unabated inflation, and rising tax levies. In an effort to increase the supply of food, a law was passed prohibiting the distillation of grain and other products into whiskey. In addition, more state saltworks were established on the coast and bushels of this scarce commodity were distributed among the people at a reduced price. Also, early in his administration Governor Vance used the embargo to strike at what he considered to be the primary cause of suffering—"the activities of speculators who bought supplies of food and held them for a rise in prices."[6] Although the embargo failed to stop speculation, the governor was still able to provide the people with some of the necessities of life. With money ap-

3. Z. B. Vance to J. A. Seddon, 21 Mar. 1863, Governors' Papers, North Carolina State Archives, Raleigh.
4. Clement Dowd, *Life of Zebulon B. Vance*, 80.
5. Richard E. Yates, *The Confederacy and Zeb Vance*, 80.
6. Richard E. Yates, "Zebulon B. Vance as War Governor of North Carolina, 1862–1865," 66.

propriated by the legislature, provisions were purchased and made available at low prices to the families of soldiers and the poor. Additional money was also made available for direct relief.

Institutions as well as individuals were hard hit by the war. Church and school both suffered, but fortunately, in Calvin H. Wiley, North Carolina had a superintendent of public instruction who would fight hard to keep school doors open. Also on the home front, new laws were passed to control the Negro labor force. In February 1865, the General Assembly expressed opposition to proposals that slaves be armed by the Confederate government but gave its consent to their being used as laborers in public service. Early in the war, however, slaves in large numbers had begun to slip away to the safety of Union lines, and in 1863 Federal authorities announced plans for the establishment of a fugitive slave colony on Roanoke Island.

While Federal authorities were making preparations to settle Negroes on Roanoke Island's unoccupied lands, the peace movement in North Carolina took on serious proportions. Early in the war there had been murmurings of discontent. In the fall of 1861 Unionists, meeting on Hatteras Island, selected Marble Nash Taylor as provisional governor of the state, but the whole movement was so fraudulent that it soon died. Then in May 1862, Lincoln appointed Edward Stanly military governor of the state with New Bern as his capital. Stanly resigned, however, in January 1863, following a bitter attack on the president's Emancipation Proclamation. Adding to the burdens of the eastern Carolinians were the activities of armed bands of Negroes and native Union bushwackers, known as Buffaloes, who terrorized the area. In western North Carolina the situation was equally unsettled. Those at home found it difficult to protect themselves against Tories (native Unionists), east Tennessee raiders, and bands of deserters who gathered in the area to plunder, murder, and rob.

By the summer of 1863 disaffection throughout North Carolina had become a matter of grave concern for state authorities. W. W. Holden, editor of the *Raleigh Standard*, emerged as the leader of the discontented. He ran for governor the next year on a peace platform but was soundly defeated by Vance whose great qualities of leadership and deep concern for the poor had made him very popular with the majority of the people. Their votes and affection made it easier for him to defeat the peace movement of 1864 and keep North Carolina in the Confederacy at a time when many people were disgruntled and tired of conflict.

By the end of 1864 much of the South east of the Mississippi had been recaptured, and the United States could now focus on North Carolina and Virginia. Lee's ability to stay in the field depended heavily upon the success of blockade-running out of Wilmington, now one of the most important cities in the Confederacy. After a fierce three-day attack by a Union fleet under Admiral David Porter, Fort Fisher, which guarded the mouth of the Cape Fear, capitulated on 15 January 1865. On 22 February Union troops marched into Wilmington. The next month Union General George F. Stoneman left Tennessee with 6,000 cavalrymen and raided into western North Carolina. By 12 April they were in Salisbury, and the productive Piedmont counties were lost. General Sherman, having ravaged South Carolina, entered the state in March at the head of a veteran army of 60,000. With little more to offer than proclamations and speeches of encouragement, Governor Vance tried to rally his despondent people. But Sherman defeated Johnston at Bentonville, 19–21 March, occupied Goldsboro, and then put his army in motion for Raleigh in pursuit of Johnston. The two generals eventually met at the James Bennett farmhouse near Durham where on 26 April Sherman granted and Johnston accepted terms similar to those Lee had received at Appomattox. The war was now over in North Carolina. All that remained was the stacking of arms at Greensboro.

North Carolina paid a terrible price for casting her lot with the Confederacy. During four years of conflict 19,673 North Carolinians were killed in battle and 20,602 died from other causes. The total loss of 40,275 was greater than that of any other southern state. Thousands of young men were also crippled for life, and on the home front countless numbers died from disease due to a scarcity of food, clothing, and medicine. Moreover, the economic resources of the state were destroyed. Not only did Confederate and local securities become worthless but also the countryside was laid waste by the Federal armies which invaded the state from the north, the south, the east, and the west, and by sea as well as land. In addition, millions of dollars worth of property was carried off by the enemy. In many respects, though, the disruptive and shocking social revolution brought to North Carolina and the South by the war was more difficult to accept than losses in property and lives. Military defeat brought with it the end of slavery and the destruction of the antebellum plantation system.

In this volume we have tried to present a well-rounded documentary history with emphasis upon the social, economic, and political aspects of Civil War North Carolina. Less than one-third of the material deals with military events which have already received disproportionate attention from writers. We hope in particular that a documentary volume will present a viewpoint of life behind the front lines that expository writing could never achieve. Certainly the suffering and worries of those at home compared with those at the front, and the toll on their morale was probably worse.

The selection of documents was based on their historical content, not literary quality. Only secondary materials were ruled out. A document which had been previously published was chosen if it expressed the particular point we were trying to make. We selected materials from as wide a variety of sources as possible: official records of the Union and Confederate armies and navies, diaries, correspondence, pamphlets, government documents, newspapers, magazines, governors' papers, manuscript collections, and local and general histories. All the materials have been reproduced from the sources without change, though most of the longer documents have parts which have been deleted.

With one significant exception—slave accounts—the choice of materials was broad. Our problem was more one of selection and deletion than search and inclusion. We have purposely omitted a special grouping on women because so many of the documents selected are either by women or deal with their roles in the war. Documents representing the experiences, attitudes, and opinions of the slaves and free Negroes were scarce. In view of the legal penalty imposed for teaching slaves to read and write, it should come as no surprise that relatively few North Carolina blacks wrote letters or kept journals. Indeed, this was probably our single most frustrating search. For, while specialists in black history assured us that there must be manuscript collections somewhere, their precise location has escaped us.

In an effort to provide the reader with a brief narrative account of the war, as well as a documentary history, and to facilitate the use of the material, each of the twenty chapters has a general introduction. Also each chapter subtopic is introduced by a statement intended to give the reader a better understanding of the material that follows. The Notes and Bibliography, we hope, will add to the utility of the volume.

ACKNOWLEDGMENTS

We are heavily indebted to others for help in the preparation of this volume. The staffs of Wake Forest University and the Preston Library of Virginia Military Institute gave us their full cooperation; and Mrs. Norris T. Aldridge and Mrs. Linda Allen, our departmental secretaries, graciously worked much of our typing into their regular duties. The Virginia Military Institute and Wake Forest University provided us with summer grants for our research. We would also like to give special recognition to the many fine research facilities and their staffs over the state, for their careful preservation of documents made our research most rewarding. Last, but never least, we must thank our modern wives, Lute and Marguerite, for patiently supporting through the years their husbands' consuming interest in the American Civil War.

John G. Barrett / W. Buck Yearns

NORTH CAROLINA CIVIL WAR DOCUMENTARY

I

A TIME FOR DECISION

The election on 5 November 1860 of "Black Republican" Abraham Lincoln to the presidency of the United States sent a shock wave through the states of the Lower South. By 4 February 1861 seven cotton states stretching from South Carolina through Texas had held conventions, seceded, and met in Montgomery, Alabama, to form a southern confederacy. To them their entire way of life was so threatened that the only recourse was refuge in a truly southern nation.

Geographic factors had steered the South into farming, and it was not long before slavery had become its chief source of labor. By the early 1800s southerners were arguing that not only their economy but also most of their basic institutions—the church, the family, government, and society—depended on the use and control of Negro slaves. In the minds of southerners developments in the North posed serious threats to southern civilization. The North's diversified economy demanded national programs—a protective tariff, a national bank, a sound currency, federal appropriations for internal improvements, free western land, and others—which would help few southerners and which would actually distress many of them. Southerners also felt threatened by the antislavery sentiment in the North, which added emotional and moral dimensions to the sectional differences. As the South saw itself becoming a minority section, its leaders sought refuge in the doctrine of state rights, the conviction that each state had retained its sovereignty when it entered the Union and therefore had the final decision on constitutional matters.

The acquisition of new territory as a result of the war with Mexico provoked the most heated sectional issue, whether Congress could ban slavery from a territory. The question was temporarily compromised by Congress in 1850, but the Kansas–Nebraska Act of 1854 revived it. This act established two territories of the remaining Louisiana Purchase and allowed the settlers of each to decide whether their territory would be slave or free. For the first time since the drawing of the Missouri Compromise Line in 1820 southerners had an opportunity to extend slavery above that line. "Bleeding Kansas" resulted, during which both northern and southern radicals struggled ruthlessly to control the first territorial government. The Dred Scott decision by the Supreme Court in 1857 supported the South's position that Congress could not ban slavery from any territory; but William H. Seward's "higher law" theory, annunciated in the Senate as early as 11 March 1850, enabled radical northerners to scorn the decision. In 1859 John Brown attempted to seize the guns from Harper's Ferry with the intention of establishing a Negro republic in the southern Appalachian mountains. Brown was captured and executed, but Horace Greeley's statement that "the noblest manhood in America swings off the gallow of a felon"[1] convinced southerners that Brown and Greeley represented the true northern spirit. Of continuing concern to the South was the organization and rapid growth of the Republican party with a legislative program catering to the North, with a pledge to bar slavery from the territories, and with implicit threats to slavery even where it already existed. The northern states already had a majority in both houses of Congress, and cotton state radicals promised that their states would secede if the Republicans ever won the presidency.

In the election of 1860 the Republicans nominated Abraham Lincoln of Illinois and promised a protective tariff, internal improvements, and the prohibition of slavery in the territories. Southerners divided themselves into three camps. Some Democrats supported Stephen A. Douglas of Illinois whose platform would leave the decision of slavery to the people of each territory. Democrats opposing such a compromise favored John C. Breckinridge of Kentucky, who maintained that neither Congress nor a territory could impair the right of slave property in a territory and that Congress must protect slavery in a territory until it became a state. Most of the former Whigs of the South supported John Bell of Tennessee, who uncontroversially simply endorsed the Constitution, the Union, and the laws. Bell carried Tennessee, Kentucky, and Virginia, while Douglas won Missouri; but all the other slave states went for Breckinridge. Lincoln, however, won 180 of the 303 electoral votes and would become president on 4 March 1861.

While cotton state "fire-eaters" had approached the election of 1860 vowing to take their states out of the Union if Lincoln became president, Upper South leaders viewed it less despairingly. The great majority of them still cherished the Union and maintained that Lincoln's election would not necessarily end all hope of an acceptable solution to the sectional difficulties. North Carolina's soil was not well suited for cotton culture, and there were relatively few large planters who felt that a Republican administration in Washington would be absolutely inimical to their best interests. In the western mountain districts and in the eastern swamp areas lived many nonslaveholders who had little vested interest in the slavery controversy. And in the central regions the Quaker and small farmer elements felt only slightly more involved. So even though Lincoln's election created dismay and concern in North Carolina, there was at first little talk of secession. While there were some who urged im-

1. Quoted in Laurence T. Lowrey, *Northern Opinion of Approaching Secession,* p. 213.

mediate secession, the great majority preferred to await some overtly antisouthern action by the incoming administration before making that fateful decision.

Events during the winter of 1860–61, however, encouraged the North Carolina secessionist minority. The states of the Lower South were seceding peaceably with the acknowledged intent of regrouping into a southern nation. Meanwhile in Congress effort after effort to reach a compromise failed, and northern radicals were seemingly determined to reject any sectional compromise. Finally in January 1861, under secessionist Governor John Ellis, the General Assembly called for a referendum on 28 February in which the people were to vote for or against a convention to consider secession and to elect delegates to this convention. In an exciting four-week campaign the convention call was rejected by a vote of 47,323 to 46,672.

---

(1) The Secessionist Argument

In November 1860 only a small minority of North Carolinians saw Lincoln's election as so dire a threat to their well-being that secession was their only logical action. This element was strongest in the eastern counties with a large slave population and most, but not all, of them had supported John C. Breckinridge in the election of 1860. Their chief newspapers were the Raleigh State Journal *and the Wilmington* Journal, *and some of their spokesmen were Congressman Thomas L. Clingman of Buncombe County, businessman Robert R. Bridgers of Edgecombe, planter Weldon N. Edwards of Warren, and attorney*

William W. Avery of Burke. Despite their small numbers, the immediate secessionists were active and well organized when the legislature met. On 20 November Governor John Ellis, a Democrat of Rowan County who had entered office with the support of the slavery and gentry interests, delivered to it a message which followed closely the ideas of the secessionists. While he did not request immediate secession, implicit in his call for a convention was the assumption that this was the necessary first step. The need for military preparedness was about the only one of his suggestions which received general approval.

MESSAGE TO THE GENERAL ASSEMBLY
OF NORTH CAROLINA

. . . The Republic has at last fallen upon those evils against which the Father of the Country so solemnly warned us in his parting advice— it is distinctly and widely divided by "parties founded upon geographical discrimination."

The great body of the people of the northern and southern states entertain diametrically opposite opinions upon the subject of African Slav-

ery: the former, that it is a social and political evil and a sin; the latter
that it is a system of labor eminently well adapted to our climate and
soil; right and proper within itself, and that so far from being a sin, its
establishment among us is one of the providences of God for civilizing
and christianizing that benighted race.

Were these sentiments entertained as abstract opinions merely, they
would occasion but little disturbance to the government. It is far otherwise, however. This sentiment, with the people of the north, has assumed
the form of a bold and aggressive fanaticism, that seeks the annihilation
of slavery. . . .

Impelled by this spirit, the people of the northern States have violated
our rights to an extent that would scarcely have been borne by any other
people on earth. They have deprived us of our property, through lawless
mobs, acting under the sanction of a high public opinion, and often too,
with the connivance of their constituted authorities. Organized societies
with them, have sent emmissaries among us to incite slaves to insurrection and to bloodshed. Inflammatory publications, counselling slaves to
rise against their masters, have been systematically circulated throughout the south by the dominant party of the north, sanctioned and endorsed by its most influential leaders. The Legislatures of a large majority of the non-slaveholding states have by solemn enactments, openly
and shamelessly annulled a provision of the Constitution of the United
States for the rendition of fugitive slaves, and have legislated directly
and pointedly, with the view to prevent the owner from recovering such
property.

Courts of justice among them have upon more than one occasion totally disregarded a law of Congress, enacted to secure our rights of property, and delivered over fugitive slaves to attendant mobs with a knowledge of their purpose to prevent their reclamation by force. . . .

The forbearance with which the South has borne these indignities and
wrongs, has utterly failed to secure a corresponding forbearance upon
the part of our aggressors. The spirit of fanaticism by which they are
influenced . . . has at last so far united the northern masses as to enable them to seize upon the general government with all its power of
purse and sword. Two persons have been elected, respectively, to the
offices of President and Vice-President, exclusively by the people of one
section of the country, upon a principle hostile to the institutions and
domestic policy of the other.—Neither of them received an electoral vote
in all the fifteen Southern States, and neither could have uttered, in
many of them, the political sentiments upon which they are elevated to
power, without subjecting himself to the penalties of the local criminal
laws. A clearer case of foreign domination as to us could not well be
presented; and that it will be a hostile domination, past occurrences and
the circumstances under which they have been elected, forbid us to
doubt. . . .

It cannot for a moment be supposed, that we could submit to have the
policy of the abolition party, upon which their candidate for the Presidency has been elected, carried out in his administration, as it would
result in the destruction of our property and placing the lives of our peo-

ple in daily peril; and even though this should not be immediately attempted, yet, an effort to employ the military power of the General Government against one of the Southern States, would present an emergency demanding prompt and decided action on our part. It can but be manifest that a blow thus aimed at one of the Southern States would involve the whole country in a civil war, the destructive consequences of which to us, could only be controlled by our ability to resist those engaged in waging it.

The civilization of the age, surely, ought to be a sufficient guarantee for the prevention of so great a calamity as intestine war. . . . But should the incoming administration be guilty of the folly and the wickedness of drawing the sword against any Southern State, whose people may choose to seek that protection out of the Federal Union which is denied to them in it, then we of North Carolina would owe it to ourselves—to the liberties we have inherited from our fathers—to the peace of our homes and families, dearer to us than all governments, to resist it to the last extremity. . . .

I therefore respectfully recommend that you invite the Southern States to a conference, or such of them as may be inclined to enter into consultation with us, upon the present condition of the country. Should such a conference be found impracticable, then I would recommend the sending of one or more delegates to our neighboring States with the view of securing concert of action.

I also think, that the public safety requires a recurrence to our own people for an expression of their opinion. The will of the people once expressed, will be a law of action with all, and secure that unanimity so necessary in an emergency like the present.

I therefore recommend that a convention of the people of the State be called, to assemble immediately after the proposed consultation with other Southern States shall have terminated.

The subject of our military defences will require your early attention. I would rcommend a thorough reorganization of the militia and the enrollment of all persons between the ages of 18 and 45 years. With such a regulation, our muster roll would contain nearly a hundred and ten thousand men.

I would also recommend the formation of a corps of ten thousand volunteers, with an organization separate from the main body of the militia, and that they be suitably armed and equipped. . . .

Noble J. Tolbert, ed., *The Papers of John Willis Ellis*, 2:510–15.

---

(2) "Watch and Wait" Conservatism

Despite the warnings of the secessionists, the great majority of   *North Carolinians did not see Lincoln's election as a cause for im-*

mediate secession. For the most part Lincoln's victory triggered great concern but little panic. The Old Whigs were roughly divided between unconditional Unionists and "watch and wait" conservatives. The latter argued that Lincoln would be powerless before a Democratic Congress and that secession would lead to a long and dreadful war. A large part of the Democracy held much the same viewpoints. These men—conservative state rights Democrats—naturally expressed more concern than did the Old Whigs, but they still did not despair of the Union. Among these temporizing Whig and conservative Democrats were Senator Thomas Bragg of North-

ampton County, Congressman Lawrence O. Branch of Wake, politician Bedford Brown of Caswell, and attorney William N. H. Smith of Bertie.

The chief spokesman of moderation was William W. Holden, editor of the Raleigh North Carolina Standard. Holden had wavered on secession for a decade, but now argued "watch and wait" and denounced Governor Ellis's message to the legislature as "tending to disunion without good cause. . . ."[2] Like other conditional Unionists, however, he refused to reject secession as the ultimate right of each state when intolerably abused. The following editorial depicts this position.

DISUNION FOR EXISTING CAUSES

A Confederacy or Union composed of the fifteen slaveholding States would, after a while, encounter some of the same difficulties which now beset the existing Union. The States south of us would produce and export cotton, while the middle or bread-stuff States would become deeply interested in manufactures. Foreigners from Europe and the North would pour into the latter, and push the slave population farther south. Manufacturers would demand and obtain protection, and free labor would contend with and root out slave labor in the middle States, until at length the latter would commence to agitate against the cotton States as the North is now agitating against us. . . .

The two Confederacies . . . would meet as rivals at foreign courts and in foreign markets. Their ministers and merchants would partake of the spirit of the people at home, and they would cripple each other and involve themselves in endless and most injurious complications in their intercourse with foreign powers.—These foreign powers . . . would insinuate themselves into the very heart of our system . . . and the end would be *foreign influence* in all our councils, foreign manners in all our social walks, and *foreign gold* in the hands of unscrupulous demagogues as the price of some portion of their country's liberties.

In case of separation party spirit . . . would rage with tenfold heat. There would be parties in each Confederacy against each; there would be parties opposed to and in favor of foreign influence; there would be parties advocating dictatorial powers in the central governments and

2. Raleigh *North Carolina Standard*, 28 Nov. 1860.

parties advocating the largest liberty or least restraint; there would be parties advocating and parties opposing the acquisition of more territory; there would be parties siding with the great body of people, and parties endeavoring to grasp exclusive privileges for the few at the expense of the many. In the midst of all this war would most probably be waged along the lines of the two Confederacies—war interrupted only by hollow truces, or by compromises made but never intended to be observed, or by mediations at the hands of foreign powers. Of course as the result of all this industry would languish, trade would be obstructed, education would be neglected, internal improvements of all kinds would be arrested, and the morals of society would be injured. War would raise up standing armies, which would obstruct civil rule and eat out the substance of the people. . . . The result would be *military despotism*. . . . *Constitutional* liberty would no longer be the birthright of our people, but instead thereof we would have discretionary powers, martial law, military rule, oppressive taxation, perpetual contentions, and civil and servile war.

Such are some of the evils which would most probably result from disunion for existing causes. Disunion at this time will certainly occasion war. If a peaceful separation in the last resort could be effected, the two Confederacies, or any number of Confederacies *might* tread their respective paths without engaging in mortal conflict. They *might* at length re-unite in a new union on foundations more lasting than the present; but if any one State shall secede, with the expectation of drawing other States after her, and if blood shall be shed, the beginning, the middle, and the end will be civil war. The States thus forced out, though they will sympathize with the State which committed them to disunion against their will, and though they may stand by her and defend her in her extremity, yet they will dislike her and watch her as an evil star in the new constellation. A violent separation would, therefore, sow the seeds of discord in the new Confederacy. It would commence its career with growing antagonisms in its members. It would be a *forced* union which time would dissolve or passion fret to pieces.

There is only one evil greater than disunion, and that is the loss of honor and Constitutional right. *That evil the people of the South will never submit to.* Sooner than submit to it they would put their shoulders to the pillars, as Samson did, and tear down the temple, though they themselves should perish in the ruins. But our honor as a people is still untarnished—our Constitutional rights, so far as the federal government is concerned, are still untouched. If the federal government should *attempt* even to tarnish the one or to deprive us of the other, we for one would be ready to resist, and ready to dissolve the Union without regard to consequences. *But not now!*—the non-slaveholder says *not now!*—the slaveholder, whose property civil war would involve in imminent peril, says *not now!*—millions of our friends in the free States say *not now!* If we *must* dissolve the Union, let us do it as one people, and not by a bare majority. Let us wait until the people of the State are more united on the subject than they are now. Depend upon it our people are not submissionists. If their rights should be assailed they will defend them. But if they should not be assailed, and if we *can* preserve the government with safety and honor, to ourselves, in the name of all that is sacred let us do so.

Raleigh *North Carolina Standard*, 5 Dec. 1860.

---

(3) Unionism

North Carolinians who considered themselves true Unionists differed from "watch and wait" conservatives chiefly in rhetoric, for only in the far western counties was there an appreciable sentiment that opposed disunion under any provocation. The other Unionists argued that the nation was indissoluble and secession unconstitutional, but they had no intention of submitting meekly to abuses by the incoming Republican party. If necessary they would agree to take the state from the Union by exercising the thoroughly recognized right of revolution. They believed, however, that the entire secession movement was being fomented by self-seeking politicians who had little support from the people. Former Governor William A. Graham of Orange County, who denied the right of secession and rejected the necessity of revolution, wondered "who can prepare a declaration of independence, appealing to a candid world for its approbation and sympathy, upon the ground that we have been outvoted in an election. . . ."[3] The Unionists' chief concession to the sectional troubles was their advocacy of a convention of all the states, not one of just the slave states as advocated by the more radical elements. The stronghold of Unionism was in the Piedmont section. Most of them were former Whigs, and some of their leaders were Graham, attorney Dennis D. Ferebee of Guilford, businessman John M. Morehead of Guilford, and attorney Josiah Turner, Jr., of Orange. Generally the Unionists worked with other conservatives to stem the headlong rush of the secessionists. In answer to Governor Ellis's message to the legislature, on 22 November, D. D. Ferebee annunciated the extreme Unionist position.

Mr. Ferebee introduced the following resolutions, viz:

1. *Resolved*, That the Constitution of the United States is not a league, confederacy or compact between the people of the several States in their sovereign capacities, but a government proper, founded on the adoption of the people, and creating direct relations between itself and individuals.

2. *Resolved*, That no State authority has power to dissolve these rela-

3. Ibid., 14 Nov. 1860.

tions, that nothing can dissolve them but revolution; and that, consequently, there can be no such thing as secession without revolution.

3. *Resolved*, That it is the duty of the State of North Carolina, under all circumstances, and at all hazards, to protect, maintain and defend, *in the Union*, all the rights guaranteed to her citizens by the Constitution of the United States.

4. *Resolved*, That the election of Abraham Lincoln and Hannibal Hamlin to the Presidency and Vice-Presidency of the United States, by a sectional vote, however much to be deplored, is not a sufficient cause for a dissolution of the Union.

And moved that the same be laid upon the table printed and referred to the Committee on Federal Relations, and the question being thereon and a division called for, there appeared fifty-four votes in the affirmative, and fifty-eight in the negative, so the motion was lost. . . .

Journal of the House of Commons of North Carolina, 1860–61, p. 47.

---

(4) The Secessionists Take the Initiative

From Governor Ellis's address until the Christmas recess on 22 December the legislature did little but debate fruitlessly the questions of secession and whether to call a state convention. Outside, the radicals, with the more positive program, took the initiative. The governor directed their campaign and saw that secessionists spoke frequently and published letters in every newspaper that would carry them. They argued that Republican rule would end slavery and thereby destroy the best features of southern civilization, and that the state must choose between remaining with the North or going with the Lower South. The best proof that this campaign was succeeding was the growing number of secession meetings, which adopted resolutions demanding either immediate secession or at least secession unless the North would give adequate guarantees to the South. At this time Congressman Lawrence O'Bryan Branch of Enfield was a strong state rights Democrat, but he was not yet convinced that secession was necessary. Meanwhile he watched developments at home closely while he was in Congress. This letter from one of his good friends describes something of the campaigning waged by both Unionists and secessionists in Raleigh and reveals the genuine quandary of a well-intentioned North Carolinian.

Raleigh Decr. 2—60

Dear Branch

Political affairs are growing more & more complicated *daily*. On Friday evening after you left, I was informed, when on my way to the post-office that Hons. Boyce & Ashmore[4] would speak that night. I went to Yarborough's [Hotel] and was soon informed that *threats* of personal violence or *insults* at least would be offered to them; and I was consulted to know if I thought such madness possible. I could not entirely suppress the fears I entertained that such might be the case, and therefore I hoped (as no previous consultation had been held; and no regular plan for the speaking formed) that their friends would not urge them to speak. I remembered that every attempt since the Charleston Convention to hold any sort of meeting in this place (looking to the *equal* protection of the South,) had been treated with indignity. The Hall of Commons had been withheld, for the reason no doubt that a formal meeting held, to be addressed by S. Car[olinian]s at this juncture, in the Capitol might operate to the prejudice of the members with their constituents. The Court House could not be got, the keepers being absent with the key. Finally it was concluded to ask Yarborough for the use of his bar room (so to speak) which was granted. Soon after which Mr. B. was introduced by [illegible]. His address was moderate, complimentary to the historical fame of our state, fair in its exposition of the *Crisis*, & emphatic in the determination of *his* State to secede! He elicited commendation for moderation from the submissionists even. Ashmore spoke more at length not so pointedly. During his address *Tar Barrels* were fired, *ringing* of *Bells* & hurrahs, were kept up in the street opposite the courthouse & *hisses* were indulged by some few persons in the room, but all the while the applause & sympathy were with the speakers, notwithstanding the surroundings of *"advalo,"* "workingmen's association, et etc." I know of few avowed secessionists here, in or out of the legislature, but if there be any, there was everything to show that the *Southern* feeling was predominant. Saturday the legislature granted the Commons Hall to the Unionists (so called), for Saturday night. I was at the office at 5 P.M. when I was accosted by Holden & told that a *Constitutional Union* meeting would be held in said Hall, that he had prepared the resolutions, wished me to see them, that he thought I would approve them, and closed by asking me to *preside* over the meeting. I declined with *promptness*, but agreed to & did attend. Well, Busbee was called to the chair. Postmaster Cooke, one Ferrell, one Brown furniture maker, and Jeff. Fisher vice. prests. Frank Wilson Secr. Holden came forward read the resolves, which were meaningless generalities, attempting, as you will see, to assume a position forbid by the circumstances of our condition. Then he attempted to make a speech, but let down after some self-laudation. Came next *Miller prepared*, who made a strong union speech but elicited little applause except when he abused S.C. *He* was for an amendment of the Const. under the ⅔ provision clause. *"So must it be, but can you get that for us!!! & if not, what?"* Then came a *boquet* from some school girls to Vance who came forward & harranged ½ hour pro-

---

4. Congressmen John D. Ashmore and William W. Boyce of South Carolina were agitating for the secession of the southern states. Joseph C. Sitterson, *The Secession Movement in North Carolina*, p. 190.

ducing little enthusiasm, and going to great extremes for the Union. This Gent.^{mn} had the bad taste to be led from Yarborough the night before over to the Court House (for by this time the key had turned up) and there addressed the new coalition of renegade dems. & simon-pure sub[missionist]s. The so called Union demonstration was respectable in numbers (many ladies in the gallery) but was obviously wanting in spirit, more like a funeral than a glorification, the only marked applause being when S.C. was abused & ridiculed! My individual opinion is that the masses are arousing to a sense of the time & that events are hastening us into disunion sooner than any prudent citizen of our State (unprepared as she is) would discern. Hence I hear with real satisfaction that the people in the *County* are holding meetings and passing quasi & only quasi resolves in favor of the Union & that Bledsoe is drawing some of these Res. such as that the militia must be reorganized & volunteers armed by *this legislature*, further that the State ought to resist the administration of the Gov.^{mt} on Republican principles, though they do not hold that the election of A. L. is per se a cause for dissolution. Should you see in our city papers resolves of the above terms you know the source & if you read the register you will see the evidence of the new coalition. I seldom write at such length to any body or on any subject but in this I'm aiming only to draw *honestly* a picture of passing events for your instruction.

I *myself* believe that this Union & slavery cannot coexist—our people must yield one or other—that sufficient cause has existed since Compro. of '50, but my fellow citizens of Missⁱ did not so think & *I acquiesced.* Now, I fear the force of events will bring the *Unionists* to the *scratch* before we should propose any action; much less separate state action. Secession is true & right, but as in private affairs must be resorted to as a means to success, not as an end to political combinations. I think I may safely say that if the Pres.^t adopts the doctrine of coercion in his message tomorrow, then farewell to this Union. North Carolina can't be held in it. Why? The issue will have been changed from the Negro to that of a question of popular liberty. He will thus have added the love of liberty to the *avarice* & the *selfishness* of *Negro Slavocracy*. I use this plain language to impress you that I have tried to see the bottom of this issue—to such an extent even unto my own imperfections, and that of our slaveholders. When two such increments are thrown into one scale & the Constitution in the other it requires little sagacity to see which will sink. You cannot unite the *masses* of any southern State much less those of N.C. against the Union & in favor [of] slavery *alone*; but change the issue & the doctrine of *force* will, & with the two the conservative submissionists will be forced into *Toryism* or a Southern Confed.^y No other choice will be left. These are [my] views. I may remark that I saw none of the Old Union *Big Guns* in the Hall last night. *T's true*, that that class are shy of their new allies. They sort with them grudgingly. *There is a fear* that coming events may translate the word Unionist into Tory. . . .

C. B. HARRISON

Lawrence O'Bryan Branch Papers.

(5) The Hope of National Compromise

Conservative North Carolinians soon realized that their negative "watch and wait" policy was no match for dynamic, emotional secessionism. They then began to suggest various compromises which might satisfy both the North and the South, and they promised that Congress would make compromise its first order of business at its next session. Above all the conservatives pleaded that the people resist being stampeded into secession by prophets of doom. Zebulon B. Vance was one of several conservatives who even considered a central confederacy to forestall complete disunion. "Zeb" Vance of Buncombe County had begun his political career as a Whig, and in 1860 he supported the conservative Bell–Everett Constitutional Union ticket. He upheld the constitutional right of secession but during the winter of 1860–61 was a vigorous advocate of compromise and Union. When he expressed his thoughts in the letter below to a member of the House of Commons from Caldwell County he was in the United States House of Representatives.

ZEBULON B. VANCE TO WILLIAM DICKSON

Ho of Reps
Washington City
Dec. 11, 1860

I replied to your dispatch rec[d] tonight, but thought it best to write also. I wish I could see you, as it is almost impossible to give you a fair idea of things here in the compass of a letter.

Since receiving your dispatch I have had a conference with Mr. Crittenden & other friends. He is of opinion that the only earthly chance to save the Union is to *gain time*. This is the general opinion of our friends here. The whole southern mind is inflamed to the highest pitch and the leaders in the disunion move are scorning every suggestion of compromise and rushing everything with ruinous and indecent haste that would seem to imply that they were absolute fools—Yet they are acting wisely for their ends—they are "precipitating" the people into a revolution without giving them time to think—*They fear lest the people shall think*; hence the hasty action of S. Carolina, Georgia & the other States in calling conventions & giving so short a time for the election of delegates— But the people *must* think, and when they do begin to think and hear the matter properly discussed they will consider long and soberly before they tear down this noble fabric and invite anarchy and confusion, carnage, civil war, and financial ruin with the breathless hurry of men flying from a pestilence—If we can gain time we get the advantage of this sober second thought, and no people on Gods earth have this in a greater degree than ours, and we also get the advantage of the developments in Congress which I hope may be favorable. Eminent and patriotic men of all parties here are maturing plans of compromise which will be offered soon, and I will not allow myself to believe that *all* of them will fail. But if they do, and we should be forced to go out at last, what difference in the name of common sense could a few months make? Fear of Lincoln when he comes into office is perfect humbuggery, and those that urge it know it to be so. If we go out now we cant take the army and the navy with us, and Lincoln could as easily employ them to force us *back* as he could to *prevent* our going out; and the Yankees would as readily fight to whip us back as they would to keep us in! Its all stuff. I tell you this great rashness that burns the public mind *must and will burn out*, and cooler councils rule the day; but it must have *time*—"Make haste slowly" is the maxim—We have everything to gain and nothing on earth to lose by delay, but by too hasty action we may take a fatal step that we *never* can retrace—may lose a heritage that we can never recover "though we seek it earnestly and with tears."

I am not only reconciled to the idea of a Convention but think it the proper course, if you can put it off as long as possible, and give ample time for the candidates for seats to canvass. I think our friends ought to lead in the Convention movement, in order that they may as far as possible control it, and that its being called may not seem a disunion victory. Say that we *confide* in the *people*: are willing to trust them with their own rights and liberties; and if, after full and fair discussion, after hearing what our Northern bretheren have to offer us, and after such mature and *decent* deliberation as becomes a great people about to do a great act, if *they* choose . . . to invite carnage to saturate their soil and desolation to waste their fields, they can not say their public servants *precipitated* them into it! The people must and should rule, but we must see to it that we do our duty in warning, instructing, and advising them, as they have made us their servants for guarding their rights. . . .

Frontis W. Johnston, ed., *The Papers of Zebulon Baird Vance*, 1:71–73.

---

(6) The Call for a State Convention

When the legislature reassembled on 7 January 1861, North Carolina moderates found their position steadily eroding. Congress had appointed committees to explore solutions to the sectional crises, but it was becoming evident that they had little chance of success. Congressmen Burton Craige and Thomas Ruffin had already signed the "Southern Address" of 13 December declaring that "the argument is exhausted. All hope of relief in the Union . . . is extinguished . . ." and urging a southern confederacy.[5]

5. Edward McPherson, comp., *The Political History of the United States of America, During the Great Rebellion from November 6, 1860, to July 4, 1864*, p. 39.

Secessionism in parts of the state was becoming so strong that on 10 January civilians from Wilmington and Smithfield seized Fort Caswell, though Governor Ellis persuaded them to evacuate it. This heated state of public opinion finally compelled the legislature to call an election of delegates on 28 February to a convention, and at the same time the people were to vote for or against having the convention. By this time even a majority of the Unionists favored the convention, hoping that it might prevent secession. However, Jonathan Worth, unconditional Unionist of Randolph County, believed that the secessionists would be unstoppable if the convention were held and argued fiercely against its supposed advantages in the following address.

TO MY CONSTITUENTS OF THE COUNTIES OF RANDOLPH AND ALAMANCE:

On the 28th of February next you are called upon . . . by your vote to declare whether or not you want a State Convention, restricted to the consideration of our National Affairs; and also, at the same time, to vote for delegates for said Convention, in case a majority of the whole State shall call it. The Act provides that the action of the Convention shall have no validity until ratified by a vote of the people. I voted against this act because neither the Constitution of the United States, nor of this State, contemplates any such convention,—and because I can see no way by which it can do any good, and I fear it may do much mischief.

Such a convention is a modern invention of South Carolina, to bring about a sort of legalized revolution. . . . Wherever such a convention has assembled, it has asserted the power to sever the State from the Union, and declare it an independent government. Under my oath to *support* the Constitution of the United States, I could not vote to call a convention to *overthrow* that instrument.

I thought it improper for the General Assembly to ask you whether you want an unconstitutional convention. What can it do? It can do nothing only as a revolutionary body. Everybody looks for a remedy for our national troubles, to an amendment of the Constitution of the United States. The Fifth Article of the Constitution of the United States prescribes two modes of amendment. . . . [Here follows an advocacy of a national convention of all the states.]

If the proposed State Convention does what its . . . advocates desire it to do, it will be what all conventions south of us have done—declare the State out of the Union. . . . Every artifice will be employed to make you believe that a convention is to be called to *save* the Union. Believe it not. It is true, many members who are Union men voted for submitting it to a vote of the people whether they would have a convention or not, throwing upon you, with little time to consider, a responsibility which I think they should have met themselves. A majority refused to pass an amendment allowing you to endorse on your tickets whether you are for Union or disunion. It will be said that the convention can do no harm since whatever it may do will have no validity till ratified by you. The disunion leaders boldly maintain that the Legislature can not restrict the convention, that it may pass whatever ordinance it pleases, regardless of the restraints attempted to be imposed upon it by the Act of the Assembly; and that it may, or may not, at its pleasure, submit its action to the people for ratification. If war begins it will probably be brought on during the sitting of the convention.

. . . Not one of the five States which seceded, though acting under no emergency, has submitted its action to the people for ratification. We have not yet exhausted constitutional remedies. We can not have exhausted them before this convention shall assemble. Believe not those who may tell you this convention is called to *save* the Union. It is called to *destroy* it. If you desire to preserve the Union vote "No Convention," and at the same time, be careful for whom you vote as delegates.

When we shall have seen what the Commissioners shall effect, who are to meet in Washington on the 4th of February, to look for a remedy for the National disturbances, when we shall have called for a National Convention and it shall be refused, or shall have failed to accomplish a pacification, it will be time enough to resort to revolution. I think that those only should vote for a convention who regard disunion as the only remedy for the disease of the times. . . .

Joseph G. de Roulhac Hamilton, ed., *The Correspondence of Jonathan Worth*, 1:129–33.

NORTH CAROLINA SECEDES

Though the referendum on 28 February temporarily stalemated the North Carolina secessionists, subsequent developments led the state inexorably toward secession. She had sent an able delegation to the Washington Peace Conference, but Congress failed to adopt the Conference's recommendations. And Lincoln's inaugural address of 4 March seemed to promise armed coercion of the recalcitrant states so clearly that it converted many conditional Unionists into secessionists. North Carolina moderates in general appeared demoralized as spring approached, and their meetings were few and noticeably lacking in enthusiasm. On the other hand, the secessionists constantly stepped up their activities.

On 22 and 23 March in Goldsboro the state convention of the Southern Rights party recommended that North Carolina immediately join the Confederacy. "Spontaneous" county meetings adopted resolutions urging secession and demanding that the governor call a special session of the legislature so that a convention might be ordered. The radical newspapers became even more aggressive, arguing that if North Carolina would "assert her independence, take the lead,"[1] the other slave states still in the Union would follow her. With little to promise, the conservative press was simply unable to cope with its aggressive opponents.

The 12 April attack by the Confederates on Fort Sumter, which the United States government had refused to vacate even after the secession of South Carolina, and President Lincoln's call for 75,000 volunteers on 15 April to quell the rebellion (or to "coerce" the seceded states, as the southerners would have it), virtually destroyed Unionist sentiment in North Carolina. Governor Ellis informed Lincoln's secretary of war that "YOU CAN GET NO TROOPS FROM NORTH CAROLINA,"[2] and he

1. Wilmington *Journal*, 4 Apr. 1861, quoted in Sitterson, *Secession Movement in North Carolina*, p. 238.
2. John Ellis to Simon Cameron, 15 Apr. 1861, in Noble J. Tolbert, ed., *The Papers of John Willis Ellis*, 2:612.

proclaimed to the state that "united action in defence of the sovereignty of North Carolina, and of the rights of the South, becomes now the duty of all."[3] He then ordered the seizure of Forts Caswell, Johnson, and Macon, and began organizing defenses, assembling volunteers, and setting up military encampments.

At the call of Governor Ellis a special session of the legislature met on 1 May and ordered elections for a convention to consider the state of the Union. The legislature then began preparing for war. After a brief campaign, in which former Unionists were almost silent, the convention met on 20 May. The question now was simply whether to leave the Union by act of secession or by exercising the right of revolution. The former device handily won the rather academic debate, and on its first day of session the convention unanimously adopted an ordinance of secession. Immediately afterward it ratified unanimously the Provisional Constitution of the Confederacy.

(1) The Failure of National Compromise

During March 1861 nothing hurt the conservative cause in North Carolina more than the outcome of the Washington Peace Conference. This conference of delegates from twenty-one states had assembled on 4 February at the call of the Virginia legislature. The border states were probably over-optimistic in reasoning that the distinguished personnel of the convention would be able to work out an acceptable sectional compromise. On 27 February the convention suggested to Congress seven constitutional amendments designed to settle once and for all the questions of slavery in the territories and in the existing slave states. But Congress found its recommendations unacceptable, and even moderates in North Carolina disliked its proposals. George Davis, former Whig and dedicated Unionist of Wilmington, had been a member of North Carolina's distinguished delegation to the Washington Convention, but even he returned home a secessionist. One of the best orators in North Carolina history, Davis delivered an address in Wilmington on his return from Washington that reverberated over the state.

SPEECH OF MR. DAVIS AT THALIAN HALL —
THE "PEACE CONGRESS" AND ITS FAILURE

When Mr. Davis appeared on the stand at 8 o'clock he . . . remarked that he was pleased to have an opportunity of submitting his course as a

3. A PROCLAMATION, ibid., p. 622.

Commissioner to the judgment of the people. . . . The . . . *project* of adjustment, known as the Crittenden resolutions, had been directly or inferentially adopted by public opinion and by the resolution of the Legislature of the State . . . as something which North Carolina might accept, and less than which she *could not* accept.

When the crisis arising out of the last Presidential election came on, . . . he held the belief that any adjustment . . . must distinctly acknowledge and guarantee *property in slaves*, and extend to such property full and adequate protection, as to any other species of property. This the Crittenden propositions distinctly did south of 36 degrees 30 minutes. The Southern Commissioners went to meet the Commissioners from the North with the Constitution of the United States in one hand, and the interpretation of that instrument in the Dred Scott case in the other. They said—"We have the constitutional right . . . to take our slaves into any part of the public territories, and to demand protection for them there . . . but we wish not to insist upon extreme rights. We *do* demand an authoritative recognition and embodiment of the principle of the Dred Scott decision so far as *property in slaves* is concerned, under the United States, being willing to concede to the North all territories above 36 degrees 30 minutes, but demanding distinct recognition and protection for our slave property below that line." This distinct recognition of the right of *property in slaves* . . . was the vital principle which alone gave value to the Crittenden resolutions. . . .

Having thus referred to his own previous position, and what he believed to be the position of the State . . . he could never accept the plan adopted by the "Peace Congress" as consistent with the rights, the interests or the dignity of North Carolina. Never! . . . Five distinct and separate times . . . the true vital principle of the Crittenden propositions . . . had been brought to a vote, and five distinct and separate times it had been voted down overwhelmingly. There is no such recognition in the most important and most debated section of the report of the congress, known as the Territorial Section. That section provides: first, that in all the present territory of the United States, north of the parallel of 36 degrees 30 minutes . . . involuntary servitude . . . is prohibited. In all the present territory south of that line the status of persons held to service, or labor . . . shall not be changed. What is meant by *status*? . . . Now the only slavery thus existing in the territories south of 36 degrees 30 minutes is in New Mexico and in the Indian Territories. . . . Congress has not yet submitted this proposition to the States, but even supposing it had submitted it, it could not be embodied into the Constitution . . . for at [least] two years, and before that time, the Republican Congress will have *abolished* the status of slavery. . . .

But this section goes on further to provide that—"No law shall be passed by Congress or the Territorial Legislature to hinder or prevent the taking of such persons from any of the States . . . to said Territory . . . but the same shall be subject to judicial cognizance in the federal Courts according to the course of the common law." . . . By whom is this common law to be administered in the Territories of the

United States? Why, by Black Republican Courts, appointed by Black Republican Presidents. This was exactly the understanding of the Republican members of the Congress, as freely admitted by some of them. . . .

The seventh section reads thus, and is, if possible, worse than anything else in the whole affair:

Sec. 7. Congress shall provide by law that the United States shall pay to the owner the full value of his fugitive from labor . . . where the marshal . . . whose duty it was to arrest such fugitive, was prevented from so doing by . . . mobs . . . or when, after arrested, such fugitive was rescued by force, and the owner . . . obstructed in the pursuit of his remedy for the recovery of such fugitive. Congress shall provide by law for securing to the citizens of each State the privileges and immunities of citizens in the several States.

The effect . . . of this section is to promote . . . the gradual abolitioning of the Border States. Congress is to buy up the negroes, making the South pay half the cost of despoiling herself. . . .

The closing sentence of this section is most peculiarly noteworthy, because of the object in view, which was plainly avowed in conference. That object was to allow Northern free negroes to come to any point South, and there claim and exercise all the rights of citizenship. . . . So that in fact all our police regulations excluding free negroes from other States . . . framed for our own protection . . . would fall to the ground. . . .

Terms more satisfactory the North will never assent to, or concede to us, in the Union. . . . It had been urged upon him to vote for this thing under protest. He didn't believe in voting wrong and shielding himself behind a "protest." He was asked to vote for this thing so as . . . he might let it still go before the people of the State. He . . . could not vote for it as any settlement—he did not think . . . he could honestly vote to lay it before the people of the State . . . for it was no settlement, but a snare and an illusion.

Mr. Davis re-stated and summed this up, by emphatically declaring that the South could never—*never* obtain any better or more satisfactory terms while she remained in the present Union, and for his part he could never assent to the terms contained in this report of the Peace Congress, as in accordance with the honor or the interests of the South. Never!

Everything showed the spirit of the Republicans.—They had passed the most oppressive tariff that had ever been heard of. They would tax us to death to protect and build up themselves, and at the same time pay the agents of the underground Railroad for running off our negroes. How could Wilmington, oppressed by a tariff of forty per cent. and upwards, expect to hold her own with Georgetown or Charleston, or any port of the Confederate States, with ten per cent. duties?

No arrangement had been made—none would be made. The division must be made on the line of slavery. The South must go with the South, and not with any new-fangled central Republic, or as the tail-end and victim of a Free Soil North. . . .

Wilmington *Journal*, 4 Mar. 1861.

(2) Fort Sumter and the End of Compromise

While North Carolina's drift toward secession seemed irreversible, she would have been a poor Confederate state had President Lincoln not committed the ultimate provocation. Her Unionists had always insisted that their "watch and wait" policy was not submission, and that they would consent to secession if the new Republican administration acted intolerably. And on 15 April Lincoln took just such a step. In response to the Confederacy's seizure of Fort Sumter in Charleston harbor, Lincoln called upon the states for 75,000 militia volunteers to suppress "combinations"

in the seven southern states which had seceded. To most remaining southern Unionists this call was reason enough for secession. They had opposed secession until now, but they were even more opposed to coercion: the central government could never use force against a state. As a historian of North Carolina secession wrote, this sudden turn of events "almost instantly destroyed virtually all Union sentiment in North Carolina."[4] In an impassioned speech delivered in Boston, Massachusetts, in 1866, Zeb Vance described his own reactions.

LECTURE BEFORE THE ANDREW POST, NO. 15, OF
THE GRAND ARMY

. . . The people of North Carolina, more, perhaps, than those of any of the eleven seceding States, were devoted to the Union. They had always regarded it with sincerest reverence and affection, and they left it slowly and with sorrow. They were actuated by an honest conviction—

1st. That their constitutional rights were endangered, not by the mere election of Mr. Lincoln, as others did, but by the course which subsequent events were compelled to take in consequence of the ideas which were behind him.

2d. By the force of neighborhood and association.

3d. By a fatality of events which ordinary prudence could not have avoided. The Union men of that State, of whom I was one, whatever may have been their doubts of the propriety of secession, were unanimous in the opinion that it was neither right nor safe to permit the gen-

4. Sitterson, *Secession Movement in North Carolina*, p. 240.

eral government to coerce a State. In their arguments therefore with the secession advocates they logically took the position that should coercion be attempted they would unite with the secessionists in resisting it. During the last session of Congress, which preceded the outbreak, the winter of 1860 and '61, the Union members of Congress from Kentucky, Tennessee, North Carolina and Virginia, after earnest and anxious consultation, constituted a committee to wait upon Mr. Lincoln, who was then in the city preparatory to his inauguration, and present him their views in regard to the situation. They did so, and my colleague, the Hon. John A. Gilmer, gave me the results of their interview. It was represented to Mr. Lincoln by them that the cotton States proper alone could not make any effectual headway in maintaining secession without the aid of the great border States of Missouri, Kentucky, Virginia, Maryland, North Carolina and Tennessee; that the population of those States was devoted to the Union, but could not be held to that position should coercion be attempted and the blood of their Southern brethren be shed. They expressed to him the opinion that the secession movement could be checked and finally broken down if those great States could be kept out of it. Mr. Lincoln appeared fully impressed with the wisdom of these views and promised that if possible he would avoid the attempt at coercion. In his inaugural address he committed himself only to the announcement that his duty would compel him to hold and possess the public property of the United States. I quote from memory. With this promise and these hopes the Union Congressmen from these States returned to their homes and began their canvassings for re-election. They promised the people that no force would be attempted, and if there should be, they could and would no longer hold out for the Union. As precarious as this position was, such was the temper of the Southern people, it was all that the situation afforded even in States so conservative.

But when Fort Sumter was fired upon, immediately followed by Mr. Lincoln's call for "volunteers to suppress the insurrection," the whole situation was changed instantly. The Union men had every prop knocked from under them, and by stress of their own position were plunged into the secession movement. For myself, I will say that I was canvassing for the Union with all my strength; I was addressing a large and excited crowd, large numbers of whom were armed, and literally had my arm extended upward in pleading for peace and the Union of our Fathers, when the telegraphic news was announced of the firing on Sumter and [the] President's call for seventy-five thousand volunteers. When my hand came down from that impassioned gesticulation, it fell slowly and sadly by the side of a Secessionist. I immediately, with altered voice and manner, called upon the assembled multitude to volunteer, not to fight against but for South Carolina. I said: If war must come I preferred to be with my own people. If we had to shed blood I preferred to shed Northern rather than Southern blood. If we had to slay I had rather slay strangers than my own kindred and neighbors; and that it was better, whether right or wrong, that communities and States should go together and face the horrors of war in a body—sharing a common fate, rather than endure the unspeakable calamities of internecine strife. To those at all acquainted with the atrocities which were inflicted upon the divided communities of Missouri, Kentucky and Tennessee, the humanity of my action will be apparent. I went with and shared the fate of the people of my native State, having first done all I could to preserve the peace and secure the unanimity of the people to avert, as much as possible, the calamities of war. I do not regret that course. I do not believe there is an honorable man within my hearing to-night who, under the same circumstances, would not have done as I did. . . .

Clement Dowd, *Life of Zebulon B. Vance*, pp. 439–42.

---

(3) How to Leave the Union?

After Lincoln's call for volunteers, events in North Carolina moved swiftly. Governor Ellis spurned the call indignantly and instead ordered the seizure of the forts along the coast and of the federal arsenal at Fayetteville. On 17 April he called a special session of the legislature to meet on 1 May. On its first day the legislature, with but three dissenting votes, ordered an election on 13 May for delegates to an unrestricted convention to meet in Raleigh on 20 May. Meanwhile Ellis and the legislature worked feverishly to put the state on a wartime basis. When the convention, which contained most of the best minds of the state, met it quickly showed its temper by electing secessionist

Weldon N. Edwards, a prominent Warren County planter, as its president over former Unionist William A. Graham. The debate on leaving the Union was largely academic. Former Unionist Whigs still denied the constitutional right of secession, and George E. Badger, an attorney from Raleigh and one of the state's most venerated citizens, presented an ordinance taking North Carolina from the Union by revolution (Document A). This was defeated 72–40, whereupon Burton Craige, Democratic attorney of Salisbury, proposed an ordinance simply repealing the ordinance of 1789 by which the state had joined the United States (Document B). It was adopted unanimously.

A.

WHEREAS, Abraham Lincoln . . . did, on the sixteenth day of April, by his proclamation, call upon the States of the Union to furnish large bodies of troops to enable him . . . to march an army into the seceded States with a view to their subjection under an arbitrary and military authority, there being no law of Congress authorizing such calling out of troops, and no constitutional right to use them, if called out, for the purpose intended by him; and, *whereas,* this call for troops has been answered throughout the northern, northwestern and middle non-slave-holding States with enthusiastic readiness, and it is evident from the tone of the entire press of those States, and the open avowal of their public men, that it is the fixed purpose of the government and people of those States to wage a cruel war against the seceded States . . . and reduce its inhabitants to absolute subjection and abject slavery; and, *whereas,* . . . the said Lincoln, without any shadow of rightful authority, and in plain violation of the Constitution of the United States, has, by other proclamations, declared the ports of North Carolina, as well as all the other Atlantic and Gulf States, under blockade; thus seeking to cut off our trade with all parts of the world:

And, *whereas,* . . . he is now governing by military rule alone, enlarging by new enlistments of men, both the military and naval force, without authority of law, having set aside all constitutional and legal restraints, and made all constitutional and legal rights dependent upon his mere pleasure, and that of his military subordinates; and, *whereas,* all his unconstitutional, illegal and oppressive acts, all his wicked and diabolical purposes, and, in his present position of usurper and military dictator, he has been and is encouraged and supported by the great body of the people of the non-slaveholding States:

Therefore, this Convention . . . in the name and with the sovereign power of the people of North Carolina, doth, for the reasons aforesaid, and others, and in order to preserve the undoubted rights and liberties of the said people, hereby declare all connection of government between this State and the United States of America dissolved and abrogated, and this State to be a free, sovereign and independent State, owing no subordination, obedience, support or other duty to the said United States, their Constitution or authorities, anything in her ratification of said Constitution, or of any amendment or amendments thereto to the contrary and notwithstanding; and having full power to levy war, conclude peace, contract alliances, and to do all other acts and things which independent States may of right do. . . .

B.

We, the people of the State of North Carolina in Convention assembled, do declare and ordain, and it is hereby declared and ordained, That the ordinance adopted by the State of North Carolina in the Convention of 1789, whereby the Constitution of the United States was ratified and adopted; and also all acts and parts of acts of the General Assembly, ratifying and adopting amendments to the said Constitution, are hereby repealed, rescinded and abrogated.

We do further declare and ordain, That the Union now subsisting between the State of North Carolina and the other States, under the title of "The United States of America," is hereby dissolved, and that the

State of North Carolina is in full possession and exercise of all those rights of sovereignty which belong and appertain to a free and independent State.

Journal of the Convention of the People of North Carolina, 1861, pp. 10–13.

---

(4) Persistent Unionism

When North Carolina joined the Confederacy overt Unionism virtually ceased except in the remote mountain counties, though it re-emerged in the Sound area once Federal armies had taken over there. A few individuals remained unreconciled Unionists, such as Charles Henry Foster, a Maine lawyer who had come to Murfreesboro and edited the Citizen, *and the Reverend Marble Nash Taylor, both of whom were forced to flee to New York. During the summer of 1861 rumors of mass disaffection circulated, but generally those whose Unionism continued after secession discreetly concealed it. The treason law would have been executed swiftly against civilians and their property. The following letter from a Washington County lawyer reports one of these treasonable combinations which never developed, if it actually ever existed.*

Plymouth, Aug. 16, 1861

His Excellency H. T. Clark ⎱
Governor of N. Carolina ⎰
   Dr Sir

    I rec^d your note of the 2nd inst. by the hands of Joseph Ramsay Esq. There are forty six muskets in the possession of the Home Guard of this place. Many of said Guard have volunteered and the Sheriff of the County has sent their muskets to Raleigh. I enclose acknowledgments of possession of muskets, and hope you will allow them to remain as long as possible. They are of service to us now, and may be of more. The condition of affairs in this County is worse now, than it was supposed to be, at the time of Mr Ramsay'^{s} visit to Raleigh. I have learned that on the 3rd inst. (Saturday) in that portion of this County adjoining Beaufort, a military organization was gotten up—regularly officered from the Captain downward—the real purposes and aims of it remain as yet a secret to outsiders. The members of the organization refuse to communicate any information concerning it, or rather but very little concerning it. I have however learned that there is some sort of an obligation & rules &c signed by the members; and from the little information I have rec^d concerning it, I feel quite safe in the inference that it is an organization for the mutual defense & protection of its members against a "draft for the war" and against any arrest that may be made or damages sustained by reason of their opinions or conduct.

I have just been informed, since writing the above, by a gentleman of this County, that he was told yesterday by a countryman, that he (the countryman) was present on the 10th inst. (Saturday) at a meeting in Beaufort County . . . at which time Resolutions were adopted declaring their determination not to muster nor to pay any tax for the support of the war. . . . Such a condition of things is most deplorable & especially at such a time as this, when it behooves every Southern man to be of one heart and of one mind, ready & willing to make any sacrifice required to secure our freedom from a state of servitude equal to, if not worse than, negro slavery. Yet the existence of such a condition of things among us here is scarcely to be unexpected, when our Representative in the Legislature . . . has not only failed to openly denounce but has been known to apologize for some of his friends, who openly declared that "Lincoln has done nothing wrong, nothing unconstitutional, nothing but what his oath of office constrained him to do." Nor is its existence to be wondered at, when the Colonel of the County . . . openly proclaims in the public sheets, in the presence of poor men, and endeavors to sustain the opinion by argument "that this present war, will, at the South, make the poor man poorer and the rich man richer. . . ." We are now reaping the harvest from the seed, sown last Summer in the "Ad valorem" canvass in this County, by the effort made to array the poor against the rich. . . .

Yours most respectfully
Wm A. LITTLEJOHN

Governors' Papers.

III

NORTH CAROLINA INVADED, 1861–1862

On 10 June 1861, at Big Bethel, Virginia, a small Confederate force, which included D. H. Hill's First North Carolina Regiment, defeated a much larger Union command. Even though Bethel was little more than a skirmish, it aroused considerable enthusiasm in the South. North Carolinians now confidentially expected another Confederate victory once General Irvin McDowell moved his Union army out of the protective confines of Washington for a push on Richmond. These expectations were fulfilled on 21 July at Manassas Junction when McDowell's forces were routed and hurled back on the nation's capital.

Following this setback Northern strategists turned their attention to eastern North Carolina. As a consequence there was little fighting in Virginia for the remainder of the year.

North Carolina's coast is indented by Currituck, Albemarle, Pamlico, Core, and Bogue Sounds, into whose shallow and sometimes narrow waters empty most of the rivers of the coastal plain. To command this strategic sound area, Union troops first had to control the long sandbank reaching from the Virginia line to Bogue Inlet below Beaufort, North Carolina. This sand strip, known as the Outer Banks, and broken by numerous inlets, separated the sounds from the ocean.

Shortly after North Carolina seceded from the Union, Governor John W. Ellis made preparations to defend the coast. Forts were constructed at Oregon, Ocracoke, and Hatteras Inlets. Of these installations Forts Hatteras and Clark were the most important because they guarded Hatteras, the main inlet north of Beaufort.

The first troops arrived at Hatteras in early May. Yet by the end of the summer there were no more than 580 men on the Outer Banks. They came primarily from the Seventh North Carolina Regiment, Colonel William F. Martin commanding, and the Tenth North Carolina Artillery.

The state's second line of defense was its navy, five small steamers jokingly called the mosquito fleet. It was under instructions to defend the sounds and rivers and to seize enemy shipping moving along the coast.

The success of these diminutive vessels, as well as Confederate privateers operating out of the sounds, caused violent repercussions in Washington, making clear the necessity of a thrust against the Outer Banks. The seven-vessel naval force assembled for this expedition was under the command of Commodore Silas H. Stringham. The land forces, consisting primarily of two New York regiments, were led by General Benjamin F. Butler.

On 26 August the Union squadron steamed out of Hampton Roads for the Outer Banks. By the evening of the twenty-ninth Forts Clark and Hatteras had capitulated, and the installations at Ocracoke and Oregon Inlets were soon to be abandoned by their defenders without a fight.

Now fully aware of the strategic importance of his victory, General Butler decided to disobey his instructions which were to abandon Hatteras after blocking the channel. Instead, upon departing for Fortress Monroe he left behind an occupation force under Colonel Rush C. Hawkins, Ninth New York Regiment. Hawkins saw not only the strategic but also the political importance of his new command. Since there seemed to be little support for secession on the islands, he proposed that a popular convention be held immediately as a step toward returning the state to the Union.

The loss of the defenses at Oregon, Ocracoke, and Hatteras Inlets was a serious blow to the Confederacy. It provided the enemy with a base for operations against eastern North Carolina and at the same time eliminated the sounds as an operational base for privateers.

Union plans for a second strike at the North Carolina coast were worked out in the fall of 1861. They called for the capture of Roanoke Island and then a push into the interior of the state possibly as far west as Goldsboro. A successful operation would cut Confederate communication lines south of Richmond as well as place Union troops in position for a flanking movement in case General George McClellan met with success in Virginia.

To carry out this rather bold plan General Ambrose E. Burnside was given an amphibious division of 15,000 men. Admiral Louis M. Goldsborough commanded the navy vessels in this highly successful expedition. By the early summer of 1862 Roanoke Island, New Bern, and Fort Macon along with much of North Carolina's sound region were in Union hands and the mosquito fleet had been destroyed. However, before General Burnside could move on the important rail town of Goldsboro, he was ordered to Richmond where McClellan was having difficulty with Lee. General John G. Foster was to assume command of the Department of North Carolina with headquarters in New Bern which was also the headquarters for Lincoln's recently appointed military governor of the state, Edward Stanly.

(1) Battle of Hatteras, August 1861

The Union assault on the Outer Banks came as no surprise to North Carolina authorities. It had *been assumed that the capture of Union prizes by the state's mosquito fleet would eventually bring* enemy troops to the coast. General Walter Gwynn, in command of North Carolina's northern department of coastal defense, nevertheless pleaded in vain for more men and guns for his command. When the Union fleet anchored off Hatteras Inlet on the afternoon of 27 August, the island's defenses were woefully inadequate.

The Union assault commenced the next morning with a heavy naval bombardment of Fort Clark. Under cover of this fire 318 men and two guns of Colonel Max Weber's Twentieth New York Regiment were put ashore by noon. A heavy surf prevented more land-ings. Fortunately for the New Yorkers, Colonel J. C. Lamb, in command at Fort Clark, had expended his ammunition by this time and was under orders to spike his guns, take off what could be carried, and evacuate his position.

During the afternoon the Confederates abandoned Clark and started making their way across the narrow marsh to Fort Hatteras. Among those racing across the sand to safety was Captain John B. Fearing of Elizabeth City. In a letter to his wife he described the fighting on Hatteras Island.

News reached us on Monday that the enemy were approaching with heavy steamers, gun boats, transports—in all, ten steamers carrying 200 guns. The ships anchored about eight miles from land. . . . We all were on our arms all night, waiting to make an attack if they attempted to land at night. None came ashore that night. Next morning (Wednesday) about ten o'clock, the steamers all came in shore and began the attack by shelling Fort Clark. We all remained and defended this fort until we were compelled to retreat to Fort Hatteras. They fired incessantly for 3½ hours. We returned the shots until we had no ammunition, then retreated under the heaviest shelling any man ever saw; we were compelled to run and fall at almost every step, to escape the fragments. Some of our men were killed, some wounded, some cut off. We were betrayed by a local preacher who the Sunday before preached and prayed for the success of our Army. He stood upon a hill, pointed out where the troops were encamped and then pointed out the best place for landing. After knowing . . . where the troops were, these ships shelled them at every step. . . . I do not think less than 2000 shots were fired the first day. Colonel Martin acted with much coolness and did all he could to defend the point. . . . They shelled us until late in the evening, but little damage was done up to this time. At the other Fort, Lieutenant Knight of Captain Lamb's company had a bad wound in the arm and was sent off to the steamer in the Sound. Colonel Martin sent dispatches to Portsmouth[1] for troops, they arrived the same evening. While landing, the enemy tried every way in the world to prevent them but they came on to the fort. We had then in all 150. . . . They all appeared in good spirits and anxious to do duty. After this, the enemy ceased firing for the night.

1. A community at the tip of Core Banks, Carteret County.

All night we were on watch; no sleep; nothing to eat; & bad water. In the morning we were aroused in an alarm "the enemy are coming to attack us by land." . . . Now we had more officers than needed; for from Portsmouth we had a full complement; and added to them, Commodore Barron[2] came with many others, among them Lieut. Murdaugh & Major Andrews. Thursday morning we were alarmed; but the enemy did not begin an attack until ½ past seven. They had [landed] under cover from the guns from their steamers, where the Preacher directed a very large force of infantry & rifle cannon. They began to storm Fort Hatteras at 7 & ½ A.M. and for four hours not a minute elapsed that a bomb did not burst in or around the fort. I never heard or read of such a bombardment . . . Commodore Barron said he never did. We returned the fire as best we could but our guns were too small, and the distance too great. They had Rifle Cannon and put almost every shell inside the Fort after they got the range.

Colonel Martin gave up the command to Commodore Barron in the morning. . . . [Portions of the letter are faded and illegible, and part has been lost.]

J. E. Wood, ed., *Year Book Pasquotank Historical Society*, 2:110–11.

---

(2) Reaction to the Union Victory at Hatteras

Throughout the North the news of the Hatteras victory was received with great rejoicing. Occurring so soon after defeat at Manassas it bolstered Northern morale. Although the operation was relatively small, it was the Union's first victory of any kind, and in the words of Admiral David Porter of the United States Navy one that "should not be forgotten. . . . as it gave us a foothold on Southern soil and possession of the Sounds of North Carolina."[3]

In the South an angry Confederate Congress, on the other hand, demanded the true story of Hatteras. Practically everyone from the engineers who built the forts to the Ordnance Department were accused. Allegations of drunkenness, inefficiency, and even cowardice on the part of the officers and men were made.

In North Carolina officials scrambled to lay the blame as private citizens and soldiers alike felt most keenly the loss of reputation to their state. Writing from Virginia a soldier lamented: "Must history record in after years that in our struggle for freedom the first repulse our cause received was on the soil of the Old North

2. Commodore Samuel Barron was chief of coastal defenses in Virginia and North Carolina.

3. David D. Porter, *Naval History of the Civil War*, p. 47.

State."[4] *An eighteen-year-old girl*   *concern in her diary.*
of Everittsville recorded similar

Aug. 28, 1861. This evening we heard the startling intelligence. That the Yankees have possession of 'Fort Hatteras' on the cape. The 17th Reg. state troops, Col-Campbell went down last evening to have a fight with the *'vandals'*! God speed them on to Victory. Let them retake the 'Fort' O My God! It makes every vein ready to burst with just indignation. When I think of such *vile* feet treading the soil of the Proud old North State. Arise, ye Men of N. Cr. Off with the cowardly hordes.

Aug. 30, 1861. Hatteras taken by Yanks—women and children fleeing. "Quick oh God! Save us from the enemy. Surely thou hast not forsaken us."

Sept. 1, 1861. The Yankees are still at Hatteras. How long must this degradation last. Men of N. Cr. Arise! Arise! Let the cry be 'Victory or Death,' But oh God! the everlasting shame of being killed by such brutes, such devils, such arch fiends. Poor Woman! How can she bear it! Nobly she will bear it. . . . Sleep not, rest not, men of North Carolina, til each armed foe expires. 'Til each vandal is made to bite the dust. God is with us! What need we more! If there is one coward among you shoot him down. We must have no cowards among us. Strike for you all—all is at stake at the mercy of such devils, mercy they have none. She is a stranger to their cowardly hearts.

Dairy of Elizabeth Collier, 28, 30 Aug., 1 Sept. 1861, Elizabeth Collier Papers.

---

(3) Union Government on Hatteras, November 1861

Colonel Rush C. Hawkins's policy, upon assuming command at Hatteras, was to create friendly relations with the local inhabitants. The commander of the Ninth New York suggested to his superiors that a popular convention be held under the protection of the Union army. Such a convention, the colonel thought, would restore a third of the state to the Union at once. A so-called convention of delegates and proxies representing forty-five counties of the state was held at Hatteras on 18 November 1861. One ordinance proclaimed Reverend Marble Nash Taylor provisional governor of North Carolina, and another declared the ordinance of secession null and void and instructed the governor to issue a call for a congressional election. The election was held and Charles H. Foster of Maine was elected to Congress. The whole Union movement was so deceptive, however, that Foster was never seated, and Taylor's

4. Diary of Williamson Whitehead, 1 Sept. 1861, Whitehead Papers.

duties as provisional governor
were short-lived.
    The following are the ordi-

nances adopted by the convention
on the eighteenth.

By the People of the State of North Carolina, as represented in Convention at Hatteras, Monday, Nov. 18, 1861.

Be it ordained by this Convention, and it is hereby ordained and published by the authority of the same:

I. That this Convention on behalf of the people of North Carolina, and acknowledging the Constitution of the United States of America as the supreme law of the land, hereby declares vacant all State offices, the incumbents of which have disqualified themselves to hold them by violating their oaths to support the Federal Constitution.

II. That the office of Governor of this Commonwealth having been vacated by the death of John W. Ellis, and by the active treason to the Union of his constitutional successor, Acting Governor Clark, therefore Marble Nash Taylor be hereby appointed and declared Provisional Governor of North Carolina.

III. That the Constitution of this State and its amendments, together with the statutes and laws thereof, as contained in the Revised Code put in operation January 1, 1856, be declared continued in full force; also such subsequent acts of the General Assembly as were not adopted in contravention of the National Constitution, or in derogation of its authority.

IV. That the ordinance of the Convention which assembled at Raleigh on the 20th of May last, proclaiming the secession of this Commonwealth from the Federal Union, such secession being legally impossible, is of no force or effect; and said ordinance, together with all other ordinances and acts of said Convention, or of the General Assembly, made and done in pursuance of the treasonable purposes of the conspirators against the Union, is hereby declared "ab initio" null and void.

V. That whereas it is desirable that this State shall be represented in the Federal Congress, and maintain her due weight in the councils of the Union, therefore the Provisional Governor be directed hereby to order special elections, in accordance with chapter sixty-nine of the Revised Code, as soon as practicable and expedient, in any district or districts now unrepresented. And, in view of the prevalence of armed rebellion and disorder in many portions of this Commonwealth, the Governor is hereby directed to issue his certificates of election upon presentation of such evidence as shall satisfy him of the fact of an election.

VI. That the Governor be authorized and empowered to fill such official vacancies by temporary appointment, and to do such acts as, in the exercise of a sound discretion, he may deem expedient for the safety and good order of the State.

The Convention adjourned, subject to be reassembled upon the call of the President.

Frank Moore, ed., *The Rebellion Record: A Diary of American Events,*

(4) Amphibious Landing on Roanoke Island, February 1862

The Union expedition dispatched to capture Roanoke Island sailed from Hampton Roads on 11 January 1862. The fleet, consisting of shallow-draft steamers, barges, tugs, ferries, and several large passenger steamers, which were guaranteed to draw less than eight feet, was a motley one. Aboard these vessels, nevertheless, was General A. E. Burnside's 15,000 man Coastal Division, the first major amphibious force in United States history. Admiral L. M. Goldsborough commanded the navy vessels in the expedition. Due to bad weather and breakdowns the fleet did not arrive off Roanoke Island until 7 February.

Scattered about the island in Forts Huger, Blanchard, and Bartow, as well as several lesser fortifications, were 1,435 Confederate effectives under Colonel H. M. Shaw. General Henry A. Wise at the time was confined to his bed at Nags Head. The mosquito fleet under Commodore W. F. Lynch, who had replaced Samuel Barron as naval commander in the sound region, took a position behind some piles that partially obstructed the narrow channel through Croatan Sound.

Around 11:00 A.M. on the seventh the Union gunboats began to shell the forts and to engage the Confederate fleet. At the same time Burnside made preparations to land his troops. The first wave landed without incident, and in twenty minutes 4,000 men were put ashore. With this first landing, however, Burnside's organizational work apparently ended, for the rest of the division did not get ashore until midnight. Still, practice had been attained in making an amphibious landing on a division scale, and lessons were available for review.

In his official report of 14 February Burnside called the landing a beautiful sight.

Headquarters Department of North Carolina
Roanoke, February 14, 1862

General: I have the honor to transmit a more detailed report of the events that have transpired in this command since my last dispatch to the General-in-Chief. . . .

At 1 o'clock P.M. . . . . I proceeded to the naval fleet, and after consulting with Commodore Goldsborough I determined to attempt a landing before night. After visiting my armed propellers and finding them doing good service . . . I received Lieutenant Andrews' report, which satisfied me that the decision to land at Ashby's Harbor was correct. . . . I accordingly ordered General Foster, who was ready with his first detachment, to attempt a landing at some point in the harbor. I had before ordered General [J. L.] Reno, who was also ready with his first detachment, to halt until the naval-boat howitzers . . . could be brought up and placed in position. They were soon taken in tow by General Reno, and in a very few minutes General Foster's boat and his had reached the shore, and were soon after joined by the boats carrying the first detachment of General [J. G.] Parke's brigade. . . . The immediate point of landing at Ashby's Harbor in the original plan was Ashby's Landing, but on approaching it General Foster discovered an armed force in the woods in the rear of the landing, and very wisely directed his leading vessel to another point in the harbor opposite Hammond's house. . . . In less than twenty minutes from the time the boats reached the shore 4,000 of our men were passing over the marshes at a double quick and forming in most perfect order on the dry land near the house; and I beg leave to say that I never witnessed a more beautiful sight than that presented by the approach of these vessels to the shore and the landing and forming of the troops. Each brigadier-general had a light-draught steamer, to which were attached some 20 surf-boats in a long line in the rear. Both steamers and boats were densely filled with soldiers and each boat bearing the national flag.

As the steamers approached the shore at a rapid speed each surf-boat was "let go," and with their acquired velocity and by direction of the steersman reached the shore line. . . . I . . . went on shore, where I met General Parke, and received from him his report of the disposition of the forces for the protection of the landing of the remainder of the division, which disposition I entirely approved of. Soon after I met General Reno, whom I left in command, General Foster having returned to his vessel to bring up his second detachment.

By 12 o'clock that night the entire division (except the Twenty-fourth Massachusetts, Colonel Stevenson, detained below by the grounding of the steamer), together with Porter's battery of Dahlgren howitzers, had been landed. . . .

Early the next morning, in pursuance of the plan of action, General Foster ordered an advance. . . .

A. E. BURNSIDE
Brigadier-General, Commanding
Department of North Carolina

War of the Rebellion: A Compilation of the Official Records of the Union and Confederate Armies, Ser. 1, 9:75–81.

---

(5) Destruction of the North Carolina Navy, February 1862

With the capture of Roanoke Island General Burnside was in a position to move against the North Carolina mainland. But to gain absolute control of the intervening sounds it was necessary first to destroy the North Carolina navy (mosquito fleet) under the command of Commodore W. F. Lynch.

On the evening of 7 February 1862, the commodore had taken his small vessels—six in number—to Elizabeth City, which lay twelve miles up the Pasquotank River from Albemarle Sound. Three days later at Cobb's Point, a few miles down stream from the city, a Union flotilla under Commander S. C. Rowan disposed of the Confederate vessels and pushed its way toward Elizabeth City where flames could be seen leaping skyward. A number of local residents had set fire to their property.

In the action at Cobb's Point the USS Commodore Perry, Lieutenant C. W. Flusser commanding, rammed the Confederate steamer Sea Bird. The collision caused the anchor fastening on the Union vessel to give way, thus anchoring both ships. It was ten, long, frantic minutes before Flusser could get the vessels separated. The lieutenant wrote his mother about the embarrassing incident.

We met the enemy on the 10th instant, a short distance from Elizabeth, and protected by a four-gun battery. They had five steamers; we had nine, but only two or three of ours got up in time to fight the rebel steamers.

I was given the lead. I singled out the largest vessel, Commodore Lynch's flagship, the Sea Bird, and ordered my pilot to run her down.

When about two hundred yards from her, and after passing through the fire of the battery and giving them some good shots in return, I fired a nine-inch shell at her, which struck her just amidships, at the water line, passing through her as if she was so much paper, and exploded a great distance beyond. I then called away boarders and ran for her, my men picking up their muskets, pistols and cutlasses for a hand to hand fight. When fifty yards or more from her she hauled down her flag and her commander appeared on the upper deck holding open his coat to signify that he had surrendered. I immediately ordered the helm put a port and the steamer stopped to avoid striking him, but my men were so crazy with excitement and made so much noise that the helmsman could not hear, and so plumb into her we went, smashing in her whole port bow. My men immediately jumped on board and I had to follow to restrain them from injuring the prisoners. The captain surrendered to my vessel, stated that he was in a sinking condition, and asked me to rescue his officers and men. I was anxious to secure another steamer and gave the order to back out, and pursue when, to my inexpressible annoyance, I found that as we struck the Sea Bird the fastenings of our anchor went and the anchor had gone to the bottom, so we were anchored and I could not move. The men were frantic with excitement and for ten minutes I could not get any one to slip the chain, then one of the engineers unshackled it. I cut the line which fastened us to our prize with my sword, and was just leaving when her captain spoke to me for the second or third time and begged me, for God's sake, not to leave his men to drown; so to save them I reluctantly gave up the pursuit. While I was at anchor engaged [in] taking the prisoners from the sinking vessel two small rebel steamers ran around us, firing with musketry at my men. I could have sunk them both with one gun each, but my men were so wild that I could not get them to their quarters at the great guns. One of these steamers came up on my starboard quarter only ten or fifteen yards off, where there was not a man but myself, and tried to train a great gun on us. I repeatedly called the men to their guns, but they would not come, so as a last chance, for I felt that if the gun was fired I was destroyed, I drew my revolver, a small-sized Colt's, and fired at the captain of the enemy's gun. I fired three or four shots with deliberate aim and saw the captain of the gun and the man on his left fall; whether I hit them or not I do not know, I only know that the gun was not fired.

The Sea Bird was sunk, the Ellis was overpowered and captured and the Fanny and the Forest were burnt, by their officers; the crews escaping to the shore. The Appomattox alone escaping up the river. It was the end of the North Carolina Navy.

Samuel A. Ashe, "End of the North Carolina Navy," pp. 3–4.

(6) Burning of Winton, February 1862

Winton, a pleasant, little village of 300 people located on a bluff overlooking the Chowan River, was the first town in North Carolina burned by Union troops. On 19 February 1862, an expedition of six gunboats, Commander S. C. Rowan in charge, with approximately 1,000 troops aboard, arrived at Winton. The purpose of the expedition was to destroy two railroad bridges above the village and to investigate the rumors of strong Union sentiment in the area.

Before the troops could disembark, Confederate musketry and artillery fire drove the gunboats down the river. When word reached Winton the next morning that the expedition was returning, most of the local residents fled, and the small band of Confederate defenders under Colonel William T. Williams hastened to the breastworks at Mt. Tabor Church several miles away.

Even though Colonel Rush C. Hawkins of the Ninth New York, in command of the Union landing party, found the village deserted, he ordered it burned. In his official report Colonel Hawkins does not mention the fact that while Winton was being put to the torch, his men proceeded to pillage and plunder the town. A soldier of the Fourth Rhode Island observed, however, that "the boys found plenty of everything and soon came flocking back to the boats loaded down with household goods, books, articles of food, and anything they found that suited their fancy."[5] Another witness to the scene was a correspondent for

5. George H. Allen, *Forty-six Months with the Fourth Rhode Island Volunteers, in the War of 1861–1865*, p. 86.

the Petersburg Express. His account of the destruction of Winton was carried in the Wilmington Journal.

The enemy in two gun boats made their appearance off the town of Winton and proceeded to land, they were repulsed by the infantry, and retiring to their boats drew off . . . [beyond] the range of our guns and commenced shelling the town. Colonel Williams then fell back to a recent fortification near Mt. Tabor on the Murfreesboro road. Here a stand was made, but the enemy refused to advance. The next morning our troops returned to Winton and found that the Federals had retired to their boats and gone down the river.

About 10 o'clock, A.M. on Thursday, 20th inst. they came up as far as Barfield's (2 miles below Winton) and commenced bombarding the town; landing 1500 men at Barfields who marched off to intercept our retreat. . . . After landing 1500 men at Barfields, the gunboats came up to Winton, and placed 300 men on the wharf. The entire force entered the village, rolled a barrel of tar into the court-house, burst it in and set it on fire. The stately building which cost the county $30,000 in 1833, is now in ruins. With the exception of a few books saved by the County Court clerk, our records are all destroyed; the entire town; from Captain Hiram Freeman's embracing Col. Jordan's Hotel and buildings, the beautiful residence of the late Jno. A. Anderson, and all buildings down to the bank of the Chowan are destroyed. The jail is uninjured. . . . In the retreat, the Confederates left some $3000.00 or $4000.00 worth of commissary stores. . . .

While at Winton the federal soldiers committed divers depredations on private property; poultry of all kinds and pigs were rapidly driven off. All the houses which the federals burned were first rifled of such valuable contents as could be taken on board the gun-boats, the rest destroyed. Before night the gunboats retired and were seen the same evening passing Coleraine, twenty miles below Winton. . . .

It should be stated that an unfortunate man named Overton, lost his clothes by the pilfering of the Yankees; was bold enough to go on board and demand his clothing from the Federal commander. A search was ostensibly made, when the clothes could not be found, whereupon the Yankee captain offered to remunerate poor Overton in money; the promise, however has not been redeemed.

Wilmington *Journal*, 27 Feb. 1862.

(7) Battle of New Bern, March 1862

After the capture of Roanoke Island and the destruction of the mosquito fleet, General Burnside moved his Union forces against New Bern on the North Carolina mainland. This strategic port, located a few miles up the Neuse River, was the second largest city on the North Carolina coast. It was defended, nevertheless, by no more than 4,000 untried troops under General L. O'B. Branch. In the main Confederate defense line about six miles below the city was the Twenty-sixth North Carolina under Colonel Zebulon B. Vance.

On 14 March Burnside easily broke the Confederate line and sent the defenders retreating to-ward Kinston. The Twenty-sixth North Carolina fought well but to avoid capture had to flee across a swamp to its right. Before the day was over New Bern was in Union hands where it remained for the duration of the war.

From Kinston Colonel Vance wrote his wife, in no unassuming terms, about his role in the Battle of New Bern.

Kinston N.C. March 20th [1862]

Again I try to write you a note—My finger is much better & I can now write without so much pain—You will see an account of the fight in the papers. It began about 7 Oclk on Friday morning and lasted till 12 M. I was stationed on the right wing with a swamp in front. By 11 Oclk every one of our regiments had left except mine, the enemy had crossed the trenches on my left gone through my camp and got a half a mile in my rear toward New Bern before I was aware of it—They had Killed Major Carmichael, Captain Rand and various others and were marching right down the works to take me in the rear when my Quarter Master Capt Young came to me and told me of my danger. Gen Branch had left without giving me any orders and when I finally started and got in sight of the River I saw the bridge in flames! After getting all the troops over but my regiment they deliberately left me to my fate! Fortunately, I knew something of the country, and striking to the left up the Trent I came to a large creek called Briers Creek, almost as big as the Trent, in fact navigable for steam boats, and there we found only one small boat that would carry three men at once. The Yankees by this time drawn up just one mile away! I jumped my horse in to swim him over but when a little way he refused to swim, sank two or three times with me and I had to jump off and swim across with my sword, pistols and cartridges box on. Once over I rode about half a mile to a house and got three boats which we carried on our shoulders to the creek and after four hours of hard labour got them all over but three poor fellows who were drowned—I cannot now speak of the thousand dangers which I passed through—Balls struck all around me, men were hit right at my feet—My men fought gloriously—the first fire was especially magnificent—It was a dark foggy morning and the men were situated in small half moon redans, they fired by company beginning on the left, and the blaze at the muzzle of the guns was bright and glorious—Many of the Yankees tumbled over & the rest toddled back into the woods—For five hours the roar of the small arms was uninterrupted, fierce and deafening. Thirty old pieces of artillery (field) were in constant play, whilst the great guns of our batteries and the enemys ships made the earth tremble. I was surprised at my feelings, excitement and pleasure removed every other feeling and I could not resist cheering with might and main. Our total loss so far as I can learn is 5 killed, 10 wounded & 72 missing—of the missing I suppose one half are killed—having to leave the field as we did it was impossible to tell our dead—Numbers were sure to fall as we left the trenches—My loss was greater I suppose than any other regiment— We feel quite proud of the good name we have obtained and are determined to maintain it—It is not known yet if the enemy are going to follow us to this place. Troops are gathering here rapidly, we will soon be able for a stand. . . .

My hand is hurting me again—Good night darling—Kiss my dear, dear children, who have a father alive preserved to them through a thousand dangers—My Kindest love to my dear Mother, and Sisters and may God bless you & preserve you all with His great right arm which has been over me is my prayer.

Johnston, *Papers of Zebulon Baird Vance*, 1:128–30.

---

(8) Governor Edward Stanly

With much of the sound region in Union hands by the spring of 1862, President Lincoln appointed Edward Stanly, a native of North Carolina then living in California, military governor of the state. Stanly assumed office on 26 May and quickly discovered that he faced an impossible task. He not only had numerous disagreements with the Union authorities in New Bern, his capital city, but he also had to endure the scorn of his own people who looked upon him as a traitor. Soon, moreover, he was in trouble with the antislavery forces because of what was termed his prosouthern attitude. Stanly also found it impossible to protect private property from what he considered the shameful pillaging of the Union troops. The last straw was Lincoln's Emancipation Proclamation to which Stanly was bitterly opposed. On 15 January 1863, the governor tendered his resignation, returning to California in March.

One of the first problems Stanly had had to face upon assuming the governorship concerned a school for Negro children which had been established in New Bern. When the governor announced that he would not support the school, he came in for severe criticism from all sides. In a lengthy letter to Secretary of War Edwin Stanton, Stanly explained his position on the school and discussed the slavery question in general.

Headquarters Department of North Carolina
New Bern, June 12, 1862

Hon. E. M. Stanton
Secretary of War:

Sir: Your letter of the 3d instant has not received the immediate answer you requested, because I was absent in Beaufort when it arrived.

You send me a copy of the resolution adopted by the House of Representatives on the 2d instant, and desire I should furnish the Department with a full and immediate answer to the following part of said resolution:

Whether the said Edward Stanley [sic] has interfered to prevent the education of children, white or black, in said State; and, if so, by what authority, if any.

On the 31st day of May last I addressed you a letter which I presume had not been received when you wrote on the 3d instant. In that letter of the 31st, in reference to matters here, I made the following observations:

The perplexing question of what is to be done with the negroes is constantly presenting itself. I have thus far managed it with discretion. Upon all occasions I say I have no hope of affording redress to the enemies of our country; that the Union is to be restored, cost what it may in blood and treasure, and this is a matter not to be argued.

One person came to me yesterday who had four slaves taken from him, and told they were free by a rude soldier, who cursed his wife. I suggested, first, he must take the oath of allegiance; this he agreed to do. Then I gave him authority to look for his property, advising him to use mildness and persuasion. He did so, and one servant voluntarily returned to the home of a kind master. This has already excited some evil-disposed persons and will be misrepresented.

Almost all the inhabitants have gone away and the belief still exists that it is dangerous for them to return.

The Confederates refuse to allow any person to come to this place, keeping away even women and children. Unless I can give them some assurance that this is a war of restoration and not of abolition and destruction, no peace can be restored here for many years to come. I am making efforts to induce Union men to come and talk with me. I feel confident I shall be successful in a few weeks. . . .

A gentleman of good Samaritan inclinations and acts had established a school for negro children. He called and informed me what he was doing, and asked my opinion. I approved all he had done in feeding and clothing the destitute white and black, but told him I had been sent to restore the old order of things. I thought his negro school, if approved by me, would do harm to the Union cause. In a few months we shall know the result of the war. If by Southern folly emancipation comes, their spiritual welfare would not suffer by the delay, for I desired he would give such oral instructions in religious matters as he thought best.

Another reason I urged was, that by one of the cruel necessities of slavery the laws of North Carolina forbade slaves to be taught to read and write, and I would be most unsuccessful in my efforts if I encouraged the violation of her laws. He acquiesced, I thought, cheerfully. If the old residents ever return, those negroes who have been taught to read and write would be suspected and not benefited by it.

You have no idea how happy the influence has been on the minds of the excellent and severely-punished people of this lonely town. This school affair has already been much misrepresented.

This extract might be sufficient to answer the resolution, but as you request not only an immediate "but a full" answer, it may be proper to add something more. . . .

In the interview with the manager of the schools I made use of no threats, used no discourteous language, and treated the gentleman referred to with all kindness. He called the next morning and informed me he had suspended teaching the negro children. I approved what he had done, but nothing approaching unpleasantness occurred during the interview, nor did the thought enter my mind I had given him offense. Not a word was said, nor any intimation given, of any intention to "enforce" the laws of this State. No such thought was in my mind nor ever can be. . . .

I believe the President to be sincere in his various public declarations, and wish to make the people of North Carolina believe him to be sincere and patriotic.

But I am grieved to say that some of the most eminent and influential of our citizens, from listening to oft-repeated slanders, have been persuaded and charge the Southern country is invaded by "an enemy who come to rob us, to murder our people, to emancipate our slaves, and who is now preparing to add a new element to this most atrocious aggression, and involve us in the direful horrors of a servile war. He proposes nothing less than our entire destruction, the total desolation of our country— universal emancipation; to crush us, to wipe out the South, to involve us in irredeemable misery and hopeless ruin." . . .

Every day's experience impresses more forcibly on my mind the conviction, felt by abler and better men than myself, that some course of policy must be adopted as to the disposition of slaves within our lines.

If the Army advances, and their numbers, already large, shall be increased, what is to be done with them? Who will support them or their owners, often loyal and true men, already reduced to want by the rebellion, who can make no crops without their aid?

The expense of feeding the negroes will be enormous. It is estimated that each negro man employed by Government will require in wages and subsistence $40 per month to support him and family, who generally accompany him.

It is my heartfelt desire to restore to my native State the countless blessings conferred by the Union. I am ready to make any sacrifice a gentleman and patriot can make to do so. But if I cannot rely upon the "perfect confidence and full support of the War Department," which was promised me, I desire to know it.

I have the honor to be, your obedient servant.

EDWARD STANLEY [*sic*]
Military Governor of
North Carolina

Official Records, Ser. 1, 9:399–402.

WAR IN EASTERN NORTH CAROLINA, 1862–1864

When General Burnside departed for Virginia, as ordered in July 1862, he took two divisions with him. This left J. G. Foster, his successor in command in North Carolina, with an insufficient number of troops to make a long anticipated move on Goldsboro. General Foster turned his attention, therefore, to strengthening the fortifications at New Bern and other places in his command. At the same time he sent raiding parties into the eastern North Carolina countryside. Union naval forces were also active on the rivers and sounds. Hamilton, Trenton, Pollocksville, Swansboro, Williamston, and Jacksonville were among the many localities visited by the Union raiders. The Confederates in turn struck at Plymouth and Washington. Finally in December 1862, Foster moved in force on the Wilmington–Weldon Railroad at Goldsboro, but he managed to damage the line only superficially. It was back in full operation within a few days.

General Lee, concerned about the threat to his supply lines in eastern North Carolina, sent General D. H. Hill to the state in early 1863 with instructions to keep the Union forces confined to their bases while Confederate supply trains moved through the fertile region. In the spring Hill made feeble demonstrations respectively against New Bern and Washington. Other than these moves he did little with his new command.

Military activity was at a minimum in North Carolina during the summer and fall of 1863. Still the times were very gloomy. The eastern counties, lying open to Union troops, were subject to numerous enemy raids including one by Negro troops under General E. A. Wild. Adding to the burdens of the eastern Carolinians were the activities of armed bands of Negroes and native Union bushwhackers, known as "Buffaloes," who terrorized the area. Furthermore, Union authorities had plans for a fugitive slave colony on Roanoke Island.

In an effort to relieve the situation in North Carolina, General Lee, in February 1864, ordered General George E. Pickett with a 13,000 man force to strike at New Bern, the chief Union base in the state. The only accomplishment of the operation, however, was the destruction of the Union steamer *Underwriter* by Commander John Taylor Wood who was in charge of the seven navy cutters assigned to the expedition.

After the New Bern fiasco Pickett returned to Virginia and General R. F. Hoke of Lincolnton took over the command in North Carolina. Immediately upon assuming his new duties Hoke commenced preparations for an attack on Plymouth. Opportunely for him the Confederate navy had under construction at this time, at Edwards Ferry on the Roanoke River, the ironclad *Albemarle*. In response to appeals from General Hoke, Confederate authorities allowed the ram to participate in the attack on Plymouth which surrendered on 21 April 1864. The capture of this important river town forced the Union to evacuate nearby Washington, but not before the community was burned by the retiring forces.

Following the successes at Plymouth and Washington, Hoke turned his attention to New Bern. He had the city under siege when orders arrived in early May to abandon the attack and return to Virginia where Lee and Grant were locked in a bitter struggle.

In the meantime the *Albemarle* had threatened the Union control of the sounds. Authorities in the nation's capital did not breathe easily until the ironclad was torpedoed at her Plymouth moorings on the night of 27 October. Lieutenant William B. Cushing of the United States Navy led this daring operation.

As a result of the ram's destruction, Plymouth was recaptured by Union troops on 31 October. Washington fell shortly afterwards. Thus by the fall of 1864 the sound region of North Carolina was once again under Union control.

---

(1) Confederate Raid on Washington, September 1862

Although Union operations in eastern North Carolina in the summer of 1862 were strictly minor in nature, the period proved to be very trying for authorities in Raleigh. Henry T. Clark, who succeeded to the office of governor upon the death of John W. Ellis, appealed to Richmond for troops to protect the rich farmlands of the east, but General Lee refused to weaken his lines in Virginia. This meant that any Confederate offensive operations in North Carolina would have to come from the few commands already in the state. The first such move occurred early on the morning of 6 September, when Colonel S. D. Pool with a small detachment surprised the Union garrison at Washington. The skirmish cost the Union command approximately fifty killed and wounded. Pool, his losses slightly higher than those of the enemy, was eventually driven from Washington. However, the capture of three brass field pieces and ample supplies, along with the sinking of the Union gunboat,

Picket, *when her magazine acci-dentally exploded, kept the day from being a total loss for the Con-federates.*

Fortunately for the Union forces when the assault started, several companies of the Third New York Cavalry were in the streets of Washington preparing to move out in the direction of Plymouth. The resistance of these troopers in the initial stages of the attack, doubt-less, was an important factor in the ultimate failure of the Confed-erate raid.

On the day following the battle,

Rowland M. Hall, a twenty-eight-year-old officer in the Third New York wrote his father a lengthy account of the day's fight. This was Hall's first experience under fire. Thus he tended to exaggerate the scope and importance of the engagement and to accept as true all accounts of Confederate atroci-ties. Yet the letter is extremely in-teresting. The young officer wrote about the excitement and thrill of battle, the "Rebel Yell," the dread-ful countenances of the Confed-erate dead, and his own inability to handle the sight of blood.

Washington, N.C.
September 7, 1862

My very dear father,

We reached this place last Tuesday . . . with four companies of the regiment. The ostensible purpose of the move from Newbern was to afford our horses and men . . . an opportunity to recruit. Yesterday Saturday morning however we were ordered to be in the saddle at 3 o'clock to make a scout to Plymouth on the Roanoke River. My company covered the rear guard of the expedition and the rear of the cavalry. Three companies and four pieces of cannon of the 8th New York Regi-ment of Artillery and the baggage wagons, having taken up their march, we were filing through the streets of Washington at half past 3 when a sudden and heavy firing of small arms told us that the town had been attacked on the west side. It soon turned out that a force of . . . rebels had eluded our picquets by passing through a field of tall Southern Corn . . . where there are no roads and had penetrated at once, broken for the most part into small squads into the streets and had scattered them-selves over every part of the town. An universal fusillade arose. My Co' quarters were attacked within 15 minutes after we had left them; the enemy's cavalry charged through almost every street & were met & every-where driven back by our cavalry, who behaved well.

Our force however, reduced by sickness did not exceed 450 men all-told, four co's. of cavalry, four incomplete Co's of Infantry of the 24th Mass. and 1st N.C. Loyalist, and one battery of cannon. The heavy bat-tery of 4 pieces . . . in the town was quickly taken having no horses and being almost entirely unmanned and with 3 light pieces brought by the enemy was turned against us. The part of the town next to the river was occupied. The condition of affairs appeared bad enough. The North Carolina troops (Loyalists) behaved *exceedingly well.* The Mass. men were surprised, some of the infantry being under arms when the attack took place, but rallied. The fighting was necessarily desultory in as much as the enemy occupied every garden fence and house. Soon the guns were got into position and opened with grape and canister down the streets. The Louisiana gunboat opened with . . . Parrott guns on the houses fronting the river and drove the enemy from the houses there. Companies G (my company) L. & D charged. The first two through the lower part of the town along the river but without meeting the enemy *hand to hand*; the latter through the upper streets into which the enemy had been driven by the heavy guns scattering them right and left. At half past seven the rout of the enemy was general and complete. . . . The cavalry now advanced in pursuit but were met by a flag of truce under a tipsy and fierce lieutenant desiring to send a surgeon into our lines. The request refused we followed passing houses full of their wounded protected by the white flag and come up with their rear guard with a battery in position and double our forces of cavalry. It was not thought provident to charge them so we kept harrassing them for ten miles and then returned to town satisfied with everything excepting the loss of our guns. These had been in the Academy green unguarded and unprovided with horses to move them and their capture had been expected. But we had defeated an attempt to take a poorly garrisoned town by a pretty strong and very desperate force . . . and perfectly confident of success. . . . It was the first time yesterday I experienced the "joy of battle." A strange excitement pleasurable while it lasts. In the afternoon being at the quarters of Captain Murphy MD desired me to help him dress the wounds of the poor negroes wantonly shot by the rebels I went; the worst wounded in appearance was one in the hand, the bone of the right side of the left hand was entirely exposed, indeed very little of the hand to all appearance was left & after the bone was removed the artery spurting blood had to be tied. I tied it up and got covered with blood & I turned deadly sick at my stomach. I find I cannot stand these things. I must see as little of the *results* as possible. Our loss is heavy at least one hundred killed and wounded. . . . Their loss in killed & wounded was double ours. Their dead lay thick about the streets dreadful countenances turned toward the sky in the beautiful morning light. It is impossible to imagine anything more repulsive than the appearance of these men, unshorn, unkempt, dirty, thin . . . hungry looking, ragged, fierce. They attacked with tremendous yells lasting throughout the battle and were met by us in silence with English coolness and defeated with English vigour. One of their cavalry knowing the wife of a man in the N.C. Loyal troops cut her down by a sabre cut over the head and then shot her little daughter through the shoulder. The child a pretty little girl of 7 years old is lying in the hospital and both are doing well. The picquet gunboat through the carelessness of a man in the magazine blew up killing [the] Captain . . . and 19 of his men. I had been talking with him the night before. I feel thankful that I am yet spared. . . . I pray that you may be well but I rarely hear from home. With more love to all than I can express I am your

Affectionate son
ROWLAND M. HALL

Rowland M. Hall to father, 7 Sept. 1862, Stickley Papers.

(2) "Buffaloes"

In eastern North Carolina the term "Buffaloes" referred to native Union bushwackers who terrorized the countryside. In August 1862, a group of Buffaloes established themselves at Wingfield, the estate of Dr. Richard Dillard, above Edenton on the Chowan River. Soon the encampment became a haven for runaway slaves, lawless whites, and Confederate deserters.

Wingfield was under the command of John A. (Jack) Fairless, a hard-drinking Gates County farm boy who had deserted from the Fifty-second North Carolina. So undisciplined were Fairless and his men that they became the concern of both the local citizens and the Union authorities. The report of a Union naval officer who visited Wingfield in the fall of 1862 confirmed the worst of the rumors about the Buffaloes (Document A), as does a letter dated 22 August 1863 from an eastern Carolinian to her cousin (Document B).

Finally in March 1863, 300 men of the Forty-second North Carolina Regiment broke up the camp and burned Wingfield. This action, unfortunately, brought little relief for the families in the vicinity. Yankee raids and plundering continued (Document B).

A.

USS *Shawsheen,*
Off Plymouth, N.C.,
September 28, 1862

Sir: In obedience to your order, I submit to you the following report in regard to proceedings of a company of home guards stationed at Wingfield, Chowan County, N.C. On my arrival there on the 18th of September I found out of sixty-three recruits only twenty present; the others had gone to their homes or elsewhere, as they chose. The captain was in a state of intoxication, threatening to shoot some of the remaining men, and conducting himself in a most disgraceful manner by taking one man's horses and making other people pay him money to pay for them, and this, too, from people who were well disposed toward our Government. He had some eight or ten horses when I went there, gotten in this way. He has no control over his men, and [by] the manner in which he conducts himself he is doing much injury to the cause of the U.S. Government. Some of the men that have gone have taken their arms or guns with them; the ammunition has all been smuggled out and sold to citizens for liquor; what remaining arms there were I took on board for safe-keeping. On the 21st, Captain Fairless went off and left his men, as he said, to go to New Berne by way of Suffolk. His men say they will serve under him no longer. They are now left in charge of a man they call lieutenant, with no clothing, no rations; are dependent on the county for subsistence.

Lieutenant-Commander
CHAS. W. FLUSSER,
Senior Naval Officer Present

THOMAS J. WOODWARD
Acting Volunteer Lt.,
Commanding

Official Records of the Union and Confederate Navies in the War of Rebellion, Ser. 1, 8:95.

B.

Stockton Aug 22ᵈ 1863

My very dear Cousin

I have such a good opportunity of writing you that I cannot let it pass without doing so. It has been so very long we have heard a word from you until a short time since Cousin Melly Dillard was kind enough to send us your dear Mother's letter, you don't know how truly glad we were to get it and hear all about you & to know too dear Cousin that you were safe from the grasp of the merciless invaders.

I would have written you before but truly & sincerely I have not the heart to write to any one. We have been in so much trouble, the war brought with it sorrow, then came to us our great grief when we were called on to give up . . . our dear old father . . . My poor Mother and myself live here entirely alone with my little children. My dear husband is still in the service of his country he was among the first that offered his services to his country and still labors for its cause with the same ardent zeal as at first. . . . Cousin dear you have no idea of the wretched condition of this part of the country—last winter we were surrounded by their [Yankee] camps the one nearest us was at E. City—there were some four or five companies quartered there besides the gunboats that constantly came up from Newbern & Roanoke Island. Then the camp at Dillards (as it was called) poor old Wingfield—dear beautiful Wingfield, now so poluted [sic] by the foot of the blood thirsty yankee not a vestige of the place remains, it lies in ashes. I feel so much for Cousin Mary. From E. City they made frequent raids in the country, with the regulars they have a company of buff[aloes] and a company of armed negroes and they looked & behaved more like deamons than any thing else in these raids they would arrest any citizen they could find. They would steal any thing they could put their hands on, they would come in a house with their heavy cavalry boots on, and go out with them filled with knives & forks, snuffers & [illegible] trays if they could get nothing else. They searched our house several times for arms. They & I had had some pretty high words about their conduct. They say we secesh women are hateful. . . . it would make your blood boil to see them rush on your premises throw out their pickets at any door & have your house completely surrounded by them white & black. I followed them wherever they went about the house, so they did not get much chance to steal. They would always demand the keys, but I never gave them up except the barn keys—there I could not much help myself. They threatened to burn our house several times, but they did not intimidate me as they hoped they had, but we might feel therefore very much blest, for many have been entirely robbed of everything they had, some families entirely broken up by them you must be sure & go see Henrietta and get her to tell you all about our poor miserable country. But you can not tell our joy when the Confederates came down, they left at a double quick, that was the time Wingfield was burned. You must get Henry to tell you how the place looked as she went there to see the Dr. while the Yanks had him a prisoner. After the Confederates broke up the camp down here we were not much troubled with them except now & then a cavalry dash through the country . . . and last week 1700 made a tramp through here coming from Suffolk down to Edenton thence through Hertford & E. City back to Norfolk. . . . They, N.Y. [troops], are known through this section as Dodges "Mounted Thieves."[1] They committed all manner of outrages they could, destroyed a great deal of property in Edenton, robbing people of all their houses, old Mr. J. C. Johnston lost a great deal & Dr Tom Warren lost about $10,oo[o]? worth. They destroyed all of the Rev Mr. Johnston's property. . . . They arrested a good many persons among them Cousin Joe Granby & carried him I have fear to Ft Norfolk. I have every reason to be thankful for they only took from us about 5 or 600 lbs of bacon [illegible] They demanded the smoke house keys so I went out and opened it myself soon as I did so some of the scamps ran up to me and said "more maggotty meat." I said yes they won't any better to eat it than I was. Then he climbed very nimbly up to get the meat, he said "I do this as if I were used to it." I told him I thought he did not at all deceive his looks. While one part was stealing the meat the others were running the horse & mules out of the pasture, after they took my mule & carried him off they could not manage him so he got loose and came home. So in all they did not make a great deal out of me. But I must not boast—as they are to be back again in a week or ten days,—yes Cousin Sally last Monday night I slept within a mile of 1700 Yankee troops. We have lost only 27 negroes and nearly all of those left when Roanoke fell. Hester is the only woman I had to leave me. She & her five children, ones that had been more human [?] than almost any. I regret losing her little children. The strength of our farm has gone but we still have many left—Cousin you don't know how desolate we feel here, so cut off. The Yanks have drawn in their lines and thrown us in despair and the water separates us from the mainland so we are in quite a strait. We never see anyone . . . nothing but Yankee papers so you may know we dont see the right side of our cause. Now for home matters. . . .

All unite with me in sincere love. . . . your affectionate cousin.

Mrs. L. J. Johnson to cousin, 22 Aug. 1863, J. L. Bailey Papers.

---

(3) Fugitive Slave Colony on Roanoke Island

General A. E. Burnside's victories   *in the sound region of North Caro-*

1. In May 1862, Colonel C. C. Dodge with the First New York Mounted Rifles had conducted a raid through northeastern North Carolina.

lina in the spring and early summer of *1862* had caused many
slaves to slip away to freedom behind Union lines. They arrived
on Roanoke Island in such large
numbers that the general appointed Vincent Colyer of New
York to be the Superintendent of
the Poor in the North Carolina
Department. With the capture of
New Bern in March *1862*, Colyer
was transferred to that city. He
was replaced on Roanoke Island
by a Sergeant Thompson. Then in
May *1863* the Reverend Horace
James was appointed to the "Superintendency of the Blacks in
North Carolina" and instructed to
establish a colony of fugitive
slaves on Roanoke Island.

He planned to settle the Negroes on unoccupied lands, give
them agricultural implements and
tools, and "to train and educate

them for a free and independent
community." James reported that
by January *1865*, a total of *591*
houses had been built and that
there were *3,091* "contrabands" in
the colony, but they were mostly
women and children. The majority
of the males were in the Union
army. The first Negro troops recruited in North Carolina, James
boasted, came from the Roanoke
Island settlement.[2] The enterprise
was finished in late *1865* when an
order was issued by Union authorities necessitating "the restoration
to original owners who had received pardon of all abandoned
property to which they could prove
title."[3]

James, in his annual report,
1864, gives an interesting description of the Negro community and
its work.

Within a month after assuming the Superintendency of the Blacks in
North Carolina, I was ordered by Major General J. G. Foster, then com-
manding the Department, to establish a colony of negroes upon Roanoke
Island . . .

I went North in June, 1863, under orders from Gen. Foster, to procure
materials and implements with which to furnish the projected colony
with an outfit, and in a few weeks raised in New England and New York
between eight and nine thousand dollars. . . .

While this work of soliciting funds was in progress at the North, Gen.
E. A. Wild received orders from Gen. Foster, to take possession of, and
assign to the negroes, the unoccupied and unimproved lands of the island, laying them out in suitable lots for families. He sent thither Serj't
George O. Sanderson (late of the 43d Mass. Reg't) as Assistant Superintendent, who made the primary surveys, and opened the first broad avenue of the new African town. . . .

I returned from the North in July, 1863, accompanied by female
teachers, and furnished with large supplies, to find that Gen. Wild had
been ordered, with his negro troops, to Charleston, S.C. He left New
Bern on the 30th of July, with his brigade of 2,154 men—and among
them, the flower of Roanoke Island—bearing the beautiful banner of the

2. Horace James, *Annual Report of the Superintendent of Negro Affairs in
North Carolina 1864*, pp. 22, 26, 31.

3. David Stick, *The Outer Banks of North Carolina, 1584–1958*, p. 165.

Republic which had been presented by the colored ladies of New Berne to the First North Carolina Regiment, Colonel James C. Beecher. . . .

The work was now prosecuted with vigor, though with little outside aid for some time. With compass, chart, and chain, and a gang of choppers, the old groves of pine, gum, holly, and cypress, were penetrated, crossed and re-crossed, and the upper, or northern, end of the island was laid out in acre lots, and at once assigned to families. Nothing could exceed the enthusiasm of these simple people, when they found themselves in possession of a spot they could call their own. . . .

It was never intended to give these people F A R M S at Roanoke, but only a homestead, and a garden spot for each family. There were sufficient reasons for this, in that the island is not large enough to divide into farms for any considerable number of people. The land is not rich enough for profitable farming, though it will produce vegetables, grapes, and other fruit, in abundance and variety. And again, invalids, aged people, and soldiers' wives and children could not be expected to improve more than a single acre. This was the plan of the settlement. Broad, straight avenues were laid out, 1,200 feet apart, up and down the island, nearly parallel with its shores and parallel with one another, which were named "Roanoke Avenue," "Lincoln Avenue," "Burnside Avenue," etc. At right angles with these were streets, somewhat narrower than the avenues, and 400 feet apart, numbered "First Street," "Second Street," & c., in one direction from a certain point, and "A Street," "B Street," etc. in the other direction. . . .

A good supply of lumber being indispensable when one would build a town, I purchased at the North a valuable steam-engine and saw-mill, thus using the larger portion of the funds which had been secured in aid of the freedmen. But as the mill could not be made immediately available, logs and boards split by hand were used at first, and chimneys of the Southern style were constructed of sticks and clay. A few sawed boards for floor, door, and window, were sometimes obtained in a boat expedition across the Sound, to Nagg's [sic] Head, Oregon Inlet or Croatan, and thus their mansions were completed. . . .

A pioneer teacher from the North landed on the Island, October 19th, 1863, and for more than three months labored alone and unattended, living in one log cabin, and teaching in another, with most commendable zeal and self-denial.

This was Miss Elizabeth James, a lady sent out by the American Missionary Association. On the 25th of January, 1864, Miss Ella Roper arrived, who was followed, on the 20th of February, by Mr. S. S. Nickerson, and a little later, by Miss Mary Burnap, transferred from a school in New Berne. . . .[4]

The wants of the island are not yet fully supplied. Besides the 1,297 children under fourteen years of age, many of the adults are eager to be taught to read and write, and will not be denied. Add to this the distribution of donated clothing, visitation of the sick, writing letters for the women to their husbands or sons in the army, and their own domestic cares, and one may readily decide whether from ten to twenty dollars

---

4. Four additional teachers arrived on the island in 1864.

per month, would tempt teachers to do this work, in banishment and obloquy, if their minds were not glowing with enthusiasm, and their hearts penetrated with benevolent love. . . .

An attempt was made, early in the year, to give the colonists an idea of governing themselves. A "council" of fifteen leading individuals was appointed, and instructed to meet and consult for the common welfare, and be a medium through which the rules and orders of the Superintendent of Negro Affairs and of the military authorities might be communicated and enforced. This was intended to be the germ of a civil government. But the plan proved unsuccessful in the main. The "councillors" were too ignorant to keep records, or make and receive written communications, were jealous of one another, and too little raised in culture above the common people to command their respect, at least while the island is under military rule. To fit these people for republican self-government, education is the prime necessity. The sword to set them free, letters to make them citizens.

The whites, who lived to the number of about four hundred on Roanoke Island previous to this rebellion, did not, for the most part, abandon their homes. They hastened, after the capture of the island, to take the oath of allegiance, which some of them have faithfully kept in its spirit, others only in "the letter which killeth." The truly loyal among them have appreciated the necessity which compelled the Government to take possession of their uncultivated lands for a negro settlement, and have accepted the fact with patriotic submission. But the other class, whose loyalty is so ill-disguised as to reveal the "copper," are loud in their complaints of the "nigger" and the "abolitioners." They would be glad to drive the colored people and their friends from the Island. . . .

Some persons have predicted that the government would fail to confirm to the Freedmen the rights and privileges they enjoy in these homesteads on Roanoke Island. I cannot believe it. These people are wards of the government. It is an element of our glory as a nation, that we can crush out a slave-holding rebellion with one hand, and sustain a liberated people with the other. The person, be he white or black, who has taken an acre of piney woods, worth two dollars in the market, and increased its value thirty or forty fold by his own labor in a single year, certainly deserves well of his country, and should be permitted to enjoy, while he lives, the fruits of his industry. When a "Bureau of Freedmen's Affairs" is created by Congress, it may well look to this matter. . . .

Horace James, *Annual Report of the Superintendent of Negro Affairs in North Carolina 1864*, pp. 21–34.

(4) D. H. Hill at New Bern, March 1863

When General D. H. Hill assumed command of the troops in North   *Carolina on 25 February 1863, most North Carolinians were* elated. He had the reputation of being a fighter which led the Raleigh Progress to comment: "We have had vastly too much stategy, too much ditching and digging in North Carolina. Had we less of these and more fighting things might have been different, than at present. . . ."[5]

Hill found it difficult with a small command to live up to his reputation. The strike at New Bern in March did little more than annoy the enemy. Yet southern newspapers carried reports of a Confederate victory in which a large number of prisoners were taken. Hill's men, of course, knew better. One young soldier even went so far as to question whether his commanding general had any real object in mind when he started the expedition.

Camp White, Above Kinston
March 26, 1863

[To Donald MacRae]
You have doubtless read full accounts of the reported recapture of Newbern, and the taking of 1500 prisoners. Our company was in most all of the fighting, except that done by General [J. J.] Pettigrew, and had the honor to be complimented for a charge made upon the Yankee picket at Deep Gully. Nobody hurt on either side—one of our horses killed. The 1500 prisoners captured at Deep Gully have dwindled down to one cross-eyed Yankee and a Buffaloe! No one down here knows what General Hill intended to do in his recent expedition, although the papers confidently assert that he accomplished his object. To the admirers of Daniel H., it would not seem exactly orthodox to say he had no definite object in view when he set out from Kinston; but I must say it looks very like it to a man up a tree. These big generals don't always have such deep laid plans as people give them credit for.

[WALTER MACRAE]

Walter MacRae to Donald MacRae, 26 Mar. 1863, Hugh MacRae Papers.

---

(5) General E. A. Wild's Raid, December 1863

In December 1863, General B. F. Butler, who had replaced J. G. Foster in command of Union forces in eastern North Carolina, ordered General E. A. Wild with two regiments of Negro troops into the northeastern counties of the state. Wild moved his command from Norfolk to Elizabeth City and then eastward across Camden and Currituck counties and then back to Virginia. Local citizens were in a state of "perpetual panic," many of whom had never before seen Negro troops. Even though the Union general

5. Raleigh *Progress*, 1 Mar. 1863.

was white, Harvard educated, and a medical doctor, he was in the eyes of many North Carolinians a "monster of humanity," a "cousin of Beelzebub" for his use of Negro troops.[6]

Wild estimated that 2,500 Negroes were released as a result of his efforts. Yet the real significance of the raid rested not upon the number of slaves freed, homes burned, and hostages taken, but upon the fact that this was one of the first raids of any magnitude undertaken primarily by Negro troops since their enlistment was officially sanctioned by Washington.

General Wild was highly

pleased with the accomplishments of the expedition and the performance of his troops, as was a Northern correspondent on the expedition (Document A). Confederate accounts present an entirely different picture of the raid. Negro soldiers, according to the Southern Recorder "ran riot during . . . [their] stay in Albemarle" and when fired upon "fled like wild deer."[7] General Wild was accused of executing a Georgia private under the false pretext that he was a guerrilla fighter. One Confederate colonel threatened to retaliate by hanging a Union prisoner and holding two more in irons (Document B).

A.

General Wild's Expedition
A National Account
Norfolk, Va., Monday,
January 4, [1864]

General Wild resolved to be absent a month, to occupy and evacuate towns at his leisure, relying upon a novel species of strategy and the bayonets of his sable braves to recross our lines in safety when his work should be accomplished.

As we rode into Elizabeth City, a little after sunrise, I was surprised to see how its appearance had been changed by the war. Three years ago it was a busy and beautiful little city. . . . Now most of the dwellings were deserted; the stores all closed; the streets overgrown with grass . . . the doors of the bank standing wide open, and a sepulchral silence brooded over the place. We found General Wild at his headquarters—the fine residence of Dr. Pool. . . .

I found that the attention of the General, after occupying the city, had been first turned to the guerrillas who infested the neighborhood. . . .

The suppression of the guerrillas was considered by General Wild subordinate [however] to the great object of his raid, which was to clear the country of slaves and procure recruits for his brigade. . . .

The material result of the raid may be summed up as follows: Between two thousand and three thousand slaves were released from bondage, with whom were taken along about three hundred and fifty ox, horse, and mule teams, and from fifty to seventy-five saddle horses,

6. "Old Times In Betsy," Elizabeth City *Economist,* 24 Aug. 1900.
7. Milledgeville *Southern Recorder,* 19 Jan. 1864.

some of them valuable animals. The guerrillas lost thirteen killed and wounded; ten dwelling-houses, with many thousand bushels of corn belonging to them, were burned, besides . . . two distilleries; four of their camps were destroyed, and one of their number was hanged; and one hundred rifles, uniforms, infantry equipments, etc. fell into our hands as spoils, with a loss on the part of the brigade of twelve killed and wounded and one man taken prisoner. Beside this, fourteen rebel prisoners and four hostages were brought in. A comparatively small number of men were enlisted—not more than one hundred in all—a large proportion of the able-bodied slaves having previously left their masters, the facilities for escaping being especially great in the region visited.

In regard to its moral and political results, however, the importance of the raid cannot be over-estimated. The counties invaded by the colored troops were completely panic-stricken. Scores of families, for no cause but a guilty conscience, fled into the swamps on their approach. . . . With regard to the guerrillas I am reliably informed that they have left this part of the state. The severe chastisement they and their friends received from General Wild rendered a longer stay not advisable. . . .

In another respect this raid possesses historical importance. It is the first of any magnitude undertaken by negro troops since their enlistment was authorized by Congress, and by it the question of their efficiency in any branch of the service has been practically set at rest. Thoroughly obedient to their officers, during a march of three hundred miles their conduct on every occasion was truly admirable. It will have been seen that they performed in the enemy's country all the duties of white soldiers—scouting, skirmishing, picket duty, guard duty, every service incident to the occupation of hostile towns, and, best of all, fighting. Colonel Draper testifies to their excellent behavior under fire, and declares that he could wish to lead no better men into battle; that he feels perfectly secure with them, and can depend upon them at a critical moment with as much confidence as upon white troops less accustomed to obey the commands of superiors. . . . When the rebellion shall have subsided into partisan warfare, so far from lasting for ever as Jeff Davis threatens, our colored troops will take care that its end is soon reached. . . .

TEWKSBURY

Moore, *The Rebellion Record*, 8:297–304.

B.

Headquarters Forces on
Blackwater,
Franklin, Va., January, 1864

General Wild, Commanding Colored Brigade, Norfolk, Va.:

Sir: Probably no expedition, during the progress of this war, has been attended with more utter disregard for the long-established usages of civilization or the dictates of humanity, than your late raid into the country bordering the Albemarle. Your stay, though short, was marked by crimes and enormities. You burned houses over the heads of defenseless women and children, carried off private property of every description, arrested non-combatants, and carried off ladies in irons, whom you confined with negro men.

Your negro troops fired on confederates after they had surrendered, and they were only saved by the exertions of the more humane of your white officers. Last, but not least, under the pretext that he was a guerrilla, you hanged Daniel Bright, a private of Company L, Sixty-second Georgia regiment, (cavalry), forcing the ladies and gentlemen whom you held in arrest to witness the execution. Therefore, I have obtained an order from the General Commanding, for the execution of Samuel Jones, a private of Company R, Fifth Ohio, whom I hang in retaliation. I hold two more of your men—in irons—as hostages for Mrs. Weeks and Mrs. Mundin. When these ladies are released, these men will be relieved and treated as prisoners of war.

> JOEL R. GRIFFIN,
> COLONEL

Moore, *The Rebellion Record*, 8:304–5.

---

(6) General George C. Pickett Fails but Commander John T. Wood Succeeds at New Bern, February 1864

In early 1864, General Lee wrote President Davis that the time had come to capture the enemy's forces at New Bern. With his own army in winter quarters Lee could spare the troops for this purpose. General George Pickett with a 13,000 man force was given the assignment, but the Virginian failed at New Bern as had D. H. Hill the previous year.

The cooperating naval force under Commander John Taylor Wood[8] was more successful. Wood and a detachment of sailors and marines were assigned the task of attacking the Union gunboats at New Bern. On the night of 1 February this fine officer and his picked crew boarded and then burned the steamer Underwriter.

Midshipman J. T. Scharf was a member of the boarding party. In his History of the Confederate Navy *Scharf wrote about the capture and destruction of the Union vessel.*

8. This remarkable officer, an 1853 graduate of the U.S. Naval Academy, would today possibly be called a commando because of his many daring exploits during the war. In January 1863, he was appointed an aide to President Davis with the statutory rank and pay of colonel of cavalry. His adventurous spirit was not content with staff duty. Thus soon he was back on the water with the rank of commander.

In the meantime, Col. Wood[9] had again launched his boats in the Neuse, and arranged them in two divisions, the first commanded by himself, and the second by Lieut. B. P. Loyall. After forming parallel to each other, the two divisions pulled rapidly down stream. When they had rowed a short distance, Col. Wood called all the boats together, final instructions were given, and this being through with, he offered a fervent prayer for the success of his mission. It was a strange and ghostly sight, the men resting on their oars with heads uncovered, the commander also bareheaded, standing erect in the stern of his boat; the black waters rippling beneath; the dense overhanging clouds pouring down sheets of rain, and in the blackness beyond an unseen bell tolling as if from some phantom cathedral. The party listened—four peals were sounded and then they knew it was the bell of the U N D E R W R I T E R, or some other of the gunboats, ringing out for two o'clock. Guided by the sound, the boats pulled toward the steamer, pistols, muskets and cutlasses in readiness. The advance was necessarily slow and cautious. Suddenly, when about three hundred yards from the U N D E R W R I T E R, her hull loomed up out of the inky darkness. Through the stillness came the sharp ring of five bells for half-past two o'clock, and just as the echo died away a quick, nervous voice from the deck hailed, "Boat ahoy!" No answer was given, but Col. Wood kept steadily on. "Boat ahoy! Boat ahoy!" again shouted the watch. No answer. Then the rattle on board the steamer sprang summoning the men to quarters, and the Confederates could see the dim and shadowy outline of hurrying figures on deck. Nearer Col. Wood came, shouting, "Give way!" "Give way, boys, give way!" repeated Lieutenant Loyall and the respective boat commanders, and give way, they did with a will. The few minutes that followed were those of terrible suspense. To retreat was impossible, and if the enemy succeeded in opening fire on the boats with his heavy guns all was lost.

The instructions were that one of the Confederate divisions should board forward and the other astern, but, in the excitement, the largest number of the boats went forward, with Col. Wood amidships.

In the meantime, the U N D E R W R I T E R, anchored within thirty yards of two forts, slipped her cable and made efforts to get up sufficient steam from her banked fires, to move off, or run the Confederates down. This movement only hastened the boarding party, and crews pulled rapidly alongside. . . .

Once on the deck of the U N D E R W R I T E R the onslaught was furious. Cutlasses and pistols were the weapons of the Confederates, and each selected and made a rush for his man. The odds were against the attacking party, and some of them had to struggle with three opponents. But they never flinched in the life-and-death struggle, nor did the gallant enemy. The boarders forced the fighting. Blazing rifles had no terrors for them. They drove back the enemy inch by inch. Steadily, but surely, the boarders began to gain the deck, and crowded their opponents to the companion-ways or other places of concealment; while all the time fierce

9. See footnote no. 8.

hand-to-hand fights were going on on other portions of the vessel. Now, one of the Confederates would sink exhausted—again, one of the enemy would fall on the slippery deck. Rifles were snatched from the hands of the dead and the dying, and used in the hands as bludgeons did deadly work. Down the companion-ways the attacked party were driven pell-mell into the ward-rooms and steerage, and even to the coal-bunkers, and after another sharp but decisive struggle the enemy surrendered. The UNDERWRITER was captured, its commander slain, and many of its officers and men killed and wounded, or drowned. The Confederate loss was over one-fourth of the number engaged—six killed and twenty-two wounded. E. F. Gill, the Confederate engineer, lay in the gangway mortally wounded, and midshipman Saunders, a gallant boy, cut down in a hand to hand fight, breathed out his young life on deck.

J. T. Scharf, *History of the Confederate States Navy*, pp. 397–99.

---

(7) Hangings at Kinston, February 1864

Although Pickett failed at New Bern in early 1864, he did manage to take approximately 300 prisoners. Among those captured were several members of the First and Second North Carolina Union Volunteers. Since twenty-two of these men had formerly served in the Confederate army, they were hanged for desertion. The executions took place at Kinston in February 1864. A great many in the North considered this wholesale murder. Most Southerners, on the other hand, thought these men received their just reward. Reverend John Paris, chaplain of the Fifty-fourth North Carolina, delivered a lengthy sermon before General R. F. Hoke's brigade, "upon the death of these men, that the eyes of the living might be opened, to view the horrid and ruinous crime and sin of desertion, which had become so preva-

lent." Paris said: "I am fully satisfied, that the great amount of desertions from our army are produced by, and are the fruits of a bad, mischievous, restless, and dissatisfied not to say disloyal influence that is at work in the country at home. If in this bloody war our country should be over-run, this same mischievous home influence will no doubt be the prime agent in producing such a calamity. . . . These malcontents profess to be greatly afflicted in mind about the state of public affairs. In their doleful croakings they are apt to give vent to their melancholy lamentations in such words as these: 'The country is ruined!' 'We are whipt!' 'We might as well give up!' 'It is useless to attempt to fight any longer!' 'This is the rich man's war and the poor man's fight,' & c."[10] The sermon was published and given

10. John Paris, *A Sermon: Preached Before Brig.-Gen. Hoke's Brigade at Kinston, N.C. on the 28th of February, 1864*, pp. 4, 8.

wide circulation. The chaplain also wrote a long letter to the North Carolina Presbyterian describing his visits with the condemned prisoners and their subsequent executions. Extracts from this letter were published both in the South and in the North.

In our late campaign against Newbern we captured in the ranks of the enemy, with arms in their hands, and dressed out in the Yankee toggery, twenty-two men who were recognized and proved to be deserters from the Confederate service. They have all been tried by courtmartial, found guilty, condemned and suffered the penalty of death upon the gallows. They were all turned over to our brigade for execution. At the instance of Brigadier General Hoke, I attended them in confinement, in the character of a minister of the Gospel, and accompanied them to the gallows. Thus I learned their history and heard their confessions. On Friday, the 5th instant, Joseph L. Hasket and David Jones, of Craven County, who deserted from the 10th regiment, were executed.

They were illiterate men; neither of them could read. Admitted they had deserted, but insisted that the Yankees compelled them to take the oath and enlist. These were the most unfeeling and hardened men I have ever encountered. They had been raised up in ignorance and vice. They manifested but little, if any, concern about eternity. They marched to the gallows with apparent indifference. Jones, though quite a young man, never shed a tear. By deserting the flag of their country they were guilty of perjury, but they seemed to regard it with indifference. With this state of feeling they were launched into eternity.

On Friday, the 12th, five more of the prisoners were brought to the scaffold. As all of these executions had to take place within twenty-four hours after the publication of their sentence, I had only that space of time to devote to their religious instruction before they went to the bar of God. The names of these men were Amos Armyett, William Irving, Mitchell Busick, Lewis Bryan, and John Stanley, all deserters from Nethercutt's battalion and from Jones county. Upon entering the cell in which they were confined, I asked if any of them were members of the church? Armyett replied that he was, and had been a Methodist for years; that he was prepared to meet his judge in peace. But as I don't admit a man's lips as test of his Christianity, I thought them only as sinners against God of the most heaven-defying character. I urged upon them the importance of making a full and complete confession of all their sins before both God and man; yet I am afraid these men were willing to look the great sin of perjury, of which they were guilty, fully in the face. Yet each one, before starting to the gallows, professed to have made his peace with his God, and two of them were baptized in the Christian faith. I suggested to them that they owed to their fellow men one duty, viz: that they should give to me the names of the men who had seduced them to desert and to the enemy. This they readily assented to, and gave me the names of five citizens of Jones county as the authors of their ruin, disgrace, and death, which names I took down in writing, and handed it into the general's office, and they will no doubt be properly attended to. At the gallows, Armyett, who was the eldest of the five, made, as chief speaker, the following confession, written down as delivered:

I believe my peace is made with God. I did wrong in volunteering after I got to Newbern. I would rather have laid in jail all my life than have done it. I have rendered prayer unto God to forgive my sin. I trust in him, and in him only. (The prisoners said, we all feel the same way.)

Mitchell Busick said: I went to Newbern and they (the Yankees) told me if I did not go into their service I should be taken through the lines and shot. In this way I was frightened into it. They all declared: We wish a statement made to the North Carolina troops that we have done wrong and regret it; and warn others not to follow our example. . . .

On Monday, the 15th instant, thirteen more marched to the gallows. I made my first visit to them, as chaplain, on Sunday morning. The scene beggars all description. Some of them were comparatively young men; but they had made the fatal mistake; they had only twenty-four hours to live, and, but little preparation had been made for death. Here was a wife to say farewell to a husband forever. Here a mother to take the last look at her ruined son; and then a sister who had come to embrace for the last time, the brother who had brought disgrace upon the very name she bore, by his treason to his country. I told them they had sinned against their country, and that country would not forgive; but they had also sinned against God, yet God would forgive if they approached him with penitent hearts filled with a godly sorrow for sin, and repose their trust in the atoning blood of Christ. They gave apparently, marked attention to my ministration of the word and of prayer. On the next morning, before they were carried to the scaffold, I visited them again and had with me as companions Rev. Mr. Thompson, chaplain of the 43d., Rev. Mr. Schenk, of Guilford county, Rev. Mr. Hines, missionary to brigade, and Rev. R. R. Michaux, North Carolina conference. After reading a chapter and prayer, I administered the ordinance of Christian baptism to eight of these poor condemned wretches, after the manner that Paul and Silas administered it to the jailer and his household, in the prison at midnight, in Philippi. They had received no religious visit from any one except the ones from myself the preceding morning, and one in the afternoon, at my request, from Rev. Mr. Thompson. I administered baptism at the request made on the morning before. . . .

The thirteen marched to the gallows with apparent resignation. Some of them I hope were prepared for their doom. Others I fear not. On the scaffold they were all arranged in one row. At a given signal the trap fell, and they were in eternity in a few moments. The scene was truly appalling; but it was as truly the deserters' doom. Many of them said I never expected to come to such an end as this. But yet they were deserters, and as such they ought to have expected such a doom. The names of these misguided men were John J. Brock, Wm. Haddock, Jesse Summerlin, A. J. Brittain, Wm. Jones, Lewis Freeman, Calvin Huffman, Stephen Jones, Joseph Brock, Lewis Taylor, Charles Cuthrell, W. C.

Daughtry and John Freeman. Ten of them were deserters from Nether-cutt's battalion.

On yesterday, the 22d, William J. Hill and Elijah Kellum were carried to the gallows, and hanged as deserters. Kellum was quite a young man, unable to read, but guilty of the dreadful crime according to his own showing. He professed to die in peace, and received the ordinance of baptism before death. The other looked very much like an impenitent man, and died leaving a wife and three helpless children to bear the disgrace of his heavy crime unto the third and fourth generation.

U.S. War Department, 39th Congress, 1st. Session, House of Representatives, Document No. 98, pp. 12–14.

---

(8) Action at Plymouth, April 1864

Shortly after taking over Pickett's Carolina command in the spring of 1864, General Robert F. Hoke turned his attention to Plymouth. This strategic little town situated on the south bank of the Roanoke River, near its mouth, was an important supply depot for Union troops in the area. It was strongly fortified and garrisoned by a 3,000 man force under General W. H. Wessels. Consequently Hoke felt that in order to take the place he would need to have both land and naval forces at his disposal. He asked that the Confederate ironclad ram, Albemarle, then nearing completion at Edwards Ferry on the Roanoke River, be allowed to participate in his planned assault.

As soon as Hoke learned that his request had been granted, he invested Plymouth on the land side and attacked the forts. This was before the Albemarle could possibly assist him. In the fighting on 18 April the Twenty-first Georgia suffered heavy casualties. One of those who fell in the day's fighting was young Sidney Richardson. It was the unpleasant duty of Captain M. Lynch to inform the young man's father of his son's death in battle.

In front of Plymouth
April 19th 1864

Mr. Richmond Richardson
Dear Sir

A few days back we left our camp at Kinston, and marched to attack the enemy at Plymouth, N.C. on reaching there we found him strongly fortified. But the attack was ordered and made on yesterday the 18th. It was a brilliant charge, but sad to tell many brave and noble youths lost their lives. And foremost amongst the brave and gallant band who gave their lives for their country, I am pained to have to say, was your son Sidney. He fell in the chase about dark yesterday evening, shot through, the ball taking effect in the left breast. Next day his remains was taken charge of by Jas. B. May and buried. He marked a head board with his name, all that by sympathy and affection could do for him was done.

I deeply regret the necessity which called forth these lines notifying you of the death of your son but it is not for us to repine we must submit to the will of Him who gives and can take away.

I must say that a truer, nobler, or more generous youth has not fallen in this cruel and unatural [sic] war, would to God, he had been spared to his country and to you.

> Very respectfully
> M. LYNCH
> [Captain, Twenty-first Georgia
> Regiment]

M. Lynch to R. Richardson, 19 Apr. 1864, S. J. Richardson Papers.

---

(9) Sinking of the *Albemarle*, October 1864

As long as the Confederate ironclad Albemarle was afloat, she was a threat to the Union supremacy of the sound region. Authorities in Washington realized the ram had to be destroyed, but how was the question. Wooden vessels were no match for her, and there was no ironclad able to cross the Hatteras bar and enter the sounds. The job finally went to William B. Cushing, a young lieutenant in the United States Navy whose daring exploits in North Carolina waters had already brought him to the attention of his superiors. Cushing's plan called for an attacking party to slip up the Roanoke River in two small boats, each armed with a torpedo and howitzer,[11] and sink the Albemarle at her moorings in Plymouth.

After the war Cushing wrote for Century Magazine *a less than modest account of his experiences.*

The Roanoke River is a stream averaging 150 yards in width, and quite deep. Eight miles from the mouth was the town of Plymouth, where the ram was moored. Several thousand soldiers occupied town and forts, and held both banks of the stream. A mile below the ram was the wreck of the SOUTHFIELD, with hurricane deck above water, and on this a guard was stationed, to give notice of anything suspicious, and to send

---

11. The open launches, outfitted at the Brooklyn navy yard, were about thirty feet long. They had small engines and were propelled by a screw. Fitted to each craft were a twelve-pound howitzer and a fourteen-foot spar with a complicated torpedo device attached to it.

up firerockets in case of an attack. Thus it seemed impossible to surprise them, or to attack, with hope of success.

Impossibilities are for the timid: we determined to overcome all obstacles. On the night of the 27th of October we entered the river taking in tow a small cutter with a few men,[12] the duty of whom was to dash aboard the [wreck of the] S O U T H F I E L D at the first hail, and prevent any rocket from being ignited.

Fortune was with our little boat, and we actually passed within thirty feet of the pickets without discovery and neared the wharf, where the rebels lay all unconscious. I now thought that it might be better to board her, and "take her alive," having in the two boats twenty men well armed with revolvers, cutlasses, and hand grenades. To be sure, there were ten times our number on the ship and thousands near by; but a surprise is everything, and I thought if her fasts were cut at the instant of boarding, we might overcome those on board, take her into the stream, and use her iron sides to protect us afterward from the forts. Knowing the town, I concluded to land at the lower wharf, creep around and suddenly dash aboard from the bank; but just as I was sheering in close to the wharf, a hail came, sharp and quick, from the iron-clad, and in an instant was repeated. I at once directed the cutter to cast off, and go down to capture the guard left in our rear, and ordering all steam went at the dark mountain of iron in front of us. A heavy fire at once opened upon us, not only from the ship, but from men stationed on the shore. This did not disable us, and we neared them rapidly. A large fire now blazed upon the bank, and by its light I discovered the unfortunate fact that there was a circle of logs around the A L B E M A R L E , boomed well out from her side, with the very intention of preventing the action of torpedoes. To examine them more closely, I ran alongside until amidship, received the enemy's fire, and sheered off for the purpose of turning, a hundred yards away, and going at the booms squarely, at right angles, trusting to their having been long enough in the water to have become slimy—in which case my boat under full headway, would bump up against them and slip over into the pen with the ram. This was my only chance of success, and once over the obstruction my boat would never get out again; but I was there to accomplish an important object, and to die, if needs be, was but a duty. As I turned, the whole back of my coat was torn out by buckshot, and the sole of my shoe was carried away. The fire was very severe.

In a lull of the firing, the captain hailed us, again demanding what boat it was. All my men gave some comical answers, and mine was a dose of canister, which I sent among them from the howitzer, buzzing and singing against the iron ribs and into the mass of men standing by the fire upon the shore. In another instant we had struck the logs and were over, with headway nearly gone, slowly forging up under the enemy's quarter-port. Ten feet from us the muzzle of a rifle gun looked into our faces, and every word of command on board was distinctly heard. My clothing was perforated with bullets as I stood in the bow, the

12. Cushing had only one launch on the night of the attack. The other vessel had been lost on the way down from New York.

heel-jiggers in my right hand and the exploding line in the left. We were near enough then, and I ordered the boom lowered until the forward motion of the launch carried the torpedo under the ram's overhang. A strong pull of the detaching line a moment's waiting for the torpedo to rise under the hull, and I hauled in the left hand, just cut by a bullet.

The explosion took place at the same instant that 100 pounds of grape, at 10 feet range, crashed in our midst, and the dense mass of water thrown out by the torpedo came down with choking weight upon us.

Twice refusing to surrender, I commanded the men to save themselves; and throwing off sword, revolver, shoes and coat, struck out from my disabled and sinking boat into the river. It was cold, long after the frosts, and the water chilled the blood, while the whole surface of the stream was plowed up by grape and musketry, and my nearest friends, the fleet, were twelve miles away, but anything was better than to fall into rebel hands. Death was better than surrender. I swam for the opposite shore. . . .

At last [some twenty-four hours later] I was on board [the Union picket vessel *Valley City*], had imbibed a little brandy and water, and was on my way to the flagship. . . .

As soon as it was known that I had returned, rockets were thrown up and all hands called to cheer ship; and when I announced success[13] all the commanding officers were summoned on board. . . .

William B. Cushing, "Destruction of the 'Albemarle'," pp. 432–39.

13. The *Albemarle* sank at her moorings.

V

BLOCKADE-RUNNING

By late 1864, Wilmington was in many respects the most important city in the Confederacy. Only Richmond was as vital to the South as this Cape Fear River port. General Lee, confined to his fortifications at Petersburg, was greatly dependent upon supplies brought in through the blockade at Wilmington.[1] Until it was cut in August 1864, the Wilmington and Weldon Railroad provided Lee with a direct line to the North Carolina coast. After August, supplies from Wilmington were transported north along a more circuitous route.

From the outset of the war the Union navy had the monumental task of blockading the Confederate coast from the Chesapeake to the mouth of the Rio Grande, and no port was more difficult to patrol effectively than Wilmington. It was ideally situated for blockade-running. Located twenty-eight miles up the Cape Fear the city was free from enemy fire as long as the forts downstream remained in Confederate hands. Moreover, there were two navigable entrances to the river. Separating the channels were Smith Island and Frying Pan Shoals, the latter jutting out into the Atlantic for approximately twenty-five miles. Protecting the lower Cape Fear were Forts Fisher, Caswell, Campbell, Holmes, Pender, and Anderson, as well as numerous batteries.

The strength of these fortifications, Fort Fisher in particular, along with the natural advantage Wilmington held for blockade-running, made the absolute closing of the port by the enemy extremely difficult. Blockade-runners slipped in and out of Wilmington with relative ease up to the last weeks of the war. It has been estimated that the sleek, shallow-draft, gray-hulled steamers designed for speed made over 400 trips in and out of the port during the war. The *Siren* alone made sixty-four trips through the blockading fleet.

Very few Southerners, however, were engaged in this business. In fact it was almost completely monopolized by English and Scottish merchants who had the ships and capital to invest in a lucrative but hazardous venture. British firms would dispatch goods, luxury items as well as

1. For additional documents on blockade-running, see Chapters IX and XVII.

materials of war, in regular cargo ships to Bermuda, Nassau, and the Caribbean islands for transfer to blockade-runners which would arrive in port laden with Confederate cotton.

Many investors in this business reaped enormous profits. With cotton selling for approximately three cents a pound in the South and in England for the equivalent of forty-five cents to a dollar a pound, fortunes could be made almost overnight. A number of successful steamers piled up millions of dollars in profits for their owners. It was possible for a large vessel loaded with 1,000 bales of cotton to realize a profit of a quarter of a million dollars in two weeks on the inward and outward run.

Even though spectacular profits were made in blockade-running, most goods brought into the Confederacy were vital to its survival. It has been estimated that cargoes valued in excess of $65 million in gold were brought into Wilmington alone during the war. In August 1864, following the Union victory at Mobile Bay, General Lee wrote Governor Z. B. Vance of North Carolina that the importance of the port of Wilmington was "such that every effort should be made to defend it. . . ."[2] A few months later the general was saying that "if Fort Fisher and Caswell were not held, he would have to evacuate Richmond."[3] However, by this time it had finally become obvious to Union commanders that an attack on Wilmington would serve as an effective strike at Lee as well. The capture of this vital port, contemplated by the Union since 1862, had now become an absolute necessity.

---

(1) Running the Blockade

Running the blockade was always an exciting experience, and one usually filled with moments of extreme anxiety. In his reminiscences, Tom Taylor describes the techniques used by the Union blockaders, and how aboard the Banshee *he made his first run into Wilmington. Taylor was only twenty-one when he arrived in town as the representative of a Liverpool mercantile firm engaged in blockade-running out of the North Carolina port.*

Wilmington was the first port I attempted; in fact with the exception of one run to Galveston it was always our destination. It had many advantages. Though furthest from Nassau it was nearest to headquarters at Richmond, and from its situation was very difficult to watch effectively. It was here, moreover, that my firm had established its agency as soon as they had resolved to take up the blockade-running business. The town

2. Letter of Robert E. Lee to Zebulon B. Vance, 29 Aug. 1864, Vance Papers.
3. *Official Records of the Union and Confederate Navies in the War of the Rebellion,* Ser. 1, 9:620.

itself lies some sixteen miles up the Cape Fear river. . . . Off its mouth lies a delta, known as Smith's Island, which . . . divided the approach to the port into two widely separated channels, so that in order to guard the approach to it a blockading force is compelled to divide into two squadrons.

At one entrance of the river lies Fort Fisher, a work so powerful that the blockaders instead of lying in the estuary were obliged to form roughly a semicircle out of a range of its guns, and the falling away of the coast on either side of the entrance further increased the extent of ground they had to cover. The system they adopted in order to meet the difficulty was extremely well conceived, and, did we not know to the contrary, it would have appeared complete enough to ensure the capture of every vessel so foolhardy as to attempt to enter or come out.

Across either entrance an inshore squadron was stationed at close intervals. In the daytime the steamers composing this squadron anchored, but at night they got under weigh and patrolled in touch with the flagship, which, as a rule, remained at anchor. Further out there was a cordon of cruisers, and outside these again detached gun-boats keeping at such a distance from the coast as they calculated a runner coming out would traverse between the time of high water on Wilmington bar and sunrise, so that if any blockade-runner coming out got through the two inner lines in the dark she had every chance of being snapped up at daybreak by one of the third division.

Besides these special precautions for Wilmington there must not be forgotten the ships engaged in the general service of the blockade, consisting, in addition to those detailed to watch Nassau and other bases, of free cruisers that patrolled the Gulf-stream. From this it will be seen readily, that from the moment the BANSHEE left Nassau harbor till she had passed the protecting forts at the mouth of Cape Fear river, she and those on board her could never be safe from danger or free for a single hour from anxiety. . . .

The BANSHEE'S engines proved so unsatisfactory that under ordinary conditions nine or ten knots was all we could get out of her; she was therefore not permitted to run any avoidable risks, and to this I attribute her extraordinary success where better boats failed. As long as daylight lasted a man was never out of the cross-trees, and the moment a sail was seen the BANSHEE'S stern was turned to it till it was dropped below the horizon. The lookout man, to quicken his eyes, had a dollar for every sail he sighted, and if it were seen from the deck first he was fined five. This may appear excessive, but the importance in blockade-running of seeing before you are seen is too great for any chance to be neglected; and it must be remembered that the pay of ordinary seamen for each round trip in and out was from £ 50 to £ 60.

Following these tactics we crept noiselessly along the shores of the Bahamas, invisible in the darkness, and ran on unmolested for the first two days out, though our course was often interfered with by the necessity of avoiding hostile vessels; then came the anxious moment on the third, when, her position having been taken at noon to see if she was near enough to run under the guns of Fort Fisher before the following day break, it was found there was just time, but none to spare for accidents or delay. Still the danger of lying out another day so close to the blockaded port was very great, and rather than risk it we resolved to keep straight on our course and chance being overtaken by daylight before we were under the Fort.[4]

Now the real excitement began, and nothing I have ever experienced can compare with it. Hunting, pig-sticking, steeple-chasing, big-game shooting, polo—I have done a little of each—all have their thrilling moments, but none can approach "running a blockade"; and perhaps my readers can sympathise with my enthusiasm when they consider the dangers to be encountered, after three days of constant anxiety and little sleep, in threading our way through a swarm of blockaders, and the accuracy required to hit in the nick of time the mouth of a river only half a mile wide, without lights and with a coast-line so low and featureless that as a rule the first intimation we had of its nearness was the dim white line of the surf.

There were of course many different plans of getting in, but at this time the favourite dodge was to run up some fifteen or twenty miles to the north of Cape Fear, so as to round the northernmost of the blockaders, instead of dashing right through the inner squadron; then to creep down close to the surf till the river was reached; and it was the course the B A N S H E E intended to adopt.

We steamed cautiously on until nightfall; the night proved dark, but dangerously clear and calm. No lights were allowed—not even a cigar; the engine room hatchways were covered with tarpaulins, at the risk of suffocating the unfortunate engineers and stokers in the almost insufferable atmosphere below. But it was absolutely imperative that not a glimmer of light should appear. Even the binnacle was covered, and the steersman had to see as much of the compass as he could through a conical aperture carried almost up to his eyes.

With everything thus in readiness we steamed on in silence except for the stroke of the engines and the beat of the paddle-floats, which in the calm of the night seemed distressingly loud; all hands were on deck, crouching behind the bulwarks; and we on the bridge, namely, the captain, the pilot, and I were straining our eyes into the darkness. Presently Burroughs[5] made an uneasy movement—"Better get a cast of the lead, Captain," I heard him whisper. A muttered order down the engineroom tube was Steele's[6] reply, and the B A N S H E E slowed and then stopped. It was an anxious moment, while a dim figure stole into the fore-chains; for there is always a danger of steam blowing off when engines are unexpectedly stopped, and that would have been enough to betray our presence for miles around. In a minute or two came back the report,

4. The blockade-runners felt relatively safe once they were under the protective umbrella of the big guns of the fort.

5. Tom Burroughs was the pilot. He was a "Wilmington Man." Pilots were paid well but the risks they ran were great for, if captured, they were never exchanged.

6. Steele was captain of the *Banshee*.

"sixteen fathoms—sandy bottom with black specks." "We are not as far in as I thought, Captain," said Burroughs, "and we are too far to the southward. Port two points and go a little faster." As he explained, we must be well to the northward of the speckled bottom before it was safe to head for the shore, and away we went again. In about an hour Burroughs quietly asked for another sounding. Again she was gently stopped, and this time he was satisfied. "Starboard and go ahead easy," was the order now, and we crept in not a sound was heard but that of the regular beat of the paddle-floats still dangerously loud in spite of snail's pace. Suddenly Burroughs gripped my arm,—"There's one of them, Mr. Taylor," he whispered, "on the starboard bow."

In vain I strained my eyes to where he pointed, not a thing could I see; but presently I heard Steele say beneath his breath, "All right, Burroughs, I see her. Starboard a little, steady!" was the order passed aft.

A moment afterwards I could make out a lone low black object on our starboard side, lying perfectly still. Would she see us? that was the question; but no, though we passed within a hundred yards of her we were not discovered, and I breathed again. Not very long after we had dropped her, Burroughs whispered—"Steamer on the port bow." And another cruiser was made out close to us.

"Hard-a-port," said Steele, and round she swung, bringing our friend upon our beam. Still unobserved we crept quietly on, when all at once a third cruiser shaped herself out of the gloom right ahead and steaming slowly across our bows.

"Stop her," said Steele in a moment, and as we lay like dead our enemy went on and disappeared in the darkness. It was clear there was a false reckoning somewhere, and that instead of rounding the head of the blockading line we were passing through the very centre of it. However, Burroughs was now of opinion that we must be inside the squadron and advocated making the land. So "slow ahead" we went again, until the low-lying coast and the surf line became dimly visible. Still we could not tell where we were, and, as time was getting on alarmingly near dawn, the only thing to do was to creep down along the surf as close in and as fast as we dared. It was a great relief when we suddenly heard Burroughs say, "It's all right, I see the 'Big Hill'!"

The "Big Hill" was a hillock about as high as a full-grown oak tree, but it was the most prominent feature for miles on that dreary coast, and served to tell us exactly how far we were from Fort Fisher. And fortunate as it was for us we were so near. Daylight was already breaking, and before we were opposite the fort we could make out six or seven gunboats which steamed rapidly towards us and angrily opened fire. Their shots were soon dropping close around us: an unpleasant sensation when you know you have several tons of gunpowder under your feet. To make matters worse, the North Breaker shoal now compelled us to haul off the shore and steam further out. It began to look ugly for us, when all at once there was a flash from the shore followed by a sound that came like music to our ears—that of a shell whirring over our heads. It was Fort Fisher, wide awake and warning the gunboats to keep their distance. With a parting broadside they steamed sulkily out of range, and in half an hour we were safely over the bar. A boat put off from the fort and then,—well, it was the days of champagne cocktails, not whiskies and sodas—and one did not run a blockade every day. For my part, I was mightily proud of my first attempt and my baptism of fire. Blockade-running seemed the pleasantest and most exhilarating of pastimes. I did not know then what a very serious business it could be.

Thomas E. Taylor, *Running the Blockade*, pp. 44–54.

---

(2) North Carolina's Success in Blockade-running

After experiencing the tribulations of purchasing supplies for the state from privately owned block-ade-runners, Adjutant General James G. Martin convinced Governor Vance that it would be to North Carolina's advantage to engage in blockade-running for herself. Thus the governor sent agents to England to purchase a steamer. They contracted for the Advance. *Later the state acquired part ownership in several other vessels.*

Vance regarded the state of North Carolina's success in the hazardous business of blockade-running as one of the most important achievements of his administration. In a speech delivered before the Association of the Maryland Line in 1885 he commented on some of the accomplishments in this field.

By the general industry and thrift of our people, and by the use of a number of blockade-running steamers, carrying out cotton and bringing in supplies from Europe, I had collected and distributed from time to time, as near as could be gathered from the records of the Quarter-Master's Department, the following stores: Large quantities of machinery supplies; 60,000 pairs of handcards; 10,000 grain scythes; 200 bbls. blue stone for wheat-growers; leather and shoes to 250,000 pairs, 50,000 blankets, gray woolen cloth for at least 250,000 suits of uniforms, 12,000 overcoats (ready-made), 2,000 best Enfield rifles (with 100 rounds of fixed ammunition), 100,000 pounds of bacon; 500 sacks of coffee for hospital use, $50,000 worth of medicines at gold prices, large quantities of lubricating oils, besides minor supplies of various kinds for the charitable institutions of the State. Not only was the supply of shoes, blankets and clothing more than sufficient for the supply of the North Carolina troops, but large quantities were turned over to the Confederate government for the troops of other states. In the winter succeeding the battle of Chickamauga, I sent to General Longstreet's corps 14,000 suits of clothing complete. At the surrender of General Johnston the State had on hand ready made and in cloth, 92,000 suits of uniforms, with great stores of blankets, leather, etc. To make good the warrant on which these purchases had been made abroad, the State purchased and had on hand in trust for the holders 11,000 bales of cotton and 100,000 barrels of rosin. The cotton was partly destroyed before the war closed; and the remainder, amounting to several thousand bales, was "captured," after peace was declared, by certain officers of the Federal army.

Dowd, *Life of Zebulon B. Vance*, pp. 489–90.

---

(3) The *Advance*

The state-owned steamer Advance *was one of the best known ships running the blockade. From 26 June 1863, the date of her maiden voyage to Wilmington, until her capture at sea a little over a year later, the* Advance *contributed much to North Carolina's war effort. At the same time she was regarded in an affectionate, personal way by the people of the state.*

Colonel J. G. Bunn of Wilmington wrote his friend James Sprunt about the Advance. *In this letter Bunn spoke of the unusual attachment North Carolinians had for the blockade-runner.*

In the spring of 1862 the ADVANCE made her first successful trip through the blockaders and arrived safely in the harbor of Wilmington, bringing a large amount of much-needed supplies. The Governor was informed of her arrival and came to Wilmington immediately, and the next day, Sunday, went down on one of the river steamers with a number of his friends to the ship, which was lying at the quarantine station about fifteen or sixteen miles below the city. After spending several hours on board examining the ship and partaking of the hospitalities of its officers, it was determined to take her up to the city without waiting for a permit from the health officers, as it was assumed the Governor's presence on board would be a justification for the violation of quarantine regulations. Accordingly, steam was raised and she came up to the city and was made fast to the wharf in front of the custom house. . . .

The ADVANCE was a first-class ship in every respect and had engines of great power and very highly finished, and her speed was good. With a pressure of twenty pounds to the square inch she easily averaged seventeen knots to the hour, and when it was increased to thirty pounds she reeled off twenty knots without difficulty. Her officers were Captain Crossan, commander; Captain Wylie, a Scotchman, who came over with her, sailing master; Mr. Hughes, of New Bern, purser; Captain George Morrison, chief engineer. The only objection to her was her size and heavy draught of water, the latter rendering it difficult for her to cross the shoals, which at that time were a great bar to the navigation of the river, and in consequence of which she could never go out or return with a full cargo of cotton or supplies.

She ran the blockade successfully seven or eight trips, bringing in all kinds of supplies that were much needed by our troops and people, thanks to the energy and wise foresight of our patriotic war governor. The regularity of her trips was remarkable and could be forecast almost to the very day; indeed, it was common to hear upon the streets the almost stereotyped remark, "Tomorrow the A D V A N C E will be in!" and when the morrow came she could generally be seen gliding up to her dock with the rich freight of goods and wares so greatly needed by our people.

James Sprunt, *Chronicles of the Cape Fear River, 1660–1916*, pp. 454–55.

---

(4) Wilmington Under Blockade

The war, and in particular blockade-running, changed Wilmington from a nice, quiet town to a rowdy, hustling seaport. Robbery and murder were not unusual occurrences. It was unsafe to venture into the suburbs at night and "even in daylight there were frequent conflicts in the public streets, between the crews of the steamers in port and the soldiers stationed in the town . . . and not infrequently a dead body would rise to the surface of the water in one of the docks, with marks of violence upon it."[7] Furthermore, the town swarmed with foreigners as well as speculators, including a large number of Jews, from all over the South. And "when a steamer came in, men, women, children rushed down to the wharves to see it, to buy, beg, or steal something." Under these circumstances it is not surprising that many of the old families moved to other localities. Those not leaving often lived "in retiracy."[8]

A Confederate officer located in Wilmington during the war years wrote for Harper's Magazine *what life was like in and around the port city at that time.*

After the capital of the Confederacy there was not in the South a more important place than the little town of Wilmington, North Carolina, about twenty miles from the mouth of the Cape Fear River, noted in peace times for its exports of tar, pitch, turpentine, and lumber. The banks of the Cape Fear had been settled by Sir Walter Raleigh's emigrants and Scotchmen, and to this day you find the old Highland names,

7. John Wilkinson, *The Narrative of a Blockade Runner*, p. 199.
8. John Johns, "Wilmington During the Blockade," pp. 497, 498.

and see strongly-marked Scottish features among the inhabitants. The people still retain many of the traits of their descent, and are shrewd, canny, money-making, and not to be beaten at driving a bargain by any Yankee that we ever saw. They are hospitable, intelligent, and polished; many old families, who for years lived in affluence and luxury, residing there, who have intermarried with each other until they form a large "cousinhood," as they call it.

Previous to the war Wilmington was very gay and social. But the war had sadly changed the place—many of the old families moving away into the interior, and those who remained, either from altered circumstances or the loss of relatives in battle, living in retiracy. When we first knew it, Major-General W. H. C. Whiting was in command. . . . His manners were brusque, but he had a kind and generous heart. He was fond of the social glass, and may have sometimes gone too far. He was not popular with many of the citizens, as he was arbitrary, and paid little attention to the suggestions of civilians. . . .

But in Whiting we [military men] had implicit faith. So, though there were constant rumors of expeditions against the place we scarcely believed they were coming. . . . In fact we had lapsed into a dream of security. . . . We ate, drank, and were merry, and there was marrying and giving in marriage, as in the days before the flood.

It seemed singular to us that the United States should so long neglect to close the only port almost of the Confederacy into which every "dark of the moon" there ran a half dozen or so swift blockade-runners, freighted with cannon, muskets and every munition of war—medicines, cloth, shoes, bacon, etc. Through that port were brought till January '65 all the stores and material needed by the indefatigable Colonel Gorgas, the Confederate Chief of Ordnance, the most efficient bureau officer the Confederacy had. Through it came those famous Whitworth and Armstrong guns sent us by our English friends. Into Wilmington was brought by Mr. Commissary-General Northrup that rotten, putrid bacon called "Nassau," because it had spoiled on the wharves of that place before shipment for Wilmington. . . .

But the cargoes of those white painted, birdlike looking steamers that floated monthly into Wilmington, producing such excitement and joy among its population, unfortunately for the Confederates, did not contain Government stores and munitions of war alone, bad as the bacon and much of the stuff brought abroad by worthless Confederate agents were. The public freight compared with the private was small. By them were brought in the cloth that made the uniforms of those gayly-decked clerks that swarmed the streets of Richmond with military titles, and read the battle bulletins and discussed the war news. . . . From it came the fine English brandies, choice foreign wines, potted meats, and conserves, jellies, and anchovy paste, etc., that filled the pantries of storerooms of many of the officials at Richmond, and were spread out in such profusion at the dinners or suppers or dejeuners given by the "court circle" (as it was called) to officials when the "circle" wanted any of their pets promoted or assigned to good positions. From it came the loaf-sugar, coffee, tea, etc., that staff-officers, blockade-runners, and their relations and friends luxuriated in, while the ragged, dirty Confederate soldier, musket in hand, broiled or soaked in the trenches before Richmond and Petersburg, watching the foe with stout heart but faint stomach; starving on a handful of meal and a pint of sorghum molasses, probably varied every other day with the third or quarter of a pound of Mr. Commissary, General Northrup's savory "Nassau Bacon." . . .

Talk about Yankees worshiping the almighty dollar! You should have seen the adoration paid the Golden Calf at Wilmington during the days of blockade-running. Every body was engaged in it save the private soldiers and a few poor line and staff officers, who were not within the "ring," and possessed no influence or position there by which they could grant favors.

When a steamer came in men, women, children rushed down to the wharves to see it, to buy, beg, or steal something. Every body wanted to know if their "ventures"—the proceeds of the bales of cotton or boxes of tobacco sent out—had come in. No people were more excited than the women, expecting gloves, parasols, hoop-skirts, corsets, flannels, and bonnets, silks and calicoes; for these things became frightfully scarce and dear in the South during the last year of the war. The first people aboard of course were the agents—on such occasions very big men. Then swarmed officials and officers, "friends" and "bummers," hunting after drinks and dinners, and willing to accept any compliment, from a box of cigars or a bottle of brandy down to a bunch of bananas or a pocketful of oranges. Happy the man who knew well and intimately the steward of a blockade-runner, or could call the cook his friend, and get a part of the stealings from the pantry or the drippings from the kitchen. . . .

Wilmington during that period swarmed with foreigners, Jews and Gentiles. In fact, going down the main street or along the river, you might well imagine you were journeying from Jerusalem to Jericho. As to the falling among thieves we will make no mention. The beggars at the gangways of the newly-arrived steamers were as thick as those in Egypt crying "bucksheesh."

At every turn you "met up," as our tar-heel friends say, with young Englishmen dressed like grooms and jockeys, or with a peculiar coachmanlike look, seeming, in a foreign land, away from their mothers, to indulge their fancy for the "outre" and extravagant in dress to the utmost. These youngsters had money, made money, lived like fighting-cocks, and astonished the natives by their pranks, and the way they flung the Confederate "stuff" about. Of course they were deeply interested in the Confederate cause, and at the same time wanted cotton. The Liverpool house of Alexander Collie and Co. had quite a regiment of these youngsters in their employ. Fine-looking fellows, with turned-up noses, blue eyes wide apart, and, their fluffy, straw-colored, mutton-chop whiskers floating in the wind, to the great admiration of their "chèr amiés," the handsome quadroon washer-women, on whose mantle-pieces and in whose albums were frequently to be found photographs strikingly resembling the aforesaid young foreigners. They occupied a large flaring yellow house, like a military hospital, at the upper end of Market Street, and which belonged to a Mr. Wright. There these youngsters kept open house and spent their pas' and the Company's money, while it lasted. There they fought cocks on Sundays, until the neighbors demonstrated and threatened prosecution. A stranger passing the house at night, and seeing it illuminated with every gas-jet lit (the expense, no doubt, charged to the ship), and hearing the sound of music, would ask if a ball was going on. Oh no! it was only those young English Sybarites enjoying the luxury of a band of Negro minstrels after dinner. They entertained any and everybody, from Beauregard and Whiting, or Lawley, the voluminous correspondent of the London *Times*, down to such "bummers" as Vizitelly [*sic*][9] or the most insufferable sponge or snob who forced his society upon them.

The tribe of Benjamin was very well represented at Wilmington, as you might imagine, the unctuous and oleaginous Confederate Secretary of State[10] having well provided for "his people." A great many gentlemen of strongly Jewish physiognomy were to be met with on the streets, in very delicate health, and with papers in their pockets to keep them out of the army from the Secretary of State, but still in hot pursuit of the "Monish." When the conscript officer became very zealous and pressing they fled away to Nassau and Bermuda. . . .

The Confederate Government used to send some queer agents abroad at the expense of the people. A Mrs. Grinnell was sent out by the Surgeon-General—so she stated—to get bandages, etc., which nobody else, we suppose, but Mrs. Grinnell could get. . . .

Mr. Mallory's[11] navy was always the laughing stock of the army and many were the jeers that the Confederate "mud-crushers" let off at his iron-clads, formidable things as they were, had he managed properly the Confederate navy. Captain Lynch was the flag-officer of the Cape Fear squadron when we first went there. His fleet consisted of the iron-clad ram NORTH CAROLINA, which drew so much water that she could never get over the bars of the Cape Fear River Inlet—except, possibly, at the highest spring tide, and then the chances were against her ever-getting back again; the *Raleigh*, another iron-clad, not completed till late in the summer of '64; and two or three little steam-tugs. They all came to grief. The NORTH CAROLINA, the bottom of which was neither sheathed nor prepared to resist worms, was pierced by them till her hull was like a honey-comb, and finally was sunk opposite Smithville.[12] The RALEIGH, after going out and scaring off the blockading fleet at the New Inlet, was beached and lost on a bar near Fort Fisher in returning. The tugs were burned on the river subsequent to the evacuation of the town. . . .

The wreck of . . . blockade-runners not unfrequently occurred by being stranded or beached, and highly diverting skirmishes would occur

9. Frank Vizetelly was a special artist and war correspondent for the *Illustrated London News*.

10. Judah P. Benjamin.

11. Stephen R. Mallory was Confederate Secretary of the Navy.

12. Present-day Southport.

between the blockaders and the garrisons of the forts for the possession. The fleet, however, never liked the Whitworth guns that we had, which shot almost with the accuracy of a rifle and with a tremendous range. The soldiers generally managed to wreck the stranded vessels successfully, though oftentimes with great peril and hardship. It mattered very little to the owners then who got her, as they did not see much of what was recovered—the soldiers thinking they were entitled to what they got at the risk of their lives. But a wreck was a most demoralizing affair —the whole garrison generally got drunk and staid drunk for a week or so afterwards. Brandy and fine wines flowed like water; and it was a month perhaps before matters could be got straight. Many accumulated snug little sums from the misfortunes of the blockade-runners, who generally denounced such pillage as piracy; but it could not be helped. . . .

Seldom, however, was there any loss of life attending these wrecks. But there was one notable case of the drowning of a famous woman, celebrated for her beauty and powers of fascination. We allude to the death of Mrs. Greenhow,[13] so well known for many years in Washington circles. . . . The small boat in which she was coming from the vessel, which was beached just a short distance above Fisher, upset. Mrs. Greenhow, after sinking several times, was brought to shore, but soon after reaching it died. It was said that the gold she had sewed up and concealed about her person had borne her down and was the cause of her death; that had it not been for that weight she would have been saved. Her body was brought to Wilmington and laid out in the Sailor's Church, where we saw her. She was beautiful in death. After her funeral her wardrobe and a great many articles that she had brought over for sale, and which had been rescued from the wreck were sold at auction in Wilmington. It was very splendid and the "venture" she had brought in for sale was most costly. It was said that an English countess or duchess had an interest in this venture, and was to have shared the profits of the speculation. . . .

Of the capture of Fort Fisher, and the subsequent inevitable loss of Wilmington, I shall not speak. These events have passed into history. My purpose has been simply to portray the aspect of Wilmington when blockaded.

John Johns, "Wilmington During the Blockade," pp. 497–503.

(5) Yellow Fever

Blockade-running not only changed Wilmington from a quiet, pleasant *community to a rowdy seaport, but it also was responsible for a yellow*

13. Mrs. Rose O'Neal Greenhow was a Washington society leader and southern spy.

fever epidemic which ravaged the town in the late summer and fall of 1862. Deaths numbered as high as eighteen in a single day and at one time there were 500 cases re-

ported. After the war Mrs. C. P. Bolles, who had almost died from the fever, wrote about the trying days of the epidemic.

The epidemic of yellow fever in Wilmington was in the fall of 1862. A vessel[14] from Nassau loaded with bacon and other food supplies ran the blockade of the Federal Fleet, came up the Cape Fear River, entered the Port at Wilmington and anchored at the foot of Market and Water streets.

The quarantine laws were over looked in our zeal and gratitude in obtaining the food and other supplies that were so much needed for our soldiers on the battle field.

This was the first week in September 1862. After a few days had elapsed, our physician Dr. James Dixon and others of the Profession reported several cases of fever, with symptoms of yellow fever, and upon investigation it was found there had been cases of yellow fever aboard the vessel from Nassau, and then it developed that some of the sailors from that vessel had been for water on the premises where we lived, "The Bank of the State," on the corner of Front and Princess Street, as was the custom before, and during the civil war, for the cashier and family to live in the Bank building. Between this building and servants-quarters on Princess Street was a narrow brick court and just in the corner was a large cistern with a pump screened from the street by a heavy board fence with a gate. Persons in passing would often stop for a cool drink of water having no ice at that time. Dr. Dixon suggested to my husband that I should immediately leave the city. Arrangements were made, but I was suddenly stricken with the disease. That was on the 17th day of September and I had to remain during the entire epidemic which lasted till the 6th of Nov.

The disease spread rapidly, after the first two weeks our physicians had more than they could contend with, and Charleston was quick in responding to the call for assistance, sending her physicians, and nurses, as many as were needed, a dozen or more "Sisters of Mercy." As I made my way over to the window one day about the middle of October to see if the weather cock across the street, on the pinnacle of the Cape Fear Bank Building, indicated any change in the weather, feeling so desperately hopeless, with no one near me but my husband who was too ill to realize the situation. As I looked out I saw all windows closed with no sign of life save the "Little Sisters of Mercy" darting across the streets—flitting from door to door, entering to administer to the sick and dying. Then as I gazed on, I saw a shabby old hearse coming across the corner, drawn by a lean horse, looking as if he had the fever and a young colored man leaning over, too sick to hold the reins, and before the setting of another sun he was laid by the side of many of his fellow men, white

14. The *Kate*.

and colored in a deep trench that had been provided for the dead in Oak-dale Cemetery.

Each physician kept a record of all deaths, and in the short space of about two months there were from 1000 to 1100 of the dead. Amongst our friends Dr. Robert Drane, Rector of Saint James Episcopal Church was one of the first to succumb to the disease, paying his last visit to me on the morning of the twenty-third September complaining of feeling sick, on the night of the 24th he passed away after giving his life for the relief of others. On the 29th Sept. Dr. James Dixon after paying his last round remarked if it had not been for my anxiety for this child, the child of my old classmate, "I would have gone home to my bed," he went home and on the following Sunday his name was added to the number of the dead.

Dr. James MacRae who then lived on 2nd St. near Princess with Mrs. MacRae and several of the children were victims of the fever. Day by day the no. of deaths increased rapidly when at the end of about 2 months a heavy snow storm on the 6th of November checked the disease, no new cases were reported, but many of those sick died within a few hours from the sudden change in the weather, leaving a pall of sorrow over the entire community.

Mr. John Dawson was then mayor of the city, and gave his entire time, and energies, in the relief of the sick and dying, and was most kind in furnishing us with nourishment during the illness of our household.

In writing of the fever I feel I must pay tribute to one of our own physicians, Dr. Frederick Cotton, he was a modest old gentleman and rather excentric [sic], but possessed decided ideas of his own, his wife was my fathers sister, and in talking with me one day about the fever said I want to tell you a little secret, "I had 104 cases, 6 died, 4 were in a dying condition when I was called, 2 could not take the treatment." He showed me a small vial he carried in his pocket containing tartar emetic. "I gave about 1 oz. [?] divided in 4 doses to each patient, which would take effect and relieve in 1 to 2 hours, then I followed it up with larger doses of quinine, and in 24 hours my patients were convalescent." He treated 16 patients of our own col-people, and not one died. He was called "Tory" [?] by many of them which annoyed the old gentleman, but it was their way of expressing their sense of his high loved character which could not be excelled.

MRS. CHARLES P. BOLLES

Account by Mrs. C. P. Bolles of Yellow Fever Epidemic, C. P. Bolles Papers.

VI

FORT FISHER

On the evening of 30 August 1864, President Lincoln's able Secretary of the Navy, Gideon Welles, noted in his diary that something had to be done "to close the entrance to the Cape Fear River and the port of Wilmington." For months he had been urging a "conjoint attack" upon the North Carolina coast. He felt such a move, if successful, would be almost as important as the capture of Richmond.[1]

The critical assignment of closing North Carolina's most important port went to General B. F. Butler and Admiral David Porter. An expeditionary force of 6,500 men, a fleet of transports, and 50 war vessels arrived off the mouth of the Cape Fear in mid-December 1864.

Fort Fisher, a mammoth earthwork below Wilmington near the tip of Confederate Point was the key to the Cape Fear defenses. It guarded New Inlet, the river's main channel. The fort was shaped like the letter "L" with the angle pointing out to sea in a northeasterly direction. People called Fort Fisher the Gibraltar of the South, and it is little wonder that Union authorities were hesitant to order an assault on this massive installation. The construction of the fort took nearly four years, and on the day that the Butler and Porter forces rendezvoused in North Carolina waters work was still in progress.

The first action occurred on the evening of 23 December and the morning of the twenty-fourth when the *Louisiana*, an old war-worn propeller of about 250 tons, filled with powder, was deliberately beached near the base of Fort Fisher and exploded. The scheme, designed to make the fort's capture a simple matter of occupancy, failed miserably as did General Butler's efforts on Christmas day to storm Fort Fisher's imposing land face. Union troops returned to their transports and the fleet sailed north.

There was little time for the victorious Confederate defenders to rejoice for on 12 January 1865 the Union fleet under Admiral Porter returned. General A. H. Terry, fortunately for the Union, had replaced the incompetent Butler as commander of the land forces. The next day the

---

1. Gideon Welles, *Diary of Gideon Welles, Secretary of the Navy under Lincoln and Johnson*, 2:127.

warships opened a deadly fire on the fort. Still the assault force had a very difficult time ashore. Fort Fisher did not capitulate until the evening of the fifteenth, following a day of extremely bitter fighting, much of it hand-to-hand combat.

Other Confederate positions along the lower Cape Fear were soon abandoned, and on 22 February Union troops marched unopposed into Wilmington. The main body of the Union army did not remain long in the port city. It moved on in pursuit of Braxton Bragg, ranking Confederate officer in the area who was retiring to Goldsboro with the remnants of his Cape Fear defense command.

---

(1) Description of Fort Fisher

The design of Fort Fisher was primarily that of its commander, Colonel William Lamb. When Lamb arrived at the fort in the summer of 1862, he found a small quadrilateral work. Part of it was constructed of sand bags, and its longest face was no more than 100 yards. Two years later, due to the colonel's untiring efforts, the Union fleet faced the largest fort on the Confederate coast.

In an address delivered after the war, Colonel Lamb described Fort Fisher.

I determined at once to build a work of such magnitude that it could withstand the heaviest fire of any guns in the American navy. I had seen the effect of eleven inch shell, and had read about the force of the fifteen-inch shell, and believed that their penetrating power was well ascertained, and could be provided against. I obtained permission of Major-General [S. G.] French, who had placed me in command of Confederate Point, to commence such a fortification, although he did not altogether concur with me as to the value of elevated batteries, nor the necessity of such unprecedently heavy works. Shortly after obtaining permission, I commenced the new Fort Fisher, and from that time, the summer of 1862, until the morning of 24th of December, 1864, I never ceased to work, sometimes working on Sunday when rumors of an attack reached me, having at times over one thousand men, white and colored, hard at work. In the construction of the mound on the extreme right of the sea face, which occupied six months, two inclined railways, worked by steam, supplemented the labor of men. Although Fort Fisher was far from completed when attacked by the Federal fleet, it was the largest seacoast fortification in the Confederate States. The plans were my own, and as the work progressed were approved by French, Raines [sic],[2] Longstreet, Beauregard and Whiting. It was styled by Federal en-

2. Either Gabriel James Rains or his younger brother George Washington. Both were graduates of the United States Military Academy from Craven County, North Carolina, and were ordnance experts.

gineers after the capture, the Malakoff[3] of the South. It was built solely
with the view of resisting the fire of a fleet, and it stood uninjured, except as to armament, two of the fiercest bombardments the world has
ever witnessed.

The morning after I took command of the fort, I noticed a blockader
lying a little over a mile from the bar, not two miles from the works. I
asked if she was not unusually close in, and was answered no. I then
remarked that she could have thrown a shot into the fort without warning, and was informed that the enemy sometimes fired on our working
parties unexpectedly and drove them from their work, and that the fort
never fired on the enemy unless they fired first. I replied that it should
never occur again, and ordering a detachment to man the rifle in the
Cumberland battery, opened fire on the blockader. The astonished enemy
slipped his cable and retreated as fast as possible, and from that day to
the final attack no blockader anchored within range of our guns, and no
working party was ever molested, not even when hundreds were congre-
gated together in constructing the mound.

When the Federal fleet appeared off the fort in December, 1864, I
had built two faces to the works; these were two thousand five hundred
and eighty yards long, or about one and a half miles. The land face
mounted twenty of the heaviest sea-coast guns, and was 682 yards long;
the sea face with twenty-four equally heavy guns (including a 170-
pounder Blakeley rifle and 130-pounder Armstrong rifle, both imported
from England) was 1,898 yards in length.

The land face commenced about 100 feet from the river with a half
bastion, originally Shepherd's Battery, which I had doubled in strength,
and extended with a heavy curtain to a full bastion on the ocean side,
where it joined the sea face. The work was built to withstand the heaviest artillery fire. There was no moat with scarp and counter scarp, so
essential for defense against storming parties, the shifting sands rendering its construction impossible with the material available. The outer
slope was twenty feet from the berme to the top of the parapet, at an
angle of forty-five degrees, and was sodded with marsh grass, which
grew luxuriantly. The parapet was not less than twenty-five feet thick,
with an inclination of only one foot. The revetment was five feet nine
inches high from the floor of the gun chambers, and these were some
twelve feet or more from the interior plane. The guns were all mounted
in barbette on Columbiad carriages; there was not a single casemated
gun in the fort. Experience had taught that casemates of timber and
sand bags were a delusion and a snare against heavy projectiles; and
there was no iron to construct others with. Between the gun chambers,
containing one or two guns each, there were heavy traverses, exceeding
in size any heretofore constructed, to protect from an enfilading fire.
They extended out some twelve feet on the parapet, and were twelve
feet or more in height above the parapet, running back thirty feet or
more. The gun chambers were reached from the rear by steps. In each
traverse was an alternate magazine or bomb-proof, the latter ventilated
by an air chamber. Passage ways penetrated the traverses in the interior

3. A Russian fort in the Crimea. Also spelled Malakov.

of the work forming additional bomb-proofs for the reliefs for the guns.

The sea face for 100 yards from the northeast bastion was of the same massive character as the land face. A crescent battery built for four casemated guns joined this. It had been originally constructed of palmetto logs and tarred sand bags and sand revetted with sod; but the logs had decayed and it was converted into a hospital bomb-proof. In its rear a heavy curtain was thrown up to protect the chambers from fragments of shells. From this bomb-proof a series of batteries extended for three-quarters of a mile along the sea, connected by an infantry curtain. These batteries had heavy traverses, but were not more than ten or twelve feet high to the top of the parapets and were built for richochet firing. On this line was a bomb-proof electric battery connected with a system of submarine torpedoes. Further along, where the channel ran close to the beach inside the bar, a mound battery, sixty feet high was erected, with two heavy guns, which had a plunging fire on the channel; this was connected with the battery north of it by a light curtain. Following the line of the works it was over one mile from the mound to the redan at the angle of the sea and the land faces. From the mound for nearly a mile to the end of the point was a level sand plain, scarcely three feet above high tide, and much of it was submerged during gales. At the point was battery Buchanan with four guns, in the shape of an ellipse, commanding the Inlet, its two eleven-inch guns covering the approach by land.

It was constructed after a plan furnished me by Reddin Pittman, an accomplished young engineer officer from Edgecombe county, and, for its purpose, was perfect in design. I remember when he gave me the plan he had named it "Augusta Battery," after his sweetheart, but General Whiting wishing to compliment the gallant hero of Mobile, directed me to call it Battery Buchanan.[4] When completed it was garrisoned by a detachment from the Confederate States Navy. An advanced redoubt with a twenty-four pounder was added after the repulse of Butler and Porter, Christmas, 1864. A wharf [on the Cape Fear] for large steamers was in close proximity to this work. Battery Buchanan was a citadel to which an overpowered garrison might retreat and with proper transportation might be carried off at night, and to which reinforcements could be safely sent under the cover of darkness.

Returning to the land face or northern front of Fort Fisher, as a defense against infantry, there was a system of subterra torpedoes extending across the peninsula five to six hundred feet from the land face, and so disconnected that the explosion of one would not affect the others; inside the torpedoes, about fifty feet from the berme of the work, extending from river bank to seashore, was a heavy palisade of sharpened logs nine feet high, pierced for musketry, and so laid out as to have an enfilading fire on the centre, where there was a redoubt guarding a sally port, from which two Napoleons were run out as occasion required. At

4. At Mobile, Admiral Franklin Buchanan aboard his flagship, the ram *Tennessee*, made a heroic attack single-handed against the entire Union squadron.

the river end of the palisade was a deep and muddy slough, across which was a bridge, the entrance of the river road into the fort; commanding this bridge was a Napoleon gun. There were three mortars in the rear of the land face.

William Lamb, "Fort Fisher," pp. 260–63.

---

(2) Powder-boat Fiasco, December 1864

After reading newspaper accounts of the explosion of an ammunition dump in England which destroyed property for miles around, General B. F. Butler hit upon the idea of exploding a powder-boat in the surf at Fort Fisher. Butler expected "that the gases from the burning powder would so disturb the air as to render it impossible for men to breathe within two hundred yards; that the magazines of the fort would be burst in and possibly the magazines themselves be exploded; that by the enormous missiles that would be set in motion, and by the concussion, many men would be killed, and if the explosion were to be followed immediately by an attack of even a small number of effec-tive men, the fort could be captured."[5] Admiral Porter, fearful for the safety of his ships, planned to order the Union fleet to fall back twelve miles. But to the chagrin of both Butler and Porter the explosion on the morning of 24 December 1864 was, in the words of a Union officer, little more than a fizzle. Colonel Lamb at the fort concluded that a blockader had run aground.

Galaxy magazine, in its January 1870 issue, carried a lengthy account of the powder-boat fiasco by one who maintained that "his opportunities for observing the details of the expedition, from beginning to end, were such as few beyond the actors in the same enjoyed."[6]

Probably no episode of the late Civil War is really so little understood as that famous attempt to disable the Confederate works near Wilmington, in 1864, known as the "Powder-boat Expedition" . . . While the crude conception of the plan was General Butler's and while the preparation of the explosive powder was the work of the Ordnance Department, the execution developed upon . . . Admiral [David Porter]. . . . The admiral's attention soon fixed itself firmly upon an officer. . . .

This man was Commander Alexander C. Rhind of New York, at this time commanding a double-ender, the Agawam. Commander Rhind had already served with great distinction in the South Atlantic Squadron.

5. Benjamin F. Butler, *Butler's Book*, p. 800.
6. "Story of the Powder-Boat," p. 77.

It was proposed to her [the Agawam] commander to take command of the Louisiana and the powder-party. He accepted at once and set about his preparation. . . .

The crew were all volunteers from the Agawam. . . .

The Louisiana was to have as consort a fast steamer, which was to tow the vessel in, if found necessary, pilot her to her destination and bring off her officers and crew. . . .

For the Louisiana was now "ready for action". . . . The vessel was taken down to Craney Island [Hampton Roads] at the mouth of the Elizabeth river and there received on board one hundred and eighty-five tons of powder. . . .

To explode this mass of powder several appliances were adopted. By the ordnance officers the movements of three ordinary marine clocks were used. . . .

There were also six slow matches . . . [They] were placed in different parts of the vessel, and connected with the powder by Gomez fuses. . . .

Besides these means . . . Commander Rhind added a third. . . . five pieces of candle cut . . . to burn one hour and three quarters. . . .

Finally, to make the explosion a certainty . . . a fire was laid in the stern composed of tallow, turpentine, cotton waste and pine wood. This was to be lighted at the last moment. . . .

It was the 13th of December that the powder-boat was finally turned over by the ordnance officers, and taken charge by Admiral Porter. A temporary crew was placed on board of her, and she was towed to sea. . . . Here [Beaufort] she received thirty additional tons of powder, making the total amount on board two hundred and fifteen tons. . . .

Everything being now in readiness, the Louisiana was again taken in tow . . . , and both vessels proceeded toward New Inlet. . . .

A gale of wind . . . sprung up on the night of the 18th and continued with great fury until the 22nd . . .

After the gale ceased, the sea went down rapidly; and the night of the 23d was clear and fine. . . . so, as he [Admiral Porter] had determined to attack on the 24th and had already sent word to General Butler, he ordered Commander Rhind to proceed in at once, and blow up the vessel.

Accordingly, the Wilderness . . . took the tow-line, and the Kansas . . . took her position as a stern range. At a quarter before eleven the two vessels passed the Kansas and stood in shore W. by S. 1/2S., running slowly. At twenty minutes before twelve, fifty-five minutes after leaving the Kansas, the Wilderness was in two and a half fathoms of water, with the beach and the embrasures of Fort Fisher plainly discernible. The signal was now made, and the Louisiana steamed in unaided to her station. Slowly, but steadily, she approached the beach; and to the spectators on the Wilderness she seemed almost on shore before she anchored. . . . Then all was quiet.

Those were solemn moments. . . . Suddenly a broad glare of light shot upward; and in an instant the powder boat was plainly visible, as if by moon-light. It was a moment like that which comes to drowning men before they sink for the last time. For to every one on board the

Wilderness, the one thought occurred—"The fire has gotten away from them!" The next instant, destruction, annihilation was expected. . . .

What closed the eyes of the sentries on the beach, and the garrison in the fort puzzled every one. The rebel newspapers which gave an account of the explosion, explained this. The Louisiana was seen, but was thought to be a gun-boat which had gotten aground, and had been abandoned and set on fire. It was impossible for them, in the obscurity of the night, to judge of her distance from the beach; and as several of our small tugs had at times during the history of the blockade been so abandoned and blown up, the glare from the Louisiana attracted no particular notice.

Soon the light was extinguished, and all was dark again. The night had become thick, and the Louisiana was scarcely discernible from the deck of the Wilderness.

Twenty minutes passed. The sentries still continued their walks on beach and parapet, and their challenges were occasionally heard. At length [acting master] Arey [of the Wilderness] announced "They are coming," and soon the boat and her crew were under the quarter. "All right" was the word from Rhind, as he came on deck; and, although orders were to cast loose the boat and let her go, he coolly remarked that she "was too good a boat for the rebels to have," and ordered her hoisted up. This being done, "Four bells!" was the word to the engineer, who had been bottling up his steam; and, the Wilderness darted away to the eastward at a speed of fifteen miles an hour.

In obedience to the Admiral's instructions, rockets were now thrown with great rapidity to notify him that the powder-boat had been duly placed, and arrangements made to explode her. This done, the party joined in congratulations on the success of the affair thus far, and hopes that the results would equal general expectation.

According to Commander Rhind's estimate, the Louisiana had been anchored within three hundred yards of the beach. It was hoped that, the wind being light, she would swing to the flood tide, with her stern toward the shore. But she swung head to wind; so that she had to be securely anchored with two anchors and short scope of chain, just sufficient to hold her firmly.

The clocks had been set at ten minutes to twelve, to run an hour and a half; and the candles . . . had been cut to burn an hour and three-quarters. The Wilderness hove to at ten minutes to one on the morning of the 24th, and awaited the explosion. The clocks should have exploded the powder at twenty minutes past one, and the . . . [candles] at twenty-five minutes before two. But it was not until twenty minutes to two that the explosion took place; and by that time the after part of the vessel was wrapped in flames.

At that moment (1:40 A.M.) a huge column of fire rushed straight upward, four loud explosions followed at intervals of about half a second, and all was darkness.

Rhind turned to his officers and quietly remarked, "There's a fizzle!" and went below. In fact he had feared all along that the arrangements for securing instantaneous explosion would fail. . . . As these arrangements, however, had been made by the ordnance officers, he did not attempt, on his own responsibility, to alter them. . . .

When day broke, the Wilderness steamed out to the flag-ship, on board of which they were most heartily welcomed as men risen from the dead. Indeed, the Admiral informed Commander Rhind that, when they had parted the previous evening, he had never expected to see any of the party again in life.

It is almost unnecessary to state here, which has been for a long time so well known to the public, that the explosion failed to damage the works. It was felt heavily at Wilmington, and distinctly at Beaufort; the former about thirteen miles from the forts, the latter about seventy. A rebel officer and a number of his men, who were lying on the ground about two and a half miles from the fort declared that "the explosion jumped them about like pop-corn." But, on the other hand, a number of wooden buildings on the point, about a mile and a half from the place where the powder-vessel was blown up, were not even injured.

The expedition did not fail; the attempt to blow up the forts did. The powder-vessel was placed and exploded according to orders; and the failure consisted entirely in the effects of the explosion not fulfilling the sanguine expectations of the projectors.

"Story of the Powder-Boat," pp. 77–88.

---

(3) Second Battle of Fort Fisher, January 1865

Three weeks after the powder-boat fiasco the reorganized Union expedition returned to the Cape Fear, and on 13 January 1865 the warships commenced a murderous bombardment of Fort Fisher. By Sunday the fifteenth it had reached a fury almost "beyond description."[7] Nearly every Confederate cannon was disabled, and the garrison suffered severe casualties. Colonel Lamb found it impossible to repair damages. He scarcely found time to bury the dead. Around mid-afternoon the main Union assault was launched, and from that moment on the fighting was constant and furious. Bayonets, knives, and gun butts came into play. The action moved from traverse to traverse and from line to line until nine o'clock in the evening when all resistance ceased. The weary Confederate troops finally surrendered to their pursuers at Battery Buchanan below Fort Fisher on the tip of Confederate Point.

During the day's bitter fighting both General W. H. C. Whiting, ranking officer at the fort, and Colonel William Lamb were wounded. The command of the installation devolved upon Major James Reilly. In a penciled account written after the war, Reilly describes in sentimental yet vivid terms the day's fierce action. He deals mostly with the heroic efforts of his small immediate com-

7. *Official Records*, Ser. 1, 46, Pt. 1:439.

mand, but he also comments on the cowardly conduct of a few men including the commanding officer at Battery Buchanan.

I saw it stated that Colonel Lamb was in command of Fort Fisher when it was captured. Such is not the case. . . . I was in command of the fort after the chivalrous Whiting and the brave Colonel Lamb were wounded. Both of these officers were wounded about the same time, Whiting first and Lamb shortly after. This sad occurrence happened about 3 oc. in the afternoon, I being the senior officer then for duty the command devolved to me. . . . I was placed in a very disagreeable situation, but I assumed it with all its responsibility and with a small number of brave men. . . . Kept the heavy assaulting column of the enemy in check all that memorable afternoon the men that did fight fought as well as any men ever fought. Shortly after the enemy got possession of the western angle of the work the fleet slackened its fire to a very great extent. This encouraged our men and I revived considerable enthusiasm and determination amongst them and it showed plainly that they meant business and the few that did come out of the chambers where they were seeking protection from the destructive and murderous fire of the enemy fleet all day fought as men ought to fight for the protection of Hearths and Homes. I availed myself of the cessation of shot and formed about one hundred fifty men in the open space in rear of the Sally Port. As soon as the formation was complete I advanced on a body of the enemy that established themselves in the open space between the western angle of the Fort and the river. This body annoyed us very much all the afternoon. I put one of the S. Ca. Regt. Colors by my side and in front of the column. As soon as the enemy observed our object they opened a very destructive fire. . . . Under such a fire our men began to waver and fall back and by the time I reached near the angle of the work I had not sixty men with me. The balance who was not killed or wounded took shelter behind the traverses and in the Sally Port. In this last effort to repel the enemy I lost heavily and that brave and gallant soldier who carried the colors was killed by my side. His loss created some confusion in the attack and I was compelled to fall back but without apparent confusion to the sand bank in front of the main magazine where I reformed and kept up as heavy and as destructive a fire on the enemy as my small command would allow [?]. . . . The fighting was very close and severe. The fleet soon found out our position and annoyed us very much all the afternoon with shot and shell and [it] had a very demoralizing effect on the men fighting in the open space behind the sand bank and exposed to such a terrible fire, not with standing their great effort . . . they were not able to dislodge us until after dark and the moon raised when I found myself nearly surrounded, this little band was completely broke down after fighting bravely all day but there was no surrender written on their face. . . . I reformed my unit with my left well up on the breast work so as to enable me to give a direct fire on the works [?] and in command of Captain McCormick, that gallant officer was killed at his post, Peace to his ashes he displayed courage and ability and kept his men well in hand up to the time of his death, about this time a white-flag was displayed from the Sally Port. I could not understand what it meant, as I knew the enemy did not get that far down the work. At the solicitation of some of the officers I ceased firing and took my handkerchief and gave it to Captain Brady who put [it] on the point of his sword. I ordered him to advance toward the Sally Port and see what was wanted. As soon as the firing ceased, and everything quiet to my surprise our men came out and instead of coming toward us they ran towards the enemy. As soon as I observed their object I recalled Captain Brady and commenced firing (I knew I gained considerable advantage by keeping up a constant & as heavy a fire on the enemy as I could. It kept them from making any formation whatever for the continuation of the assault and they were content to keep behind the captured banks and would not make any demonstration until after dark) and the men fought with more determination than ever, and my gallant troops [were] greatly incensed at the dastardly conduct of their comrades.

I maintained my position until about seven P.M. Under cover of darkness the enemy made their . . . attack simultaneously at several points. This concentrated attack compelled me to fall back from one position to another until we were driven from the Fort, not however [until] sometime after I sent General Whiting and Colonel Lamb to Battery Buchanan with the expectation that they would be able to get over the river, as I was under the impression that Captain Chapman had everything in readiness to render what assistance he could (for he and a portion [?] of his command was not engaged during the day that I am aware of) in getting our wounded officers and men away from the Battery. After allowing sufficient time to escape for the officers before mentioned . . . I formed my brave little [immediate] command of thirty-two into a column of fours. . . . with saddened hearts marched away from the fort we defended with all our might. . . . I consider the defense one of the most determined of the war. It was from traverse to traverse, from traverse to the main magazine, from there to the breast work where the last and most determined stand was made and we [did] not leave until we were attacked on both flank and front. I wish I could know the names of the thirty-two men who stood by me that evening. Well might their names be put on the Roll of Honor of N.C. troops, for none fought more gallantly or with more determination or valour, our march was directed to Battery Buchanan where I expected to reform . . . and to be in a position to engage the enemy under more favorable circumstances the command was badly disorganized from the position they were placed in and the mode of fighting we had to resort too, they were subject to the demoralizing effect of the destructive fire of the enemies fleet (which a portion of the time fired over one hundred shots per minute into the Fort. I was ordered by Genl. Whiting to count the number on several occasions myself) on the land forces, I was pretty confident I might [?] be able to reorganize, for when I came within sight of the Battery I halted my little column for two objects. First to see if we were pursued. Second to inform Captain Chapman, as I presumed he was in a position to render me what assistance I needed, by having his men and armament ready for action, and on my approach to the Battery not to fire on us. For this reason when we halted I sent Captain Powell to the Battery with a verbal message to Captain Chapman not to fire on any organized body approaching the work. I was confident Chapman was still in the Battery for I thought him too good a soldier to abandon us for we were all sailing in the same ship and let us all go down together. What . . . gave me more confidence was that I [had] sent Capt. Adams . . . to him about 4 P.M. with a verbal message to this effect not to abandon the Battery for when I was forced out of Fort Fisher I would fall back on Buchanan and fight the enemy there. Capt. Adams returned to me and said he saw Captain Chapman and gave me as a reply "very well." But what surprise mortification came upon me when Captain Powell returned and informed me that Chapman and command was gone with few exceptions, the Battery abandoned and the guns spiked. And on my arrival I found about six hundred officers and men perfectly disorganized. With considerable effort of myself and several officers we secured in getting their Battery re-organized but three fourths of them had no arms and we had no means . . . of defending our position against an organized and victorious enemy. We had a splendid opportunity to retrieve our defeat and get away, if the armament of the Battery had been serviceable. It was as bright as day, the enemy advancing on the two fronts of the Battery, with our guns pouring shell and canister on them as they advanced down the sandy plain. Our men free from the destructive and demoralizing effect of the fire of the fleet, with the officers in charge of their respective commands and sure that their men kept a well directed fire of musketery on the lines as they came within range. . . . The whole mode of fighting was changed we would have regained coverage and the enemy would not have captured us, not that night at all events, for the position was very strong, and I have always been confident we were able to hold it. I could have communicated with Genl. [L.] Hebert and got means for there was plenty at his disposal at Fort Pender, for to get all the troops across the river. I knew from their activity the enemy displayed in the latter part of the attack on the fort that they would soon advance upon and attack Buchanan and as soon as they would come within range they would open fire on a defenseless mass. When I saw there was not a possible chance of defending ourselves, I took Major Hill and Captain Van Benthusen [*sic*] of the Marine Corps and went some distance in advance of the Battery and awaited their coming. We had a white flag with us and met the enemies skirmish line under the command of Captain Eldridge and I told that officer we surrendered and requested him to halt and retire his line and not let them fire on our defenseless troops. Captain Eldridge with the instinct of a true soldier complied with my request and reported I think to General [J. C.] Abott [*sic*] who came up and was conducted by Major Hill to General Whiting. . . .

Yours Respectfully,
JAS. REILLY

Account by James Reilly of the Second Battle of Fort Fisher, W. L. de Rosset Papers.

(4) Criticism of Braxton Bragg

While the garrison at Fort Fisher was engaged in a life and death struggle on 15 January, a sizeable Confederate force under General Robert F. Hoke was at Sugar Loaf a few miles above the fort. For various questionable reasons, General Braxton Bragg, in overall command of the Cape Fear defenses, would not allow Hoke to enter the fight. For this Bragg was severely criticized. One of his bitterest critics was General W. H. C. Whiting whom Bragg had replaced at Wilmington. Shortly before he died in a Northern hospital of wounds received on the fifteenth, Whiting wrote his friend Blanton Duncan that Braxton Bragg was primarily responsible for the loss of Fort Fisher. The letter was never finished and remained unsigned, but after the war Duncan, to vindicate the reputation of his friend, had it published in the Philadelphia Times. *Southern newspapers also carried the story.*

Hospital, Goat Island,[8]
March 2, 1865

Colonel Blanton Duncan:

My Dear Duncan—I am very glad to hear from you on my bed of suffering. I see the papers have put you in possession of something of what has been going on. That I am here and that Wilmington and Fisher are gone is due wholly and solely to the incompetency, the imbecility and the pusillanimity of Braxton Bragg, who was sent to spy upon and supersede me about two weeks before the attack. He could have taken every one of the enemy, but he was afraid.

After the fleet stopped its infernal stream of fire to let the assaulting column come on, we fought them six hours from traverse to traverse and parapet to parapet, 6,000 of them. All that time Bragg was within two and a half miles, with 6,000 of Lee's best troops, three batteries of artillery and 1,500 reserves. The enemy had no artillery at all. Bragg was held in check by two negro brigades while the rest of the enemy assaulted and, he didn't even fire a musket.

I fell severely wounded, two balls in right leg, about 4 P . M . Lamb, a little later, dangerously shot in the hip. Gallant old Reilly continued to fight hand to hand until 9 P . M ., when we were overpowered.

Of all Bragg's mistakes and failures, from Pensacola[9] out, this is the climax. He would not let me have anything to do with Lee's troops. The fight was very desperate and bloody. There was no surrender.

The fire of the fleet is beyond description. No language can describe

8. Governors Island, N.Y.

9. On 10 March 1861, Bragg took over command of Confederate forces near Pensacola, and on 6 April President Davis authorized him to attack Fort Pickens. Davis would have preferred that Bragg maneuver the enemy into firing the first shot. Instead, the general strengthened his defenses.

that terrific bombardment, 143 shots a minute for twenty-four hours. My traverse stood it nobly, but by the direct fire they were enabled to bring upon the land front they succeeded in knocking down my guns there.

I was very kindly treated and with great respect by all of them.

I see that the fall of Fisher has attracted some discussion in the public prints of London. So clever a fellow as Captain Cowper Coles, R. N., ought not to take Admiral Porter's statement and reports "au pied de lettre," and he ought to be disabused before building theories on what he accepts as facts and which are simply bosh.

The fight at Fisher was in no sense of the word a test for the monitor Monadnock (over which Porter makes such sounding brags), or of any other monitor or iron-clad.[10]

Newspaper clipping, W. L. de Rosset Papers.

---

(5) Surrender of Wilmington, February 1865

When the telegraph announced the fall of Fort Fisher on 16 January 1865, the seal of doom was put on the Confederacy. The loss of the mouth of the Cape Fear destroyed the last major contact of the South with the outside world. Soon Wilmington, abandoned by Bragg, was in Union hands. On the morning of 22 February Mayor John Dawson surrendered his city to General A. H. Terry. The Reverend Mr. Burkhead witnessed the meeting between the mayor and the Union general.

At the North Carolina Annual Conference held in Mocksville, Davie County, December, 1864, I was appointed the Pastor of the Front Street M. E. Church, South, Wilmington, North Carolina. I reached Wilmington December 24, 1864. On the 25th—the birthday of Jesus Christ, the Saviour of the world—which was the holy Sabbath, I preached to a small congregation. Early in the day an attack was made on Fort Fisher at the mouth of Cape Fear, by the United States fleet, and a furious shelling kept up throughout the whole day which was heard in the city. The reports of the guns averaged, I suppose, some forty to the minute. This was the first time in my life I had attempted to preach the blessed gospel of PEACE with the sound of WAR ringing in my ears. After preaching, in company with Rev. R. S. Moran, I dined at Mr. Peterson's. The probable fall of Fisher and Wilmington and the effects these events

---

10. A number of monitors or ironclads, including the *Monadnock*, were in the Union fleet which shelled Fort Fisher. The *Monadnock*, in Admiral Porter's opinion, was the finest monitor in the world.

would have upon the military situation, were of course the prominent topics of conversation. . . .

The evil could not be deferred. Again on January 13, shot and shell commenced to rain upon the Fort, and after a most heroic resistance the little garrison, under the command of General [Whiting] and Colonel Lamb, was compelled to surrender to a vastly superior force, and the "Stars and Stripes" waved in triumph over the captured Fort. A few days and nights of anxious solicitude and the 22d of February dawned upon us—a day to be noted in the history of this City, for on this day the Confederates retired and the Army of the United States took possession. I had just seen the last squad of Confederate cavalry dash along our streets, repaired to the foot of Market Street and was watching the approaching U.S. Army on the west side of the river when my attention was attracted to a small company of horsemen who came galloping down the street, and halting near where I was standing inquired politely for the Mayor of the City. "His Honor" John Dawson being in the company stepped forward and said, "I am the man." The officer stated to him that "General Terry would meet the Mayor and Commissioners at the City Hall in five minutes." In company with the mayor and several other gentlemen I walked up to the City Hall to witness the meeting between General Terry and Mayor Dawson. Here we stood for perhaps half an hour, during which time horsemen were dashing in hot haste through all the streets picking up the Confederate stragglers who had fallen behind General Hoke's retreating veterans. Then came General Terry at the head of a column up Front Street, with the strains of martial music, and colors flying. Leaving the main column at Market Street, heading a squadron of splendidly equipped men mounted on superb charges— every horse a beautiful bay—he dashed up to the City Hall, instantly dismounted, and said, "Is this the Mayor?" The Mayor replied, "It is." Whereupon General Terry took off his hat; the Mayor did likewise, and they shook hands with formal and graceful cordiality and together ascended the steps of the City Hall. The troops came pouring through the City, white and colored, and marched directly towards "Northeast" in pursuit of General Hoke's braves.

L. S. Burkhead, "History of the Difficulties of the Pastorate of the Front Street Methodist Church, Wilmington, N.C.," pp. 37–38.

VII

WAR IN THE CENTRAL AND WESTERN COUNTIES

The central and western counties of North Carolina, although generally free of Union troops during the first two years of the war, experienced difficult times. This was due primarily to disaffection in the region which by 1863 had reached an alarming stage. As early as November 1861, Governor Henry T. Clark had become concerned over conditions in the mountains. On this date he wrote authorities in Richmond that he was receiving "numerous communications from the North Carolina counties bordering on East Tennessee" requesting help against traitors.[1]

The situation grew worse in the spring of the following year when the Confederate congress passed the first of three laws which were particularly obnoxious to the mountain people. This was the Conscription Act of April 1862. The other two pieces of legislation which brought the war home forcibly to the region were the tax-in-kind and the impressment acts passed in 1863. For mountain folk, accustomed to individual freedom, these acts were especially galling. Of the three pieces of legislation, the Conscription Act of 1862 was the most distasteful. Having responded most generously to the early call for troops, the mountain counties in many cases were already stripped of young men by the time conscription went into effect. The additional demand for troops, therefore, met with considerable opposition, as did future legislation expanding the draft.

Furthermore, many western Carolinians placed little or no stigma on desertion, and the warm welcome they accorded army deserters caused the mountains to fill up with the disloyal from all of the southern states. The heavily armed deserters many times formed bands to plunder and murder. They perpetrated every sort of outrage.

The war was hardly a year old when Secretary of War George W. Randolph wrote Governor Vance and other governors that "our armies are so much weakened by desertion . . . that we are unable to reap the

1. *Official Records*, Ser. 1, 52, Pt. 2:209.

fruits of our victories. . . ."[2] A year later General Lee wrote Secretary Seddon that "desertion of the North Carolina troops from this army is becoming so serious an evil that, unless it can be promptly arrested, I fear the troops from that State will be greatly reduced."[3] This rapid desertion rate was confirmed by deserters fleeing north and telling their story, and by letters from Confederate soldiers to their families and friends. One soldier wrote "At least half would desert if they had an opportunity. . . ."[4] Newspapers were full of advertisements by officers offering rewards for the capture of deserters. In an exhaustive study on the subject, Professor Richard Bardolph writes: "A rough estimate suggests that the average number of [Confederate] absentees without leave comprised one-fifth of the [entire] enlisted force before May, 1863, one-third in the latter part of 1863 and early 1864, and two-fifths in late 1864 and early 1865."[5] Specific figures show that North Carolina's 428 officers and 23,694 men who deserted were almost twice that of any other Confederate state.[6]

Both Confederate and state authorities tended to see the causes of desertion as rather simplistic. While General Lee finally admitted that desertions were "occasioned to a considerable extent by letters written to soldiers by their friends at home,"[7] almost everyone in high position attributed desertion to "the pernicious press and judiciary at home."[8] General James Johnston Pettigrew wrote: "I can attribute these desertions to but one cause, the unfortunate state of public opinion at home, produced, I am convinced, by a small but very active portion of the community."[9] Certainly Chief Justice Pearson's rulings and Editor William W. Holden's despairing editorials induced many to desert, but they would have had little effect had much deeper causes not already existed. Persistent Unionism, hatred of conscription, the hardships of camp life, infrequent furloughs, the length of the war, the feeling that North Carolina was being discriminated against by the central government, "fathers gone mad" by news of suffering at home, the growing idea that the war was lost, and innumerable personal factors were also important causes of desertion.

Governor Vance sympathized with deserters somewhat, but he also realized that if unchecked they could render the southern cause helpless. When proclamations and appeals bore too little fruit, he began to send militia units over the state to seek out deserters and return them to the army.

Hiding out was difficult in central North Carolina and the militia seems to have had a fair record of recapture there. But the mountains of the western counties were ideal retreats for deserters and "Tories," as

2. *Official Records*, Ser. 4, 2:7.

3. *Official Records*, Ser. 1, 25, Pt. 2:814.

4. Richard Bardolph, "Inconstant Rebels: Desertion of North Carolina Troops in the Civil War," p. 165.

5. Bardolph, "Inconstant Rebels," p. 165.

6. Ella Lonn, *Desertion During the Civil War*, p. 231.

7. *Official Records*, Ser. 1, 47, Pt. 1:170.

8. D. H. Hill to Zebulon B. Vance, 3 May 1863, Governors' Papers.

9. *Official Records*, Ser. 1, 51, Pt. 2:712.

Unionists were known in the west, and Vance's efforts to enforce conscription and other laws resulted in virtual civil war. By 1864, home guard units operating in the west were almost helpless to cope with the bands of "bushwackers" roaming at will, and all semblance of Confederate control had vanished in large areas.

Adding to the unsettled conditions in western North Carolina was the threat by 1864 of Union cavalry raids from east Tennessee on the vital rail lines east of the mountains. With much of Tennessee in Union hands and disaffection widespread in North Carolina's mountain counties, Confederate authorities had every reason to be concerned. Their fears became a reality in June when Colonel George W. Kirk led a daring raid from east Tennessee on Camp Vance near Morganton. Kirk, a native of Greene County, Tennessee, was considered a "bushwacker" by Confederates, but among the Unionists he was known as an officer who could conduct guerrilla warfare necessary in the mountains.

Then in March 1865, General George Stoneman with a sizeable cavalry force left Morristown, Tennessee, for a raid through southwest Virginia and western North Carolina. In many respects Stoneman's operations, which carried him into North Carolina as far east as Salem and southward to Rutherfordton, were a brilliant military feat. His accomplishments were overshadowed, nevertheless, by the rush of events which were fast bringing the war to a close. As his cavalrymen tore up railroad tracks and destroyed property in Virginia and western North Carolina, Grant and Sherman were applying the death blows to the Confederacy.

---

(1) Causes of Desertion

In his study of the desertion of North Carolina troops, Professor Richard Bardolph states that the "causes of desertion were more numerous and diverse than may at first appear." In his analysis, the causes seem to fall into four broad categories, and the documents below are illustrative of these groupings: the hardships of army life (Document A), letters of distress from home (Document B), disagreement with the management and/or professed purposes of the war (Document C), and demoralizing news from the press (Document D). It should be noted, however, that analyzing personal motivation is such a sensitive task that the Bardolph article must be studied carefully in order to understand the many variables at work on the Confederate soldier.

A.

To come more particularly to the treatment of the Confederate rank and file by those in authority over them, I often remarked the little consideration shown the humble musket-bearer. There was a difference in companies, regiments and brigades, of course; but on the whole, the disregard for the feelings, comfort, health, and welfare of the private soldier was something wonderful.

The sick were generally left to languish in their tents, liable any day to a drenching from the rain, or to be overturned in a storm. The surgeons were often incompetent to dissect even a chicken's leg, and surgery on the battlefield was sheer *butchery*, resulting, oftener than not, in the death of the sufferer. The troops were often exposed to all the rigors of winter, while thousands of tents lay rotting in warehouses; thousands of men marched and fought (I myself fought at Manassas No. 2, Boonsboro, and Sharpsburg with bare and bleeding feet), with torn and festered feet because of lack of shoes, while plenty lay idle at some depot, or in a Quarter Master General's stores: men were denied a furlough when they could easily have been spared for a day or two, and when every letter from home told of starvation, misery, and death among the dear ones there.

Often we were without rations for three or four days because no care had been taken to secure a supply; often the whim of some epauletted, whiskey-drinking colonel or brigadier forced a sudden change in camp and consequent discomfort to the troops, who perhaps had been fixing themselves comfortable for weeks. Often the men were rushed off on some wild goose chase, generally in the night time, and after marching until their feet were blistered and legs stiff as iron, ordered to countermarch, and return to their camps—having endured all this hardship by reason of some blunder or absurd experiment, and when weary from frequent marches perhaps kept "drilling" for hours to gratify the ambition of some young officers anxious to show off his corps.

The truth is the Confederate private soldier could give only a part of his patriotism to the repulse of the foe as fully one-half of it was needed to sustain him in patience against the blundering discouragements that assailed him from his own side.

Was it wonderful that in many instances the quality of the article of patriotism proved unequal to the double strain upon it. . . .

After a while the spirit of the men became broken. Constant marching and fighting were sufficient of themselves to gradually wear out the army; but it was more undermined by the continual neglect and ill-provision to which the men were subjected. . . .

Pestiferous vermin swarmed in every camp, and on the march—an indescribable annoyance to every well-raised man yet seemingly eradicable. Nothing would destroy the little pests but *hours of steady boiling*, and of course, we had neither kettles, nor the time to boil them, if we had been provided with ample means.

As to purchasing clothes, the private soldier did not have an opportunity of so doing once in six months, as their miserable pittance of $12 per month was generally withheld that length of time, or longer—(I only drew pay *three* times in *four years*, and after the first year, I could not have bought a *couple of shirts* with a *whole month's pay*. . . .

It is impossible for such a state of things to continue for years without breaking down one's self-respect—wounding his *amour propre*, stirring his deepest discontent, and very materially impairing his efficiency as a soldier.

Starvation, rags, dirt, and vermin may be borne *for a time* by the neatest of gentlemen; but when he becomes habituated to them, he is no longer a gentleman. The personal pride which made many a man act the *hero* during the first year of the war was gradually worn out, and undermined by the open, palpable neglect, stupidity, and indifference of the authorities until during the last year of the war, the hero became a "shirker," and finally a "deserter."

Hamilton, *The Papers of Randolph Abbott Shotwell*, 1:129–30, 315–16.

B.

> Marshall, Madison County, North
> Carolina
> July 20 [?], 1863

H. W. Revis:

Dear Husband: I seat myself to drop you a few lines to let you know that me and Sally is well as common, and I hope these few lines will come to hand and find you well and doing well. I have no news to write to you at this, only I am done laying by my corn. I worked it all four times. My wheat is good; my oats is good. I haven't got my wheat stacked yet. My oats I have got a part of them cut, and Tom Hunter and John Roberts is cutting to-day. They will git them cut to-day.

I got the first letter yesterday that I have received from you since you left. I got five from you yesterday; they all come together. This is the first one I have wrote, for I didn't know where to write to you. You said you hadn't anything to eat. I wish you was here to get some beans for dinner. I have plenty to eat as yet. I haven't saw any of your pap's folks since you left home. The people is generally well hereat. The people is all turning to Union here since the Yankees has got Vicksburg. I want you to come home as soon as you can after you git this letter. Jane Elkins is living with me yet. That is all I can think of, only I want you to come home the worst that I ever did. The conscripts is all at home yet, and I don't know what they will do with them. The folks is leaving here, and going North as fast as they can, so I will close.

Your wife, till death,

MARTHA REVIS

Official Records, Ser. 1, 23, Pt. 2:951.

C.

> Fayetteville NC 27th Feb/63

Gov Vance
Dr Sir

Please pardon the liberty which a poor soldier takes in thus addressing you as when he *volunteered* he left a wife with four children to go to fight for his country. He cheerfully made the sacrifices thinking that the Govt. would protect his family, and keep them from starvation. In this he has been disappointed for the Govt. has made a distinction between the rich man (who had something to fight for) and the poor man who fights for that he never will have. The exemption of the owners of 20 negroes & the allowing of substitutes clearly proves it. Healthy and active men who have furnished substitutes are grinding the poor by speculation while their substitutes have been discharged after a month's service as being too old or as invalids. By taking too many men from their farms they have not left enough to cultivate the land thus making a scarcity of provisions and this with unrestrained speculation has put provs. up in this market as follows Meal $4 to 5 per Bus, flour $50 to 60 per Brl, Lard 70¢ per lb by the brl, Bacon 75¢ per lb by the load and every thing else in proportion.

Now Govr. do tell me how we poor soldiers who are fighting for the "rich mans negro" can support our families at $11 per month? How can the poor live? I dread to see summer as I am fearful there will be much suffering and probably many deaths from starvation. They are suffering now. A poor little factory girl begged for a piece of bread the other day & said she had not had anything to eat since the day before when she eat a small piece of Bread for her Breakfast.

I am fearful we will have a revolution unless something is done as the majority of our soldiers are poor men with families who say they are tired of the rich mans war & poor mans fight, they wish to get to their families & fully believe some settlement could be made were it not that our authorities have made up their minds to prosecute the war regardless of all suffering since they receive large pay & they and their families are kept from suffering & exposure and can have their own ends served. There is great dissatisfaction in the army and as a mans first duty is to provide for his own household the soldiers wont be imposed upon much longer. If we hear our families are suffering & apply for a furlough to go to them we are denied & if we go without authority we are arrested & punished as deserters. Besides not being able to get provs. the factories wont let us have cloth for love or money & are charging much over 75 per ct profit. Now Govr you are looked upon as the soldiers friend and you know something of his trials & exposures by experience. But you do not know how it is to be a poor man serving your country faithfully while your family are crying for bread because those who are enjoying their property for which you are fighting are charging such high prices for provs & the necessaries of life and still holding on for higher prices.

I would also request in behalf of the soldiers generally (for I know it is popular with the army) for you to instruct our representatives in Congress to introduce a resolution as follows. That all single young men now occupying salaried positions as Clerks Conductors or Messengers in the Depts of Govt & State & Rail Road & Express Cos. be discharged immediately & sent into the services and their places filled by married men & men of families who are competent to fill the positions.

Such a move as this would enable many a poor man to support his wife & family & prevent them from becoming public charges & at the same time it would fill our ranks with a very large no. of young active men who have no one dependent upon them for a support and who are shirking service. This would be very acceptable to the army generally. Our soldiers cant understand why so many young magistrates are permitted to remain at home and especially so many militia officers there being no militia and two sets of officers.

Respy your obt svt
O. GODDIN
Private Co D. 51st Regt. N.C.T.
on detached service

O. Goddin to Zebulon B. Vance, 27 Feb. 1863, Governors' Papers.

D.

Pro Marshal's office Rodes Division
Feby. 9th 1864

Col. Bryan Grimes
Coomdg. 4th N.C. Reg.t
Colonel

I deem it my duty to make known to you the last words of Private James King Co. E. of your Reg.t who was executed for desertion on the 30th of January ult. After bandaging his eyes, I told him that he had but two minutes more to live, and asked if he had any message he desired to send to his relatives or friends: he replied: "I have no message. I only wish that my body may be sent to my friends; but I want to say to you, Lieutenant, though others persuaded me to do what I did, the reading of Holden's Papers[10] has brought me to this; but thank God I shall soon be

As it may be the wish of his relatives to know in what spirit he died, I make this statement that if you think proper you may convey it to them.

Very respectfully Colonel
Yr. Ob.t Servt
J. M. Goff 1.st Lieut
Co. J 5th Ala. Reg.t & Pro
Marshal
Rhodes Division [sic]

Respectfully forwarded with the request that this paper be submitted to his Excellency the President, inviting his attention to the pernicious effects of the teachings of the Raleigh (N.C.) Standard.

This is not by any means an isolated case, there is another now to my own knowledge—an ignorant but *good soldier*, Sentenced to undergo the same penalty for a like offense who attributed his Misfortune to the evil influence of the Same sheet upon his friends at home and many who have suffered milder punishments say the Same Nathan McDaniel of Co at peace."

10. W. W. Holden was editor of the Raleigh *Standard*. See below, pp. 292–305.

"G" N.C. Troops is the offender alluded to above whose sentence has been suspended until the will of the President can be Known

BRYAN GRIMES
Co.4th N.C. S' Troops
Hd. Qrs. Ramseur's Brig
Feb. 12, 1864
Resp.y forwarded.
S. D. RAMSEUR
Brig Gen. Com.d

J. M. Goff to Bryan Grimes, 9 Feb. 1864, Governors' Papers.

---

(2) An Appeal to Deserters

Governor Vance never quite abandoned the hope that personal and official appeals from him would induce deserters to return to camp. On 26 January 1863, he published a proclamation in which he urged them to return, promising pardon if they did so and punishment if they refused. Apparently large numbers did return, and it was reported that about 300 men rejoined the Sixty-first North Carolina Regiment alone. But by spring, desertion was once more decimating the ranks. On 11 May Vance published the proclamation below, this time phrasing it in dramatic appeals and threats, and now only promising that returnees would not be shot. Once again the appeal was only temporarily effective.

BY THE GOVERNOR OF NORTH CAROLINA
A PROCLAMATION

Whereas, I have learned with great pain that there have been latterly numerous desertions from the ranks of our gallant army, and that there are many persons in the country who incite and encourage these desertions and harbor and conceal these misguided men at home, instead of encouraging them to return to duty.

Now, therefore, I, Zebulon B. Vance . . . do issue this my proclamation, commanding all such evil disposed persons to desist from such base, cowardly, and treasonable conduct, and warning them that they will subject themselves to indictment and punishment . . . as well as to the everlasting contempt and detestation of all good and honorable men. Certainly no crime could be greater, no cowardice more abject, no treason more base, than for a citizen of the State, enjoying its privileges and protection without sharing its dangers, to persuade those who have had the courage to go forth in defense of their country vilely to desert the colors which they have sworn to uphold, when a miserable death or a vile and ignominious existence must be the inevitable consequence:

no plea can excuse it. The father or the brother who does it should be shot instead of his deluded victim, for he deliberately destroys the soul and manhood of his own flesh and blood. And the same is done by him who harbors and conceals the deserter, for who can respect either the one or the other? What honest man will ever wish or permit his own brave sons or patriotic daughters . . . to associate . . . with the vile wretch who skulked in the woods, or the still viler coward who aided him when his bleeding country was calling in vain for his help? Both are enemies—dangerous enemies—to their country. . . . Rest assured, observing and never-failing eyes have marked you, Every one. And when the overjoyed wife welcomes once more her brave and honored husband to his home, and tells him how . . . in the lonely hours of the night, you who had been his comrades rudely entered her house, robbed her and her children of their bread, and heaped insults and indignities upon her defenseless head, the wrath of that heroic husband will make you regret . . . that you were ever born. Instead of a few scattered militia, the land will be full of veteran soldiers, before whose honest faces you will not have the courage to raise your eyes. . . . You will be hustled from the polls, kicked in the streets . . . and honest men everywhere will shun you as a pestilence. . . . Though many of you rejected the pardon heretofore offered you, and I am not now authorized to promise it, I am assured that no man will be shot who shall voluntarily return to duty. . . . Unless desertion is prevented, our strength must depart from our armies; and desertion can never be stopped while . . . they receive any countenance or protection at home. I therefore appeal to all good citizens and true patriots . . . to assist my officers in arresting deserters, and to frown down on all those who aid and assist them. . . . Unless the good and patriotic . . . arise as one man to arrest this dangerous evil, it will grow until our Army is well nigh ruined. . . . You can arrest it, my countrymen, if you will but bring to bear the weight of a great, a patriotic, and united community in aid of your authorities. . . .

Done at the City of Raleigh, this 11th day of May, A.D. 1863.

Z. B. VANCE

Proclamation of Governor Vance, 11 May 1863, Governors' Papers.

(3) Deserters in Central North Carolina

Vance was determined to hunt down those deserters who did not respond to his proclamations. Beginning in the spring of 1863 he ordered the state militia to guard all public highways and river crossings and told Secretary of War Seddon that he was using "every imaginable effort" to ferret them out.[11] When a few months later the legislature abolished the militia and created the "Guard for

11. *Official Records*, Ser. 1, 51, Pt. 2:715.

Home Defense," Vance used these troops, sending detachments to find deserters wherever they could be reached.

The counties of central North Carolina had fewer deserters than those of the west, and the relatively flat terrain made hiding more difficult. Consequently, deserters from here hid singly or in small groups and were no match for the state troops sent to capture them.

In fact it was not until the last months of the Confederacy that deserters in central North Carolina became numerous enough to band together and openly defy the authorities.[12] Document A illustrates some of the techniques used to avoid capture. Document B relates a highly publicized incident revealing the extent to which the militia would go to capture a deserter.

A.

For the first year or more after the passage of the conscription act, the deserter had little to fear so long as he avoided public places, or even gave the conscription officer an excuse for not seeing him. . . .

But after the Confederate ranks were thinned by the desperate fighting of 1863, the lines of the deserter fell in hard places. The Richmond government set energetically to work to bring every available man to the front. . . .

Then it was that the deserters . . . had recourse to a mode of hiding which they had learned from runaway slaves. . . . He either enlarged and concealed some natural cavity, or dug a cave in which he hid by day, to sally out under cover of darkness in quest of poultry, pigs, sheep, fruit, roasting-ears, watermelons, and other good things in season. . . .

The deserter made a vast improvement on the burrow of the runaway negro. . . . Banding together in squads of two or three, some unfrequented place would be chosen, generally on a hillside to avoid moisture, and as near a stream as practicable, for the easiest and safest way of disposing of the earth thrown up in digging the pit was to dump it in running water. The site being carefully selected . . . a watch was set, and work was begun and pressed with the utmost dispatch. . . .

Every hand that could be trusted,—old men, women, and children,— was called in to assist. To these auxiliaries fell the hardest part of the task, that of disposing of the dirt, which of course could not be left near the cave. This was generally "toted" away in buckets and piggins, and dumped in the adjacent stream. . . .

The proper depth . . . being attained, a fireplace was cut in the earthen sides of the cave and connected with a flue cut through the adjacent earth. Across the pit, and slightly below the surface, were then placed stout poles, and on these the roof of pine boards, while over all the earth and leaves were carefully replaced so as to conceal all signs of having been disturbed. . . .

12. A good description of the increasing boldness of deserters in Randolph County, for instance, is to be found in Joseph G. de R. Hamilton, ed., *Correspondence of Jonathan Worth*, 1:343–64.

Even under the best of circumstances . . . a cave was a dismal abode. . . . When rainy weather came, and the walls oozed water, only heat made it habitable. Care was taken to use the driest and most smokeless fuel, but as even that . . . would cause some smoke, various plans were hit upon to minimize the danger of betrayal from this source. When practicable, the cave would be dug near a dead tree, which was first blackened by fire. . . . The object . . . was, of course, that, should any unfriendly eye discover the smoke, it would be attributed to one of the accidental fires which sometimes smouldered in dead timber for weeks at a time. . . .

Entrance to the cave was usually had by means of a small trapdoor in the roof, in the concealment of which much care and ingenuity were also expended. In addition to the leaves always kept on it, a tree would often be felled over the spot, the boughs serving not only to screen the entrance from view, but likewise to lessen the danger of anyone walking directly over the cave. . . .

To insure greater safety, a band of deserters would have several caves in different places, occupying the same one but a few days at a time. A timid man is still being twitted with having done nothing but dig cave after cave during the whole war. . . .

The deserter while "hid out" was fed by his wife or some female of the family. . . . Nearly every woman had her own code of signals to guide the movements of her deserter husband. Sometimes a certain bedquilt hung on the fence meant danger, and another of different color or pattern meant safety; or a certain song sung on the way to the spring conveyed the necessary information. But hog-calling was the favorite signal.
. . .

The tedium of deserter life was broken by all sorts of pranks and practical jokes played by rollicking members of the fraternity. One very effective but somewhat dangerous pleasantry was for several deserters to don uniform and personate Confederate guards. Some timid deserter or band of deserters, chosen as least likely to shoot, would be ousted from their caves, and at intervals chased around the neighborhood for a day or two. . . .

The war over, almost as many absentees came back to our midst from the woods as from the camp. The meeting between deserter and deserter-hunter was at first very awkward, but the world moved faster now than of old, and the friction disappeared with surprising quickness. . . .

David Dodge, "The Cave-Dwellers of the Confederacy," pp. 515–20.

B.

Lexington
Oct. 4, 1864

His Excellency
   Z. B. Vance
      My Dear Sir:
         I wrote you that after investigating the matter I would report in full the conduct of the officers towards Owens wife. Last week in Ash-

boro I commenced to make some inquiries, but was soon relieved of all trouble by Col Alfred Pike himself. He called on me at my room and stated that I need have no trouble in sending for witnesses as he could report the facts himself. I informed him that I was getting up the facts in order to lay them before your Excellency & that if he chose to make a statement he could do so. His statement is as follows in substance & I think nearly in words "I went with my squad to Owens spring where his wife was washing & inquired of her as to Owens whereabouts, she said he was dead & buried. I told her that she must show us the grave. She thereupon began to curse us and abuse us for every thing that was bad. Some of my men told me that if I would hand her over to them they would or could make her talk. I told her to go some twenty steps apart with them, she seized up in her arms her infant not twelve months old & swore she would not go—I slaped her jaws till she put down her baby & went with them, they tied her thumbs together behind her back & suspended her with a cord tied to her two thumbs thus fastened behind her to a limb so that her toes could just touch the ground, after remaining in this position a while she said her husband was not dead & that if they would let her down she would tell all she knew. I went up just then & I think she told some truth, but after a while I thought she commenced lying again & I with another man (one of my squad) took her off some fifty yards to a fence & put her thumbs under a corner of the fence, she soon became quiet and behaved very respectfully. The rails were flat and not sharp between which I placed her thumbs. I dont think she was hurt bad. This is all I have done Sir, and now, if I have not the right to treat Bill Owens, his wife & the like in this manner I want to know it, & I will go to the Yankees or anywhere else before I will live in a country in which I cannot treat such people in this manner." I told him simply to make that report to you, he said he would do so but was no hand at writing, he said perhaps he could get Geo. A. Foust to do so— I learn that Geo. A. Foust and Alfred Moffitt with others were present & witnessed it all—

Allow me Governor in this connection to call to your attention a matter in which you certainly must be misunderstood although your orders on their face bear the interpretation which the officers gave to them. I found in Chatham, Randolph and Davidson that some fifty women in each county & some of them in delicate health and five advanced in pregnancy were rudely (in some instances) dragged from their homes & put under close guard & there left for some weeks. The consequence in some instances have been shocking. Women have been frightened into abortions almost under the eyes of their terrifiers. This matter has been called to the attention of Judge French and in his charges to the grand jury he forcibly and at length instructs them that all such proceedings are against the law, and that unless a magistrate first issues a warrant there is not and cannot be any authority for such arrests. . . .

I know that your Excellency never has intended by any order to justify torture, & yet in many cases where the treatment has been equally as bad as it was in Owens Case, the officers boldly avow their conduct & say that they understand your orders to be a full justification—

I shall continue to prosecute all these cases for I am sure that many things are done in your Excellencys name which you do not now nor never did sanction. Last week in Randolph I tried a man who had actually hung his neighbor until he was senseless in order to extort confessions from him it was a most aggravated case & the Judge sentenced him to six months imprisonment. . . .

> With great respect—
> Your Obt Servt.
> [Judge] THOMAS SETTLE

Thomas Settle to Z. B. Vance, 4 Oct. 1864, H. L. Carson Papers.

---

(4) Deserters and "Tories" in the West

Deserters whose homes were in the more westerly counties had an excellent chance of remaining free once they reached the hills and coves of home. The yeoman farmer citizenry, containing strong elements of disaffection, was sympathetic to the deserters' plight, and the "Tories" already in hiding welcomed them to their bands. George W. Lay, the inspector of conscription for North Carolina, wrote his superior officer that deserters "leave the Army with arms and ammunition in hand," and that when home they organized into bands "up to hundreds" and made camp in easily defended places. The disaffected citizens fed them out of sympathy and the loyal, out of fear. Lay confessed the "utter inadequacy" of his forces to capture them.[13] Peter Mallett, the colonel commanding conscriptions in North Carolina, wrote Governor Vance that it was literally unsafe for his enrolling officers to enter western counties without armed guard.[14]

For his part, Vance reported that the "evil has become so great that travel has been almost suspended through the mountains,"[15] and that the strength of discontent there had rendered his Home Guard "timid by fear of secret Vengeance. . . ."[16] On one occasion "an armed Company of deserters" entered a church "during service . . . stacked their guns and assumed conspicuous seats."[17] For any hope of success against the lawless bands the governor needed an engineer for mountain warfare and a brigade of experienced soldiers from the Army of Northern Virginia. He finally begged for a suspension of the draft in the mountain counties because they were "filled with

13. *Official Records*, Ser. 4, 2:783–85.
14. *Official Records*, Ser. 4, 2:733.
15. *Official Records*, Ser. 1, 18:821.
16. *Official Records*, Ser. 1, 29, Pt. 2:676.
17. O. S. Hamer [?] to Zebulon B. Vance, 17 Apr. 1863, Governors' Papers.

tories and deserters, burning, robbing, and murdering." [18] Of his requests, Vance received only the engineer. Furthermore, in October 1863, a 150-man force under General Robert B. Vance, the governor's brother and commander of the newly formed Western Military District of North Carolina, was so soundly beaten in Madison County that for a while Asheville seemed in danger.

The result was that most deserters recaptured there were those taken by surprise either singly or in small groups. Document A describes the defiance of these disloyal bands; Document B relates an incident when a group of soldiers was able to overcome such a band. The Shelton Laurel "massacre" (Document C), a particularly notorious affair, occurred after a band of "Tories" from the Shelton Laurel section of Madison County raided Marshall, the county seat, to get salt and clothing. They also did some plundering and pillaging. By the time Colonel J. A. Keith, Sixty-fourth North Carolina, reached the scene, most of the raiders were in hiding and could not be found. So the colonel went into the Laurel Valley (known locally as Shelton Laurel) and rounded up thirteen suspects, among them old men and boys. As it turned out, a majority of those arrested had not participated in the raid. Yet Keith had all of the prisoners shot and under the most cold-blooded circumstances.

A.

HDQRS. FIRST BRIGADE,
NORTH CAROLINA HOME GUARDS,
Mars Hill College, Madison County, N.C., April 12, 1864
Governor Z. B. Vance:

A dispatch reached me last night that a band of tories, said to be headed by Montreval Ray, numbering about seventy-five men, came into Burnsville, Yancey County, on Sunday night last, the 10th instant, surprised the guard, broke open the magazine, and took all the arms and ammunition; broke open Brayly's store and carried off the contents; attacked Captain Lyons, the local enrolling officer, in his room, shot him in the arm slightly, but accidentally he made his escape. They carried off all the guns they could carry; the balance they broke. . . . They also took off the bacon brought in by my commissary. . . . On the day before about fifty women assembled together, of said county, and marched in a body to a store-house . . . and pressed about sixty bushels of Government wheat and carried it off. I very much regret the loss of the arms. On Monday previous to the robbery I wrote to one of the captains in that county . . . to either remove the guns and ammunition or see that a sufficient guard was placed there to protect them. It seems that neither was done. I also urged on the citizens to lay to a helping hand in this hour of danger, but all done no good. The country is gone

18. *Official Records*, 53:324.

up. It has got to be impossible to get any man out there unless he is dragged out, with but very few exceptions. There was but a small guard there, and the citizens all ran on the first approach of the tories. I have 100 men at this place to guard against Kirk,[19] of Laurel, and cannot reduce the force. . . . In fact it seems to me that there is a determination of the people in the country generally to do no more service in the cause.

Swarms of men liable to conscription are gone to the tories or to the Yankees—some men that you would have no idea of—while many others are fleeing east of the Blue Ridge for refuge. John S. McElroy and all the cavalry, J. W. Anderson and many others, are gone to Burke [county] for refuge. This discourages those who are left behind, and on the back of that conscription [is] now going on, and a very tyrannical course pursued by the officers charged with the business, and men conscribed and cleaned out as raked with a fine-toothed comb, and if any are left if they are called upon to do a little home guard service, they at once apply for a writ of habeas corpus and get off. . . . What are we to do? There are no Confederate troops scarcely in the western district of North Carolina. . . . This emboldens the tories, and they are now largely recruited by conscript renegades and very soon it is possible our country may be full of Yankees. Give me your advice and orders. . . . If something is not done immediately for this country we will be ruined, for the home guards now will not do to depend on. . . .

Very respectfully, your obedient servant,

J. W. MCELROY,
Brigadier-General,
Commanding First Brigade,
North Carolina Home Guards

Official Records, Ser. 1, 53:326–27.

B.

Yadkinville, N.C.,
February 19, 1863

Dear Sir: We have had a startling occurrence in this county, of which you have doubtless heard before this time, which has greatly exasperated every intelligent and good citizen of the county. I mean the murder of two of our best citizens, magistrates of the county, by a band of deserters and fugitive conscripts. The circumstances are these: There has been a strong feeling against the conscript law among the uninformed part of the citizens here ever since its passage. Many of that class swore that they would die at home before they would be forced off, and when the time came for them to go perhaps nearly 100 in this county took to the woods, lying out day and night to avoid arrest; and although the militia officers exerted themselves with great zeal, yet these skulkers have always had many more active friends than they had and could always

19. The writer was evidently referring to Colonel G. W. Kirk, Third North Mounted Volunteer Infantry (Union). See above, p. 95.

get timely information of every movement to arrest them and so avoid it. The militia officers have been able to arrest very few of them. This state of affairs has encouraged the dissatisfied in the army from this county to desert and come home, until, emboldened by their numbers and the bad success of the militia officers in arresting them, they have armed themselves, procured ammunition, and openly defied the law. They have even sent menacing messages to the militia officers, threatening death to the most obnoxious of them and all who assist them. Last Thursday 12 of the militia officers came on 16 of these desperadoes in a school-house about 4 miles from this town, armed, fortified, and ready for the fight. The firing immediately commenced; which side first fired is not positively certain, but from the best information I can get I believe it was those in the school-house. They finally fled, leaving 2 of their number dead and carrying off 2 wounded, after killing 2 of the officers. In the school-house were found cartridges of the most deadly and murderous quality, made of home-made powder (one of the men known to have been among them has been engaged in making powder). Four of the conscripts who were in the fight have since come in and surrendered and are now in jail here, but the leaders and the most guilty of them are still at large; and the section of the country in which they lurk is so disloyal (I grieve to say it), and the people so readily conceal the murderers and convey intelligence to them, that it will be exceedingly difficult to find them, even if they do not draw together a larger force than they have yet had and again give battle to the sheriff and his posse. But my principal object in writing this letter is to ask you what we shall do with those four murderers we have and the others if we get them? Suppose we try them for murder, do you not believe that our supreme court will decide the conscription act unconstitutional and thus leave these men justified in resisting its execution? I believe they will, and tremble to think of the consequences of such a blow upon the cause of our independence. It would demoralize our army in the field and bring the first horrors of civil war to our own doors and then perhaps subjugation to the enemy, which no honorable man ought to want to survive. . . . I hope you know I am conservative and for the rights of the citizens and the States, but for my country always, and for independence at all hazards.

Your obedient servant,

R. F. ARMFIELD

Official Records, Ser. 1, 18:886–87.

c.

Asheville, N.C.,
February 24, 1863

[HON. ZEBULON B. VANCE:]

GOVERNOR: In obedience to your directions so to do, I have made inquiries and gathered facts such as I could in reference to the shooting of certain prisoners in Laurel Creek, in Madison County. I have to report to you that I learned that the militia troops had nothing to do with what was done in Laurel. Thirteen prisoners, at least, were killed by order of Lieut. Col. J. A. Keith. Most of them were taken at their homes, and none of them made resistance when taken; perhaps some of them ran. After they were taken prisoner the soldiers took them off to a secluded place, made them kneel down, and shot them. They were buried in a trench dug for the purpose. Some two weeks since their bodies were removed to a grave-yard. I learned that probably 8 of the 13 killed were not in the company that robbed Marshall and other places. I suppose they were shot on suspicion. I cannot learn the names of the soldiers who shot them. Some of them shrank from the barbarous and brutal transaction at first, but were compelled to act. This is a list of the names of those killed: Elison King (desperate man); Jo Woods (desperate man); Will Shelton, twenty years old (of Pifus) [sic]; Aronnata Shelton, fourteen years old . . . ; James Shelton (old Jim), about fifty-six years old; James Shelton, Jr., seventeen years old; David Shelton, thirteen years old . . . ; James Madcap (Metcalf) forty years old; Rod Shelton (Stob Rod); David Shelton (brother of Stob Rod); Joseph Cleandon (Jasper Chandler), fifteen or sixteen years old; Helen (Halen) Moore, twenty-five or thirty years old; Wade Moore, twenty or twenty-five years old. . . . The prisoners were captured on one Friday and killed the next Monday. Several women were severely whipped and ropes were tied around their necks. It is said Col. L. M. Allen[20] was not in command and that Keith commanded. Four prisoners are now in jail, sent here, as I learned, by order of General [W. G. M.] Davis. These are Sipus Shelton, Isaac Shelton, William Morton, and David Shelton, son of Sipus. I think the facts stated are about true. One thing is certain, 13 prisoners were shot without trial or any hearing whatever and in the most cruel manner. I have no means of compelling witnesses to disclose facts to me, and I do not know that I shall be able to make a fuller report to Your Excellency at any early day. I hope these facts will enable you to take such steps as will result in a more satisfactory development of the true state of the matter. . . .

A. S. MERRIMON
[Solicitor for the Western district]

Official Records, Ser. 1, 18:893.

---

(5) Desertion and the North Carolina Courts

Even in counties where militia and home guard units were cap- *able of apprehending deserters, Vance found his efforts hampered*

---

20. Colonel L. M. Allen of Marshall commanded the Sixty-fourth North Carolina, but at the time of the raid his status was unclear.

by Richmond M. Pearson. The chief justice issued many writs of habeas corpus freeing such captives on the ground that enforcement of the conscription laws was the task of the Richmond and not the Raleigh government. Men resisting arrest by state troops, therefore, were committing no offense. Vance wrote President Davis that Pearson's decision "went abroad to the army in a very exaggerated and ridiculous form. Soldiers were induced to believe that it declares the conscript law unconstitutional, and that they were entitled, if they came home, to the protection of their civil authorities."[21] In the words of General W. D. Pender "the whole trouble lies in the fact that they believe when they get into North Carolina they will not be molested, and their belief is based upon the dictum of Judge [R. M.] Pearson. . . ."[22] Vance, nevertheless, continued to use the home guard to find deserters until finally in July 1863, the General Assembly gave him formal authority to do so and made it a high misdemeanor to aid or harbor deserters. The following document was published in the Raleigh Standard at Pearson's request on 1 April 1863, and reveals how he reasoned that one might harbor a deserter with impunity.

State of North Carolina,
Forsyth County

To the Honorable R. M. Pearson, Chief Justice of the Supreme Court of the State aforesaid:

The petition of Chordy Whitehart, of Guilford County, respectfully showeth unto your Honor that your petitioner aforesaid was, on the 12th day of March, 1863, arrested at his home in said County of Guilford, by R. P. Kerner, Captain of a portion of the Forsyth County Militia, and other persons, acting under his command, without any precept or process of law whatever, and carried by force from his said home into the County of Forsyth, where he is now kept, held, and in false imprisonment, detained, by said R. P. Kerner contrary to the laws and constitutions of the State and of the Confederate States.

Therefore your petitioner prays your Honor to grant to him the writ of *habeas corpus* to be directed to said R. P. Kerner, requiring him to bring before your Honor the body of your petitioner, with the cause of his capture and detention, that the same may be enquired into and relief may be afforded to your petitioner.

C. WHITEHART

Sworn to and subscribed before me, this 13th day of March, 1863

JOSHUA BONER, J.P.

North Carolina

To R. P. Kerner, Greeting:

Being informed by the annexed petition and affidavit, that you have in your custody the body of Chordy Whitehart, unlawfully, and without the authority of law, (as he says;) you are therefore commanded to have

21. *Official Records*, Ser. 1, 51, Pt. 2:709.
22. *Official Records*, Ser. 1, 25, Pt. 2:746–47.

the body of said Chordy Whitehart, together with the cause of his arrest and detention, forthwith at Chaffin's Hotel, in the town of Salem, in Forsyth County, before me, R. M. Pearson, Chief Justice of the Supreme Court and said State, to the end that the matter may be enquired of by me and such proceedings has as are agreeable to law. Herein fail not.

R. M. PEARSON, C.J.C.S.

Salem, March 13, 1863

I acknowledge the services of the above process.

R. P. KERNER

March 13, 1863

In obedience to the above writ I herewith produce the body of Chordy Whitehart before his Honor.

The cause of his arrest and detention is as follows:

One James H. Conrad, and two others, to me unknown, professing to be detailed and authorized by a Confederate officer, to arrest conscripts and deserters, ordered me as Captain of Militia, in Forsyth County, to arrest said Whitehart, a citizen and resident of Guilford County, who they alleged had been harboring one Wm. Beeson, a conscript or deserter. I objected to going out of the county; they said I had authority to go out of the county, and that they had authority to look after the Militia Officers, and see that they did their duty; and made threats that if I did not obey their orders, that they would report me, and that they gave me full power to tie or shoot if resisted. And I made the arrest under these orders.

R. P. KERNER, CAPT.

North Carolina:

Upon the facts set out in the return of R. P. Kerner, I am of opinion that the arrest and detention of Chordy Whitehart was unlawful and without authority of law. I am not apprised that the Legislature have, at their recent session, passed an act making it an indictable offense to harbor a recusant conscript or a deserter; but if any act of the kind was passed, it could only authorize the arrest of the party by process of the civil authorities; that is, by a warrant issued by a Judge or Justice of the Peace on belief of probable cause stated upon oath and directed to the sheriff, constable, or other lawful officers. A Confederate officer or a militia officer has no authority to execute the laws of the State of North Carolina.

It is therefore considered by me, that the said Chordy Whitehart be discharged with liberty to go wherever he will. It is further considered that the cost of said Whitehart, allowed by law, in this proceeding, be paid by said Kerner, to be taxed by the clerks of the Superior Court of Guilford County, agreeable to act of Assembly, in that case made and provided.

R. M. PEARSON, C.J.S.C.

At Salem, 13th March, 1863

On the testimony of Whitehart and Kerner, the Chief Justice, issued a Bench Warrant for the arrest of Conrad for the unlawful arrest of Whitehart.

Raleigh *Standard*, 1 Apr. 1863.

(6) The "Heroes of America"

One of the three major treasonable secret peace societies of the Confederacy was the "Order of the Heroes of America" (sometimes called the "Red Strings" or the "Red String Band") which was found in North Carolina, eastern Tennessee, and southwestern Virginia. While it was strongest in western North Carolina, it seems to have extended into the east as well. Federal officers were well informed of its existence, let its members pass freely through their lines, and promised them amnesty after the war. Loyal North Carolina Confederates discovered its existence in 1864, and the following newspaper account of its organization and purposes created a sensation. Lack of records actually make it impossible to assess the Heroes properly.

TREASON STALKS ABROAD — THE CONSPIRACY EXPOSED!!

A secret oath-bound Society, of a treasonable character, exists in North Carolina. There can be no doubt of the fact. The proof has been gradually accumulating and is now overwhelming. The names of some of its traitorous leaders are known. Their places of assemblage has been ascertained. Their channels of "communication" have been discovered. And as an evidence alike of the extent to which treason has ventured to promulgate its flagitious doctrines in our midst, and of the positiveness of our knowledge respecting the organization through which it seeks to destroy the Confederacy, we would call the attention of the public to the following *facts*, which have been discovered by the initiated.

1. The organization is known as the H.O.A. Society—the letters standing for the words 'Heroes of America.'

2. Its motto is *Truth, Honor, Fidelity* and *Justice.*

3. The Oath is as follows:

I, A. B., of my own free will and accord, and in the presence of Almighty God, do hereby and hereon most solemnly swear, or affirm, that I will never reveal the secrets of the H.O.A. to any person, except it be to a true and lawful brother Hero. I furthermore promise to swear, that I will not confer the degree of the Hero upon any person in the world, except I am authorized by a brother who has power to do so. I furthermore promise and swear, that I will not give the secret words of the *Heroes* in any other manner than that which I shall hereafter receive it. I furthermore promise and swear, that I will not write, cut, paint, print, or stain on anything moveable or immoveable, whereby the secret words of the H.O.A. may be made known. I furthermore promise and swear, that I will not speak evil of a brother *Hero* before his face or behind his back; but will give him timely notice of all approaching danger, binding myself under a no less penalty than that of having *my head shot through* —so help me God and keep me steadfast in the due performance of the same.

This Oath is preceded by an injunction to read the 2d Chapter of Joshua; and by the questions, 'Are you willing to keep a secret? Are you willing to be qualified to it?' If affirmative answers are given, the candidate is told to 'repeat his name and begin.'

4. The signs are these: Ordinary Sign: Two fingers on the mouth. Answer—One finger passed by the eye.

Signs of distress. Right fist closed on the breast and left hand across the mouth.

5. The words of the H.O.A., are: 'These are gloomy times.' 'Yes, but we expect better.' 'Why do you expect better?' 'Because we look for the cord of our deliverance.'

Also the words '*Three*,' '*Days*,' 'Duty,' and 'Washington,' will be comprehended by the informed.

6. The scriptural allusions refer to the story of Rahab the Harlot, who hung a *scarlet cord* from her house to secure the protection which had been promised by the spies of Joshua, for the assistance afforded them while in Jericho. The idea is to hand out the same or same similar sign to the Yankees, so that they may recognize their friends and afford them protection and relief.

From this exposition of the *secrets* of the association, it must be plain, even to the most confident of its members, that their machinations are understood; while, at the same time, it must serve to convince the unwary of the existence of a most dangerous conspiracy against the Confederacy. We expect to be able to obtain in a short time an accurate list of all the members of the H.O.A., together with its officers, places of meeting, mode of communication, &c; and though we may be induced to spare many who have been unwittingly inveigled into the organization, its ringleaders had better *beware*.

The objects of this association are preeminently treasonable. An unsuspecting man is approached, and questioned as to his desire to have his property protected in the event of raids. If the bate [sic] takes, he is made to believe that subjugation is inevitable; the story of the Harlot is related to him as a mode of escape from the evils of such a fate; the Oath is then administered, and the objects of the society fully made known to him.

The *Hero* finds to his surprise, perhaps, that, in this attempting by ungenerous and unpatriotic efforts to secure favorable terms for himself and his household—in thus seeking to prosper upon the miseries of his friends and the downfall of his country—he has become the member of an association *devised by the Yankees themselves*, as a covert and cowardly means of effecting the subjugation and slavery of the Southern people. He is placed in as direct antagonism to the authorities and laws of the Confederacy, as if he had taken the Oath to Lincoln, or had enlisted in the northern army. He becomes really a spy, a conspirator, and a traitor, in the fullest meaning of these words—subject to the penalty of death at the hands of the hangman, and with no redemption before him save that afforded by the utter ruin of the land which gave him birth.

Since the above was written, we have received the following communication from the Rev. O. Churchill, of Chatham County, which will fully explain itself. . . . The order of the 'Heroes,' it has been ascertained, was imported from Yankeedom, and it was expressly devised . . . for the purpose of sowing the seeds of disloyalty and treason in the Confederate States, under the specious pretext of affording protection and giving amnesty to those who should become initiated . . . in the event the Yankee army should get possession of the particular section of the country in which they might reside. . . .

We . . . [include] the communication of Rev. O. Churchill, who is an upright man and a minister of the gospel, of the Baptist persuasion, in the county of Chatham. . . .

Mr. Editor—*Sir;*—I wish to state a few facts for the benefit of the public, generally. There is a secret concern in this, and other counties, of our beloved Old State. Its name is 'Heroes of America.' Its objects, or main objects, are protection from the enemy. It has one of the hardest oaths attached to it, that has ever been invented, so as to prevent its subjects from telling the secrets. . . . I, a poor deluded soul, went into this unholy thing and for a short time thought it was all right, and during that time, was the cause of some four or five others becoming deluded with myself. But, thank God, my eyes were opened to see what I had done for myself and others. I at once declared non fellowship with the concern, and I prayed to God to forgive me for doing so vile a thing. . . . I think I am a loyal man, and always have been, and I do not want to be in anything that has a disloyal tendency.

Again, I thought of my brave boy, who was fighting for our independence and of all that I had done.

It was said too that those who belonged to this concern were expected to vote for Mr. Holden. I know that I could not do that, for I had ever been a warm supporter of Z. B. Vance, and expect, if permitted to live . . . to vote for him again. I would, as a friend, say to all of those who have been deluded and misled, to come right out of this thing *at once.* . . . Our authorities say it is treason, and I fear it is. So all of you, who are now keeping its secrets, come right out . . . and you will be pardoned at once, for we have a Governor who tries to do right. . . .

Raleigh *Daily Conservative,* 2 July 1864.

---

(7) Colonel George W. Kirk's Raid on Camp Vance, June 1864

In June 1864, Colonel G. W. Kirk, Third North Carolina Mounted Volunteer Infantry [Union], led a successful raid from east Tennessee on Camp Vance, near Morganton, North Carolina. This camp for Confederate conscripts and junior reserves was easily captured, but the colonel failed to achieve the main object of the raid, the destruction of the railroad bridge over the Yadkin River north of Salisbury. This move was foiled when Confederate authorities in Salisbury learned of Kirk's presence in Burke County.

Captain C. N. Allen arrived at Camp Vance on the morning of 29 June, the day following the raid. He immediately wrote Colonel Peter Mallett, Commandant of Conscripts for North Carolina, about what he found and what he could learn about the affair.

Camp Vance, N.C., June 29, 1864

Colonel: On my arrival here this morning I found Camp Vance a heap of ruins, and after strict investigation beg leave to submit the following report:

Major McLean left this place Monday morning, the 27th instant, leaving Lieutenant Bullock, the senior officer present, in charge of the camp, with instructions to organize and arm the three remaining companies of Junior Reserves at this place. Lieutenant Bullock proceeded to organize them that day, and it being late in the afternoon when the organizations were completed, he postponed arming them, intending to do so next morning, I suppose, apprehending no difficulty on account of the delay; but on the following morning, the 28th instant, ere the sound of reveille hushed in camp, it was resumed by an unknown band, and a squad, under cover of a flag of truce, proceeding to headquarters demanded an unconditional surrender of the camp, by order of Colonel [Captain] Kirk, commanding a detachment of the Third Regiment North Carolina Mounted Infantry Volunteers, the same notorious tory and traitor, vagabond and scoundrel, who organized those four companies of thieves and tories at Burnsville, North Carolina, last April.[23] Lieutenant Bullock seeing his men scattered all around the camp, sent out Lieutenant Hanks to endeavor to make terms of surrender, which Lieutenant Hanks reported that he succeeded in doing, and that the terms were that the men and officers should be paroled immediately, and private property respected. The officers present secured their goods and chattels, and then the incendiary's torch was stuck to every building except the hospital, which the surgeons by their blarney and ingenious persuasion saved intact. The officers and men were all taken off under guard except the surgeons, who were paroled, and about seventy men, whom they managed to get on the sick list and crowd in the hospital. The surgeons succeeded in saving about all of their supplies, all the cooking utensils of the camp, and extinguished the flames in two double cabins of officers' quarters and one row of privates' cabins. There were 250 bushels of corn burned, about 6,500 pounds of forage, some 100 bushels of rye, and 50 of oats; also some 250 guns and accoutrements, a goodly number of which were in bad condition, about 1,500 rounds of ammunition, &c. They burned all the office books and papers and all papers and documents in the quartermaster's and commissary departments. They took off 4 government mules and 4 private horses, leaving the 2 wagons and

23. The Third North Carolina Mounted Infantry (Union) had on its rolls seventy-nine recruits from Yancey County.

1 set of harness. I am not informed as to the amount of commissary stores on hand, though no considerable quantity.

There were some 240 of the Junior Reserves in camp here on the morning of the capitulation besides the officers. The raiding party numbered, so far as I have been able to learn, between 150 and 200 men, being composed of a very few soldiers, some 25 Indians, and the remainder of deserters and tories from Tennessee and Western North Carolina. All of them were armed magnificently, the most of them with Spencer repeating rifles. They released some recusant conscripts and deserters from the guard-house here and armed them immediately. They are retreating and gathering horses and negro men, whom they arm instantly. The home guard and some two companies from the garrison at Salisbury are in pursuit.

I will let you hear from me again soon. The surgeons had sent all the men who were in the hospital home, with orders to report to their respective county enrolling officers, before my arrival. I will have what little they failed to destroy well stored.

I am, colonel, with great respect, your very humble servant,

C. N. ALLEN
Captain (retired)

Official Records, Ser. 1, 39, Pt. 1:236–37.

---

(8) Salem Spared by Stoneman's Cavalry, April 1865

Union General George F. Stoneman left east Tennessee on 20 March 1865, with a 6,000-man cavalry force for a raid into western North Carolina and southwest Virginia. From Wilkesboro, North Carolina, he moved north to destroy the railroad between Salem, Virginia, and Wytheville to the west. He returned to North Carolina on 9 April and the following day was at Salem in Forsyth County. This Moravian village was one of the more fortunate localities visited by the Union troopers.[24] There was little destruction of property or pillaging in the community. The day-by-day record kept by the Moravians in Salem pictures the raiders as both orderly and well disciplined.

After we had enjoyed the solemn meetings on Palm Sunday we were greatly startled the next day, April 10th, by the Intelligence that the same portion of the federal army, looked for on the 3rd would pass through Salem to-day and indeed towards evening, about 4 o'clock they

---

24. Asheville was thoroughly ransacked by a detachment of Stoneman's command under General S. B. Brown.

took us completely by surprise, as they appeared all at once in our midst. Before we could realize it, soldiers were seen at every corner of the streets, had taken possession of the post office, and secured our whole town. Some of our brethren had gone out to meet . . . [Colonel W. J.] Palmer, the commander of the troops seen coming our way. Bro. Josh Boner and our Mayor addressed him personally. When commending our town and community to his protection not only on our account but also of our large female boarding school, the General assured him that persons and property should be safe, and thus that no destruction of any kind would be allowed, and that we might feel perfectly secure from harm during their stay with us. Other persons had gone out to reconnoiter, of them two were captured and taken to the federal camp; they were however released the next morning. [Colonel] . . . Palmer established his headquarters in the house of our Br. Josh Boner. In very great comparative silence about 3000 cavalry passed through our town, pitching their tents on the high ground beyond the creek. Had it not been for the noise of their horses and swords made, it would have been hardly noticed that so large a number of at the time, hostile troops were passing through our streets. The strictest discipline was enforced, guards rode up and down every street and very few indeed, comparatively were the violations of proper and becoming conduct on the part of the soldiers. The night was as quiet as any other, except there was a great deal of riding to and fro in main street, and some of us could not divest . . . [ourselves] of apprehensions that . . . [we] and . . . [our] houses would be in danger, in case the cotton factories in town should be molested. Providentially government stores were in town, in considerable abundance, so that individuals were not called upon to contribute anything, except bread and the like, for which the men would generally ask for politely and return thanks in the same manner. Fears were however entertained by some, whether their good behavior would continue to the last, and no doubt many a prayer ascended to the throne of a prayer hearing and answering God; and not in vain. For no outrages except the pressing of horses of any kind were committed and even the cotton manufactories were spared by the federals. Without any fault on the part of their officers some of whom had been scholars at Lititz and spoke feelingly of that happy time, entrance was effected into one of these establishments and considerable damage done. During the afternoon of the eleventh a large number of the federals came back from the railroad which they had tapped in several places, they brought with them 50 prisoners. By some mistake they came into the graveyard avenue and passed through the graveyard part of the cemetery, having shifted their camp to a place above town, but passing through those hallowed grounds almost all of them dismounted and led their horses, some even uncovered their heads. Before dark they had all left, passing through Winston towards the river, and though other soldiers said to be less disciplined than that portion of Palmers Brigade, which had been here near our town, they were not allowed to enter it.

Memorabilia of the Congregation at Salem, 1865, Moravian Archives. Moravian Church in America, Southern Province.

(9) Salisbury Visited by Stoneman, April 1865

Since late February 1865, Salisbury, crowded with refugees from South Carolina, had been in a state of near panic. First Sherman was expected, and then it was Stoneman. When orders came to remove all government property from the town, many of the people moved on. But for those remaining behind the "excitement . . . [was] perpetual. The news comes in constantly," wrote a minister, "rumor after rumor—from various directions."[25] The situation became so chaotic that the Daily Carolina Watchman *felt compelled to review for its readers all of the various rumors circulating at the time.[26] Stoneman finally arrived on 12 April.*

Harriet Ellis Bradshaw was but a child when the Union troopers rode into town. Yet the raid etched a "vivid impression . . . upon her memory."[27]

On a never-to-be-forgotten Monday morning, Mamma, Mrs. Barringer, a house guest, and I were already seated at the table laid for breakfast. Suddenly the . . . day was rent by an uproar of war whoops. . . .

"The Yankees! The Yankees have taken the town!" Mamma cried. . . .

I slid from my chair. Mamma caught hold of my hand. Together we hurried to the parlor and from the window looked out onto Innis Street along which our house fronted. The roadway was jammed with a surging mass of mounted soldiers. . . .

It was frightening, curiously thrilling to see the capless cavalrymen standing erect in their stirrups as they rode. . . .

Almost at once we overheard the sound of . . . voices, set eyes on a squad of bluecoated Yankees pushing roughly through the open gates which shut off our private driveway from Innis Street. . . . Their emphatic demand for liquor sounded as if they had come for strong drink rather than for conquest. . . .

A small-sized wooden keg rewarded a successful search. It was placed on end on the porch floor. Mamma told York to stave in the head of the little keg. . . .

Thirsty troopers filled their canteens with the liquor drawn from the wooden keg. Amazed, I thought, "These Yankees certainly do love our corn-whiskey!" . . .

How dreadful sounded in our ears the shouts of "Fire!" "Fire!" On the note of wild alarm came the sight of dense brown smoke billowing in rolls between the shingles of our barn roof. . . . Mamma gazed terrified. . . .

25. A. W. Mangum to Lucy Mangum, 25 Feb. 1865, Mangum Papers.
26. Salisbury *Daily Carolina Watchman*, 12 Apr. 1865.
27. Harriet Ellis Bradshaw Papers, "General Stoneman's Raid on Salisbury, North Carolina," p. 1.

"This outrage has gone far enough," she [Mamma] said. "I'll ask General Stoneman for protection; it's the only way."

Mrs. Barringer consented to go with Mamma to the headquarters of General Stoneman. When the two ladies had put on dainty bonnets, had drawn fringed crepe shawls about their shoulders we three sat out hurriedly to the front door, opened it and stepped forth into Innis Street.

Rapidly we walked the short distance to the Mansion House Hotel, where General Stoneman had set up his headquarters. A brick-paved floor of the hotel verandah extended the whole length of the ancient inn. Sitting beside a deal table, in a shaded part of the piazza, were General Stoneman and his officers. Their blue uniforms were red-clay powdered, evidently gathered from the dirt roads over which they had ridden the previous night to attack Confederate troops. . . .

Mamma accosted a fine upstanding Yankee orderly. "I wish to speak to the gentleman who is in authority here," she said. . . .

The orderly saluted gravely, turned, then approached the seated group headed by the Commander, and saluted. "General," he said, "two ladies wish an interview." The words were quite audible to me but I could not follow the Commander's reply. Again the orderly saluted, walked to the place where Mamma and our house guest were waiting; then he stood immobile at attention.

"Madame," he said, addressing the message to Mamma, "General Stoneman will listen to what you have to say."

The ladies moved forward, bowed courteously. The Commander seemed to hesitate for the fraction of a second, then he stood up, and with grace touched the wide brim of his plumed hat. On their feet, promptly the officers followed the General's example and offered the salute.

No time was lost in preamble. . . . "General," she [Mamma] began, "Will you kindly assign a guard to protect my dwelling house. . . ."

"Madame," the General replied, "Your request for the protection of your dwelling is granted. A guard will be detailed immediately to attend you to your home." . . .

The orderly . . . smartly saluted, faced the ladies, and stood rigidly at attention to await their leave. Mamma thanked General Stoneman, nodded her head to the Yankee guard. We three set out at once for home; the Yankee guard marched behind us. During the long day that followed, he paced the sidewalk in front of our house. . . .

It was long past ten o'clock that same night when our friendly-enemy-guard received instructions to report at headquarters. He carried away the remnant of a Confederate flag which had been hauled down from the entrance of the Yankee prison.[28] Fastened to a short pole set up against the outside frame of our front door, the flag had rippled its rebel folds all the day long. . . .

Next morning, Tuesday, a spectacle of the high-piled rows of military supplies, greeted our astonished eyes. Out of every storage warehouse in Salisbury had been carted wagon loads of army blankets, army over-

28. See below, p. 120.

coats, army shoes, army underclothing, in fact every oddment listed in the military stores, and then were heaped in piles on the roadway of Innis Street. Yankee ready-lighted torches touched ablaze the piled up loot. . . . "Poor white trash" and a horde of daring Negroes were carrying and dragging way as much of the pillage as they could loot by hand; chanting weird allelujahs. . . .

The final day of the raid was moving to an end; the stir of excitement pervaded the ranks of idle riders, their unsaddled horses stabled at the curbstone. Stoneman's pursuing cavalry was coming back to Salisbury after a battle lost. But no wild cheers, no war whoops of victory marked their return to the town. [Confederate] . . . defenders had saved the Yadkin River railroad bridge.

In the yellow glow of the late afternoon sun the Yankee columns swung round the corner of Main Street at the Mansion House Hotel, and General Stoneman and his officers rode into view. I noticed that they checked their horses to a slowing pace as they passed our house. Behind the General and his officers jogged the jaded cavalrymen with swords eased in the scabbards and the holster straps released. . . .

With emotions of angry disgust, like the other unhappy folks of Salisbury, our household watched the invaders depart; a departure that left behind a destruction that promised a future resultant poverty, bitter indeed. . . .

Harriet Ellis Bradshaw, "General Stoneman's Raid on Salisbury, North Carolina," pp. 3–8.

(10) Salisbury Prison

For Stoneman's cavalrymen Salisbury was especially attractive. A large Confederate prison was located there. In November 1861, a vacant cotton factory in town had been turned into a prison. "It is quite a little village . . . on the site of an obsolete cotton factory which some deluded capitalist once tried to establish here," wrote a Union prisoner in the summer of 1862. "A high palisade fence encloses 15 or 20 acres, the large factory building, overseer's former residence, 3 little log houses, 3 small brick ditto, & a two story

temporary wooden structure used as an hospital of which there is need. Within, & about the centre of the large enclosure is a second containing an acre or two perhaps, a tumble down shanty or two; in which pen are confined citizens under various accusations affecting their loyalty."[29]

Late in the war with supplies running low and the compound greatly overcrowded, Confederate authorities decided to transfer the prisoners to a new location. The news of Stoneman's raid hastened the move. By March 1865, all of

29. Diary of Charles Carroll Gray, Gray Papers.

the prisoners except the infirm had been evacuated. Thus on April 12–13 the hard-riding Union troopers had only a few abandoned prison buildings to raze.

One of the more graphic descriptions of prison life was that of New York Tribune correspondent Junius Henri Browne who was at Salisbury from February 1864 until his escape in January 1865.

On the afternoon of the second day we reached Salisbury, and, entering the inclosure of the Penitentiary, we were warmly greeted by prisoners we had known at the Castle,[30] and officers, held like ourselves as hostages, whose acquaintance we had made at the Libby.[31] At the Penitentiary there were Rebel convicts, Northern deserters, hostages, Southern Union men, and all persons that the enemy designed to hold for a long time. There were then but six or seven hundred inmates of the place, which we preferred either to the Castle or Libby, because we had the privilege of the yard, and had a daily opportunity to breathe the external atmosphere, and behold the overarching sky.

The quarters in which we were confined were very undesirable, being about ninety by forty feet, with barred windows, dirty floors, partially occupied by rude bunks, and two broken stoves that gave out no heat, but a perpetual smoke of green pine-wood that made the atmosphere blue, and caused us to weep as though we had lost the dearest mistress of our soul.

There, with rags and vermin, filth and odors, as little Sabean as possible, we passed the long, cold, desolate nights, shivering in our light blankets, and striving, for many a dreary hour, in vain to sleep. What a dismal den it was. . . .

Vermin swarmed everywhere; they tortured us while we tried to sleep on our coarse blankets, and kept us in torment when awake. Not a square mile of Secessia seemed free from them.

No light of any kind was furnished us; and there we sat, night after night, in the thick darkness, inhaling the foul vapors and the acrid smoke, longing for the morning, when we could again catch a glimpse of the blue beaming sky. . . .

Few persons can have any idea of a long imprisonment in the South. They usually regard it merely as an absence of freedom—as a deprivation of the pleasures and excitement of ordinary life. They do not take into consideration the scant and miserable rations that no one, unless he be half famished, can eat; the necessity of going cold and hungry in the wet and wintry season; the constant torture from vermin, of which no care nor precaution will free you; the total isolation, the supreme dreariness, the dreadful monotony, the perpetual turning inward of the mind upon itself, the self-devouring of the heart, week after week, month after month, year after year.

30. Castle Thunder was the name of Confederate prisons in Richmond and Petersburg. Castle Pinckney was a prison in Charleston, South Carolina.
31. Libby Prison was in Richmond.

Most strange that captives there do not lose their reason, or die of inanition and despair. How hard it is to kill a man, I had not fully learned, until fortune threw me into Rebel hands.

After nine months of confinement, at Salisbury, some ten thousand enlisted men were sent thither from Richmond and other points; and then began a reign of pain and horror such as I have not believed could exist in this Republic under any circumstances.

Our poor soldiers had been robbed of their blankets, overcoats, often their shoes and blouses, and were sent there in inclement weather and turned for some weeks into the open inclosure without shelter.

After a while they were given tents capable of accommodating about half their number; and there they began to sicken and died from cold and hunger—the rations being sometimes only a piece of corn bread in forty-eight hours, until the daily mortality ranged from twenty-five to forty-five per day.

The soldiers dug holes in the earth and under the different buildings in the yard, constructed mud huts and shelters of baked clay, showing extraordinary energy and industry to shield themselves from wind and storm. But their attire was so scant, and their diet so mean and meager that they died necessarily by hundreds.

Hospital after hospital—by which I mean buildings with a little straw on the floor, and sometimes without any straw or other accommodation —was opened, and the poor victims . . . were packed into them like sardines in a box.

The hospitals were generally cold, always dirty and without ventilation, being little else than a protection from the weather.

The patients . . . had no change of clothes, and could not obtain water sufficient to wash themselves.

Nearly all of them suffering from bowel complaints, and many too weak to move or be moved, one can imagine to what a state they were soon reduced.

The air of those slaughter-houses, as the prisoners were wont to call them, was overpowering and pestiferous. It seemed to strike you like a pestilential force on entrance, and the marvel was it did not poison all the sources of life at once.

Imagine nine or ten thousand scantily clad, emaciated woe-begone soldiers . . . in an inclosure of five or six acres, half of them without other shelter than holes they had dug in earth, or under the small buildings employed as hospitals. . . .

Look into those hospitals—strange perversion of the name!—which are small brick and log buildings, twenty-five by sixty feet. . . .

What a ghastly line of faces and of figures! To have seen them once is to remember them always. They are more like skeletons in rags than human beings. Ever and anon some of them strive to rise and obey such calls as Nature makes; and a companion, less weak and wasted than they, bears them, as if they were children, over the dirt-incrusted floor, and lays them down again to suffer to the end.

Through all the day and night corpses are carried from the hospitals to the dead-house, where the bodies are piled up like logs of wood, until the rude cart into which they are thrown is driven off with its ghastly freight.

All day long, one sees wretched, haggard, sick, and dying men in every part of the inclosure. Their faces tell their story—an unwritten epic in the saddest numbers. . . .

Not a single face relaxes into a smile; every eye is dull with despondency; every cheek sunken with want; every lip trembling with unuttered pain.

Disease and Death there hold high carnival, and the mirror of misery is held up to every vacant stare.

The air is heavy with plaints, and prayers, and groans, and over the accursed camp hangs the pall of despair. . . .

Suffering everywhere, and no power to relieve it. In every tent and hole in the ground, wherever you tread or turn, gaunt and ghastly men, perishing by inches, glare on you like accusing spectres, until you find yourself forced to exclaim, "Thank God, I am not responsible for this." . . .

On the 25th of November last, a few of the prisoners perhaps a hundred or two, feeling that their condition was entirely desperate; that they were being deliberately murdered by starvation and exposure, determined to attempt an outbreak. . . .

Some of the guard resisted, and a fight occurred, in which two of the Rebels were killed and five or six wounded, with about the same loss on the part of the insurgents.

The alarm was immediately given. The whole garrison mounted the parapet; and though, in a minute, the E M E U T E was suppressed, the effort to get out of the gate having failed, they began firing indiscriminately upon the prisoners. . . .

For fully half an hour the shooting went on, and in that time, some seventy men were killed and wounded, not one of whom, I venture to say, had an intimation of the outbreak before it was undertaken, and who were as guiltless of any attempt at insurrection as infants unborn.

At the Penitentiary in Salisbury, Mugging was reduced to a system.

Men were frequently mugged in the Prison yard. Several of the band would gather round the intended victim, who on a sudden would be thrown to the ground; his pockets turned inside out; his coat and hat, sometimes his shoes, taken; after which he would be let alone until he obtained more money or clothes to invite a fresh attack.

The Rebel Room, in the third story, where the convicts were confined, was the principal field for mugging. The wildest cries of pain and terror emanated from that quarter every night or two; and daylight would reveal some poor fellow with black eyes, swelled lip, and badly cut face, deprived of all his valuables and a large portion of his clothes.

In Prison, the inmates think and talk of little beside escape.

To them, freedom is everything; all else, nothing.

Long shall I remember the fresh, free air that greeted me like a benison when I stepped out of the Prison limits on that murky, rainy evening. The old worn-out feeling, the inertia, the sense of suppression, seemed to fall from me as a cast-off garment; and I believed I could walk to the ends of the Earth, if I could but find the sweet goodness of Liberty—dearest and best of women—at the end of my long, long journeying.

Junius H. Browne, *Four Years in Secessia: Adventures within and Beyond The Union Lines*, pp. 315–61.

VIII

THE CALL TO ARMS

One historian wrote that "North Carolina's greatest contribution to the Confederacy was man power—the high number of soldiers who bore the brunt of scores of battles."[1] She had one-ninth of the population of the Confederacy and furnished over one-seventh of its troops: 111,000 men organized into seventy-two regiments, 10,000 reserves comprising eight regiments, and 4,000 home guardsmen. North Carolinians killed in battle numbered 19,673, more than one-fourth the Confederate total. One-fifth of the Confederate losses in the Seven Days Battle around Richmond, one-fourth of those at Gettysburg, and one-third of those at Fredericksburg were North Carolinian. One-fifth of Lee's men who surrendered at Appomattox were North Carolinian. Those who died of disease numbered 20,602. North Carolina's total war casualties were greater than that of any other state. Since the United States had two and one-half times the population of the Confederacy, this great drain of manpower was the state's supreme sacrifice for southern independence.

Because of the South's long and strong military tradition, each state that joined the Confederacy possessed a well-organized volunteer militia system. In previous wars they had formed the basis of the national army, and in his inaugural address President Davis advised Congress to continue this practice. During the spring of 1861 Congress established the system that was to be used until the adoption of conscription. On the local level men would form a company, elect their officers, and then offer the company to the governor. He would organize companies into regiments, appoint the regimental officers, and send them all to camps of instruction for basic military training. Finally the governor would offer the regiments to the president for specific terms of enlistment, generally for twelve months but frequently for only six if the company's term of enlistment so stipulated. The president would then organize the

1. Hugh T. Lefler and Albert R. Newsome, *North Carolina, The History of a Southern State*, p. 430.

regiments into battalions and larger units and appoint the field officers.

After the first battle of Manassas the United States began vast military preparations, and in turn the Confederate Congress authorized President Davis to raise an army of 400,000 men. Davis, however, considered this number excessive and accepted militia units rather selectively. By the summer of 1861 the War Department had begun accepting only regiments and independent companies which would volunteer for three years or other units which had already been armed and would volunteer for twelve months. This policy was both embarrassing and expensive to the individual states, for they now had thousands of unaccepted volunteers idling in camp at state expense.

The enthusiasm that in the spring of 1861 had induced so many young—and even quite old—North Carolinians to volunteer for twelve months had, by the autumn of the same year, noticeably subsided, quickly dampened by the miseries of camp life. The worried Confederate secretary of war reported to President Davis that the terms of 148 regiments would soon end and that most of them would not reenlist. In the face of northern manpower superiority, conscription became increasingly attractive to Confederate leaders, and even General Lee began drafting such a law for Richmond's consideration. President Davis submitted Lee's ideas to Congress and on 16 April 1862 Congress enacted the first American conscription law. It authorized the president to place in the army all white males between eighteen and thirty-five except those legally exempt. Men already in service were to be continued for three years or the duration. By February 1864 the draft had been extended to include all those between seventeen and fifty. Besides assuring the Confederacy of an army, the first conscription law also solved the problem of those regiments that President Davis would not accept, for now all men within the draft age were placed on the same basis and subject completely to Confederate jurisdiction.

The Confederate War Department established a Bureau of Conscription to carry out the laws of Congress. Section 3 of the first draft law specified that state enrolling officers be used, and only on a governor's failure to cooperate could Confederate officers be used. So many problems, however, eventually developed that gradually the War Department took over the entire operation. By April 1863, the Bureau of Conscription had about one-half million men enrolled, but only about half of them were present for duty, the others being lost either by poor law enforcement or by good draft dodging.

Obviously if all able-bodied men were placed in the army the home front would collapse in short order. One North Carolina editor wrote: "In order that the war should be carried on efficiently—that our soldiers should be fed, clothed, supplied with munitions, forage, etc., that the agriculture and business of the country should also, as far as possible, be carried on, and the machinery of civil government kept in motion, and thus the life of the country be sustained, and its credit supported, it has been deemed necessary that certain exemptions should be made."[2]

2. Wilmington *Journal*, 17 Mar. 1863.

Consequently, on 21 April 1861, Congress established a system of "class exemptions" conferring blanket exemption from service on certain individuals, professions, and occupations. Among these were the physically unfit, government officers, printers, teachers, apothecaries, tanners, blacksmiths, iron workers, mail carriers, and others.[3] The list was gradually reduced—toward the end of the war it was pared to a minimum—but the principle of class exemption was never abandoned.

Avoiding military service soon became the consuming interest of thousands all over the Confederacy. Labor was scarce and farm families already operating at a bare subsistence level could scarcely afford to spare even one son. Often badly educated men were reluctant to fight for a cause which they hardly understood. And southerners of that era in general were notoriously unreceptive to any kind of regimentation. But while dodging the draft seems to have been particularly rampant in North Carolina, actually the execution of the laws there differed from that in other states in only two significant ways: North Carolina exempted almost twice as many state officials as any other state; and Chief Justice Richmond M. Pearson flagrantly used the power of his office to keep men out of the army. These two types of deliberate obstructionism, however, are of minor significance when measured against North Carolina's total contribution of army manpower as described above.

---

(1) The Volunteer Company

By the time of North Carolina's secession the General Assembly had already overhauled its volunteer system. On 8 May it authorized a division of state troops constituting ten regiments with 10,000 enlisted men who were to volunteer for the duration of the war and whose officers were to be appointed by the governor. The law of 10 May authorized the governor to accept as many as 50,000 twelve-month volunteers. The enlisted men elected their company officers who then elected the field officers. The governor then was to organize the regiments into brigades and divisions and to appoint the general officers.

In both organizations each captain was responsible for raising his own company, generally doing so by placing a notice in the local newspaper stating "ONE HUNDRED MEN WANTED For the First Regiment of State Troops . . . to meet an enemy now ready to . . . invade our homes and subjugate a free people."[4] After each company had been

3. For all the classes exempt under the law of 21 April, see James M. Matthews, ed., *Public Laws of the Confederate States of America*, pp. 51–52.

4. Henry T. King, *Sketches of Pitt County, A Brief History of the County, 1704–1910*, p. 124. This announcement is printed in full herein and is almost identical to scores of others printed in most of the newspapers of the state.

accepted it would be assigned to a camp of instruction where supposedly the men would learn the rudiments of army life. To take charge of the entire operation of turning "plow-boys and clerks into soldiers,"[5] *Governor Clark chose General James G. Martin, a graduate of West Point and a one-armed veteran of the Mexican War. To cover the expenses the General Assembly authorized a five-million-dollar bond issue.*

In the first flush of enthusiasm thousands of men rushed to the colors. When it was time for a company to depart, either by foot or train, the entire town turned out, the women waved handkerchiefs and proffered food, the bands played stirring and sentimental songs, and the older men left behind determined to organize themselves into home guard units. The following document describes a company's departure.

One of our venerable survivors of war times . . . is Richard P. Paddison, of Point Caswell. . . . He tells us that . . . "this part of North Carolina was wild with excitement and rumors of war, and a public meeting was called at Harrell's Store, in Sampson County, for the purpose of organizing a military company to be tendered to the Governor. In a short time an organization was effected, and a man named Taylor was elected captain. At the next meeting they voted to call the company the 'Wild Cat Minute Men.' Next the question came up as to where the company should go. After considerable talk it was voted that the company should remain around Wild Cat as a home protection. There were a number of us, however, who did not take to the Wild Cat idea, and quietly withdrew and marched to Clinton, where a company was being organized by Capt. Frank Faison, called the 'Sampson Rangers,' composed of the flower of the young men of the county. I joined as a private in this company. We had a good time drilling and eating the best the country could afford, and every fellow was a hero in the eyes of some pretty maiden. But this easement was suddenly cut short by orders to go with utmost dispatch to Fort Johnston. The whole town was in excitement. We were ordered to get in marching order, and to my dying day I shall remember that scene—mothers, wives, sisters, and sweethearts all cheering and encouraging their loved ones to go forth and do their duty; such love of country could only be shown by true Southern womanhood. After a good dinner and a sweet farewell under the inspiring strains by the band of 'The Girl I Left Behind Me,' we took up our march to Warsaw, where we boarded the train for Wilmington and arrived before night. We were met by the officials and marched up Front Street to Princess and Second; here we halted and the fun began. On the northeast corner stood a large brick house built for a negro jail and . . . this was to be our quarters for the night. Now picture in your mind . . . a hundred and twenty wealthy young men . . . being forced to sleep in a

5. Robert D. W. Connor, *North Carolina: Rebuilding an Ancient Commonwealth*, 2:176.

negro jail. We marched into the house and deposited our luggage, which in after years would have been sufficient for Stonewall Jackson's army. The rumbling noise of discord and discontent rose rapidly. . . . At this juncture, Judge A. A. McKoy, who was a private, said he would stand sponsor for the boys to be on hand next morning. . . . This was accepted, and there was a hot time in the old town that night. Next morning, promptly on time, every man was present. We boarded a river steamer . . . and arrived in good shape at our destination, where we had a good time until the organization of the Twentieth North Carolina Regiment, when our trouble began. Our captain was elected lieutenant colonel, and an order was issued for the election of a captain. The candidates were James D. Holmes and William S. Devane. . . . The Devane men, of whom I was one, said we would not serve under Holmes. I can not remember how long this trouble lasted, but the matter was carried to Governor Ellis, who settled it by ordering each faction to send out recruiting officers and make two companies, which was done."

Sprunt, *Chronicles of the Cape Fear River*, pp. 354–56.

---

(2) Problems of Volunteering

During the process by which North Carolina volunteers became Confederate troops, two rather serious problems arose. The Confederate laws of 6 and 8 May authorized President Davis to receive into service such companies, battalions, and regiments of militia as he deemed necessary. He was then to organize them into brigades and divisions and appoint the general officers for such units. These laws meant in effect that the brigade and divisional organization which the North Carolina law of 10 May established was unacceptable to the Confederacy. And, more important, since President Davis did not have to accept all militia units offered by the states, he chose for the most part to accept the state troops who had volunteered for longer service

under the state law of 8 May.

This conflict caused North Carolina considerable embarrassment. The right to appoint general officers was a precious political plum for a governor, and Governor Ellis would dearly have liked for the brigades and divisions organized under state law to enter the Provisional Army intact. Furthermore, Davis's refusal to accept immediately all volunteers offered meant that the expense of maintaining them until they were called up was borne by the state treasury.

Governor Ellis sent two prominent citizens, William A. Graham and former Chief Justice Thomas Ruffin of Alamance County, to discuss these problems with the Confederate War Department. Secretary of War Leroy Pope

Walker's letter below explains the
Confederate position on these matters.

Richmond, June 23, 1861

Hon. Messrs. Graham and Ruffin,
COMMISSIONERS FROM NORTH CAROLINA:

Gentlemen: I herewith transmit you the acts passed by the Provisional Congress . . . and in relation to the conversation between us had on yesterday deem it proper to say that by reference to the act "to provide for the public defense," and the emendations to that act, you will find the law regulating and controlling the organization and service of the provisional forces of the Confederate States. It will be seen that volunteers . . . are received and mustered into service by "companies, squadrons, battalions, and regiments" only. When thus organized . . . they uniformly are accepted with the company and field officers selected by themselves. It is quite apparent this Department cannot receive under the law a higher military organization than that of a regiment, and it has always claimed and exercised the right to make all staff appointments. . . . Brigades are organized and general officers appointed by the authorities here. The Congress wisely confined both the one and the other to the military experience of the President, and the reservation of staff appointments to the War Department was essentially necessary to the harmonious administration of a . . . field so extensive and ramified as that now existing.

Some of the States, before joining . . . the Confederates, found it necessary to make independent military preparations and to raise troops under their own laws. These troops had been generally passed under Confederate authorities through agreements between their respective States and the Confederate Government. In view of the controlling necessity of the case and to avoid confusion the Confederate Government may, perhaps, in this manner have taken into its service troops not thoroughly organized according to the requirements of Congress, but in no instance has the Confederate Government stipulated to receive from a State a brigade as such, or a general officer, or yielded to a diminution of its power to regulate staff appointments at will. The organization of the Regular Army . . . has been entirely suspended for the present, in view of the public necessities and the immediate demand for large forces in the field, only to be supplied through volunteers. This Department has been enabled the more readily to take this step in consequence of the law passed at the second session of Congress, in order to meet the proclamation issuing from the Government at Washington calling for enrollments for three years and enlistments for the war. . . . Thousands have so tendered, and by the fall the chief bulk of the Army now in the field from the original States composing the Confederacy will stand on the same basis as regulars. . . .

It is understood here that North Carolina has organized ten regiments for the war, to be passed under Confederate authorities, and it gives me pleasure to say that these regiments will be mustered into the service and received into the pay of this Department at the earliest moment after notification from Governor Ellis of their actual organic formation. But concerning the fact mentioned by you, that a number of volunteers in addition to the ten regiments reported for the year are being raised in North Carolina, it is proper for me to state that the President, under the laws of Congress authorizing him to make requisitions upon the States, will call for these troops from time to time as the public exigencies may demand. He now more especially desires to embody in the different States a reserved army corps, to be placed in camps of instruction and thoroughly prepared as regulars to meet the casualties of the battle-field and possible reverse of arms. To this end these forces will be enrolled for the war, will be received by companies, and as thus mustered into service will be paid and subsisted by this Department. The numbers necessary to the entire corps will be determined upon and the quota of North Carolina made known to Governor Ellis in the course of a few days. . . .

L. P. WALKER
Secretary of War

Official Records, Ser. 4, 1:396–98.

---

(3) Reaction to Conscription

North Carolinians reacted to the shock of compulsory military service in varied fashion. Merely the idea itself disgusted many, who argued that Confederate patriotism would always provide the army with enough volunteers. Soldiers often described it as unethical and discriminatory. William W. Holden of the Raleigh Standard *termed it "despotism." Nevertheless the majority of the people seem to have reconciled themselves to the necessity of conscription. Actually the concept was not new. North Carolina had enacted a modified draft law as early as 1778, and the principle had been thoroughly debated during the War of 1812.[6]*

The following are the reactions of a governor who accepted conscription as a necessary evil but who privately questioned its constitutionality[7] (Document A); two editors of opposing parties and principles (Documents B and C); and a resigned enlisted man (Document D).

6. For a thorough analysis of conscription and its ramifications in North Carolina, see Memory F. Mitchell, *Legal Aspects of Conscription and Exemption in North Carolina, 1861–1865.*

7. Governor Clark wrote "The conscript act is very distasteful to our people and doubts of its constitutionality have been raised and it has only been acquiesced in as a necessity of our welfare." Henry T. Clark to Peter Mallett, 24 June 1862, George F. Mordecai Papers. Governor Vance held much the same opinion.

A.

STATE OF NORTH CAROLINA,
EXECUTIVE DEPARTMENT,
Raleigh, April 24, 1862

Hon. GEORGE W. RANDOLPH,
Secretary of War, Richmond, Va.:

SIR: I desire to carry out the conscription act fairly and to the fullest extent of the wants of the country; and presume, as a guide, that you will publish some regulations and instructions in detail to aid in understanding the method in carrying it out. But in the meantime I am so circumstanced as to be compelled to make some immediate inquiries, which I trust you will indulge me with a consideration. The late Secretary of War made a call on the State for her quota (being one-sixth of the white population, 631,000), amounting in round numbers to 38,000. This number is now in field from North Carolina. Twelve regiments of troops originally for the war-service have been fully recruited. The twelve-months' regiments have very generally re-enlisted, taking the furloughs and bounty. Those over thirty-five years who have taken the bounty, I presume, will not be relieved under the ninety-days' clause. Besides the above troops in the Confederate service, within the past two months I have recruited for the war about 10,000 troops, who are mostly now in our camp of instruction (Camp Mangum) near this place, and some companies are still recruiting. These troops were intended to be drilled and disciplined here, and turned out for the defense of the State when required or turned over to the Confederate service if a larger number were required from us. First. I desire now to inquire if the State has her present quota in the field? Until another quota is called will the conscript act be enforced? Second. If more are required, will the recruits now in our Camp Mangum be received in lieu of the conscription; and will the volunteers over thirty-five years be accepted in place of the conscripts? Third. Is the volunteering stopped on the passage of the conscription? Fourth. Will the Confederate bounty be paid to any one who volunteers subsequent to the passage of the act? Fifth. Will the conscription act take in the militia officers as well as privates? Sixth. If North Carolina has not in the field her requisite number or quota, will the new volunteers be received; or will there be a conscription to fill up to the maximum the companies of the present regiments? The twelve regiments now in camp of instruction, and organized by election of field officers, are being regularly drilled, . . . but they are not armed, and I see but little prospect of procuring arms unless you will capture them from the Yankees. Whenever these regiments can be made available they shall be in service. When and upon what grounds are they to be turned over to you? The solution of these inquiries will aid me much— in fact, are necessary for me to fulfill my engagements to the Confederate States. One answer I would like to have by telegraph—whether volunteers can be received since the passage of the conscript act.

Most respectfully, yours,

HENRY T. CLARK

Official Records, Ser. 4, 1:1091–92.

B.

Let the people have the names of those who voted for it. It is an extraordinary fact that this act, which ignores the rights of the States, and assumes summary and absolute control over some six hundred thousand of the militia, was debated and passed in secret session.

This act breaks the faith of both the State and Confederate Governments with the twelve months men, by compelling them to remain two years longer in the war. It also designates the mode of appointing the officers, which is in direct conflict with the Confederate Constitution. It also provides for substitutes. There ought to have been exemptions, even under so sweeping a law as this; but they should have been such only as were rendered necessary by mental or bodily infirmity. The idea, for example, of one of the correspondents of the Macon (Ga.) *Telegraph*, who advocates conscription, that it will "put the rich and the poor—the *noble* and the *peasant*," as he calls them, "on the same footing" is not realized. "The *noble* and the *peasant!*" Are we in Europe or America? The substitute system, though wrong in theory, may work well, and has worked well in our volunteer armies; but when a levy is made *en masse* on a certain portion of our population, it is wrong to put wealth in one scale and the compelled and inevitable service of the poor man in the other. But we shall not dwell longer at present on this measure. We regard it as inexpedient, unnecessary, oppressive, and unconstitutional. It places the rights of the States and the liberties of the people at the feet of the President. . . . We can only hope that this measure will not seriously injure the Southern cause, and that good results, and not calamitous ones, may flow from it. But we enter our protest against it; and if evil comes of it, it shall not be said that we were the advocate of, or the apologist for, so monstrous and dangerous a measure. Again we admonish the people, who are fighting against despotism from without, to look well to the encroachments of power within. The price of liberty is not only treasure and blood, but sleepless vigilance.

Raleigh *Standard*, 23 Apr. 1862.

C. CONSCRIPTION

The events of the last few weeks and those now in progress have stirred and will continue to stir both sections of the former Union to their centres. The fruits of all the enemy's victories in the spring campaign are melting away before the heats of summer. They are calling for three hundred thousand more men. They must have them, and if not otherwise they will obtain them by conscription. This conscription may react upon the powers that be,—it may help, with other things, to make the war unpopular at the North, but it will be done. The three hundred thousand men they want promptly, and they will have them.

The Southern armies must be not only kept up but augmented to meet this fresh burst of the enemy. The thinned ranks of our gallant regiments must be recruited. The invader insists on having more men to subserve the ends of conquest and aggression. The invaded must have them to defend the country against the worst horrors of ruin and subjugation.

Under these circumstances a cheerful compliance with the Conscription law and a full and complete enforcement of its provisions becomes a necessity of our national existence, a necessity equally pressing with the carrying on of the war itself. We may regard it as a most painful necessity. So is war. But it is now no less a necessity because of its being painful.

Wilmington *Journal*, 18 July 1862.

D.

The passage of the "Conscript Act" as it was called, though not unexpected, and understood to be necessary by the more intelligent soldiers, naturally created a profound sensation, throughout the army, especially the "Virginia Army," which was mainly composed of twelve month volunteers, whose terms of enlistment would nearly all expire in April and May.

The term of the eighth Virginia expired April 25th and the men had all the winter looked forward to that day as one on which they should be free to start home and see their people, who were now within the enemy's lines, though not occupied by his troops.

To find all their fond anticipations blasted and years of service before them, with very little prospect of one in a dozen of them ever seeing home again unless as a cripple, or diseased wreck of his former self, stirred, as may be imagined, a strong feeling and not a little indignation.

The following will serve as a sample of camp-fire grumbling in the Eighth Regiment, on the night of the 20th of April, when the news reached Yorktown:

"I think it is pretty d——d hard that we, who have fought, suffered and marched for a whole year; leaving our wives and children to shift for themselves away off yonder inside the Yankee lines, while we are here fighting to defend another part of the State, that we must be held for the Lord knows how many years to come, and be placed on the same footing as those cowardly conscripts who have been at home having a good time all this while, and we not even git to see the old woman for a day or two! D——d if I like it."

"Yes," quoth another, "Of course we mean to keep a fightin' till she wins, and we gain our independence; but we was solemnly promised a discharge when our time was up, and I mind that Colonel Hunton swore he'd lead us home himself soon as our term expired. But that's all forgot *now*, and we is without even a thirty-days' furlough to go home and fix up things a little for the folks there in case we never do get to go back no more hereafter. I'll be derned if I ain't a mind to cut out after night."
. . .

I, fully as much as my comrades, felt the indignity of being changed, after twelve months of faithful service from the venerable position of "Volunteers" cheerfully lending their lives and labors to their country, to the condition of worse than mere hirelings—almost—slaves,—conscripts! And had the war been an ordinary one . . . I would not have submitted even if I had been compelled to fly for life!

But I could well understand that the conscript law was an imperative necessity; and it must be enforced, or the whole country delivered up to the enemy, and not even the most unappeasable growler was ready to consent to the alternative.

Hamilton, *Papers of Randolph Shotwell*, 1:184–86.

---

(4) Exploiting the Exemption System

The Confederate exemption system was designed to excuse from military service enough men to keep the home front operating with at least fair efficiency. One historian of Confederate conscription estimated that 44.9 percent of all men called out for conscription were eventually exempt. While well intended, the system of class exemptions afforded many able-bodied men a chance to avoid the hardships of army life. Vocations affording exemption became popular overnight, and many well-to-do men abandoned profitable careers to become teachers, apothecaries, tanners, justices of the peace, or government clerks. The following letter from a sergeant in the 26th N.C. Regiment demonstrates some of the ruses used.

GEORGE RICHARDS TO Z. B. VANCE

Monroe Union County N.C.
Decr. 19 1862

After my respects to you, I would say that I have had a long & sevear spell of sickness, allmost ever since our retreat from Malvern Hill, My recovery has allmost been a miracle. When I became convalescent & received a sick furlough to visit this place where my brothers & sisters live hoping that good nurseing & kind attention would restore my broken health & shattered constitution, and it is with pleasure I state, that my fondest hopes have been realized, & I hope soon to be able to join my Regt the gallant Old 29th N.C. that still look with fondness on you, their gallant leader.

To day I have witnessed a rich & extraordinary seen, To wit, The enrolment of conscripts from 18 to 40, and just here I wish to inform you of the many subterfuges adopted by some of those who are—subject to the act. First & foremost I believe there is a collution between the Malitia Capt & some of his favorites, with whome the most flimsey excuse is sufficient to pass them over & lay them on the Shelf.

One man by name of John W. Rose a man of some property about 35 or 36 years of age, who attempts to get out by buying an interest in a contemplated tannery, just started build a house for that purpose, or rather, to avoid going into service—No Mechanic himself but purely a Speculator in every sense of the word, ever since the war broke out.

The next is one Marshel Broadway a very stout able young man about 24 or 25 years old who bot out a little mail contract carried on horseback once a week 10 or 12 miles, and he in his turn, hires another conscript one Moses Gordon very stout & able about 35 or 36 years of age to ride for him, so this little 10 mile mail (formerly carried by a little boy) once a week deprives the service of 2 very stout able men.

The next one John Shute a speculator about 36 or 37 who has Managed to get 2 or 3 neighbors to pretend to have him as an Overseer but realy attends to speculating & not to their business, & one of those persons pretending to hire him is only 35 or 36 years of age, but he is a Post Master,—So this favorite slips the noose—

The next one is one John Holm, with a little sore on his leg that no one heard of before, got a certificate from a hired Physician of disability and he slips through also, The next, a pretended "Doctr" Henry Tribble who never obtained diploma or perhaps never heard a Medical lecture a man of Very limited education a near-quack, who has been trying to practice physic in a very obscure neighborhood no more than 3 or 4 years & he too runs through. There are 2 others John Irby & William Woolf what they feign, I have not heard, All the above, with one exception are in the little Town of Monroe Union County N.C.—

The name of the Capt of this Beat is Stanly Austin.

Perhaps there are many others who never came under my observations I saw enough however to disgust a member of the Old 26th N.C.

I hope all the above will be attended too by an impartial officer as well as many others who are trying to evade the Conscript.

Johnston, *Papers of Zebulon Baird Vance*, 1:441–43.

---

(5) The Exemption of State Officials

For some time Vance insisted on his right to exempt from conscription all men necessary to the proper conduct of state affairs. Finally General Gabriel J. Rains, chief of the Bureau of Conscription, explained that "the law exempts judicial and executive officers of State governments, except those liable to militia duty," and no other state employee.[8] Vance responded heatedly that he was "not quite willing to see the State of North Carolina in effect blotted

8. G. B. Rains to Z. B. Vance, 25 Mar. 1863, *Official Records*, Ser. 4, 2:458.

from the map and her government abolished by the conscription of her officers." [9] The same day he repeated his arguments more calmly in the letter to President Davis below. Meanwhile Vance had been receiving innumerable letters asking for exemption. One justice of the peace wrote that all justices should be exempt, for the matter was "one almost of life and death with our people . . . , and in the name of God what is to become of them if I am taken away?" [10]

On 1 May Congress exempted "all State officers whom the Governor of any State may claim to have exempted for the due administration of the government and the laws thereof. . . ." [11] Under this sweeping concession Vance submitted a list of exemptions which even included all justices of the peace, and which the Bureau of Conscription reported on 20 November 1864 had kept 14,675 men out of the army.

STATE OF
NORTH CAROLINA,
EXECUTIVE DEPARTMENT,
Raleigh, N.C. March 31, 1863

HIS EXCELLENCY PRESIDENT DAVIS:

SIR: I have this day addressed a letter to General Rains . . . in regard to the enrolling of certain State officers, but as the case is urgent and may assume important proportions, I have thought it best to address you directly and beg your attention thereon at as early a moment as your heavy duties may permit. The extreme rigor (and I am proud to be able to add good faith) with which the conscript law has been executed in North Carolina has stripped it so bare of its laboring and official population as to render its further operation a matter of anxiety in various respects. In addition to sweeping off a large class whose labor was, I fear, absolutely necessary to the existence of the women and children left behind, the hand of conscription has at length laid hold upon a class of officials without whose aid the order and well-being of society could not be preserved nor the execution of the laws enforced, and whose conscription is as insulting to the dignity as it is certainly violative of the rights and sovereignty of the State. Having heretofore exerted the utmost powers with which I am entrusted, in the execution of this law, . . . at this point I deem it my duty not only to pause, but to protest against its enforcement. In my letter to General Rains I assumed the position that the Confederate authorities should not conscribe any officers or agents of the State whose services were necessary to the due administration of her government, and that the State authorities (not the Confederate) must judge of this necessity. In this class I should certainly place justices of the peace, constables, and the police organizations of

9. Z. B. Vance to G. B. Rains, 31 Mar. 1863, ibid., pp. 465–66.
10. W. A. Houck to Z. B. Vance, 3 Apr. 1863, Governors' Papers.
11. Matthews, *Public Laws of the Confederate States of America*, p. 159.

our towns and cities. There being no attempt made to enroll the officers
of the militia, I shall not urge as to them, though I understand the right
is claimed under the law to conscribe them. The exemption bill of October 11, 1862, provides that the executive and judicial officers of the State
be exempted, except such as may by State law be subject to militia duty.
This would render every able-bodied man in the State liable to conscription, as our laws expressly provide that in case of invasion or insurrection no person shall be exempt whomsoever. If this construction prevails
you will perceive that it is in the power of the War Department to abolish the State government by a very simple process; but, taking it for
granted that such construction is not intended, I beg leave to say that
the present proceedings of the Bureau go very far toward it. I need not
inform you of the character and duties of the magistracy. You can but
be aware of their importance. I will only say in brief that, in addition
to their being conservators of the peace generally, they constitute our
courts of pleas and quarter sessions and have jurisdiction over a far
more extensive, and in many respects more important, range of subjects
than the superior courts; in fact, the superior courts cannot be held without them. They levy more than half the taxes of the State, assess all the
property for taxation, provide for the poor (now a doubly important
function), and in many cases the law requires a certain number to be
present to render their proceedings valid. The constable is the sheriff of
the magistrate's court, and as absolutely necessary to the community as
the sheriff himself, since our sheriff can be compelled to execute no process except those addressed to him by a court of record.

It is no answer to all this to say that we have more justices than are
actually necessary, and that some might be dispensed with. The Legislature of the sovereign State of North Carolina recommended their appointment to the Executive according to the forms of the constitution,
and it is to be presumed they deemed them all necessary, and no one
has the right to say otherwise. The municipal officers present, if possible, a still stronger case. The mayor and police of this city have been
enrolled and ordered into camp, which, of course, abolishes the government of the corporation at once and turns over the inhabitants to a state
of lawlessness and anarchy. With the magistracy, the militia, and the
municipal officers of our incorporated towns, constables, and such like
officers of the State, swept into a camp of instruction, I am at a loss to
know what would be left of the power or sovereignty of this State or any
other. So obvious is the great damage and disparagement which this latitudinous construction of the law could work against the States that I
cannot believe its framers so intended it, and with all due respect I doubt
the wisdom and the policy of the War Department in urging it so far.
Having made no question of its constitutionality and interposed no obstacle to its faithful execution, but on the contrary acquiesced in it as a
great measure of necessity and assisted with zeal in its enforcement, I
am content now to state my opinion simply upon a fair construction of
its terms. . . .

Soliciting again your earliest convenient answer, and begging you to

accept assurances of my highest consideration and esteem,
I am, sir, very truly, your obedient servant,

Z. B. VANCE

Official Records, Ser. 4, 2:464–65.

---

(6) Overseer Exemption

The Exemption Act of 11 October 1862 exempted one white male, either owner or overseer, on every plantation with twenty slaves or more on it. Most North Carolinians abhorred this "20 Nigger" law as the grossest class legislation. Vance threw at President Davis the common denunciation that they were now fighting "a rich man's war, and a poor man's fight;" and the General Assembly asked Congress to end an exemption which "made unjust discrimination between such persons, and their less fortunate fellow-citizens. . . ."[12] Overseer exemption was later modified but, for purposes of farm production and slave control, it was never ended.

The letter below is an extended justification for exempting overseers.

Hayes 17th June 1863

To His Honor
Governor Vance
Sir

It is with great reluctance that I again trispass on your time which I am well aware is fully occupied on more important matters. A letter dated the 7th inst from Mr Henry J Fentrill my manager on my Roanoke farm near Halifax informs me that he is advised that he's liable to be called out as a conscript & unless I swear that I cannot procure a person over 45 yrs of age to supply his place. Which I am willing to do before any competent authority and I am well satisfied that it would be utterly impossible to do so even if I had twelve months time to do so Besides Mr Fentrill is an infirm man & weakly constitution being afflicted with piles some times and frequently with a bleeding at the nose which exhaust him so that he is unable to attend to the plantation business in person. He has 300 negroes under his care and his nearest white neighbor is four or five miles off except one who is three, He manages these negroes well & keeps them in proper subjection but if he is taken away they would be at large on the community & entirely demoralize the corn crop

---

12. *Public Laws of the State of North Carolina Passed by the General Assembly, 1862–'63*, p. 50.

now growing & wheat now harvesting would be totally lost—I well know that negroes cannot be controuled by a new overseer let his talents be what they may as they can by overseer who has disciplined them for years & with whom they are acquainted & have confidence in—Mr Fentrill has had the management of my farm upwards of twelve years and the negroes are perfectly under his controul & obedient to his orders, Some shallow pated persons believe that any man can be an overseer and manage a farm & gang of negroes but from an experience of sixty year & the employ of a great number, I have found but four in all that time on whom I could rely, And in my opinion it requires more sense & talents to direct a large farm a number of negroes than it does to be a short sighted Politician & statesman, The loss of my crop of corn & wheat would be a serious one to me and not a small one to the quar master when he wanted supplies in the present scarcity.

The present year I sold the Confederate qr^t masters 2400 bus of corn & that was not more than one fourth of my usual crop having my crop cut off last year by a destructive freshet. The feeding of an army in my opinion is of as much importance as equipping it with arms for no men can fight without food let them be ever so well armed, Besides the conscription list might be easily filled by supernumerary sinecure do nothing office holders & their worthless assistants who scuttle into some insignificant office to protect them fr enrollment & then pride themselves on their sneaking ingenuity in cheating the government of their services in the army—

Under these circumstances Sir I beg the favor of you to have Mr Henry J. Fentrill of Halifax Co exonerated from the conscription list, if in your power. Your prompt attention to a former request encourages me to make the present one. A line to him by the bearer Mr Norfleet will greatly relieve and oblige me & I think will be of some public service.

With the highest & personal respect & great admiration of yr Administration,

Y^{rs}

JA. C. JOHNSTON

Governors' Papers.

---

(7) Executive Detail of Soldiers

President Davis considered the system of class exemptions too rigid and preferred the more adaptable system of detail, whereby he could transfer a soldier from place to place, job to job, or even return him to the army, all the while retaining full control over him. Before 1864, however, the only latitude that Congress conceded the president was the right to detail men to industry as he wished. The conscription law of 17 February 1864 allowed him to detail overseers, artisans, mechanics, and scientists as he saw fit.

Despite the specifics of the law, most people only knew vaguely that a detail was one way of avoiding military service. And since most plain folk never accepted the fact that once a man had been drafted he was beyond his state's control, the governor's office received most of the petitions for detail, begging for temporary assignment at home to help a family in distress, to "make a crop," or to manufacture scarce items. Governors Clark and Vance could only respond by endorsement "Gov has no power to detail him—Secy of War alone can do that."[13]

Below are two requests for detail, the first in conformity with the law (Document A) and the second born of desperation (Document B).

A.

COMMANDANT'S OFFICE,
NAVAL STATION,
Charlotte, N.C., May 5, 1864.

COMMANDER JOHN M. BROOKE,

Chief Bureau Ordnance and Hydrography, Richmond, Va.:

SIR: In answer to your letter of the 2d instant, directing me to inform you more clearly of the necessity of detailing additional mechanics to be employed in these works, I have to state that a number of our most important tools are idle a large portion of the time for the want of mechanics to work them, and some of these tools, the steam hammer for instance, are the only tools of their class in the Confederacy, and many of the large forgings required in the building and arming of war vessels can only be made with the assistance of these tools.

In addition to this there are now six locomotives on the railroads between Wilmington and Richmond thrown out of use owing to their crank axles having been broken, and new axles can only be forged at this establishment. The Secretary of the Navy has ordered this work to be done here, as the locomotives are greatly needed to transport supplies to the Army and Navy, but it is impossible to make any considerable headway on them, as our present force is inadequate to manufacture projectiles, gun carriages, &c., for arming vessels as fast as they are required. At this time we are working night and on Sundays and still are not able to fill orders for munitions of war as is desired.

I understand from you that the iron-clad Virginia at Richmond is now in readiness for action except her gun carriages and wrought-iron projectiles, which are being made at these works. If we had a full force of mechanics this work would have been finished in one-half the time.

The following is a list of the additional mechanics required to give employment to the tools, forges, and furnaces now in operation:

13. John H. Martin to Z. B. Vance, 9 Mar. 1863, Governors' Papers.

Seven machinists, eight blacksmiths, eight gun-carriage makers, two blockmakers, one pattern maker, one coppersmith, two molders.

Very respectfully, your obedient servant,

H. ASHTON RAMSAY,
Chief Engineer, C.S. Navy,
in Charge

Official Records, Ser. 4, 3:521–22.

B.

ELIZA A. THOMAS TO GOVERNOR VANCE

Oct. the 25 1864

I suppose you turn a deaf ear to all of my entreaties whoso stoppeth his ears to the cries of the poor he shall cry himself and not be heard—I know you possessed the power of retaining my husband—I lived in hope of his getting detailed at raleigh—he wrote me word he went to gen. holmes and he would listen to nothing he had to say he said he was ordered to the 13th regiment—oh my god I have at this time 5 sick children I cannot attend to them my health is so feeble, I can get no one to stay with me, I can only sit over them and cry god be merciful to us I mentioned in my first appeal what I will mention again thinking it probable you never got it that I have six small children and will if god spares me that long be confined on that account in a month from this time my oldest is not eleven my youngest cannot walk with the winter approaching what is to become of us this is no false tale made up to save some one from the army as you may think I would not tell a lie to get my husband back I could get truthful men to qualify to this as there is to his petition—my reason for not doing so is that there is a great deal of falsehood used to keep men out of the army and you might be troubled with more petitions but if you doubt the truth of this matter you know men in this vicinity—I am willing to have the matter tested you may send any man or board of men to test it you please—Mr Thomas tried to get his petition to take an appeal on it but the enrolling officer told him he had orders to hold them he has a small crop in the field probbable enough to support his family if it could be taken care of but the prospect is for it to remain there I have no relations that is able to help me my husband has none that is able to [do] anything for us if the country has come to the pass that such a man cannot be spared to his family I suppose we must take what follows—I have not heard a person express their sentiments but what said they did not know of a man that could not be better spared from his family than Mr Thomas if all the men was called out I would not think so much about getting him back but there are men here whose chance is far better to go than his he has such a helpless family as I said to you before he substituted petitioned and spent pretty well all that he had if I had means to hire there is no one to hire he was our all I have been an invalid for the past ten years I still beg of you to send him back to stay the winter with us if he can be spared no longer I think you have the power to write to gen. Scales that he be detailed or if it is necessary to petition to the secretary of war you know how it ought to be done I expect this the last time you will hear from me if you turn a deaf ear to this I shall despair and if he can be spared and will not, I fear when Judgement shall be laid to the line and righteousness to the plumet there will be a fearfull reckoning somewhere, we live in a few 2 or 3 mile of the piedmont railroad or I should have said of the reidsville depot on that road   my husband name is James F Thomas perhaps you will think me very bold but when one sees nothing but suffering before them it is enough to make them bold there has been provisions made for feeding soldiers families but there has not for clothing and waiting on them when they are not able to wait on themselves which is the case with us such as getting wood and making fires we are scarcely able at the best time we have to cook our own food, with a hope you will intercede in our behalf I subscribe myself

Your humble servt

E L I Z A   A .   T H O M A S

Governors' Papers.

---

(8) Requests for Discharge

Requests for discharge or special exemption from the army differed from requests for detail only in the length of absence desired. The following petitions reflect genuine problems at home rather than any shirking of duty. Once again it should be noted that only the War Department could discharge Confederate soldiers.

[10 July 1863]

To Governor Z. B. Vance.

We the undersigned Citizens of Burke would most respectfully petition you to grant a special exemption under the late militia law to John P. Janes a citizen of said County, for the reason that we feel that his services are indispensible in the neighborhood where he resides—. He is the only mechanic in the neighborhood—he makes looms, bed-steads, trays, chairs, tables, chests, stocks scythes, plows &.C &.C—He is almost constantly engaged in the above work & during the present summer he has only worked upon his farm about three days; We would also represent to your Excellency that he has been engaged in work of the above description for the last ten or twelve years, and that said Janes works now for the same prices which he charged in times of peace; We would also represent that Mr. Janes and one other person in our neighborhood are the only persons who make coffins—. We feel that it will be a great loss & inconvenience to our neighborhood for him to be taken from us; He is about 43 years of age & has a wife & ten children the youngest of which is about 10 months old—his oldest a son not 19 years of age, has been in the army as a volunteer for more than six months—For the reasons set forth we trust that your Excellency will deem it proper to cause Mr. Janes to be exempted from the service—.

[Thirty-five signees]

Governors' Papers.

August the 23rd 1863

To Your Exelency, Z B Vance

Sir, Beliving you to be a true friend to the Soldiers their wives and Mothers, and believing you have the power invested in you to befriend them I being a Widdow and a Mother of a Soldier, I earnestly beg of you a favor which I believe your Excelency will grant—My Husband Died a few months ago and the Conscription Act has taken my only Son and only help from me—I further more declare that my Son in plain words is not a man and he is not able to stand the hardships of war, and knowing that the Confederacy wants Men, and men that are robust and healthy, to stand the hardships which a soldier has to endure, I beg of you that you will permit my Son William R Tise To return home. I am a true friend to the Southern cause and I would freely give up my Son to fight for the South and protect our homes from the raveges of a merciless foe, but knowing my Son is not able to stand, as I have said before said the hardships of war, I beg of you to let him return home and if others are needing to fill his place, that you will take those extortioners who are extortioning on the verry lives of the poor Soldiers wives and widowed Mothers. I will mention one Cavine Hine who is public tanner in Salem—I went to him a day or two ago in a manner barefooted, and tryed to get enough leather to make me a pair of shoes no he said as an excuse he did not have any. I asked then if I could not get enough to half sole a pair shoes—no I could not have that much even, and I know he has got leather, but none for the poor Soldiers wives and widows. This man I think Gov is a very suitable man to take my sons place in the army—He is a hale healthy robust man and pretends to be a friend to the Southern cause but I tell you he shows no friendship to the Soldiers and their families—Just so he can stay at home and extortion on the Poor Soldiers their wives and widowed Mothers. This is the friendship which he has for the Southern cause. I will mention another instance to testify the truth that he is a true Southern man and friend to the Soldiers. A poor crippled soldier who had been fighting for this same Cavine Hine, and who had one arm and one leg shot off went to this man to get leather enough to make straps for a wooden stump for his mutilated limb, and Hines charged the poor crippled Soldier $2.75 Saying he would drop five cents becase he was a Soldier. My Son is in the 10 eng N C Regiment What I have told you in regard to my Son is true, though if You deem it necessary that evidence should be given Your Exelency will write to me and I will send Evidence to testify the fact

Please write to me as soon as possible whether there is any chance of my Son's getting to come home and if you will let him off Yo will Please write to Col Pool or Capt Cogdell as the case may require

So nomore from your obedient
Servent
TEMPERANCE TISE

Governors' Papers.

---

(9) Absence Without Leave

Inevitably some enlisted men could not conform to army regulations, and when unable to secure a discharge or a detail they either overstayed a furlough or went home without leave. Technically they were deserters, but many promised to return if guaranteed that they would not be imprisoned or executed. Governors Clark and Vance could make no such hard promises, but their endorsements on many letters in the Governors'

Papers recommend toleration for these simple men. Other Confederate records indicate that such returnees were generally only docked the proportionate part of their pay—$11 a month! Below are letters from two men who found themselves in this predicament. It might be added that Peedin was accepted back and died in service and Harris received his detail.

Pine Level, Johnston Co. NC
January the 22nd 1864

Mr. Z. B. Vance,   Sir.

I wil now Send to you by my Father for you to accomdate me so far as to send me papers that wil Return me to my Regt. without any punishment I wil now State to you my name an Regiment and company

H. F. Peedin Co. C. 50,th Regt N,, C. Troops when my Regt left the Eastern part of N,, C an went to Georgia I was left sick at Wilson Hospital an Remaind thare one month and was to Report to my Regiment, when at the same time Being Barefooted and Badly clothed goin within sixteen miles of home I Come home after Some Shoose and clothes I have bin absent without leaf 20 dais I have bin Rite at home an is now a having chills Evry other day Pleas send me those papers to Return to my Regt.

Yours Respectfuly
H. F. PEEDIN
Co. C. 50,th Regt N.C. Troops

Governors' Papers.

July the 13th 1863

Dear Govenor

With hartily sorrow I am bound to Communicate to you that I was taken from home a Conscript and after serving in Co I 26th N,, C,, about Six months my better informed Judgment was over Ruled by my Sympathy for my family an there well fare for i have a larg family of little children the eldest ones being girls my wife but very weakly her self and dependent on my dayly labors for their subsistance knowing to that provision were all most out of the Reach of the poor I therefore left my Company with out furlow and made my way home to se after the well fare of my kneedy family for which i pray and beg you in mercy pardon me an help me with your name back to my Company if you pleas If you pleas send a paper of transportation so that i may get back to my Company and Escape punishment for i was honetstly in search of all that was near and dear unto me one Wife and 8 little children and their wellfare Your Excellency can imagin my feelings &C immediately on my arrival home i sent for the—Commishioned officer of my former Malitia and did Report immediately to the—pleas give me your aid in assisting me to my Comp and save me from any Savere punishment and in duty my Family will ever Remember you

Yours most Sincerely

pleas write and inform me for the best my adress is Lovelady Po Caldwell Co N,,C,,

GOODWYN HARRIS

Governors' Papers.

---

(10) Requests for a Temporary Suspension of Conscription

Early in his administration Governor Vance began receiving requests from outlying districts for a suspension of conscription there. The arguments were that it had "well-nigh stripped us of our laboring population,"[14] that the few remaining able-bodied men were needed for protection from Union soldiers and bushwhackers, or that conscription was literally unenforceable. Vance would then add as an endorsement "I know all the facts set forth to be true,"[15] and forward the petition to the War Department. But such requests received short shrift from Richmond, Secretary of War Seddon on one occasion replying that he objected to "yielding to the disaffection classes. . . ."[16] Included below is one of these petitions.

14. C. D. Smith et al. to Jefferson Davis, 11 Dec. 1862, *Official Records*, Ser. 4, 2:247–48.

15. Z. B. Vance to Jefferson Davis, 19 Dec. 1862, ibid., p. 246.

16. J. A. Seddon to Z. B. Vance, 23 Apr. 1864, Governors' Papers.

JUSTICES OF THE PEACE OF PERQUIMANS COUNTY
TO GOVERNOR VANCE

To His Excellency Gov. Z. B. Vance

We, the undersigned, Justices of the Peace of Perquimans County, at Nov. Term A . D . 1863 of said County Court, respectfully show unto your Excellency, that in view of the many dangers which surround the people of this County, (and we believe the people in all the Counties East of Chowan River) a suspension of the Conscript Law in this Region is demanded as a measure of just leniency and on grounds of high expediency.

In the beginning of the war a large portion of the able bodied men in this section volunteered in the service . . . leaving at home few but those upon whom families of women and children were dependent for support.

Before the fall of Roanoke, this country was full of provisions of all kinds; the knowledge of the plenty left behind and the large amount of labor at the command of those at home, stimulated volunteers to leave their families for the war. . . .

After the Capture of Roanoke Island, the production of provisions in the counties East of Chowan River was stopped almost entirely, except what little could be raised by the white population; for the slaves, especially the laborers amongst them, left suddenly and almost in a body. The surplus of provisions on hand has been delivered to the Government, our most valuable and fertile lands are lying waste and idle and the labor remaining now to us, scarcely can supply an amount of food necessary to sustain our people even could they make sure of what is raised. The families of many in the army are now suffering and must continue to suffer, without the hope of any but a scant alleviation. Our County Courts have made large appropriations for the relief of these families, but the immense loss of property and the total cessation of all profitable business have stopped this source of charity. Stripped of all their paying property, our citizens cannot pay the large taxation demanded for State and county purposes and in addition thereto raise sums sufficient to support the needy wives and children of the many soldiers our section has furnished to the army. Our slave property is gone and every man is dependent upon his own labor for his support. Where there is no male labor the condition of the women and children is that of pensioners upon others and we have no resources with which to meet their demands. Hard work, scanty living and the little relief that private donations can afford, where none have any thing to spare, are the only helps that our needy poor can look to to avoid starvation.

Every laborer taken from us leaves his own family destitute and destroys another chance of food to those whose husbands and sons are now in the field.

In addition to the privation we now feel from the scarcity of food, we stand in hourly fear from the invasions of the enemy. . . . Instead of complaining of neglect from the State and Confederate Authorities, we see that they cannot yield us protection yet; and whilst we live, hoping to see our soil rescued from the invader, until that time does come, we know that we shall experience his exactions and cruelties. Nor are our fears of those exactions imaginary. He has already taken all the laboring slaves, he has robbed us of the best portion of our stock, private homes time and again have been entered, robbed of their contents and deprived of every particle of food. Bands of armed negroes domineer in the homes of their masters and spread terror over the land. We need more labor than we now have to repair the ravages of the enemy.

Scenes of distress such as these greet us often and human endurance fails at the thought of exposing tender women and children, reared in peace and ease, unprotected and helpless, to an experience such as this.

Owing to the absence of our young unmarried men in the service those now at home subject to conscription are men upon whom women and children are entirely dependent for food, clothing, fuel and protection from insult. . . .

Could our men leave their homes secure from the incursions of the enemy, could they feel that their families were surrounded by neighbors who have labor to spare to haul their fuel in the snows of winter and to raise a surplus of food upon which charity could found a claim: could they feel that their wives and daughters would be safe from the insolence and insults of armed and brutal negroes, they would have no excuse for wearying the ear of your Excellency with cries for relief. We expect no exemption from the evils incident to War. We have borne the common sufferings of war without a murmur and we have felt its bitterest fate in being subject to the will of the enemy. Our condition is more intolerable than that of most of our Countrymen and we think we can ask for relief without injustice to others.

To take away from their homes the men now left and force them into service, will be to add additional and grievous sufferings, without corresponding advantage, to a people already tried far beyond the common fate, and will cause *extreme* suffering to a large class of our people who are entitled to receive our sympathy. For these reasons, we respectfully ask your Excellency to suspend the execution of the Law within this County until such time as we may be relieved from some of the trials by which we are now surrounded. . . .

Governors' Papers.

(11) Substitutes and Principals

The first conscription law allowed men, upon their own arrangement, to submit as substitutes any able-bodied man not subject to the law. A market for substitutes immediately opened, and news- *papers carried such advertisements as Frank I. Wilson's in the Raleigh* Standard: "PERSONS WISHING TO ENGAGE THEMSELVES AS SUBSTITUTES, *and those desiring to* employ substitutes, will do well to call on or address me by letter. Native North-Carolinians . . . preferred for substitutes."[17] Soon large numbers were serving in the army and the cost of hiring one of them rose from $100 to as much as $5,000.

When the draft age was extended to forty-five in September 1862, many substitutes were now included within the new conscription age limits. The War Department ruled that principals—who had expected permanent exemp-tion by offering substitutes—were now liable for service once their substitutes had been enrolled. Amos T. Johnson's letter below shows him to be in this unexpected predicament (Document A). The need for more soldiers and the public hostility to this class legislation finally compelled Congress on 5 January 1864 to end all substitution, draft the principals, and retain the substitute, provoking such outrage as expressed in Document B.

A.

May the 30 1863

Mr Govner Vance   I hierd a substitute March the 22 1862 and had him sowin in for the war and he is in survice yet in the 53 Regt in company C under Captain Joseph Ritchenson and is sound and Dos his part of survice in the war But he is under 40 and tha have arrested mee on it and Brought Mee to camp holms and in tends to keep mee in survice and tha ar going to send Mee to the 49 Regt of NC. T. and some men tells me wher A Man Put in A substitute Bee fore the Conscript Law Past he is exempt tha told mee when I Put him in survice I was Clear for the war and now tha tha Brought Mee A way from my farm and ef tha keep Mee my farm is lost and My wife is not able to work at this time and she wont Bee soon and I think I have don My Part to wards this war for it cost mee all the Money I had in hand and I cant Drill not without suffering from it verry much for I have hurna on the left side verry bad and I think my farm would doo more god than I can doo in the war and I want you to write to me wheather my substitute Clears mee or not or wheather you think I ought to Bee clear or not Sow I Remain yours and Co writ soon as you get this Direct your letter to Camp Holms

AMOS T. JOHNSON

Governors' Papers.

B.

Eagle Mills, Iredell County
At home January 23[d] 1864

To his Exelency Govenor Z. B. Vance
Dear Govenor . . . In March in 1862 two Young men who had been

17. Raleigh *Standard*, 10 Sept. 1862.

living with me in my imploy for several Years volenteered and went to the army and in august of the same Year my son then a weakly boy of eighteen Years old went also to the army and they all three served faithfully untill my son's health utterly failed so that he was not able to do duty and on the 29th of October 1862 I took an able bodied man 47 Years old to the regment in Verginia where my son was serving presented him to the officers of Company and regment who had him examined by the Sergeon and willingly accepted of him as a Substitute for my son and firnished my son with a discharge from Millitary duty during the war. I paid the Substitute $1800 and a suit of good clothes and took my son home paying all expense which all put together with the Substitute money made about $2100 money that I made not by speculation but by honest industry. the Substitute served on with the two young men that went from my house & in the Battle of Fredricksburg 13th Dec. 1862 one of the young men was killed the other & the Substitute served on and in the Battle of Chancelorville 3d May 1863 the Young man & Substitute were both killed. In addition to the above since the war began I have given more than $500 worth of corn & flour to the support of the families of the Soldiers. All of which I done in good faith thinking that I was Supporting a just Cause and an honest Government strugling for indipendence. But now I am gravly told by the legeslation of Congress that there was no contract upon the part of the Government and the putting in of a Substitute was all a mere farce! and my Son is Called upon to give up his Substitute paper and go back into the Service and Sacrifice his poor feeble life for what! Ah my God for what. I forbear. Now dear Govenor I address these lines to You to ask in the *name* of *common honesty* in the *name* of *common justice* is honest North Carolinians to Submit to these things. is there no redress is there no escape from such odious legislation I have thus laid my case before You in simplicity and honesty! & I would further add that my son never received one cent from the Government for all the time he Served; and also that he is at home helping to Cultivate the farm when he is able to do any thing. all of the above is very respectfully and humbly submitted to Your notice hopeing that You will favour me with a Speedy answer.

Very respectfully
Your most Obedient
THOMAS A. NICHOLSON

Governors' Papers.

---

(12) Substitution Before the Courts

The War Department's ruling that principals were no longer exempt when their substitutes became liable to conscription precipitated *a major state rights confrontation between North Carolina and the Confederacy. When John N. Irvin's substitute became liable, the*

Confederate enrolling officer arrested Irvin with the intent of
placing him in the army. Irvin obtained a writ of habeas corpus,
which forced the arresting officer
to take him before Chief Justice
Richmond M. Pearson of Surry
County. In the Irvin case (Document A), Pearson, sitting in chambers at Richmond Hill, ruled on
9 July 1863 that the second Conscription Act did not specify that
principals were liable to service
and ordered Irvin's release.

When Secretary of War Seddon
ignored Pearson's ruling, Vance
warned him that as governor he
was forced to execute the law as
expounded by the state's courts,
and that "an attempt on the part
of the Confederate officers to seize
citizens in defiance of their decisions . . . might lead to unpleasant and unprofitable consequences."[18] In June 1863, in the
key case of In the Matter of J. C.
Bryan the Supreme Court ruled
"that it has jurisdiction and is
bound to exercise it, and to discharge the citizen whenever it
appears that he is unlawfully restrained of his liberty by an officer
of the Confederate States."[19]

This should have settled the
dispute, for the Confederacy had
no supreme court and generally
respected state court rulings, but
the War Department stubbornly
kept arresting principals, and just
as speedily Justice Pearson continued to release them. Finally in
December 1863, Congress abolished substitution and drafted all
principals; in February 1864, it
attempted to foil state courts by
suspending the right of habeas
corpus for those attempting to
avoid military service. Needless
to say, Pearson ruled that drafting
principals violated the obligation
of contract and was therefore unconstitutional. Justices William H.
Battle and Matthias Manly, however, were known to disagree with
Pearson, and it was expected that
at the approaching June session
they would overrule the decision
of a single justice sitting in chambers.

But the War Department would
not wait and now ignored Pearson's writs, hustling principals
into camp at will. In a remarkably
restrained letter (Document B)
Vance explained the situation to
Seddon, who then promised to
make no more arrests of men
temporarily discharged by Pearson. In June the Supreme Court
overruled Pearson in the case of
Walton v. Gatlin and the long constitutional struggle was over. Pearson, however, had managed to
keep hundreds of men from service for months at a time.

A. IN RE IRVIN

The facts are: John N. Irvin, being liable as a conscript under the act
of April, 1862, offered in July, 1862, one Gephart as his substitute. Gep-

18. 22 May 1863, Governors' Letter Books.
19. *North Carolina Supreme Court Reports*, 60 N.C. 1(1863), p. 3. For a
thorough discussion of this case, see Mitchell, *Legal Aspects of Conscription
and Exemption*, pp. 40–43.

hart was 36 years of age, and in all aspects a fit and sufficient substitute for the war, and was accepted by Major Mallett, commander of conscripts, who thereupon gave Irvin an absolute discharge. . . .

It is admitted that, under the regulations of the War Department, Major Mallett had full authority to accept substitutes and give discharges; but it is insisted that Irvin's discharge was afterwards, by the action of Congress, rendered of no effect; for the act of September, 1862, makes all persons between the ages of 35 and 45 liable as conscripts; so Gephart became liable as a conscript, by reason whereof he was no longer a sufficient substitute; and thus Irvin's discharge had no further effect. If one who is at the time liable as a conscript should be offered and accepted as a substitute, it may be conceded the discharge obtained in that way would be void, because no consideration is received by the Government, and the officer exceeds his authority. So, if after the conscription act of April one who is under 18 years of age is offered and accepted as a substitute, it may be conceded that the discharge would only be of effect until the substitute arrives at the age of 18; for as it was known to the parties that the substitute himself would become liable at that date under a law then in force, . . . the officer had no authority to grant a discharge for a longer time.

But in our case there was at the time no law in force under which it was known to the parties that the substitute would afterwards be himself liable as a conscript; on the contrary, he was in all respects fit and sufficient substitute for the war, and was accepted as such, and an absolute discharge given, so there was full consideration received by the Government and full authority on the part of the officer. The question is, Does the subsequent action of Congress, to wit, the act of September, 1862, by its proper construction and legal effect, repudiate and make void the contract and discharge?

The construction of acts of Congress, so far as the rights of citizens, as distinguished from the military regulations, are concerned, is matter for the courts.

Whether Congress has power to pass an act expressly making liable to conscription persons who have heretofore furnished substitutes and received an absolute discharge, is a question not now presented, and one which, I trust, public necessity never will cause to be presented, as it would violate natural justice and shock the moral sense.

In my opinion, the act of September, 1862, . . . does not embrace men who were before bound, as substitutes, to serve during the war. It is true, the act in general words gives the President power to call into military service all white men, residents, etc., between the ages of 35 and 45; but this manifestly does not include men who are already in military service for the war, for this plain reason: there was no occasion to include them—they were bound before; and the true meaning and intent of the act is to increase the army by calling into service men who were not before liable. . . .

A decent respect for our lawmakers forbids the courts from adopting a construction which leads to the conclusion that it was the intention, by the use of general words, to include within the operation of the act substitutes who were already bound for the war not for the purpose of affecting them, but for the indirect purpose of reaching parties who had furnished substitutes, and in that way asserting a power which is at least doubtful, and certainly involves repudiation and a want of good faith.

As the conscription act does not include substitutes, the conclusion that Gephart is no longer sufficient as a substitute, and that Irvin's discharge is of no further effect, fails.

It is considered by me that John N. Irvin be forthwith discharged, with liberty to go wheresoever he will.

North Carolina Supreme Court Reports, 60 N.C. 60 (1863).

B.

STATE OF NORTH
CAROLINA, EXECUTIVE
DEPARTMENT,
Raleigh, February 29, 1864

HON. JAMES A. SEDDON,
Secretary of War:

DEAR SIR: I desire to call your attention most earnestly to the difficulties and complications arising from the conscription of principals of substitutes in this State.

Chief Justice Pearson has decided recently that the law is unconstitutional, and further that the act of Congress suspending the privilege of the writ of habeas corpus does not apply to these men. He therefore continues to grant the writ, and the execution being resisted by the enrolling officers by orders from the Conscript Bureau, the result will be a direct and unavoidable collision of State and Confederate authorities. I have taken the ground that the decision of a single judge at chambers does not possess the binding force and effect of an adjudicated case, but it only operates to discharge the individual. It certainly does this much, and until it is overruled it is final and absolute, made so expressly by the statutes of this State. It cannot be overruled except by the supreme court, which does not meet until June next. In the meantime, if the man is discharged I am bound to protect him, and if the process of the court is resisted I am forced by my oath of office to summon the military power of the State to enforce it. There is no escape from this conclusion. . . .

Knowing, as I trust you do, my great anxiety to avoid collision with the Confederate authorities and everything else that might tend to hinder its efficiency, yet it cannot be supposed that I am to omit a plain and obvious duty prescribed by my official oath. I therefore earnestly request that you will order a suspension of the enrollment of the principals of substitutes in North Carolina at least until time sufficient be allowed to exhaust all efforts at an amicable arrangement. I do not know a better one than that made at Salisbury, and which, though it would deprive the Government of the services of these men until June, would yet give still greater advantages by preserving that peace and harmony between the respective governments without which all our labors will be in vain.

You will observe that I make no comment whatever upon the correctness of the chief justice's opinions. As an executive officer I consider that I have no right to do so; neither, with all due respect, do I consider you to have any such discretion; and however unfortunate it may be to the efficient and equal working of the Government that the laws of Congress are at the mercy, so to speak, of the various judges of the various States, I submit that it is not possible to avoid it, in the absence of the Supreme Court of the Confederacy to give harmony and uniformity of construction. We can only obey the judges we now have, and even this is infinitely preferable to the assumption of judicial power by executive officers, and making their will the law.

Hoping an early response, I am, sir, very respectfully, yours,

Z. B. VANCE

Official Records, Ser. 4, 3:176–77.

General B. F. Butler's Union troops landing at Cape Hatteras, August
1861 (drawing by Civil War artist A. R. Ward)

The Confederate ironclad *Albemarle*, torpedoed at her moorings in
Plymouth on the evening of 27 October 1864, was later raised by Union
authorities, stripped, and towed to the Norfolk Navy Yard, where this
photograph was taken (official United States Navy photograph)

Builder's model of the blockade-runner *Banshee* (Merseyside County Museums, Liverpool, England)

Front Street, Wilmington, 1865 (North Carolina State Archives)

Interior of Fort Fisher, January 1865, showing three traverses on land
front (Alexander Gardner photograph, 1865)

Confederate prison at Salisbury, 1864 (North Carolina Collection, The University of North Carolina at Chapel Hill)

The Fayetteville arsenal (North Carolina State Archives)

Cotton cards, used for straightening fiber preparatory to spinning (Old
Salem, Inc., Winston-Salem)

The Cedar Creek trestle (North Carolina State Archives)

Much of the hard labor on railroads was performed by slaves or free Negroes, impressed by both the state and the Confederate governments (North Carolina State Archives)

Imaginative drawing of a runaway slave in a swamp and a Negro from a neighboring plantation carrying food to him (North Carolina State Archives)

Portrait of Governor Zebulon B. Vance at the time of his inauguration,
1862 (North Carolina State Archives)

One of Sherman's "Bummers" (G. W. Nichols, *Story of the Great March*)

The Harper residence, Bentonville, used as a Confederate hospital during and after the Battle of Bentonville (North Carolina State Archives)

The earliest known photograph of the Bennett house, scene of the
Johnston-Sherman surrender negotiations in April 1865 (North Carolina
State Archives)

Restoration of the Bennett place; the frame structure on the left was the scene of the Johnston-Sherman surrender negotiations and the log building on the right was a kitchen (North Carolina State Archives)

PROBLEMS OF PROCUREMENT

After the war, Zeb Vance observed "a nation in prison we were, in the midst of civilized society, and forced to rely exclusively upon ourselves for everything."[1] This isolation, caused by the increasingly effective blockade, found the South woefully unfit to equip its armies by its own resources. Like her sister slave states, North Carolina had few manufactories or skilled laborers, less than one percent of her population being employed in manufacturing, and the tools and accoutrements of war would always be scarce. "Not an ounce of lead was mined in the state, and hardly enough iron was smeltered to shoe the horses. Revolvers and sabres were above all price, for they could not be bought."[2]

Secessionist leaders knew that their success might lead to war and began early preparations for it. In January 1861, the legislature appropriated $300,000 for arms and equipment and established a military commission to help Governor Ellis administer it. Ellis then dispatched agents northward with long lists of military needs, and, not surprisingly, the northern manufacturers were more than willing to sell the state whatever she could afford to buy. The attack on Fort Sumter made secession inevitable and soon war took precedence over everything. By the end of May $5,300,000 which had been appropriated by the legislature for military preparedness had been spent, and $6,500,000 more was needed. The cost of such goods mounted steadily and soon some supplies were unavailable at almost any price.

Chief among the state's needs was a continuing supply of weapons and ammunition. All ordnance that could be saved from the Norfolk Navy Yard was moved to Charlotte. There land was bought; machineshops and workshops were erected for continuing the manufacture of projectiles, gun carriages, and other necessary naval purposes. At one time the operation employed over three hundred workers. There were also several federal arsenals in the South which had served as repositories for small arms manufactured in the North, and from these the Confederacy

1. Dowd, *Life of Zebulon B. Vance*, pp. 453–54.
2. Ibid., 454.

obtained 163,800 pieces, most of them old smoothbore muskets that had been altered from flint and steel to percussion locks. In North Carolina the state troops on 22 April seized 37,000 of these from the arsenal at Fayetteville, but were allowed to retain only about half of them, the rest being assigned to other Confederate states. In May the legislature appropriated $200,000 for gun purchases, and agents were appointed to scour the state for whatever they could find, even hunting and sporting rifles. This collection went slowly, however, for, as the governor informed the War Department, people were "hugging" their shotguns and rifles "to their own bosoms for their defense."[3] So great was the shortage of small arms in 1861 that one regiment was accepted by the War Department armed only with hunting rifles, many of them flintlocks used in the Revolution.

The Confederacy was worse off in ammunition and accoutrements. At the opening of hostilities, besides the stores seized from the Navy Yard at Norfolk, there were in the Confederacy only 60,000 pounds of powder, no stockpile of lead, one-quarter million percussion caps, and 716 heavy guns. There were no cavalry arms, bridles, harnesses, or blankets; copper and iron were scarce, and the entire South depended on imports and the Wytheville mines for lead. Shortages were everywhere. Wooded North Carolina even had a wood shortage.

The American talent for improvisation was never more evident than in the rapidity with which Governor Clark and his staff contracted with individuals for what they could not seize or manufacture. One of the ablest organizers in the state at this time was Adjutant General James G. Martin, the guiding genius behind these preparedness activities. With indefatigable energy he negotiated contracts with local craftsmen for whatever seemed needed: gunpowder, saddles, clothing, blankets, guns, sabres, boots, and other items. As Professor Connor summarized it:

> The state also [contracted] for the manufacture of cartridges, swords, sabres, bayonets, and powder. Rifles were made at Jamestown, in Guilford County, and at Asheville; sabres at Raleigh, Kenansville, and Wilmington; bayonets at Raleigh and Kenansville; rifle stocks at High Point; shells at Raleigh, Wilmington, Fayetteville, and Charlotte; powder and percussion caps at Raleigh; cartridge paper at Raleigh, Fayetteville, and Lincolnton; knapsacks and canteens were made at many points because their manufacture did not require special machinery. Pistols were being made at New Bern when that city was captured in 1862.[4]

By the end of 1863, the secretary of war reported happily to President Davis that the Confederacy was now able to arm itself.

At the outbreak of war North Carolina, with its thirty-nine cotton and nine woolen mills, was better off in clothing production than any other Confederate state. Consequently in September 1861, the legislature in-

---

3. Henry T. Clark to J. P. Benjamin, 25 Oct. 1861, *Official Records*, Ser. 1, 4:690.
4. Connor, *North Carolina*, 2:194.

structed Governor Clark to collect from the Confederate government the yearly allowance due to each North Carolina soldier for clothing and to pay this into the public treasury so that it could be spent to provide suitable clothing for North Carolina volunteers. The Confederate quartermaster general was so delighted at the arrangement that he promised to keep his purchasing agents out of the state. Adjutant General Martin and Governor Clark had assumed that the state could buy, contract for, or manufacture sufficient clothing, but the approach of winter found the supply still insufficient and Martin was forced to appeal to the people for help. They responded generously, giving blankets, quilts, socks, pants, "pantaloons," pans and plates, and even making "carpet blankets" out of old rugs when cloth gave out.

During the summer of 1862 Martin increased the number of contracts with cloth and shoe mills, and state agents roamed far and wide buying wool and hides for these mills. But still more was needed, and Martin proposed that the state send a purchasing agent to Europe who should also buy an interest in several vessels to get his purchases back to North Carolina. Though advised against it, Vance finally decided in favor of the experiment and appointed John White to the position of purchasing agent. Though the state had to spend two dollars for each one dollar of goods obtained abroad, by the summer of 1863 so much had been imported that in September Vance ordered White to cease purchasing.

Though the makeshift nature of all these arrangements prevented the Civil War from propelling North Carolinians into industrialization, at least they were productive enough on the short-term basis to make the average North Carolina soldier moderately well armed and equipped. In November 1864, Major General Bushrod R. Johnson wrote Vance from Petersburg, Virginia, that because of the state's activities his soldiers would be "not only comfortably, but genteelly clad, this winter."[5]

---

(1) Early Purchasing Operations

Governor Ellis, strong secessionist that he was, began preparing North Carolina for war as soon as it became evident that the state might leave the Union. Other than textiles, the state contained few manufactories of military equipment and until home production could be developed, war material had to be purchased from the North. As soon as the legislature made the money available, Ellis began his purchasing operations. Included below are Ellis's instructions to one of these purchasing agents, a man who had graduated from West Point and who had served as a 2nd lieutenant of ordnance in the United States Army. Apparently these agents

5. 19 Nov. 1864, Governors' Papers.

could operate freely, for one of them wrote "I do not think there is any danger of the police at- *tempting to take any thing sent to N.C. as things is now. . . ."* [6]

JOHN W. ELLIS TO CHARLES C. LEE

Executive Department
Raleigh, Jan 19, 1861

You will proceed North, stopping at Richmond Va., Baltimore, Wilmington Del. Philadelphia, New York, New Haven, Springfield Hartford, and such other places as you may think desirable for the purposes herein stated.

Receive written proposals for such arms and munitions of war as you find listed in the annexed schedule signed by Maj. D. H. Hill and Col. C. C. Tew, to be delivered at Norfolk Va.

Forward these proposals to me from each place as soon as you receive them, and place the parties making them in correspondence with me. You will also receive proposals for 8 & 10 inch Columbiads.

In all cases have the time stated at which the articles can be furnished with certainty.

Have regard always to the responsibility of the parties proposing to make contracts.

Procure all the information on the subject of arms and munitions of war which you may be able to do.

Endeavour to get each establishment to make proposals for as many articles as you can so as to reduce the number of persons with whom we may have to deal. [The schedule referred to includes a list of almost $400,000 of varied arms and ammunition.]

Tolbert, *Papers of John Willis Ellis*, 2:562–63.

---

(2) The Fayetteville Arsenal

Colonel Josiah Gorgas, a Pennsylvanian who became chief of the Confederate Ordnance Bureau, wrote in April 1861, that "no arsenal, except that at Fayette- *ville, N.C., had a single machine above a foot-lathe."* [7] *This deficiency was partly remedied when the machinery at Harper's Ferry fell into Confederate hands. Ma-*

6. Thomas McKnight to John W. Ellis, 6 Feb. 1861, Tolbert, *Papers of John Willis Ellis*, 2:586.

7. Josiah Gorgas, "Notes on the Ordnance Department of the Confederate Government," p. 69.

chinery for making Mississippi rifles (.54 caliber) was sent to Fayetteville and by the fall of 1861 the arsenal was in full production. Before the machinery arrived, the arsenal, under the supervision of William Bell and with a force of eighty-five or ninety hands, was engaged in changing flint and steel muskets to percussion, in rifling smoothbore muskets, and in making ammunition. When running at full capacity with the new machinery, which was seldom, the arsenal could produce 10,000 rifles a year. Operations continued until Sherman's men burned it in 1865.

Below is a description of the arsenal soon after the new machinery had been installed.

THE C. S. ARSENAL AND ARMORY

A few evenings ago, we enjoyed a stroll through the grounds and some of the buildings of the Arsenal and Armory on Haymount. It was always pleasant to walk there; for the grounds are tastefully laid off, the numerous buildings are admirably designed, located and built, and the position itself commands a fine view of some miles. But the attractions of a visit are wonderfully enhanced now by the activity which has suddenly displayed itself throughout the establishment. There is a never ending train of wagons with brick and other material; and sawing machines, planing, morticing, dovetailing, turning, and machines of that ilk ad infinitum, buzz and whir and spit off their white flakes, while everywhere forges glow and trip-hammers let fall their ponderous masses.

The machinery in the original work shops is driven by a 80-horse engine, and is employed, besides other things, in the manufacture of tubes and hammers for the old flint and steel muskets, pistols and rifles. A very fair weapon is thus made of the old muskets, while a most efficient arm for cavalry is made of Hall's breech-loading rifle . . . by cutting off nine inches of the barrel and substituting percussion locks for the others. 300 of the ordinary horse pistols, found throughout the country, have been collected together and are now undergoing the repairs and alterations necessary to their efficiency. 1000 old muskets have been recently sent off much better than new, and large numbers were piled up ready for alteration.

The greater part of the rifle machinery brought from Harper's Ferry is placed in a large two-story building, 150 feet in length. . . . Just beside this, there has gone up . . . an engine house. . . . In this latter house are placed two steam engines of 75-horse power each, now nearly ready in Richmond, the motive power for all the machinery for the manufacture of rifles. At right angles with the main building spoken of above, the foundations of another 130 or 140 ft. in length have risen some 4 feet above the ground . . . When completed, this will contain forges and trip-hammers, and, at the South end, some half dozen enormous grind stones are to be revolved with terrible rapidity, upon which the rifle barrels will be polished. Two wings, 50 feet each, are to be added to this building. . . . The plan has just been submitted and the ground staked off for a building at the rear of the main Arsenal building, to contain eight offices for the heads of departments. . . .

As soon as the engines arrive—less than three weeks hence, we are informed—the manufacture of rifles on a large scale will be commenced.

At present there are 220 persons, machinists, laborers, &c., employed within the grounds.

Fayetteville *Observer*, 21 Oct. 1861.

---

(3) The Manufacture of Gunpowder

Charcoal, sulphur, and saltpeter (or niter) were needed to make gunpowder. All were easily obtained except niter, and private production was so well stimulated by liberal contracts and by state aid that soon enough was being produced. In 1864 North Carolina produced 237,000 pounds, most coming from nitrified soil under home outbuildings but large amounts also being taken from mountain caves. The Confederate Ordnance Department bought all that was produced and sold it to gunpowder manufacturers at cost. In September 1861, Governor Ellis reached an agreement with George B. Waterhouse and Michael Bowes of Charlotte whereby they would build a powder mill in Raleigh and the state would buy and install up to $10,000 of machinery. Waterhouse and Bowes agreed to make 700 pounds a day and received a profit of 15¢ a pound for it. The undertaking was a success and provided the Confederacy with over a half-million pounds of powder. The following letter from Haywood W. Guion, a Charlotte lawyer who was a member of the state Military Board and president of the Wilmington, Charlotte, and Rutherford Railroad, describes the beginning of the negotiations.

Lincolnton July 22ᵈ '61

Dear Sir

Our late Governor was very solicitous to procure an ample supply of powder, and requested Co¹. Bradford & myself as members of his Board to give our attention to the matter, and aid him if we could. Co¹. Bradford twice was so much occupied with the duties of his office as were also Co¹. Winslow, that the inquiries as to the Powder devolved chiefly upon me.—We for some time meditated & actually commenced preparing to send the Steamer North Carolina to Europe, in quest of both powder & arms. Other inquiries induced us to look to our own resources, and we despatched an Agent Mr. C. S. Smith to Tennessee & Kentucky to look up the Saltpetre—We opened negotiations with two gentlemen with the view of procuring the Sulphur—from our own mines and our object & intent was to establish Powder Mills on State account. These matters were all approved by Governor Ellis & he concurred in the proposition however, that if individuals could be induced to engage in the manufacture that they should be encouraged to the fullest extent. Learning that a Company of reliable gentlemen in Charlotte, were desirous of engaging in the manufacture, an interview was invited with them. Messrs Waterhouse & Sanders came to Raleigh, and reported that much of the Capital had been subscribed, & more was necessary. We gave them the benefit of our reports as to Saltpetre—and agreed that Mr. Pigott who was to furnish Sulphur to the State, might furnish them if they could agree—And they agreed to return to Charlotte forthwith & commence the manufacture, and if they could not raise all the Capital the Governor instructed us to say he would make them a loan upon proper securities, to enable them to proceed vigorously—On their part they were to commence furnishing powder in Sixty days, and not to sell or give away any to other parties, until the State was fully supplied and the State they were assured would need 200.000 lbs.

I learn from them that they have taken some steps toward the work, but leave them to make their own report & state their own views—The object in this communication being solely to inform your Excellency as to the relation existing between them & the State—that you may act understandingly in the matter—and that you may give to the enterprise initiated by us such measure of encouragement as you may think its importance demands.

With Sentiments of high respect

I am your most obt
H. W. GUION

Governors' Papers.

---

(4) Coercing the Cloth Manufacturers

When it became evident that the Confederacy would have difficulty clothing the troops, the North Carolina legislature on 20 September 1861 agreed to clothe all its volunteers in return for the fifty dollars allocated to each soldier to buy his own clothing. North Carolina was the only Confederate state to make such an arrangement with the central govern-ment. By this time the legislature had consolidated upon Adjutant General James G. Martin all the duties of the Quartermaster, Commissary, Ordnance, and Pay Departments so as to make him thoroughly responsible for equipping and outfitting all North Carolina troops. Martin soon found that fifty dollars would not pay half the cost of clothing needed and was able to induce the War Department to pay the actual cost of all clothing and shoes furnished.

One of Martin's first acts was to organize a clothing factory in Raleigh and appoint Captain I. W. Garrett to manage it. During its first year of operation the factory made 6,000 overcoats, 49,000 jackets, 68,000 pairs of pants, 12,000 blankets, and numerous other items. Much of its success was due to the veiled threat which Governor Clark made to all cotton factories in the form letter printed below.

STATE OF NORTH CAROLINA,
EXECUTIVE DEPARTMENT,
Raleigh, Nov. 6th, 1861

To
The Proprietors of Cotton Factories in N.C.

Gentlemen,

I am informed, through the Adj't Genl's Department, that our state is in absolute want of cotton goods, especially domestic cloths, for the use of our volunteers; and to enable the State to comply with her contracts to clothe our troops now in the Confederate Service,—it is indispensably necessary to secure at once the requisite supply from some source.

I know of none to which I can appeal with as strong hopes of success, as to yourselves,—the owners of the Factories in our own State. I learn that many, if not all of your mills, are already occupied in furnishing goods to individuals, upon contracts for resale. I am sure that when the urgent wants of your own State and her gallant soldiers are made known to you, that I may rely, with the most confident expectations, on your patriotism and your zeal in the good cause against our common foe, to supply these wants without compelling the authorities of the State, upon the ground of military necessity, to resort to more stringent measures to obtain that supply without which our troops cannot be prepared for the field.

If there are existing contracts with individuals, you ought not to hesitate to suspend them, at least for a while, and give your State the preference,—when she pays you prices equally remunerative, and when it is impossible, as it is now ascertained to be, to procure supplies elsewhere in time to meet our necessities.

These necessities, as well as the object of this circular, will be more fully explained to you by *Captain Sloan* of the Quarter Masters' Department, who is authorized to make contracts with you for the supplies required by the State.

Very respectfully
Your Obt. Servant,
HENRY T. CLARK,
GOVERNOR EX OFFICIO.

Governors' Papers.

(5) Contracting for Army Supplies

North Carolina had hardly left the Union when the state quartermaster general wrote Governor Ellis that only "trifling purchases could be made from retail merchants, as the volunteer companies had exhausted their stocks. . . ." [8] He added, however, that he had already begun making contracts with small manufacturers for uniforms and assured Ellis that the volunteers would be well clad by winter. But by the fall of the year, even with the output of the Raleigh state clothing factory, North Carolina troops were still short of clothing and almost everything else. Consequently, Governor Clark had to continue negotiating private contracts for clothing and to begin contracting for other needs of war. He also began sending agents around the state to see that these contracts were being filled properly. When Vance became governor he continued the system and also required the agents to see that the contractors were complying with the conscription and exemption laws. Below is a letter from one of these agents, Hal W. Ayer of Wake County.

Bethania Forsythe County
Nov. 10th. 1862

I have been busily engaged since my last communication to you, but have not a great deal to show for it. Those iron works I alluded to in my letter from Salem have been visited and have an outward appearance of honesty, but there are some rumors afloat against them, which I could not trace up as true. The one owned by Stephen Hobson is situated in Yadkin County, he has at present 50 employees, detailed to him from Forsythe, Iredell, Davidson and Yadkin Counties by the Cols. of the Regts to which they respectively belong. In addition to these he has 17 others, who have not been enrolled, being between the ages of 18 & 45 at the last enrollment. He has no state or Govt. contract, further than a sub Contract, from Jno. P. & J. J. Nisson of Waughtown, who have a Govt. Contract for wagons and horse shoes, which sub Contracts Hobson agrees to furnish 3000 lbs iron every two weeks—He now runs two fires and one forge—is interested in 3 other new forges now being erected, and wishes to have some 38 hands more in addition to the 50 he now has detailed, Thinks he will be able then to furnish 1000 lbs iron pr day The opinion of some of his neighbors is that he is erecting the new forges for the purpose of screening some of his friends from the army, as he is a *Quaker*, but my own opinion is he is doing it for the dollars and cents he can make by it, as he employes these conscripts for $10, pr month He has a foundry also—and has been engaged in the manufacture of Iron with one forge. . . . You can make your own calculation whether

8. Lawrence O'Bryan Branch to John W. Ellis, 26 May 1861, Tolbert, *Papers of John Willis Ellis*, 2:788.

the amt. which he now produces to the Govt. (3000 lbs. in two weeks with 50 hands) is a paying business or not, and whether it will pay to raise the number of operatives to 88 for . . . 1000 lbs, pr day—Jesse Wooten near him has one forge completed . . . & two others on the way . . . 15 conscript hands . . . and furnishes 15000 lbs, every two weeks—at least that is his contract. . . . I would not have visited either of these establishments, had I not heard that they were frauds upon the Govt. [Hobson] has been heard to say "That he would *ease the conscience of as many of the neighbors as he could, from fighting in the war. . . .*

I visited also the Shoe Shop of Mess[rs] Kerner & Gentry at Kernersville, Forsythe Co. find the working 13 hands—12 whites, 1 Blk. 11 Conscripts, Contract with State, for 1000 prs pegged and sewed shoes. . . . Enclosed find . . . the report of Mess[rs] Fries & Fries—Salem, for woolen goods—and Mess[rs] Hine & Co—for Leather, The report from the Cotton factory of Gray & Wilson Salem has not been made out yet oweing to the absence of Mr Gray—It will reach me at Greensboro—and will be for[d]. in my next. I am authorized and requested by Chief Justice Pearson to lay before your Excellency the following facts, There is a man in Yadkin county near Mount Nebo—75 Regt, N.C. M named Elkanah Willard, who openly defied the law. First, By rescueing his brother who is a conscript (he himself is not) from a guard who had him in custody by a display of arms and open force Secondly, By putting Capt Flemming of that district and the men accompanying him at defiance, in such a way that they were obliged to shoot him down or rush upon him armed as he was at the iminent danger of their lives. . . . Anything else coming to my knowledge will be promptly reported to your Excellency.

Johnston, *Papers of Zebulon Baird Vance*, 1:330–31.

---

(6) Contributions from Home

With the manufacturing efforts described above, plus generous gifts from patriotic homes, the North Carolina soldiers fared well enough through the first winter. Adjutant General Martin reported that "before cold weather most of the troops were supplied with clothing and blankets, at least so far as to prevent any suffering."[9] But during the spring and summer of 1862 the state was hard pressed to clothe the new soldiers brought in under the conscription law, and those men already in uniform had to depend even more on gifts from home. One young officer wrote to his father "I wrote to ask your aid in getting some clothes for the 'Alamance Regulators.' They are here without any thing, except the few rags that they have on."[10] On

9. "Governor's Message," *Public Documents of North Carolina, 1862–'63,* p. 25.

10. Thomas Ruffin, Jr., to his father, 15 May 1862, Joseph G. de R. Hamilton, ed., *The Papers of Thomas Ruffin*, 3:235.

15 October, in a proclamation which the North hailed as an announcement of "The Wants of the Rebel Army," Governor Vance admitted that it was "impossible to clothe and shoe our soldiers without again appealing to . . . the private contributions of our people." He appointed all militia colonels as agents to collect goods and to pay for what was not donated gratis. In closing, he begged the people to remember that "the soldier is sitting upon the cold earth . . . when you come forth in the morning well fed and warmly clad. . . ."[11]

The following documents are examples of cooperation by home enterprise (Document A) and by the collectors designate (Document B).

A .

THOMAS RUFFIN TO THOMAS RUFFIN, JR.

Alamance—May 21st, 1862

My very Dear Son

I received your letter . . . and on the same day wrote to Govr. Clark for an order on Messrs Fries for the cloth for the Regulators Coats and pantaloons; having learned, that those gentlemen had repeatedly refused to let any person have cloth without such an order. This morning I have the reply of the Governor, declining to furnish the order, for reasons which seem to me very good. . . . I have to assure you, that not only I, but all the Ladies and all the men of the neighbourhood feel the utmost interest in and sympathy for our brave boys. All were so alert to supply their wants, that if we could have procured the cloth *every body* was ready to go to work and complete the job with very little delay. Mr. John Faucett or I would have gone to Salem, that we might make sure of it, and all our Ladies were desirous of doing all that diligence and patriotism and admiration for the men could prompt or effect. As it was, money was made up in a day to buy materials for shirts and drawers for the Company, and I went up to Mr. Holt's Factory and got them,—and Mary tells me, that by Saturday night enough for the whole Company will be completed; which we propose to commit to the Express Company, to go off Monday morning, in order to insure their safe and speedy transportation to Richmond, we expect Mr. Green Andrews will also go with them, for the purpose of seeing them safe from Richmond to the Camp. But I shall direct him to apply to your agents, Messrs Hill and Norfleet, at Richmond, for directions and assistance in carrying out the purpose of his mission; and I think you had better advise those gentlemen of our intention, that they may be the more inclined and ready to co-operate with us. Let your men know, that *this supply* is the *voluntary* offering of their fellow-citizens, male and female, as evidence of their sense of the noble patience, endurance, and heroism of our men. They will, therefore, not have to account for these things to either Government. If we could have procured shoes and socks, they should be sent also. But they are not on hand and can not be got up in a short time. But, as we shall soon

11. Frank Moore, ed., *The Rebellion Record*, 4:23–24.

begin to spin wool again, I doubt not every effort will be made to send them socks before long.

Hamilton, *The Papers of Thomas Ruffin*, 2:237–38.

B.

Yanceyville, N.C., Nov. 6th, 1862

MESSRS. EDITORS: In obedience to General order No 9, of the Adj't General, and in accordance with Gov. Vance's noble and patriotic appeal to the people of N.C., in behalf of our soldiers, I have ordered the commandants of the different districts in this regiment, to visit *every family* and appeal to them for donations of clothing, shoes, blankets, &c, for the soldiers, and to purchase such articles as they find, that cannot be given. We want the *goods* in preference to the money; clothing, &c., the soldiers *must* have, but if any one cannot possibly give an article of clothing, we will be glad to have from him or her twenty, fifty, or seventy-five dollars to purchase from those who have for sale; five or ten dollars is a *very* small matter, it will only buy one or two yards of cloth, so out with your fifties if you have no clothing to give. The object of this communication is to say to the people of this county, to get the articles ready by the time the officer comes; don't say I have nothing to spare, but wish the soldier was clothed and comfortable; your wishes and desires, not loud boasting of sympathy for the soldier will warm him in a cold winter storm. . . . I intend to have a list of the donations, also of purchases, with their worth or price published, and a copy of the paper sent to the Captain of each company sent from this county, to be read to his company. . . .

I have a special permit from Gov. Vance to carry or send directly to the companies such articles as may be given at State expense. If the officer should fail to visit any family we hope they will send the article of clothing to the officer.

Yours respectfully,
JOS. C. PINNIX, COL. COM'G
47th Reg. N.C.M., &c.

Milton *Chronicle*, 14 Nov. 1862.

(7) State Purchasing Agents

All during the time that the state was manufacturing, contracting for, and begging clothes and equipment for its soldiers, Adjutant General Martin and his staff had purchasing agents combing the state, buying whatever was needed from rawhide to guns.

Governor Clark ordered the agents to have the county solicitors prosecute anyone refusing to sell his gun. After 1861 the main search was for cloth and food. The Confederate War Department had agreed to keep its purchasing agents out of the state if the latter would sell the Confederacy all its surplus products. But since there was no surplus, the department felt justified in sending its own agents into North Carolina to compete with those of the state. Vance soon reported to the General Assembly that the country was "swarming with agents of the Confederate Government, stripping bare our markets and putting enormous prices upon our agents."[12]

The agent who wrote the following report to Governor Clark seems to have been chiefly interested in buying whatever weapons he could find.

Raleigh N.C. 7th Nov 1861

To His Excelency
   H. T. Clark
      Present
Governor

On the 8th of October I proceeded to Lexington to collect the State arms at that point I could find only 13 muskets & 9 rifles which I boxed up & sent to Capt Lawrence—I called on Col Hargrave & by him was referred to Col Park who gave me the following information as to the distribution of the arms which he had collected. Fifty muskets & twenty swords to L[t] Col Leech 11th vol sixty rifles. Thirty nine p[rs] Pistols. Nine swords & 4 boxes of rifles & muskets (n[o] not recollected) to Hon Warren Winslow. To Capt Hargrave 4th Reg[t] NC vol 8 swords. To Liut Cogren 8 swords. To a company of dragoons in Davie County 3 Pairs Pistols & 2 swords. To Capt Lawrence 15 Pairs Pistols 17 swords & the Box named in the first part of this report.

From Lexington I proceeded to Statesville to complete a contract previously made for a lot of bacon, which was accomplished. I then proceeded to Morganton where I received about 11000 lbs bacon which I inspected, weighed & dispatched to the western extension of the NC R Road. I also purchased shoes over coats Blankets Jeans Boots &c which I also forwarded.

From Morganton I proceeded to Asheville where I paid the bounty money to the 29th Reg[t]. In Asheville I bot a few guns & found 3 good Harpers Ferry Rifles with Bayonets which I boxed & turned over to the Quarter Master there to be forwarded to Cap[t]. Lawrence. Whilst at Asheville I learned that 400 rifles were in Macon County in charge of Col Moore. The Roads being impassible I sent a messenger over to Col Moore. On his return he informed me that the number would not reach 200 but that they were boxed & would be sent over as soon as the Roads were open I visited the new Rifle works and regret to say that their progress towards

12. Z. B. Vance to the General Assembly, 17 Nov. 1862, *Official Records*, Ser. 4, 2:183.

completion has been retarded by the heavy freshets They lost at one time 500 Rifle Brls completed and only wanting lock & stock. The same cause has retarded the arrival of their machinery I much fear they cannot render much service before late in the Spring. The work they do is well done but their scale of prices is much higher than further East. I had them to alter some Halls carbines for guard service in the 29th Reg[t] & the work was well executed.

At Morganton I found Capt Walton had anticipated me & collected all the arms in his vicinity which he is having boxed & will come forward immediately.

At Morganton I went to Caldwell & Wilkes counties. At Wilksboro I found the sheriff had charge of a few guns which after my promise to have the transportation & boxing expense paid he graciously agreed to receive written instructions from me to send them on to Statesville. There is also an iron howitzer there a fine piece which I ordered to Statesville.

This Governor embraces the substance of my journey which I sincerely wish could have been of more advantage. . . . For the disbursements for Payment to Troops and Commissary Department for articles under that department, as also the Quarter Master & Ordnance stores purchased & paid for I beg to refer you to the separate accounts & vouchers in each Dep't. . . .

> Your Ob[t] Serv[t]
> W. W. PIERCE
> Capt ordnance

Governors' Papers.

---

(8) Imports from Abroad

When President Lincoln in April 1861, ordered a blockade of the entire Confederate coast, he had twenty-four fit steamers with which to patrol 3,549 miles of coastline. By the end of 1862 there were about three hundred blockaders, but they were bunched near ports, and the odds still favored a small ship attempting to dash through this thin cordon of enemy vessels to the protection of large coastal guns. So Confederate and European businessmen quick-ly established a system whereby large vessels would take goods from Europe to the Caribbean Islands and return with Confederate cotton; while speedy, light-draft vessels would run these goods into Confederate ports and return with cotton. After the fall of New Orleans, Wilmington, with its good harbor and protective fort, became the best of the blockaded ports. Document A describes the activities of successful Wilmington entrepreneurs. Donald Mac-

Rae was a member of a family with large interests in manufacturing, railroading, and shipping; John W. K. Dix was a prominent merchant.

In mid-1862 Adjutant General Martin, seeing that clothing was still in short supply, conceived the idea of large-scale purchases in Europe. Against the better judgment of most of his advisers, Vance finally agreed to implement Martin's concept. On 1 November he appointed John White, a prominent Warrenton merchant, as state commissioner to sell cotton bonds in England and to "purchase supplies with the money thus raised. . . ."[13] With part of the two million dollars which the legislature appropriated, Vance bought a large amount of cotton as the basis for the operation.

In May 1863, White negotiated a £100,000 loan with Alexander Collie & Co. which enabled him to begin operations. He bought the steamer Clyde—renamed Advance—and 250 tons of merchandise. He then traveled about making other purchases while the Advance carried his first purchases to Wilmington and returned to England with cotton. The success of this operation induced Vance and the legislature to buy one-fourth interest in three more vessels, while selling half interest in the Advance to Power, Lowe & Co. of Wilmington. By the summer of 1863 so much freight had reached the state that on 3 September Vance wrote White not to buy anything else and to devote his energies to shipping out what had already been bought. Document B is White's detailed account of his work in England.[14]

A.

Wilmington N.C. August 11/62

Dear Don.

I am to day in receipt of your letter of the 8th & will reply in detail. first I will give you the "sad particulars" of our foreign fleet as you will know the "hard is gone," which was No 1: The Howard now the Br[itish] Ida left Nassau under command of the Mate Capt. Guthrie loaded with salt. About the time he was due a small schooner was taken off the sound & I fear it was her, thus goes No 2 in part. Capt. Carrow of the Howard purchased a fine schooner in Nassau called the Alexander one-half of her for a/c of the owners of the Howard. she will be loaded about the middle of the month and expects to arrive at Topsail the last of the month. He had $2200 left which he would remit by next Steamer. Shantung is now selling 225, this will bring the amount up to enough to pay out the adventure but if the Alex gets in we will make a good thing out of it, and make No 2 all OK. The Spray No 3 arrived at Nassau and has

13. Z. B. Vance to John White, 1 Nov. 1862, Frontis W. Johnston, ed., *The Papers of Zebulon Baird Vance*, 1:289.

14. For a detailed account of North Carolina's foreign commerce during the Civil War, see Daniel Harvey Hill, *A History of North Carolina in the War Between the States*, 1:329–97.

changed to the Br Sloop Lizzie. she was loaded with 220 barrls. Salt, 1 bale flannel, 1 bale cloth 1 bale Arrow Root, 2 casks lard ashe & 2 casks caustic soda costing about $1200—her outward cargo of Cotton & Tobacco was shipped to Liverpool. She sailed from Nassau on the 23ᵈ under charge of Capt Green of Charleston SᵒCᵃ. This was a Sloop taken off the New Inlet on the 30ᵗʰ which I fear was her last. Mr Cameron says it could not be her as she could not make the run with the winds she had, but I fear it was her—Bob Brown played us a mean trick, he would not trust his life on the Sloop as he says she was unseaworthy without an addition of $500 for his services which Mr Cameron would not pay— Brown came home passenger in the Br Steamer "Kate" which arrived here last Thursday with a full cargo of arms & goods. thus ends all the particulars of No 3. Now, for No 4 the Ann E. Berry out at Bermuda all safe, but the people there are not as easy as Nassau and they could not get a Br register for her, consequently laid her up, after shipping her cargo to London. the Crew went over to Nassau & there Mr Cameron bought the Br Schooner "Emma" and she is now expected on our coast. Now comes the No 5, which is the "Belle" or rather was, but is now the schʳ "Maggie Fulton" named after Rod[s] sweet heart at Cambridge. She arrived out all O.K. he sold his cargo and bought a return cargo consisting of 200 sack salt, 20 doz. cotton cards & some [illegible]. he sent home before he sailed a bill of exchange which will pay us 100% profit on the venture. So there is not much lost on that Spec. on Saturday morning Rod walked into the office and reported the M. F. safe at McMillians, and we have sent down a lot of Govt. teams to haul it up, will have it all here by Wednesday. I think the cargo will value about $10.000 cost about $500. Now what have you got to say about Rods imagination. Rod bought on his account 1 bag coffee 200 lbs 1 bll coffee & 1 bll sugar, on which he can make $1000 profit. this ends No 5. We think of sending him back immediately. No 6—Mary Abigail will sail from Challotte[e?] this week —& No 7 Lavinia will sail from New River this week. So far we have made enough to double our investment, so I do not think the particulars *so bad* after all—. . . .

Hidden still keeps in luck. his Schooner "Argule" arrived out safely with a full load of cotton. Parsley & McEtheridges vessel was taken just as she was going to Nassau. . . . just about now the Jones are in luck picking up Steamers, among them they got a large one called the Sodonia with a cargo that cost $750.000 in hull. They also took the Steamer Memphis getting out of Charleston with a cargo of 1950 bales cotton worth to them about $400.000. . . . They got their Schooner "Jane Campbell" released from New York and took her out to Nassau and shipped the cargo on the Leopard when it arrived safely & pays them enormous profits. . . . More of Rods cargo has just come up among them are some Pine Apples, as fine as I ever saw he has some cocoa nuts also will send you some of them. . . . would write you more, *but have spun out all I know.*

Yours truly
J . W . K . DIX

MacRae Papers.

B.

REPORT OF JOHN WHITE, COMMISSIONER

[1864]

To His Excellency

Governor Z. B. Vance

The subscriber having been appointed by you a special commissioner for the State of North Carolina to visit Europe and make sale of Cotton, Bonds of the State, and the Confederate States of America, and also to purchase clothing and other articles for her troops, respectfully submits the following report.

On the 15th of November 1862 at Charleston South Carolina I embarked in the steamer "Leopard" for Nassau. . . . I left Nassau for Liverpool . . . in the steamer "Bonita" and arrived . . . on the 23rd of [December]. I reached London about the 5th of January 1863, and spent nearly all of my time there and at Manchester while in England.
. . .

About the 1st of May 1863 I sold at London & Manchester Nine Hundred & Ninety nine (999) Cotton Bonds or warrants as they are there called, at One Hundred pounds each. . . . The Bonds numbered from 1000. to 1395 were deposited with Alex^r. Collie & Co. in . . . Manchester where they are now. The Bond numbered 1396 was returned by me to the State as a sample. The Bonds numbered from 1397 to 1500 were deposited with Isaacs & Samuel of London as security for a contract entered into between them & myself acting through Alexander Collie & Co. All the Bonds issued by me were obligations which . . . bound her [North Carolina] to deliver to the holder thereof 12 Bales of Cotton weighing 400 lbs each ginned packed and in sound Merchantable condition at the port of Wilmington, Charleston, or Savannah or if practicable at any other port in possession of the Confederate States Government, except the ports of Texas, on receiving sixty days notice of the port at which delivery is required said Bonds bear interest at the rate of 7% pr annum payable half yearly in Manchester and reckoned from the 1st of July 1863. . . .

I employed Mssrs Alexander Collie & Co. to negotiate for the sale of the Bonds for 5% commissions, with the understanding that I was to pay the solicitors fees and Bank Commission. . . . I made no contract for the sale of cotton except that for which Bonds were given. I also carried with me to England Five Hundred Thousand Dollars of State Bonds bearing 8% interest. . . . The . . . said bonds were deposited with Alexander Collie & Co and others as trustees for the faithful performance of the contract on the part of the State for the delivery of the Cotton hereinafter mentioned.

You also sent me One Million of Dollars of North Carolina Bonds in accordance with my request made in a letter dated May 20th 1863 in order to secure the performance of a cotton contract on the part of the State which I expected would be shortly entered into at the time when I wrote; . . . but I was only able to negotiate a sale to the amount of

Ninety-Nine-Thousand Nine Hundred pounds (£99.900) and therefor
. . . the bonds . . . are now deposited in the Manchester and County
Bank . . . for safe Keeping. . . .

While in England I purchased chiefly through Alexander Collie & Co.
for the State and shipped to Bermuda 150.115 yards of Gray Cloth 6/4
wide, 11023 yards ¾ Gray Cloth 28582 yards 6/4 Gray Flannel 83173
yards ¾ Gray Flannel 2978 yds. Brown Canvass Padding 25887 pairs of
Gray Blankets 37092 p^{rs} of Woolen Socks 26096 p^{rs} of Army shoes 530
p^{rs} of Cavalry Boots 1956 Angola shirts, 7872 Gray Flannel shirts 1006
Cloth overcoats 1002 Cloth Jackets 1010 pairs of trousers besides other
articles of clothing for the North Carolina Troops, all being of good
quality and as I believe at as cheap prices as they could be purchased for
in England. I also purchased and shipped a considerable quantity of
Leather, Sole, upper & Harness and a considerable quantity of Cotton &
Wool Cards.

I also purchased 20,000 pairs of Army shoes 10,000 pairs of Gray Blankets 160 dozen Flannel shirts 5800 yards 6/4 Army Cloth 10,000 of Gray
Cloth of finer quality and 70,000 pairs of Cotton and Wool Cards. 5 Card
setting machines with wire and other furnishings sufficient to keep them
running for perhaps twelve months and probably some other articles of
small value not now recollected. The last mentioned articles or most of
them were expected to be shipped about the first of January 1864 but as
I left England early in December I do not know whether they have been
shipped or not. . . .

A statement of my transactions with Alexander Collie & Co. will appear in papers B & C with the exception herein before mentioned. They
acted as my agents in the purchase and shipping of Goods as well as in
the Sale of Bonds, and an agency of the Kind is necessary to the transaction of such business according to the uniform custom in England. . . .
[A]ccording to your directions I paid the purchase money amounting to
Thirty-Five Thousand pounds (£35.000) for the "Ad-Vance" formerly
called "Lord Clyde" which was purchased by Col. T. M. Crossan for the
State under your authority. . . .

The State has also embarked in another enterprise which I think has
been a fortunate one upon the whole. I allude to the contract entered
into on the 27th of October 1863 between Alexander Collie in behalf of
himself and his friends on the one part and myself as commissioner for
the State of North Carolina on the other. I entered into the contract without any directions from you, but it was made with the distinct understanding that it should be void unless it should meet with your approval
and you afterwards did approve it. Under the contract M^r. Collie & his
friends were to furnish four Steamers of suitable construction and speed
for blockade running as soon as practicable, the State to pay One fourth
of the Cost and that the other persons interested the remaining three
fourths and the parties to be interested in the profits & loss in the same
proportion. The Steamers were to be furnished, and the business commenced shortly after the date of the contract and is still going on. Two
of the Steamers the "Hansa" and the "Don" cost at Bermuda or Nassau
Twenty Thousand pounds each. I have not now before me the data to

show the cost of the other two steamers, but suppose they will cost Fifteen to Seventeen Thousand pounds each. The claim against the State for her interest in the above Steamers is payable according to the terms of the Contract in Cotton Warrants of the State at par. . . .

J N° W H I T E

Governors' Papers.

STATE SOCIALISM

Armies are like hungry animals, demanding so very much but contributing nothing to the economy, insisting that their needs be satisfied and leaving to the civilians only what remains; and often destroying the very means of their own survival. So while feeding and equipping the armies became part of the states' new economic responsibility, the economy of the home front also demanded attention. The rural individualism of most Confederate civilians was an almost automatic block to voluntary cooperation for the common good, and as the war developed the several state governments found it at times necessary to intervene in some areas of the economy that were not directly related to the war.

Certainly nothing like modern state socialism occurred. Conservative American economic attitudes would not have accepted any regulation so radical. Nevertheless, North Carolina and her sister Confederate states endeavored in a cautious and limited fashion to exercise certain regulations which presumably would benefit both civilian and soldier. Every southern state curtailed or stopped the distillation of grain. Several limited the planting of cotton and/or tobacco. Most legislatures authorized their governors to impress slaves and use their labor where needed. Most states tried some form of price control. And all states undertook certain business operations when private resources proved inadequate. Considering the many problems of North Carolina's economy, the interventionism of the government seems quite inadequate, but it exceeded that of the northern states. In his provocative volume *The Confederacy as a Revolutionary Experience*, Emory M. Thomas states that "the wartime South became more centralized, more nationalized than her Northern enemy."[1] The same might be said of the southern state governments as well.

1. Emory M. Thomas, *The Confederacy as a Revolutionary Experience*, p. 59.

(1) Prohibiting the Export of Necessities

The productivity of North Carolina's fields and mills lured speculators and purchasing agents from other states, and on 28 March 1862 Governor Clark felt compelled to ban the shipment out of state of all cotton and woolen products except by order of the North Carolina or the Confederate governments. In addition, Article 4 of General Order No. 9 instructed each colonel to seize all shoes and leather leaving the state in the hands of speculators. Vance continued the ban until May 1863. He apparently decided to discontinue it because by this time North Carolina had its own agents "drawing large supplies" from other states.[2]

The following letter describes the interception of goods being smuggled out of the state and the citizenry's reaction to the seizure. William M. Shipp was a lawyer of Lincoln County who was captain of a volunteer company stationed in Hendersonville.

Hendersonville Nov. 1st

Hon. Z. B. Vance
    Dear Sir.
    You will probably receive a letter, mailed to day, from Stansil the colonel of this county in reference to certain goods, leather &c which he has stopped in transit & which belong to M.[r] B. F. King of Georgia. I think it due to our citizens & to myself that I give you a full statement of the facts in reference to this matter. For the Colonel has acted at the request & by the approbation of the people generally: M.[r] King was a captain in the Confederate army from the State of Georgia & resigned . . . some time last summer. Shortly afterwards he came to this place & stated that he was an agent of the confederate government. . . . In that character he purchased a quantity of jeans & woolen goods in this and the neighboring counties and brought it to this place & packed it in boxes for the purpose of shipping to Atlanta Georgia. He also contracted for a large amount of leather. I think 4000 lbs. Some 900 lbs of this he has sent off & a portion has been brought to this place & is now in the hands of the Colonel. . . . Some week or two since & particularly after your late appeal to our people for aid to the soldiers this accumulation of goods by M.[r] King attracted special attention. Our people were anxious to get leather for the soldiers & for themselves & found that the tanners had engaged so much of it to King that they would not or could not furnish them. You know the difficulty upon the subject of leather. not only soldiers, but women & children I fear must suffer this winter for the want of *it* so to some extent with woolen goods—our tanners have sold most of the leather heretofore made out of the State—Under these circumstances—a public meeting was held in this town to do something in be-

2. David Outlaw to Z. B. Vance, 1 Jan. 1864, Governors' Papers.

half of our soldiers & in response to your call. A handsome subscription was made at once. In the progress of the meeting the subject of woolen goods & leather came up—and especially the goods &c purchased by King—It was doubted by many that he was a *bona fide* agent—& asserted that he had no authority: He was called upon for his appointment—He showed a paper from the Quarter Master at Atlanta stating in substance—"That he was a loyal citizen & engaged in purchasing goods for the Army." This was the only written authority. . . . It was ascertained that he had made contracts with Davis [illegible] manufacturers of shoes for a large number out of the leather purchased: The meeting was adjourned untill Davis & [illegible] could be written to in regard to their contract—They signified their willingness to release King: Thereupon a meeting was held & resolutions passed instructing the colonel to prevent the removal of the goods & leather & tender the same to Yourself for the benefit of the State & our own soldiers at cost—the money to be paid to King—also requesting the Colonel to prevent the exportation of leather & woolen goods, untill our own soldiers & women & children could be supplied—There is a good deal of excitement in the county about the matter & a general impression that King is engaged in a private enterprise, and upon a speculation—our people too are poorly provided with leather & we think that our first duty is to our own soldiers & women & children—North Carolina would derive no immediate benefit from sending goods to Atlanta. . . .

Yours &c
W. M. SHIPP

Governors' Papers.

---

(2) The Ban on Distilling

To protect the food supply, the state convention ordered that after 15 April 1862 the distillation of corn, wheat, rye, or oats would be illegal, and it placed a tax of one dollar on imported liquors. In the fall of that year the General Assembly added peas, peanuts, sorghum cane, syrup, molasses, rice, dried fruit, and potatoes to the list of prohibited ingredients. The patriotic elements of society accepted the ban in principle (Document A), though physicians considered whiskey indispensable in medication and received some concessions from the state. From letters in newspapers and in the Governors' Papers in the North Carolina Department of Archives and History, however, enforcement of the ban on distilling must have been spotty, as evidenced by a letter from a well-to-do farmer from the community of Henrietta (Document B).

A . STOP THE STILLS ! — SAVE THE COUNTRY ! !
AND FEED THE POOR.

The Ladies of Catawba appeal to the lovers of their country and the friends of humanity, to co-operate with them in stopping the manufacture of whiskey, and traffic in the same.

It is but the common and spontaneous voice of the land, that if our country is lost, whiskey will be the cause of it. Drunkenness and riot have already demoralized our camps to an appalling extent. . . . Whiskey has sapped the courage of the people throughout the land. . . . Stop the stills, or ruin is our certain doom. We plead for our country. . . .

As a country, we are hemmed in on all sides. We must make our bread, or perish for the want of it. A bountiful Providence has given us enough for man and beast; but distillers have already converted so much corn into poison, that prices look like famine ahead. . . . And now distiller, we ask you, in heaven's name, is it manly is it brave, is it not dastardly and unutterably mean, to force such prices for bread on us and our children? . . . Are you not a sordid race to fill your own base coffers with the price of innocent blood? . . . Distillers, beware how you grind the faces of the poor!—God hears their cry, and He will avenge them with judgments of terrible servility [*sic*]. . . .

It will send joy to our hea[r]ts . . . if you will . . . stop this accursed business. We hope you will. But if not . . . then it will become our sacred duty . . . to use all the means that God and nature have put into our hands, to deliver the land of a direful curse and a burning shame. We are resolved to perform this duty.

The signatures to this appeal are too numerous to publish.

Newton, No. Ca., March 18 1862.

Mr. Editor.—The above appeal was made and circulated in this community some weeks ago. It has been pressed upon the consideration of those directly engaged in the whiskey business. It failed to still them. About two weeks ago the ladies gave them a certain time in which to cease operations. The time expired and still the wicked work went on. A large quantity of the stuff was being brought to the Depot on its mission to private gain and public ruin.

The resolution had been taken—to-day it was carried out. The ladies of Newton, armed and equipped with short-range axes, marched to the depot, and then and there began one of the most glorious battles fought in these days of wartime. Bold men sat astride the barrels, and thought of the dollars under them and the axes over them—bold men, I say for their adversaries were ladies, and their beloved traffic was in danger. With uncommon courage they talked of pistols and shooting—"cused" heroically—and cried aloud for private rights.

"But, sirs," said the ladies, "your private rights, are public wrongs. Could Rothschild buy up all the corn in the Confederacy, and destroy it, and then inocently plead 'private rights?' "

"But, ladies, you will ruin us." "Well, when you put gold in your pocket, what shall we put in our children's mouths?"

"But, my all is invested here."

"Well, sir, it ought to be in better business."

"We appeal to the laws of the country."

"And while you are crying, 'law,' our little ones will cry, 'bread'— 'bread.' "

The parley was a short one. Blows followed words. Barrels roll—hoops fly—head split—staves burst asunder—ladies stand ankle deep in the flowing "elixor," and ply their weapons, if somewhat awkwardly, yet with terrible slaughter,—they are *in the spirit*.

The struggle was soon over. When the fumes of its conflict had cleared away, it was found that its killed were nine hundred or a thousand gallons, and the wounded were some half dozen speculators. The missing were three or four hundred bushels of corn, and, the deserters were the doughty heroes who threatened to shoot the ladies.

. . . Three times three cheers for the resolute ladies were given by the large crowd which had by this time collected to witness the assault upon toryism. It then gently dispersed, feeling assured that while a large proportion of the men of its country were away in the army, the ladies were fully competent to protect its interests at home. If any of our neighboring counties are afflicted as we were, and need help, let them call for the ladies of Catawba.

Greensboro *Patriot*, 27 Mar. 1862, taken from the Charlotte *Bulletin*.

B.

North Carolina ⎫ Apr 18th / 64
Rutherford County ⎭

To our Exilency Gov Vance honored Sir after my strongist desires for your wellfar in the present camppaign I feel it to bee my duty to repoart to you the condishion of a part of this county thar is now and has bin for the last three months Sum Twelve or fifteen Stills running night and day and we have made Several indevers to git at the root of this evil but it seames to bee a matter of impossibility as the most of the men who own the stills lives in south Carolina and tha have imploid the poorist men tha can find so as to ignore the fine and I was present at several of those houses a day or two ago in company with sum two or three magistrates and I wanted them to sias the stills and hold them as that is the only way where by this wicked and abominable thing can bee Stopt and if it is not stopt I arnistly say to you that the poor people must and will starve for the want of bread those abominable law brakers ar paing from Thirty to forty Dollars fir bushel for corn—and I ernistly pray you as the head of our State that we may have the right to take all the Stills we can find in operration and put them under lock unless that is dun I tell you most ernistly at this seson of the year tha will set them upon the secret placis and those still with out the shape of a hous and unless the still is taken a way from them tha will still not respectting the Law nor the wants of the poor and we wish to no if a man who alows a Still put upon his land fer the purpos of distilling grain aint as guilty as the man who stills we hope to hear soon the right to take and hold the stills of those men who will not respect the Law I am happy to say to you that the people ar all most unanimous fer you in the present campaign thar has bin a package of Mr Holdens paper sent to this Settle ment fer distribution but to no affect I hope pleas pardon me fer bothering you with this lengthy letter

> I am as ever your most
> Obet Servt
> J A S. O. S I M M O N S

Governors' Papers.

---

(3) Encouraging Food Crop Planting

With the blockade gradually strangling foreign commerce and with hunger looming everywhere, eventually each Confederate state took some action to encourage food production by limiting the cotton and/or tobacco acreage. Some states imposed strict acreage limitations; others simply requested a voluntary limitation, the proclamation of Governor Vance's print-ed below being of this type. In response, a Warren County resolution asked farmers to plant no cotton and not more than "fifteen hundred hills of tobacco to each hand,"[3] and most other counties followed suit. The total program was successful, and the southern cotton crop of 1863 was only one-ninth that of 1860.

GOVERNOR VANCE'S APPEAL
TO THE PLANTERS OF NORTH CAROLINA

The peculiar calamities which often befall a nation struggling for its existence are about to come upon us in the shape of a scarcity of provisions and a threatened famine. While it is still believed there is enough in the country, if fairly distributed, it is certain there is none to spare, and there is danger that insufficient preparations will be made for the ensuing season, and that a considerable proportion of the labor of the country will be devoted to the production of crops other than breadstuffs.

. . . I have deemed it my duty to address you in this extraordinary manner, praying you of your own will avert it. And I am confident that the large-hearted patriotism—the wonderful generosity which last year filled to overflowing the storehouses of our quartermasters, in response to my call in behalf of our naked soldiers, has not yet deserted the farmers of North-Carolina.

By universal consent there is allowed to be but one danger to our speedy and triumphant success, and that is the failure of our provisions. Our victorious soldiers now constitute the best army in the world. Arms

3. Raleigh *State Journal*, 13 Apr. 1861.

and munitions are abundant. . . . Every thing depends now upon the industry and patriotism of the farmer. . . .

Without bread the soldier has neither strength nor courage. Without bread, the cries of his little ones at home will reach his ears . . . and cast a sickening chill to his heart. No bravery, no skill, nor device, nor human wisdom can cope with that dreaded enemy—Famine. . . .

And as the soldier who shirks the conflict and deserts his comrades in the hour of battle, is a coward or a traitor, as equally is he who withholds his hands from the plough, or guides it to the production of those crops which produce money and not bread. . . .

The bright sunshine again warms and dries the earth. We must use it to our salvation, or neglect it to our destruction. Plant, sow, dig and plough; corn, oats, potatoes—any thing and every thing which will support life. Let every body take to the fields, where the plough, not the maddening wheels of artillery, furrow the generous soil. These will prove the real fields of victory and independence. . . .

Let none be idle. And above all, my countrymen, let none plant cotton or tobacco. Though the prices are high, and the temptation great, your profits would be made from the blood of brave men and the suffering of helpless women and children. Your children and your children's children would reap an abundant and enduring harvest of scorn, and the remembrance of the manner in which your wealth was gained would burn into your conscience to the hour of death. . . . Ninety days will bring us to harvest, and I am confident we can reach it without actual suffering, if all parties will do his duty and Christianity prompt. Let all who have to spare divide liberally with those who have not. Sell to the county and State agents when your neighbors are supplied, and do not wait for it to be impressed. . . .

I earnestly recommend that meetings of the farmers and planters of each county of the State be held immediately to express their condemnation of cotton and tobacco planting, and to devise means of mutual aid and assistance in the trials of the coming season. Much good can be done in this way, and a wholesome public opinion set forth, more powerful, perhaps, to steer us past our impending dangers than the fines and penalties of a statute.

> Very respectfully, your obedient
> servant,
> J . B . V A N C E [sic]

Raleigh, April 2, 1863.

Moore, *The Rebellion Record*, 6:524–25.

---

(4) Price Control

The combination of scarcities and high prices made the terms "ex- *tortion" and "speculation" among the most common of the day. On*

11 December 1861 the convention ineffectively made it a misdemeanor to buy food or leather with "the intent to sell the same again at unreasonable prices. . . ."[4] On 11 October 1862 the Confederate exemption law attempted a more precise control by forbidding cotton and woolen manufacturers with exempt workers from making more than a 75 percent profit. The North Carolina legislature followed suit by putting a 100 percent tax on profits above 75 percent over the cost of production. Governor Vance then secured contracts as the one below (Document A) with all the cotton mills in the state, whereby the owners agreed to abide by the profit restriction and to sell the state a fixed part of their production. Vance had little success in getting similar agreements with the woolen manufacturers.

These efforts at price control were ineffective because no agreement could be reached on how to figure the cost of production.[5] Vance once ordered the draft of workers in two Gaston County mills accused of making excessive profits, but he only succeeded in curtailing production (Document B). As one purchasing agent expressed it, "we are in the hands of the manufacturers I fear without relief. . . ."[6]

A.

Fayetteville NC Nov 1, 1862

C. W. Garrett A G M.
    Dr Sir
    Yours of 31st ult to hand—We have called on M[r] Haigh and read your Letter to him of same date—
    The stockholders of the "Fayetteville Mill" have been consulted upon the subject of your proposition, and are willing to comply with the requirements of the State to the extent specified viz: furnish one third of the manufactured goods for its use at 75% on cost of production— Such compliance as we understand, securing to us the continued Services of any conscripts employed in the Mill—
    After we have furnished you say ten Bales, we shall then feel at liberty to dispose of the next twenty Bales to other customers, Some of which are crowded out who had special contracts with us previous to the reception of your orders
    As to the price, that we cannot name in this communication; some little figuring and estimates will have to be made before we could specify according to the requirements of the *"Exemption Act"*
    It may not be necessary to state, however that the cost of production has materially advanced within the past few months, as for instance,

    4. *Ordinances Passed by the State Convention, 1861–1862,* p. 22.
    5. For a good example of questions in the minds of those attempting to figure costs of production, see F. & F. Fries to Z. B. Vance, 13 Oct. 1862, Johnston, *Papers of Zebulon Vance,* 1:262–64.
    6. James Sloan to Captain John Devereux, 25 Dec. 1861, Civil War Collection, Quartermaster Department Correspondence.

the high rates of oil & leather, large quantities of which enter into the daily consumption in running the mill.

All this however will be fairly adjusted in short—the Law shall be *complied with*

> Yours truly
> J O H N S H A W Agent
> Fayetteville Mills

Civil War Collection, Quartermaster Department Correspondence.

B .

> Catawba Station N.C.
> March 30 1863

Capt. Wilson A. G. M.
        Raleigh N.C.

Sir Your favor of 20' ordering 3000 yds sheeting H. Hughes High Point was duly recd—We had the day of its Recpt sent Messrs Howard & Beard Salisbury 580 yds in previous orders but are unable to say at present when we can furnish any more, as the Superintendent and operatives have been conscripted and ordered off to camp, and without them can not run our mill at all, as there are no men over conscript age in the County but what are engaged that are competent to run and keep up repairs. The cause of their conscription we can not divine as we had complied with the requirements of the law on our part—but was not permitted to file an application with the Enrolling officer but directed to the Sec. War, where we met with a similar repulse he declining to consider any "original applications." So the door is shut to us on both sides —We have made application to Col. Mallett also hoping to finally succeed in finding some officer whose duty it is to give us the benefit of the law—and if we shall be so fortunate will take great pleasure in filling your orders as far as possible but in the mean time unless we can beg time of the Col of the Reg our men will be taken from us at a time when not only the state but the people at large are *greatly* in need of our labor —but if we are permitted to run will ship as [illegible] & apprise you of the same

> Very Respectfully
> Your most obt st
> P O W E L L & S H U F O R D

Civil War Collection, Quartermaster Department Correspondence.

---

(5) The Failure of Debtor Relief

In fairness to men in the army, the legislature on 11 May 1861   *forbade the sale of any property for nonpayment of debt unless by* the consent of both parties. This indefinite postponement of all collection of debts was patently unfair to creditors, and on 12 September it was repealed. Proponents of another, but this time a fairer, stay law then demanded that the state convention take some action at its November session. Oppo-

nents of a stay law were meanwhile arguing that it "vastly depreciates every kind of property"[7] and that it violated the "good order of society."[8] Despite arguments like the one included below, neither the convention nor the legislature gave debtors any further relief.

Mr. Editor.—As the Convention is now in session . . . I am pained to see so little in favor of some means of relief for a class of people who are unfortunately in debt at this terrible juncture, many of whom are serving as common soldiers in the army of the Confederate States. . . . I am unable to see how any man can take a different position without evincing a want of either information or sympathy touching the class for which such laws are intended. . . . What is the use of fine spun theories on the operations of stay laws at a time like the present? We have facts to deal with. One fact is, that our people . . . are more or less in debt. When the debts they now owe were contracted they were not apprised that men in high places were plotting a dissolution of the Union. . . . Unexpectedly these men are called upon to leave everything near and dear to them, and take up arms in their country's defence. Now sir, when these men return (if ever) shall they find that a foe as bad or worse than the one they have been facing, has devastated their homes, and that their wives and children are homeless? . . . But the opponents of the law tell us of a large class of individuals whose means consists in notes, and talk about their barefooted children, and their debtors snapping their fingers in their faces, &c. . . . If this class demands our especial care and sympathy, who is to take care of the man who . . . bought land in flush times to provide a home for his family? He pays what little money he can raise and gives his note for the balance. The war comes upon him. He has worked hard and made many improvements on the premises. Suppose he is pressed on his note, what becomes of him? . . . I honestly believe if the sheriffs . . . were turned loose upon the people at this time that it would produce a revolution; and who could blame the class, whom it is well known are doing most of the hard work in this war. I heard of a remark made by a very honest man some time ago, when he expected his property to be forced into market at a cash sale, that if everything he had was to be sacrificed at a time like this, he would as soon that Lincoln had it as any body else. . . . I say let the people sustain the government, and let the government protect the people. . . . I was called on yesterday by a lad with a message from his father, to know if I could let him have $250. I asked what was the matter. He said the sheriff had filed on all of Uncle ———'s negroes, and if the money

7. B. F. Moore to Thomas Ruffin, 27 Sept. 1861, Hamilton, *Papers of Thomas Ruffin*, 3:189.
8. Raleigh *Standard*, 29 Jan. 1862.

is not paid they would have to be taken to town Monday to be sold. This *Uncle* has been in the army since June, and is at this time dangerously ill, I am informed, at Manassas. J .

Raleigh *Standard*, 4 Dec. 1861.

---

(6) State Aid to Production at Home

Despite the fact that the needs of the army seemed bottomless, the state did not completely neglect the more simple needs of domestic production. Widespread state aid to the general economy was beyond the economics of the day, but occasionally the state helped solve problems caused by the war. Farm tools wore out rapidly and Governor Vance sometimes used space on the Advance *to import replacements. The fact that Paul C. Cameron, wealthy railroad president and agriculturalist of Hillsboro, suffered from such shortages (Document A) indicates their universality. Among the supplies brought from England were 60,000 cotton and wool cards and wire for repairing them. The governor's office was flooded with requests from women for new cards, and Vance's aide had to allocate them rigidly (Document B). One contemporary wrote that she had "seen tears of thankfulness running down the cheeks of our soldiers' wives on receiving a pair of these cards by which alone they were to clothe and procure bread for themselves and their children."[9]*

A .

Hillsboro N.C. Jany 27th 64

Dear Sir

It may be that your provident foresight may have anticipated the suggestion that I now make & in which as a citizen & farmer I feel no little interest—We shall be put to it to save our crops & small grain & hay unless we can obtain by the first of June an importation of *Sythe & mowing blades*—We have had no addition to the old Stock—now pretty well worn out—May we hope for a distribution of cotton cards! . . .

With best wishes
Yours very truly
PAUL C. CAMERON

I have ordered ten thousand scythe blades &c
Z B V

Governors' Papers.

9. Cornelia P. Spencer, *The Last Ninety Days of the War in North Carolina*, p. 20.

B. GEORGE LITTLE TO THOMAS RUFFIN

Raleigh 28 Oct., 1863

Your letter to Gov. Vance has been received in his absence to Asheville to look after the troubles in that vicinity, I make a reply.

There are a few cotton cards here, which the Governor deemed advisable to keep on hand, until another arrival, which it is hoped will be in a few days. And then he will commence to distribute them to the various Counties, through such agencies as you suggest responsible and reliable private persons, when properly recommended, or the officers (*civil*) of the Several Counties. I shall take occasion to keep the Governor reminded of the name of Col. Gant as a suitable person, for your County.

As Alamance is the first county in alphabetical order, she will stand a chance to be first supplied.

Hamilton, *Papers of Thomas Ruffin*, 3:342.

---

(7) Meeting the Salt Scarcity

The per capita consumption of salt in the antebellum South had been fifty pounds a year, it being used chiefly in diet, preserving, and the tanning of hides. Though the South had bought most of its salt from the North, it could have supplied itself during the war by boiling sea water and from saline artesian wells, but labor and transportation problems, compounded by speculation, created a serious shortage in many areas. On 6 December 1861 the North Carolina Convention ordered the appointment of a salt commissioner to make salt wherever he thought best and to deliver it at cost to the justices of the peace, who were then to distribute it fairly to the people.[10] John Milton Worth, planter and businessman of Randolph County, was the first commissioner, and he was succeeded by his nephew Daniel G. Worth. After being driven from Currituck Sound and then from Morehead City, the commissioners finally located their works eight miles from Wilmington in an area where enemy vessels could not approach and where private manufacturers were already operating. The state saltworks lasted here until 15 November 1864, when General W. H. C. Whiting, then in charge of the area's defenses, ordered it closed and the workers drafted. His stated purpose was that most of the workers were members of the Heroes of America and were relaying information to the enemy, but he may simply have wanted the men for his army. The following is a report to Governor Vance by Commissioner J. M. Worth.

10. In 1862 the state also negotiated a contract with Virginia for enough saltwater from the Saltville wells to make 300,000 bushels a year. Nicholas W. Woodfin was in charge of this operation and he contracted with Stuart, Buchanan & Co. to prepare the salt. An account of the beginning of this operation may be found in the Fayetteville *Observer*, 22 Sept. 1862.

Wilmington Sept. 19th. 1862

An ordinance of the Convention passed about the 1st. Dec. last making an appropriation for the purpose of manufacturing salt makes it my duty to report to you monthly. To enable you to understand the whole thing, I will go back to the beginning. Immediately after my appointment as Commissioner I visited the coast & found the most eligible places at Morehead City & Currituck Sound & was prepared to make one hundred Bu salt per day when Newbern fell. I had done nothing at Currituck Sound but bargained for Supplies. I lost all the pans I had & was thrown back to a ground start at Wilmington. Private individuals had already engaged in the manufacture of salt much more extensively here than at any other place in the State or on the Coast. Prices of everything was already high & it was very difficult to get the pans & other material. The extreme high prices of Salt induced private parties to pay most extravagant prices & to step in when I had contracts for pans & other material & bid two or three prices & get them away from me. With all these difficulties I have only been able to make up to this time a little over two hundred Bu Salt per day, which will be increased to two hundred & fifty Bu with what pans I now have. I am now paying from $1— to $1⁵⁰ pr cord for wood on the Stump two miles distant from the works & should be entirely unable to get the teaming done so as to sell the salt at any reasonable price but for the exemption from military duty of the hands. I have furnished all the counties in the State with from two to four hundred Bu Salt . . . at from 3 to 4 dollars per Bu—Private parties have gotten from 8 to 13 dollars for all the salt they have made. . . . Although I condemn extortion I think it fortunate for the country that salt went so high early in the season, for there has been & continues to be a perfect rush from all quarters to get into the business. . . . There is now about 1800 Bu salt made per day here, which will be increased to 2500 by Oct. 15th. I understand Mr Woodfin promises to make 200 Bu pr day for the State. If that be true & the Salt be kept in the State it will soon be abundant at far less prices—4000 Bu pr day would in 100 days give every inhabitant in the state 20 lbs—We have just 100 days before the pork season is over. . . . There has been a great deal of Salt brought in from Virginia & several small cargoes ran the blockade, all of which has gone to the country & there is a large number of persons supplied, yet the great fear of the article being short makes them (the supplied) very quiet on the subject & leaves it very difficult to tell who or how many are supplied. The difficulty & expense of making salt increases rapidly as the distance to team the wood increases. I am now trying to bring the water 2½ miles into the woods. If I succeed it will be a great advantage. I have many letters from county agents saying the salt is doing great good for the soldiers families; but all speak of the quantity being insufficient. . . . I have about 200 men that are liable to military duty who are exempt by an ordinance of the State Convention; one third of whom are quakers, whom at my suggestion Gov Clark directed me to take at the time of the draft, another third are all men of limited means, who furnish their own teams, the other third are men of weak constitutions & men that are afraid of the board of surgeons & would be of no use in the

Army & are but little use to me. If the teams were taken from me I would be helpless. . . . The teamsters work for 3^{50} per day finding themselves & teams . . . while private parties pay $6—for the same Service, so that they are contributing more to the Country by far than could be got from them in the field. . . . I could have been making more salt if I had been regardless of the cost of making it but could see no advantage in outbidding private parties thereby making the State salt cost the people as much as if they bought it from private individuals. . . . I feel confident that if this place does not fall into the enemies hands we will have enough salt to squeeze through.

All of which is respectfully submitted

Johnston, *Papers of Zebulon Baird Vance*, 1 : 206–9.

XI

BEARING THE COSTS OF WAR

WARTIME FINANCE

During the first days of the Confederacy its best financial minds asserted that most expenses of government could be met by the income from a moderate revenue tariff. Until that machinery could be set up they expected to meet expenses with an issue of $1 million of Treasury notes and a loan by means of a $15 million bond issue. The outbreak of war ended this delusion, but in most unimaginative fashion Secretary of the Treasury Christopher G. Memminger steered the Davis administration into merely expanding rather than changing the lines already taken. Consequently the financial history of the Confederacy was marked by consecutive issues of notes and bonds into the hundreds of millions. Since the Treasury notes were backed only by faith in the government's promise to redeem them in gold after the war, their value steadily declined, and the spiraling inflation that resulted wrecked havoc on public and private finance. This same inflation made government bonds a poor investment, and by mid-1863 Congress began trying to force people to buy bonds by making older Treasury notes worthless after a certain date. But even the threat of repudiation failed to halt the deterioration of the currency.

Inevitably the Confederacy had to devise more practical methods of obtaining income. The produce loans allowed planters to pledge part of their crops to the purchase of bonds; Congress began to levy a variety of taxes; and in April 1863, it levied a 10 percent tax in kind on food crops.

North Carolina's financial record during the Civil War was no more imaginative than that of the national government. In all, the convention and the General Assembly authorized $13,131,500 in bonds and $20,-400,000 in Treasury notes. By November 1864, a $100 state bond sold for $7.40 and even this was better than the performance of Confederate bonds. The counties borrowed approximately $20 million, most of which was used to aid destitute families of soldiers. The tax rate on real estate was raised from one-fifth of one percent to one percent; and slaves, inheritance, and income were added to the list of subjects taxed. By 1864 the tax income had doubled, but as inflation had eroded both state and national currency so badly by this time, the tax burden was actually diminishing. Both state and nation seem to have been managing their finances only in the hope that victory would come before bankruptcy.

---

(1) The Effect of Inflation on Banking

Both state and national governments issued interest-bearing as well as non-interest-bearing Treasury notes. The former were issued in large denominations and were transferable only by endorsement, the intention being to curb inflation by making them such an attractive investment that people would save rather than spend them. But in January 1862, serious objections arose in the General Assembly to a bill proposing a new issue of $3 million of notes bearing 6 percent interest and redeemable in four years. Its opponents argued that people would not hold them as an investment when coupon bonds bearing the same interest and payable semiannually were a better investment; and that neither banks nor businesses wished to bother with tabulating the accrued interest each time anyone wished to spend one.[1] These arguments prevailed, but as the letter below illustrates, banks also disliked having large amounts of non-interest-bearing notes lying in their vaults and steadily depreciating in value. The authors of the letter, Francis and Henry William Fries of Salem, were among the state's most successful manufacturers of cotton and woolen goods.

Salem N.C. Feby 7th '62

Judge T. Ruffin
Gov. Wm. A. Graham.
  Raleigh, N.C.
  Dear Sirs.—
    . . . When the Quartermaster advised us that from that date he could pay only in Treasury notes issued under a former ordinance of the Convention, and bearing interest; we were content to receive such payment. First, we were willing to carry as large a portion of those notes, as our means and business would permit; secondly, we felt confident that by parting with them to individuals seeking investments, or making some arrangement with the Bank, we could convert a sufficient amount into available funds to enable us to carry on our business. The recent action of the Convention however in striking out the interest features of these notes, caused us serious uneasiness. We saw, or thought we saw, that if

---

1. For a good description of the discussion on this question, see Journal of David Schenck, 4:204–6.

in addition to the already inflated currency of our State, three or four millions of Treasury notes must be forced upon the community as circulation, without the safety valve of having at least a portion absorbed as investments, there was great reason to fear an explosion. Our judgment told us that those banks that have a scrupulous eye to their own solvency and the public welfare must . . . decline to take indiscriminate general deposites. Hoping that our apprehensions might not be well founded, we at once went to the cashier of the Bank at this place to inquire whether he would take these new Treasury notes on deposite, and give us on our checks such currency as would be available to us. We, however, found him entertaining the same views and fears that harrowed our breast. He has now a large mass of currency in his vaults, which brings the Bank no advantage, and he felt himself constrained, with the lights before him, to decline swelling his deposites by taking in these Treasury notes. We forthwith addressed the Prest. of the Bank of N. Carolina and requested to open a deposite account with this institution for such funds as we might receive from the state. He . . . felt constrained to decline opening such account. Though our judgment approves his decision . . . we are now left in an extremely embarrassing condition. To close our transactions with our State department brings no inconvenience to us as manufacturers . . . but as citizens of N. Car. it is painful to us to refuse to work for the State. . . . We might work up our present stock and let the State have the cloth, and in the end have our pockets full of Treasury notes, and our mills standing idle for want of material, nearly all of which must be brought from beyond the limits of the State, and for the purchase of which, these new Treasury notes, unless bankable and convertable, will avail us nothing. . . .

Our intercourse with the Quartermaster department leaves no room for complaint . . . but the late action of the Convention leaves them powerless. For our part we are anxious to do our full part . . . but we doubt whether the closing of our mills in the manner above pointed out, would benefit the country any, whilst at the same time it would be very disastrous to ourselves. Now we think you have the case, and we sincerely hope that you may point out to us the way in which we may reconcile our views as manufacturers with our feelings and earnest desires as citizens of the State. We will delay giving the Quartermaster our ultimatum until we hear from you. . . .

Respectfully

FR. FRIES

H. W. FRIES

Hamilton, *Papers of Thomas Ruffin*, 3:211–12.

---

(2) Confederate Inflation Controls

By the spring of 1863 the war's end was nowhere in sight, and the *blithe confidence that fiat money would suffice had ended. The orig-*

inal expectation was that people would invest their surplus cash in government bonds, but only about $3,500,000 a month were actually sold, an amount not even approaching that of the new notes being poured into circulation. To force people to buy bonds with the redundant currency, Congress enacted the funding law outlined below, while the states made Confederate Treasury notes receivable for all state taxes. But the system did not work. All notes were eventually redeemable in specie after the war, and until then currency holders could invest them in anything more profitably than in bonds. All currency continued to circulate, therefore, at a constantly diminishing value. In the letter below State Treasurer Jonathan Worth is instructing sheriffs and tax collectors how to act until it was seen how far the legislature would support the Confederate funding law. Worth himself feared that forced funding would "take away the little vitality now in the present currency,"[2] and soon Governor Vance was receiving complaints that "there is some men in the cuntray that is refusing to take Confederate Money of any instance. . . ."[3]

TREASURER'S OFFICE, ⎱
Raleigh, N.C. June 13, 1863, ⎰

To the Sheriffs and Tax Collectors of North Carolina:

Under the act of the Confederate Congress of the 23d March last, relating to the funding of Confederate Treasury notes, these fundable notes are divided into three classes:

1. Those dated prior to December 1st. 1862.
2. Those dated between 1st December, 1862, and 6th April, 1863.
3. Those dated on and after 6th April, 1863.

The first class is fundable in 7 *per cent.* bonds until the 1st August next, after which they are not fundable at all.

The second class are also fundable in 7 *per cent.* bonds until the 1st August next, after which they are fundable in 4 *per cents.*

The third class are fundable for one year from the first day of the month printed in red ink across the face of them in 6 *per cent.* bonds, after which they are fundable in 4 *per cents*

The faith of the Confederate government is pledged for the ultimate payment on all of these issues, and all of them are receivable in payment of taxes and other dues to the Confederate government at any time. . . .

The second section of ordinance No. 35, February session of our Convention, compels you to receive any Confederate notes in payment of taxes, and gives me no power to forbid you to receive any class of it; and as it may turn out that the effect of the act of Congress may be to make one or both of the first mentioned classes of notes uncurrent after the 1st of August, whereby the State and County Treasuries may be supplied with unavailable money, the Governor, with the advice of his Council,

2. Jonathan Worth to Daniel Worth, 10 Feb. 1864, Hamilton, *The Correspondence of Jonathan Worth,* 1:294.

3. J. M. Galloway to Z. B. Vance, 27 Aug. 1863, Governors' Papers.

has ordered an extra session of the General Assembly to convene on the 30th inst., to consider and decide what ought to be done in the premises.

It is expected, therefore, that you will abstain from collecting taxes in the old issues until the action of the Legislature shall be known.

In the mean time there should be no panic among the people on this subject. All have an opportunity to fund till the 1st of August, and to pay the large tax to the Confederate government in these notes; and if the General Assembly should decide to continue to receive the issues of the second class, which will continue to be nearly as good as those of the third class, after the 1st of August, the people will not be incommoded materially, in paying the State and County taxes. . . .

Until you receive further instructions, you are, therefore, advised to receive only in payment of State and county taxes, the Treasury notes of this State, the notes of all the Banks of this State, gold and silver coins, and Confederate Treasury notes dated on and after 6th of April, 1863, and the interest bearing Treasury notes of the Confederate States.

Very respectfully,
JONATHAN WORTH,
Public Treasurer

Wilmington *Journal*, 18 June 1863.

---

(3) The Produce Loan

One of the few successful Confederate loans was an early one designed to appeal to the patriotism of the planters. On 16 May 1861 Congress authorized the secretary of the treasury to issue $50 million of bonds "to be sold for specie, military stores, or for the proceeds of sales of raw produce or manufactured articles, to be paid in the form of specie or with foreign bills of exchange. . . ."[4] Secretary Memminger designated, with the advice of Governor Ellis, P. K. Dickinson, O. G. Parsley, and William A. Wright as North Carolina's "Central Board of Commissioners" to administer the law. They divided the state into eleven districts and appointed three local commissioners in each district to solicit subscriptions. The form letter below was sent to each district commissioner, and they in turn appealed to the planters, with gratifying results. The fact that William S. Pettigrew, one of the wealthiest planters in eastern North Carolina, was designated commissioner might indicate that the Central Board was trying to attach as much prestige to the system as possible.

4. James M. Matthews, ed., *Statutes at Large of the Provisional Government of the Confederate States of America*, pp. 117–18.

TREASURY DEPARTMENT,
C.S.A.
Richmond, June 18, 1861

Wᵐ S Pettigrew Esq
  Scuppernong P O
    Washington Co N C

Sir: The Congress of the Confederate States at its last session passed an act authorizing the issue of bonds for the proceeds of the sale of raw produce and manufactured articles.

It has been deemed advisable in carrying out this law to circulate, in advance, lists for subscription in which every planter can indicate the portion of his crop which he is disposed to lend for the support of the Government. It is proposed that no disturbance shall be made of the usual arrangements of each planter for selling his crop; but that he shall simply indicate the portion he is willing to subscribe, the time and place of delivery, and the factor in whose hands it is placed for sale; and shall order the factor to exchange the proceeds of sale of the subscribed portion for Confederate Bonds bearing 8 per cent. interest.

Several of these lists are herewith sent to you, and you are requested to act as Commissioners in bringing the same to the attention of the people of your District or County. You will use your discretion as to the best mode of bringing the matter forward; but it is suggested that it would be desirable to use any public occasion, and to induce as many gentlemen as you can to make individual applications to their fellow-citizens.

As soon as you shall have procured as many signatures as you can to any one list, you will please forward it to this Department. To provide against loss of any list, it is desirable that they should be signed in Duplicate, and forwarded by different mails.

Respectfully,
C. G. MEMMINGER
Secretary of Treasury.

Pettigrew Family Papers.

---

(4) The Tax in Kind

While the Confederate government never mustered the courage to impose heavy monetary taxation upon a resistant citizenry, the tax law of 24 April 1863 contained a device that yielded great quantities of goods for army use and foreign trade. After reserving specified amounts for his own use, each farmer and planter had to deliver to a nearby post-quartermaster's depot one-tenth of his slaughtered hogs and also one-tenth of most of his crops. Not only did having to pay in kind prevent producers from exploiting the market, but they were being taxed at a rate far higher than those who were assessed a monetary tax. By June 1864, North Carolina producers had paid 3 million pounds of bacon, 770,000 bushels of wheat, 75,000 tons of hay, and other produce worth $150,000.

However profitable this tax might have been to the Confederacy, producers argued with considerable truth that it dangerously threatened their small food reserves. Even such a relatively wealthy planter as Jonathan Worth instructed his overseer: "Feed the cows no more with meal, unless to keep them alive. I give up the butter project."[5] To add insult to injury, the Confederacy's deteriorating transportation facilities often caused perishable goods to be left rotting at the depot. The following editorial reveals what sometimes happened to accumulations of hay, even though lack of forage was a major army problem.

PUBLIC FORAGE

The Government hay, fodder, &c., stacked at this place last year, is going to waste in the most shameful manner. Our people paid the tithe tax with more or less willingness as they were able to spare the produce, and if they can have a reasonable hope that it will be properly taken care of and appropriated to the public use, will continue to do so, hard as it was in some cases when a man had no more than his own necessities required. But if they afterwards see it going to waste as it is here at the forage yard, and have reason to fear, also, that the tithe corn is run into the mammoth distillery on the East side of this town, their good disposition on the subject will forsake them, and they will become offended. Can't President Davis issue some order that will make the responsible agents in these matters do their duty? We understand that thousands of pounds of hay have already been wasted. The cattle of this town feed on it at will, (for it is in a common) and tramp and spoil more than they eat. War, every one knows, is a great waster, and the Southern people will doubtless submit to it as an incident inseparable from their condition with as much patience as any people in the world. But they have long been in the habit of requiring agents to render an account, and they will continue to hold them responsible for the faithful performance of the public duties for which they are hired and paid. . . . Let President Davis *slash* around among them with a vigorous hand, and the people will stand right square up to him, and all our affairs will prosper.

Salisbury *Daily Carolina Watchman*, 4 Apr. 1864.

5. To James Russell, 22 Apr. 1864, Hamilton, *Correspondence of Jonathan Worth*, 1:305–6.

(5) State Taxation

By 1864 North Carolina state taxes had reached their peak. The property tax had risen from 20¢. to $1 on each $100 valuation, and numerous new taxes had been added. In his own patronizing way the editor of the Fayetteville Observer *explained to his readers in the article below what and when taxes must be paid.*

A very large tax is to be paid to the Government . . . in a few days. This tax to be at once paid is 10 per cent. on "all profits made in 1863 by buying and selling spiritous liquors, flour, wheat, corn, rice, sugar, molasses or syrup, salt, bacon, pork, hogs, beef or beef cattle, sheep, oats, hay, fodder, raw hides, leather, horses, mules, boots, shoes, cotton yarns, wool, woolen, cotton or mixed cloths, hats, wagons, harness, coal, iron, steel or nails." Also, 10 per cent. on "all profits made by buying and selling money, gold, silver, foreign exchange, stocks, notes, debts, credits, or obligations of any kind, and any merchandise, property or effects of any kind not enumerated above." Also, 25 per cent. on all "profits exceeding 25 per cent. made during 1863, by any bank or banking company, insurance, canal, navigation, importing and exporting, telegraph, express, railroad, manufacturing, dry dock, or other joint stock company of any description, whether incorporated or not." These taxes are to be paid in the notes about [sic] $5 at their par value, dollar for dollar. Every man who has paid his taxes due in January . . . knows exactly the profits taxed 10 or 25 per cent. . . . as the case may be, and [let him] go to work to collect (or hold if now in possession) notes above $5 to an amount sufficient to pay these taxes. *They will be needed,* for the tax will absorb very many millions of dollars—in this community alone hundreds of thousands of dollars of these large notes will be needed for this purpose. There will be no need of "funding" them, an operation which is unfortunately understood by comparatively few. Mr. Hardie and his co-laborers elsewhere will "fund" them very rapidly and most effectually. We think this is plain enough for the dullest comprehension, and hope to hear no more of panic-stricken people trying to rid themselves of the notes or refusing to receive them.

Next. There is a large tax due on the 1st of April. This is the quarterly business tax of 2½ per cent. on all sales made during January, February and March. There is no man who cannot tell with . . . accuracy what his sales are or will be for the quarter. His taxes are to be paid by means of these notes above $5. Not, if the tax-payer is wise, in the notes themselves; for if he does so pay the notes will be received only at 66⅔ cts. on the dollar. The remedy is: find out the amount of your tax, take your notes above $5, leave them with the Depositary, (Mr. Broadfoot here,) receive in exchange a certificate of such deposite, and on the first of April pay the tax with it, *dollar for dollar.* . . .

Next again: On the 1st of June comes the big tax of all. On that day is due 5 per cent. on "the value of property, real, personal and mixed, of every kind and description, not exempted or taxed at a different rate;" 10 per cent. on "the value of gold and silver wares, and plate, jewels, jewelry and watches; 5 per cent. on the value of all shares or interests held in any bank, banking company or association, canal, navigation, importing, exporting, insurance, manufacturing, telegraph, express, railroad, and dry dock companies and all other joint stock companies of every kind whether incorporated or not; upon the amount of all gold and silver coin, gold dust, gold or silver bullion, whether held by the banks or other corporations or individuals, and upon all moneys held abroad, or upon the amount of all bills of exchange, drawn therefor on foreign countries; upon the amount of all solvent credits, and of all bank bills and all other papers issued as currency, exclusive of non-interest bearing Confederate treasury notes, and not employed in a registered business, the income derived from which is taxed."

Now to find out your tax due in June 1st, refer to your taxes in 1860 and see what all your property which you still hold was valued at; 5 per cent. on the amount will show the amount of Confederate notes needed for the purpose, *except* in cases where property has been bought since Jan'y 1st, 1862, when it is 5 per cent. on the price paid for it, and in stocks, when it is 5 per cent. on the market value. What then shall every man, town or county do? Find out about what his June tax is—an easy operation—take the notes to a Depositary, receive a certificate, and on the 1st June pay your taxes with it *dollar for dollar*.

Next: the quarterly business tax for July 1, and October 1 of 2½ per cent. on sales. These can be estimated for with an approach to accuracy, and are to be provided for in the same way by exchanging the amount in notes for 4 per cent. bonds or certificates.

Fayetteville *Observer*, 25 Febr. 1864.

THE IMPRESSMENT OF ARMY SUPPLIES

Sometimes groups of soldiers on active duty found that arbitrary seizure was the only practical method of obtaining certain necessary army supplies. This was particularly true of food and forage. Transportation deficiencies were partly responsible for these shortages, but speculation seems to have been the chief cause. Farmers would withhold their produce from sale in anticipation of rising prices, and when goods finally reached market the army commissary agents would have to compete with civilians for their purchase, forcing prices even higher. As early as 1861 some field commanders were assigning special impressment agents to seize produce either on the farm or en route to market, paying for it whatever they considered a fair price. Often these agents simply seized what their army needed at the moment, chiefly food but at times horses, wagons, and even slaves. Abuses in this system seem to have been quite common: failing to concede the owner any profit, taking food needed on the farms, concentrating impressments in the more accessible areas, and many others.

On 26 March 1863 Congress finally attempted to regulate army impressments. Prices for goods held by the producer were to be determined by agent and owner on the spot; prices on goods held for resale were set by a state commissioner who published his price schedules in the newspapers. Disagreements between producers and impressers were to be settled by "disinterested" ad hoc appraising committees, though in disputes involving scheduled prices the impressing officer could appeal to the state commissioner. Vicinage arbitration generally provided near market prices for goods taken from producers, but prices of scheduled goods were often ridiculously low. Despite a resolution of the North Carolina legislature on 1 February 1865 that the state commissioners should "allow the market price for articles at the time and place of impressment,"[6] and similar pressure from other states, the law remained in effect and without radical revision until 18 March 1865. It proved to be, from the army's standpoint, one of the most successful of all Confederate laws.

---

(1) Early Impressment Abuses

Before Congress began regulating impressments the chief complaint was against the arbitrariness of the so-called "hog-impressers." These abuses occurred most frequently in outlying districts of the state where supply depots were often inconveniently far away. Early in 1863 Governor Vance received a letter stating that "a troop of 500 cavalry, or men with old worn out horses, are traversing every part of Burke, Caldwell, McDowell and are now on their way to Rutherford and Polk Counties, in search of all the corn they can find."[7] Vance relayed the complaint to the War Department, commenting that "When the ques-

tion of starvation is narrowed down to women and children on the one side and some worthless cavalry horses on the other I can have no difficulty in making a choice."[8] The accused officer vowed that "he has impressed forage from but two men in N.C., and that these men were speculators, and were unwilling to sell grain to the Government at any price."[9] Upon investigation Vance found that conditions were worse than reported, so he reiterated his protests in the letter of 21 March printed below. As might have been expected, little was, or could have been, done for the long-suffering populace.

6. *Public Laws of the State of North Carolina Passed by the General Assembly at the Adjourned Session of 1865*, p. 36.
7. R. L. Abernethy to Z. B. Vance, 20 Febr. 1863, Governors' Papers.
8. Z. B. Vance to J. A. Seddon, 25 Febr. 1863, *Official Records*, Ser. 1, 18:895.
9. A. F. Cook to Major General Samuel Jones, 3 Febr. 1863, Governors' Letter Books.

STATE OF NORTH CAROLINA,
EXECUTIVE DEPARTMENT,
Raleigh, N.C., March 21, 1863

Hon. JAMES A. SEDDON,
    Secretary of War:

SIR: Yours of 7th instant, inclosing letters from Lieutenant-Colonel Cook and General Jones, in relation to impressment of forage by a detachment of General Jenkins' cavalry, has been received. I am sorry to see that the charge of impressment is denied upon the authority of Sergeant Hale. The concurrent testimony of the citizens of about twenty counties with at least fifty letters to that effect in my office would seem to be sufficient to establish a fact of general notoriety. Those men were in several detachments, operating in as many different counties, and Sergeant Hale hardly could know what they were all doing at the same time. Their method was to go to a farmer's house and tell him they wanted corn at $1.50 per bushel, and if he did not sell it they would take it. In some instances their quartermaster attended public sales and publicly notified the assemblage (most of them families of absent soldiers) that they need not bid for the corn; that they were determined to have it. Yielding where resistance would have been useless they (the cavalry) took the corn at such price as they saw proper to pay, and this is not impressment! I beg leave also to assure you that the imputations indulged in by General Jones and Lieutenant-Colonel Cook against the loyalty of the people of that region (I suppose also upon the authority of Sergeant Hale) are entirely without foundation in fact, the refusal to take Confederate money, if such was the case, originating solely in the fact that they did not have the corn to sell. Neither North Carolina money nor gold could buy an article which was not in the country. That country, to my personal knowledge, may safely challenge any similar region in the South to show a better muster-roll in the army. But that is not the matter at issue. I complain that a large body of broken-down cavalry horses are in North Carolina, eating up the subsistence of the people in a region desolated by drought and reduced to the verge of starvation; impressing it at prices about one-half the market rates. The people or the horses must suffer. I ask for the removal of the horses. Is it denied or refused? That is the question. I beg leave to disabuse your mind of the impression which it seems to entertain, that I objected to these impressments because they were for Virginia cavalry. By no means. I did not term them such, at least did not so intend to term them. I have no prejudice against the troops from any State engaged in defending the common cause, but I am unwilling to see the bread taken from the mouths of women and children for the use of any troops, when those troops might be easily removed to regions where there is corn to sell, and I earnestly request once more that they may be so removed.

Very respectfully,
your obedient servant,
Z. B. VANCE

Official Records, Ser. 1, 18:934–35.

(2) The Danger to Goods in Transit

While the law of 26 March 1863 brought some order into a haphazard system, it made foodstuff in transit even more enticing to army agents, who would assume that only speculators would be moving wagon loads of food from one county to another. Consequently, those responsible for feeding large numbers of people, such as factory owners, planters, or school principals would need permits to ensure their purchases from impressment en route (Document A). On the other hand, commanding officers disliked seeing food removed from the environs of their camp, and Document B shows the concern of one such commander.

A .

Salem N.C. Dec 13ᵗʰ/64

His Excellency
   Gov. Z. B. Vance
     Raleigh N.C.
      My Dear Sir
      May I trespass upon your time & kindness to beg your assistance in procuring "Permits" from the Confed & State authorities to purchase & carry away supplies, especially of Pork & Corn from the Eastern Counties of our State for our Institution. Unless I shall be permitted to draw supplies from abroad I fear I shall not be able to keep up the school. In view of the fact that there are but few schools like ours still existing & that we have under our care so many *homeless young ladies* from *all parts of* the Confederacy, I trust the authorities will grant me permission to procure such supplies of corn & pork and I would very respectfully beg of you to help me in getting such permits—I have requested Dr. Wm Wheeler who returns to Raleigh today to hand this to you & he has consented to try upon your recommendation to get permits for me from the Commanding general at Goldsboro.

            I am very respectfully
            Your obᵗ Servt
            R O Bᵗ D E S C H W E I N I T Z
              Pres. S[alem] F[emale]
              A[cademy]

Governors' Papers.

B .

        Head Quarters 1ˢᵗ Brigade N. C. H. Guards
        Burnsville—Yancy County N.C.
        October 28ᵗʰ 1863

Gov. Z. B. Vance
    I received the communication sent you from high Shoals Iron works

dated October 21ˢᵗ. 1863, and also your reference on the back of it and it now becomes my duty to give you a fare statement of the facts in the case. When it became apparent that a force would have to be raised and kept up in this mountain Country, so long as the Yankees held East Tennessee or be over run I at once ordered my Quartermaster and Comissary to commence laying in Supplies, but no Beef cattle could be bought only where men would bring in one at the time and sell us the Beef and keep the hide for the reason that speculators wer giveing forty and forty forty cents when the Government price was only 28 and 30 cents per pound of course none could be bought for our soldiers. Capt Chandler told me he wanted to buy some cattle that he would pay a high price &.C. I told him plainly I would suffer no Cattle drove out of the counties That Troops had to be kept here for the defence of the State and it would take all the provisions that were here to support the troops. That we had to depend entirely on our own resources. That no supplies could be furnished us by Railroad and that no provisions of any kind should be caried out of these mountain Counties—he left this county and went to Mitchell and was buying all the cattle he could there—When I ordered D. M. Young my C. S. not to allow him to take the cattle out of the county, Capt Young in obedeance to my order impressed the cattle and recepted for them at the Government price and kept the cattle for the use of the soldiers and I have ordered several other lots impressed in the same way, a part of them on my own order and a part under a General order from Brigadier Gen R. B. Vance published in the Ashville news. I do not know whether any one has complained of the matter but Chandler or not, one thing is certain if I had not have persued the course I did there would not have been Beef Cattle enoughf left to have supported the force that will be required here one week, and I concidered it at the time and does yet, a case of needcesity for it was utterly impoable to buy cattle at the fixt Government price. and speculators biding up at the same time ten and fifteen cents per lb more. Therefore I shal hold the cattle so impressed and impress all that an attempt is made to be run out of the County at the same time haveing due regard for your instructions 25 and 30 cts per lb for beef ought to be sufficient to satisfy the most avaritious of the human family. . . .

> Very Respectfully
> Your Obt Servant
> J. W. MCELROY
> Brig. Genl 1ˢᵗ Brigade
> N C Home Guards

Governors' Papers.

---

(3) Continuing Impressment Abuses

Despite legislation and War Department directives, need and/or callousness caused all too many authorized impressment officers and even unauthorized enlisted men to seize indiscriminately whatever they needed. One complainant wrote, "These things are seldom done by actual violence, but with such a parade of numbers & a show of determination, as to disarm resistance & ensure compliance." He added that the "more ignorant classes are utterly intimidated & submit to any treatment. . . ."[10] Governor Vance wrote the War Department that "if God Almighty had yet in store another plague worse than all others . . . to have let loose on the Egyptians . . . it must have been a regiment or so of half-armed, half-disciplined Confed-erate cavalry,"[11] and the legislature asked him "to put a stop to all such illegal proceedings and public nuisances."[12] But neither the department nor Vance had much success. Men from the commands of Generals John C. Vaughn, Joe Wheeler, John H. Morgan, and James Longstreet were particularly ruthless. Tyre York was a planter, physician, and future congressman of Wilkes County, and his description (Document A) of the unbridled rapacity of some of these soldiers must have carried some weight in Raleigh. Document B is a typical War Department rejoinder to Vance's many letters of complaint.

A.

Trap Hill N C
May 5 1864

To His Excellency
    Gov. Vance
        Dr Sir

As we have been badly imposed upon throughout this & adjoining Counties I have concluded to write your Excellency a few lines concerning the matter—Last week a detachment of Genl. Morgans command eight hundred Strong passed through & I will venture to say 50 of the best horses the lower part of Wilkes the upper part of Surry & the adjoining part of Alleghany County was stolen & among the No your humble servant lost his only riding horse and in nos of cases they stole horses from the wives of volunteers the only horse their husbands had left them to tend their little crops while they offered up their lives as a sacrifice for the good of their Country and not only did they steal horses but plunder any thing else that could be carried with them. But alas they did not stop at stealing horses after leaving this County and going to Alleghany some 5 or 6 of them undertook to rape a very nice decent white woman & some of the neighbors heard her scream & immediately went to her assistance and relieved her from their foul hands then after the affair was all over some 7 or 8 of the Home Guard started on to inform the Commanding

10. W. P. Bynum to Z. B. Vance, 7 May 1864, Governors' Letter Books.

11. Z. B. Vance to J. A. Seddon, 21 Dec. 1863, *Official Records*, Ser. 4, 2: 1061.

12. *Public Laws of the State of North Carolina Passed by the General Assembly at the Adjourned Session of 1863*, p. 31.

officer of their helish work & a parcel of the soldiers learning they were coming on stoped & waited for them & when the H[ome] G[uard] got up in reach they fired into them killing one of the H. G.   from that the H G fired into them killing one of the guilty reches, after the shooting affair the H G had to turn back & the guilty reches went unpunished Well Gov I could write you a week concerning their dirty work but must stop & turn my attention to one Regiment of Genl Vawns [Vaughn's] Brigade that has just left   I have not time to go into particulars but if any difference they are worse than Morgans men stealing horses plundering houses &c and in many instances they have jerked helpless women from their horses bruising & crippling them up considerably. A few weeks ago we were badly damaged by a parcel of men pretending to be press agents from Genl Longstreets army   they robed the County of every yoke of oxen & cows that could go & pretended to have receipts for them that are not worth carrying & since they left I understand they have authority, and such conduct as this is getting to be an every day business & what to do no one knows   any man that is so fortunate as to have a horse left has to keep him hid out in the mountains farmers cannot plant their crops and starvation seems to be inevitable. Now Gov. I am a good friend of yours & I ask you in behalf of the suffering women & children of the county if something cannot be done to prevent this unfortunate state of affairs   I tell you honestly we cannot live under such treatment we cannot pay such taxes our tithes are a true horror our horses property are stolen from us   Something must be done soon or we are bound to suffer considerably—hoping you will write me by return mail I am Gov your friend &c

                         TYRE YORK

Governors' Papers.

                              B.

                              CONFEDERATE STATES OF
                              AMERICA
                              WAR DEPARTMENT
                              Richmond Va. Mar 26, 1864

His Excellency Z. B. Vance
   Governor of N.C.
      Raleigh N.C.
Sir,
   I regret to learn from your letter of the 21st—inst. of the necessity for the impressment of Corn in Burke County, N.C., to sustain the Artillery horses of Genl Longstreet's command, and that such impressment may cause inconvenience and perhaps some suffering to the people of the county. Genl Longstreet, however, I know from recent communication with his Chief Quarter Master, has directed essential supplies to be left in all cases, and it is certain that the Artillery cannot with safety be removed to a greater distance. Some compensation for the loss, it is hoped,

will be found by the people of the county in the reflection that to the presence of Gen Longstreet's forces, to which this Artillery is essential, is due their protection from greater ills.

Very Respectfully
Your obt Servt.
J A M E S A . S E D D O N
Secretary of War

Governors' Papers.

THE WAR AND THE RAILROADS

When the Civil War began there were approximately 9,000 miles of railroads in the South, with slightly less than 900 of these being in North Carolina. Its chief lines were the state-owned North Carolina Railroad connecting Charlotte with Raleigh and Goldsboro, the Raleigh and Gaston, the Wilmington and Weldon, the Atlantic and North Carolina running from Beaufort to Goldsboro, and the Wilmington and Manchester extending from Wilmington to the South Carolina border.

These lines, like all Confederate railroads, went through lightly populated areas, carried relatively light freight, and consequently were lightly and even carelessly laid. Ties were generally put on bare ground with little ditching beside them, and bridges were spindly. Even the rails were made of rolled and wrought-iron "T" sections which scarcely lasted ten years. Fuel was invariably wood, which the companies contracted to be piled up along their lines at regular intervals, a cord of wood being generally used every seventy-five miles. On these rickety, rusting rails the wheezing and patched-up engines pulled passenger trains at an average of about sixteen miles an hour under favorable conditions, while freight trains did well to average twelve.

But the weaknesses of the Confederate railroad system were not all physical. In all it was a patchwork of short lines, most of them connecting a seaport with the immediate hinterland. Rates differed, equipment varied, schedules were uncoordinated, and worst of all the gauges differed, causing disgraceful delays for passengers and freight attempting long passage. On 1 May 1863 Congress finally authorized the War Department to seize and manage the railroads and thereafter the use of the deteriorating facilities improved, but the authority here was chiefly that of coordination. It was not until 28 February 1865, too late to be of any value, that Congress finally established complete War Department control over all transportation and communication.

Nevertheless, under the most trying circumstances, its railroads were of the utmost value to the Confederacy. Indeed, one of the many ways in which the Civil War might be considered the first "modern war" was in its use of railroads, for both participants gradually saw the advantage of railroads in concentrating large supplies of men and material with speed and facility. In fact the Confederacy, without good water transportation, was forced to base its defensive strategy chiefly around its railroads. One historian writes "Rebel railroads almost beat the odds, almost supported the war. Spread too thin, run too far, they brought diminishing returns from dwindling resources and wrote a tantalizing chapter in the history of Confederate logistics."[1]

(1) The Danville Connection

The most significant improvement made in the entire Confederate railroad system was to be the construction of the "Danville Connection," a forty-mile-long line connecting Greensboro on the North Carolina Railroad with the Richmond and Danville. Such a link would be relatively immune from enemy raids and would connect Richmond with the productive states to the south. In February 1862, the state convention chartered the Piedmont Railroad Company, and two days later Congress appropriated $1 million in bonds towards its construction.

But Governor Vance was the leader of a large minority of North Carolinians who feared that the Danville Connection would permanently end the state's dream of an east-west trunk line serving North Carolina for North Carolinians. The following letter shows how Vance refused to help either with the Piedmont's labor needs or with the adaptation of its gauge to fit that of the Richmond and Danville. The line was finally completed in May 1864, and a historian of Confederate railroads believed that it "added months to the length of the Civil War."[2]

STATE OF NORTH CAROLINA,
EXECUTIVE DEPARTMENT,
Raleigh, N.C., February 12, 1863

HON. JAMES A. SEDDON,
  Secretary of War:

SIR : I have the honor to acknowledge the reception of your letter of the 4th instant, invoking the aid of the authorities of the State to procure labor for the completion of the Danville railroad and also asking my influence with the Legislature in securing the gauge of that road to correspond with that of the Virginia road. The object is a most important one and commends itself strongly to my favor; but under all the circumstances I feel compelled to decline impressing slaves to aid in its completion. For many months past the eastern part of this State has been

1. Frank E. Vandiver, *Their Tattered Flags*, p. 246.
2. Robert C. Black, *The Railroads of the Confederacy*, p. 228

furnishing labor upon all the public works from Wilmington to Petersburg, and no less than twenty counties are now so employing their slaves. In the region through which this road runs there are very few slaves, and the very existence of the people requires them to labor on their farms. In addition to the fact that this road is viewed with almost universal disfavor in the State as entirely ruinous to many east of it, and that the charter never could have been obtained but as a pressing war necessity, I feel it due to candor that I should add there exists a very general impression here that upon the completion of the Danville connection, as it is termed, the eastern lines of our roads would be abandoned to the enemy. How far this opinion does injustice to the purpose of the War Department I am not able to say; I merely state the fact. For these reasons, with the additional one that this road is constructed by private contractors, I do not feel that I could be justified in forcing the labor of citizens upon it. I assure you I regret this exceedingly, not only on account of the importance of the work itself to our military operations, but also because it is exceedingly unpleasant for me to refuse to do anything whatsoever which is requested by the Confederate authorities and regarded as important to the general cause. I would suggest, however, that a large number of free negroes might be obtained in the adjoining counties of Virginia and North Carolina, and if this species of labor could be made available, my assistance in gathering it up shall be promptly rendered. In regard to the gauge of the road I have to say that the proposition to make it conform with the Virginia road had been disposed of in the negative before yours was received.

Very respectfully,
your obedient servant,
Z. B. VANCE

Official Records, Ser. 4, 2:393–94.

---

(2) Physical Deterioration of the Railroads

It was not long before the enormous increase in traffic plus the lack of sufficient labor and replacement parts took their toll on the Confederate railroads. No new rails were produced in the Confederacy after 1861 and few were imported. By 1863 only six of the North Carolina Railroad's twenty-six locomotives were in good running order. By 1864 the average speed of passenger trains had fallen to ten miles an hour, and some rails and roadbeds were in such poor shape that five miles an hour was considered dangerous. The following documents reveal something of the general effects of the war on two of the state's major lines, the state-owned North Carolina and the privately owned Wilmington and Weldon railroads.

DIFFICULTIES

. . . In former years supplies of all kinds could easily be procured; though often hard pressed for money, yet our credit was good, and an order from this company always obtained the articles desired. But now neither love nor money will enable you to obtain the necessary material requisite for the repairs of your engines and cars, much less to build new ones. When this war . . . was forced upon you, the equipment of the road was not sufficient to do its business. You needed several more engines and a number of cars, both for passengers and freight. Every exertion has been made to procure them; but we could neither buy nor rent, until the misfortunes of other roads gave us an opportunity in May, to procure a partial equipment.

The avalanche of troops, passengers and freights have been carried with your old equipment; and the tables will show that the work has been immense. Your road has been of incalculable advantage to the Confederacy. Both the Confederate and State authorities have reason to congratulate themselves that in it they have had a powerful auxiliary for their defense. Nevertheless, while doing this heavy business, we have not been able to satisfy the public. The government officials, at many points on the road, have been clamorous for transporting their material and supplies, each one demanding that his own should be attended to immediately, the general government, at Richmond, demanding of us immediate transportation for all public freight in preference to that of private persons, the State authorities, at Raleigh, demanding the immediate transportation of provision and forage and lumber for Camp Mangum, the General in command at Goldsboro, needing our engines and cars to transport his troops even on other roads, the clamors of speculators to get off their freight, and the urgent, but respectful application of private persons to bring them stores for the support of their families, have caused the officers of this road to be up and doing, to be instant in season and out of season, to spend sleepless nights and anxious days. . . .

Loss and Damage

From the insecure condition of our cars, caused by dilapidation, and injury from soldiers knocking off the boards, and the impossibility of procuring locks, a large amount of sugar, bacon, molasses, whiskey, &c., has been stolen from the cars at the stations where they were loaded, or remained over during the night. These depredations have not been confined to any particular locality, but complaints come from every point. Charlotte, Shops and Raleigh have been the principal sufferers. . . .

Freights

Great complaint has been made of the want of promptness in moving Freights. This has been unavoidable, and has arisen from our limited equipment and the immense demands made upon us by the Government. Situated as we are at the end of the line of 4 ft. 8 inch gage, with the large amount of outgoing freight, it has been impossible for us to keep our Cars upon the road. Our cars have been taken by Government many times when those of connecting Roads have been standing ready to receive the freight. Every exertion has been made to keep the equipment on the Road. . . .

Proceedings of the Thirteenth Annual Meeting of the Stockholders of the North Carolina Railroad Company, Held at Hillsboro, July 10th & 11th, 1862.

On the Weldon R.R. 45 miles from
Weldon & 115 from Wilmington
Sept. 16th 1863. 3 o'clock P. M.

To Genl. S. Cooper
    Adj. & Inspt. Genl.
      Genl.
      I deem it my duty to report through you to the Secy. of War the utter deficiency & neglect of transportation on this R. Road. I was ordered to be ready at Rice's Station, Monday the 14th inst. at 4 o'clock P. M. I notified the Rail Road Agent that I would require transportation for 2.500 Infantry and 67 horses. At 2½ P. M. the troops were at the station. The cars arrived at 5½ P. M. and with transportation enough for 1200 men only. These were forwarded to Petersburg, the rest were left at the station, and it was not until 5 A. M. the 15th inst. that all reached that city.—We were not started thence until near 10 A. M., and there, too, transportation in the morning was furnished for but 1200 men. The rest followed at 6 P. M. The 4th & 26th Regmts. which started at 10 A. M. passed Weldon last night, and I arrived there with the 2d train at about 5 A. M. to-day. We were detained at Weldon 5 hours, until 10 A. M. and reached where we are now broken down, 45 miles from Weldon, at 2½ P. M. inst. The Engineer very openly and ingenuously confesses or avers that this is owing to willful and very culpable neglect on the part of the chief machinist of the Road at Wilmington. The tie of one of the driving wheels of the locomotive bursted entirely off and all the wheels are in a condition unfit for use. The Engineer states that this was duly reported by him at Wilmington to the proper agent of the Company; and yet the locomotive was sent to Weldon without repairs to take on troops.—The cars at Weldon & Petersburg both are in very filthy condition, and at the former place my men this morning were required to occupy cars from which horses or cattle had just been taken; and I could find neither conductor nor R.R. Superintendent to have the matter removed. In short the R.R. from Rice's here is in bad condition, not superintended or conducted with any system or arrangement, is shamefully out of time with its appointments; and will, in case of serious emergency, demanding prompt, precise & efficient transportation, disappoint & defeat the operations of our armies. The R.R. is either under the charge of the govt. or of the Company; if of the former *its* officers and agents ought to be held to strict accountability; if of the latter, the Company is a contractor with the Govt. and ought to be made to meet the conditions of the contract—those conditions can't possibly be as bad as the condition and superintendence of the road now

are. The agents of Gov^t. transportation at Weldon & Petersburg, will, I presume, confirm these statements & views. I know the deficiency of material & labor is great & we must not expect complete arrangements for transportation at this crisis, but there is no excuse for the present condition of things on this R.R. A general agent, inspector or Superintendent for Gov^t. ought to be placed on each road. The delays at junctions could easily be avoided, the cars & locomotives could be kept in order, and negligent employees & officers be held accountable.

Yr. obd^t. Servt.

HENRY A. WISE,

Brig. Genl.

John D. Whitford Papers.

---

(3) The Sacrifice of Secondary Railroads

Lacking the ability to maintain all its lines in good working order, Confederate authorities were compelled to cannibalize some of them. In January 1863, the government created an Iron Commission whose chief task was to transfer rails and rolling stock from the less important to the more important lines. The commission would first try to buy what it needed from the former companies, and if this failed it would order its impressment. One of these secondary railroads was the Wilmington, Charlotte, and Rutherford. As early as September 1862, the War Department *began considering impressing some of its rails. President Robert H. Cowan objected strenuously and sought Vance's support. First by refusals and then by court injunctions, Vance held off all impressment until October 1864, when the General Assembly decided and President Cowan agreed to release the rails "not laid down" for transfer to the Wilmington and Manchester.[3] The following letters explain the position of the Confederate government (Document A) and the counter arguments of Governor Vance (Document B).*

A.

Confederate States of America
War Department Engineer Bureau
Richmond Va 5th - Augt. 1864

To His Excellency

Z. B. Vance, Gov. of N. Carolina

Executive Dept. Raleigh N.C.

Sir

I have the honor to invite your Excellency's attention to the State of things presented below and to request your cooperation. . . .

3. R. H. Cowan to Z. B. Vance, 3 Oct. 1864, Governors' Letter Books.

The Wilmington and Manchester R Road forms an essential link in the great line of Southern Rail roads; and there is no exaggeration in affirming that the safety of our people and the possibility of maintaining the present contest with success depend to a great degree, on the preservation of this Road in an efficient condition for the transportation of troops and provisions, of imported articles and of Cotton for exportation. The condition of this Road seriously impaired and worn by the constant call upon it for heavy transportation, has long excited apprehension: it is now represented on good authority that, unless thoroughly repaired, the road must in three months become wholly incapable of furnishing the transportation which the interest of the Government require. In order to repair it, ten or fifteen miles of R.R. Iron are absolutely necessary, and . . . it is evident that the only means of Keeping up the efficiency of the main trunklines of the Confederacy consists in repairing them at the expense of other lines of secondary and merely local importance. The commissioners, acting on this principle, have recommended that the iron required for repairing the Wilmington & Manchester R.Rd be taken from the western terminus of the eastern section of the Wilmington, Charlotte & Rutherford R. Road, from the tract namely beyond Laurenburg where are situated the work shop of the Company. . . . It is much to be regretted that in the execution of this measure, loss and inconvenience must unavoidably be experienced by a portion of your State. The interest affected will however be purely local, and it will be the object of the Confederate Government to act in all such cases as liberally and leniently as is consistent with the attainment of its object. The Government therefore, in removing the iron, will pledge itself to replace it within six months after the conclusion of a treaty of peace between the country and the United States—to pay interest in the mean time on the value of the iron estimated at schedule rates and to protect the interest of the State of North Carolina by such security as may be recommended as fair and just. . . . It is impossible to over estimate the importance from a national and military point of view, of a thorough repair of the Wilmington & Manchester R Road: it will, I think, be found equally impossible to effect this by any course other than the one recommended above. The highest interest of our Army and our Government are involved in the question; and it is in my opinion, only by the earnest and united action of the State and Confederate authorities, that the danger of a permanent and disastrous interruption of R.R. transportation can be effectually obviated.

I respectfully ask for a prompt expression of your views, and am

Very Respectfully
Your Obt. Servt.
J. F. GILMER
Maj. Genl. & Chief & Engr. Bureau

Governors' Letter Books.

B.

State of North Carolina
Executive Department
Raleigh September 10ᵗʰ 1864

Maj Genl J. F. Gilmer
    Chief of Engr Bureau
        Genl

Your letter . . . in regard to the removal of a portion of the rail from the Wilmington Charlotte & Rutherford R.R. has been duly received and its contents considered. In reply I must say, that desirous as I am . . . to aid the Confederate States' Government in every way that I can . . . I can see no good reason why I should grant that consent to the removal of said rails. . . . You seem Genl to entertain the opinion that this Road is one of merely "local interest." But in this you are surely very much mistaken. . . . It is upon supplies of provisions carried down by this road that the people of Wilmington, in a large degree depend for subsistence, and without which they would probably starve, and the place be lost . . . for all the purposes of business. . . . It seems to me in the highest degree, impolitic, just now, when an attack on Wilmington at an early date is deemed probable, to cripple this road which furnishes the only certain means of retreat to both citizens & soldiers in case of disaster. And I am informed that it is now doing a large amount of Government work which the Chief Engineer of the Department declares to be indispensable to the defense of the place. Nor is this all, the State has at great expense erected Salt Works below Wilmington upon which its citizens largely depend for this indispensable article. . . . These works are dependent upon this very road for all their supplies and if it is mutilated or destroyed, they will be destroyed with it; and the citizens of the whole State suffer also. This I submit is something more than a merely "local interest" indeed one of sufficient magnitude to render it expedient to undergo the comparatively triffling inconvenience of transporting rails a little greater distance from some of the branch roads further South, rather than sacrifice it. These branch roads in South Carolina, we were told, several months ago, as [sic] now were upon the point of being torn up to repair the main trunk; but they still remain intact. But even if it were impracticable to bring iron from other Roads, I would remind you that the Genl Superintendent of the Wilmington & Manchester RR in his report of the condition of his road in October last, said that "in this particular (meaning the condition of the railing) we are probably in no more critical situation than most roads on the main line of business" So it would seem that the road cannot become unserviceable before the Company can, enriched as they have been by its large earnings, and owning a large interest in a Steam Ship for running the blockade, import the iron necessary to repair the Road. You lay some stress in your letter upon the fact that "it is not proposed to remove all the Eastern Division of the Road." You cannot be aware of the fact that the Company is operating under a charter granted by the Genl Assembly of the State which requires that the road shall be furnished by sections at stated times, and upon a failure to comply the charter is forfeited, so that the removing of the portion of the road proposed would be equivalent to the removal of the whole, as it would render the forfeiture of the charter inevitable. The State moreover is by the terms of the Charter, largely interested in said Road, and would by its destruction, lose millions of money. Again Colonel Garrett, several months ago took some steps toward the removal of the rail from the same portion of this road, when his proceedings were stopped by an injunction from Judge Battle, one of the Justices of our Supreme Court, and this injunction is still in force and cannot now be ignored by me, even if there were not other sufficient reasons for me to withhold my consent to the removal of the rails.

I herewith enclose a letter to you from Robt H. Cowan, President of the road, to which I would invite your careful attention.

> I am very Respectfully
> Your obt servant
> Z. B. VANCE

Governors' Letter Books.

THE ECONOMY OF SCARCITIES

Not very long after the Civil War a writer questioned whether "there was ever before a great people so far from self-sustaining as was the South in 1861."[1] Most Confederates originally believed that the war would not last long enough for this to be of much import, but their optimism was short-lived and by the fall of 1861 the seriousness of shortages was becoming grim. As the war progressed, the declining imports, the loss of labor, the needs of the army, the deterioration of machines and tools, and the lack of capital planning by manufacturers made the Confederacy a land of scarcity, needing everything "from a hair-pin to a tooth-pick, and from a cradle to a coffin."[2] Each family's welfare depended largely on the ingenuity of its women, and living with scarcity and devising substitutes became harsh realities of life.

The most serious shortage was of food. Early in the war the Confederacy was self-sustaining only in corn and bacon, and supplies of the latter became inadequate after the loss of Kentucky and Tennessee. But other shortages were less serious only in kind. The little local tanneries that sprang up required about eighteen months for a tanning process, and sole leather was particularly difficult to make. Despite the state's salt making activities, people often had to dig up the dirt floors of their smokehouses to get the salt from years of meat drippings. Iron was scarce, and women half believed that northern manufacturers had deliberately sold them poor quality pins before the war with an eye to the future. Of all the manufactured articles, the scarcity of cotton cards created the most anxiety, for they were fragile, difficult to replace, and absolutely necessary for making lint useable.

But not even frugality and economy could compensate for some shortages, and substitutes had to be found. Confederate ingenuity was remarkable here, and eventually women were able to devise substitutes for almost every item in short supply. One writer estimated that southern

1. David Dodge, "Domestic Economy in the Confederacy," p. 229.
2. Mary Elizabeth Massey, *Ersatz in the Confederacy*, p. 4.

women had to "manufacture or devise a substitute for three-fourths of the articles in common use. . . ."[3] Most such ideas and innovations passed over the state by word of mouth, from family to family.

It was inevitable that the combination of severe shortages and an inflated currency would cause prices to soar. Purchasing practices accelerated them even more, for people spent money as rapidly as they obtained it, knowing that the longer money was saved the less valuable it became. Meanwhile speculators were heightening the distress by buying quantities of goods and holding them from market as long as possible. The great profits to be made by speculating prompted one of Jonathan Worth's correspondents to write: "Such as could do so speculate instead of work in the field. The rush about market house is distressing by the time it is light. . . ."[4] Editor W. W. Holden wrote that "the spirit of extortion and speculation pervades all classes."[5] And Governor Vance warned "extortion and speculation have attained such proportions that . . . it will be impossible to clothe and shoe our troops this winter without . . . submitting to the most outrageous prices."[6] Undoubtedly speculation and extortion were common in North Carolina. Certainly the consumers blamed the rapid inflation of prices almost entirely on them. Possibly, though, opinion on where speculation ended and good business practices began depended on one's side of the counter.

(1) "The worst of all is the scarcity"

That Confederate civilians suffered shortages of virtually everything is distressingly evident in their letters. Document A describes the staggering comprehensiveness of the problem. A concerned Fayetteville manufacturer wrote that "our Cuntry Women would have no difaculty in making a very desent living by their Labor if they could git Cards and Factory Thread,"[7] and Document B re-

counts efforts of two desperate women to do so. Document C indicates that even factory owners were having difficulty buying provisions for their workers and were bartering their goods for food. Most consumers believed, probably with much justification, that the owners sold in Virginia at a good price much of the bacon and corn received by bartering.

3. Mrs. Charles R. Hyde, "The Women of the Confederacy," p. 23.
4. J. A. Worth to Jonathan Worth, 23 Jan. 1863, Hamilton, *Correspondence of Jonathan Worth,* 1:225.
5. Raleigh *Standard,* 17 May 1862.
6. Z. B. Vance to W. N. Edwards, 18 Sept. 1862, Hamilton, *Papers of Thomas Ruffin,* 3:260.
7. A. A. McKethan to Z. B. Vance, 10 Aug. 1863, Governors' Papers.

A. THE CONDITION OF THE COUNTRY

We publish below some extracts from letters from various parts of the State, showing the condition of our people with respect to supplies for the coming year. . . .

A friend writing from Transylvania County, says:

"I see every body appears to be after the speculators, but the more you abuse them the worse they get. There is likely to be as great a mania for speculation now, as there was for whiskey making ten months ago. . . . My impression is that . . . the condition and excess of the currency has had a great deal to do with it, but the worst of all is the scarcity. You can have very little idea how hard our people are pressed to live even comfortably. The ground is frozen here, and is . . . bitter cold. . . . Nearly all our people have more or less work to do out of doors—men, women and children. Not one-half of them have the sign of a shoe on their feet; not one-third have shoes that will keep their feet dry, nor do I know how they are to get them. They are nearly all scarce of wearing clothes. Cotton and wool is pretty hard to get—but the worst is, cotton and wool cards can scarcely be had at all, the old ones being about worn out. We would all be glad to do something for our famishing soldiers, but how can we, when we have more suffering at our doors than we can possibly relieve? Then we are getting scarce of almost every article of necessity, from a needle to a scythe blade. Not a few are out of knives, forks, spoons, plates, dishes, tin cups and coffee pots.—Then we may turn to edibles. Take out a very few families, and there is not one pound of salt to every white inhabitant in the county. We got from Wilmington some weeks ago, what we call government salt, and divided it out, one pound to every white person in family, but did not get quite around to all. That cost us fourteen cents per pound. . . . A gentleman told me the other day he traveled 40 miles without grain for his horses. He says he offered one dollar for ten ears of corn, and could not get it. . . . Very few of us have half hogs enough to make our meat for next year; I would say not half as much in the county as we ought to eat—nor can we spare the corn to fatten what we have. Numbers of people . . . think they had better keep the corn, and depend on bread and milk, than to lose both corn and pork for lack of salt. My opinion is that numbers must perish before another crop is made, unless we can alarm the people in time to take better care of what they have than they have ever done before. . . . Our rulers understand raising an army better than feeding and clothing one. . . ."

Raleigh *Standard*, 18 Nov. 1862.

B. ELIZA ARMON & OTHERS TO GOVERNOR VANCE

Hookerton green County
September the 6 1863

Mr Z B Vance governr of the Staite of North caralina your excellency I seat my self to wright you A letter for The first time how cousin Nancy Vines and I my self was treated at lowell factore we left home Sunday afternoon And reached theare tuesday eavning an our by the Sun we went to the factory and informed Mr Ben Bordan that we wanted some cotton And he told me to go to Mr Cox and And he promest that we might have cotton The next day we staide theare that night next Day we wente to the factory and wente in the house and asked Mr Bordan to let us have our cotton Soas we might go home he said we Sould not have Eny cotton untill three oclock we saw A Man theare by the name of webe we hired him [to] tell Bordan that he had come for his cotton Ready paid for we went to Mr webe and told hime our situation and that we ware some forty five or fifty miles from home I told him that my husban was ded and that I had four Childrin And that thay ware [illegible] Cusen Nancey told him That hir husband was inn the Sirvis and she had too Childrin and we wanted to get cotton Too cloth them he asked hoo we ware and wheare we lived we told him that we ware from green County and what our names ware he said he wold give us twelve bunches of his cotton then Soas we could get some cotton and he wold come A Nother time and get it——we thanked him for his kindness Mr webe wint to Mr Bardon and And Told hime what he wold do abut The cotton and he refused to let us have it we went to Bardon our selves and he said he Should not let us have it we encisted that he should After webe was gon he said that webe said we Told Storyes that he dide not say eny sutch thing And that we could not have enny I took holt of a bunch he had in his hand we asked him to let me have that and he held on to it and said you Cant have it he tooke hold of my arm and Said to me you go out of hear I told him I should go out when I got redy he said he wold have me Put out I said to him no you wont I told him my My situation cusen Nancy told him that hur husband was in the war and she had too Children he said he did not car hoo was soldiurs wives and hoo wert not who was widows and hoo was not and hoo was nakd and hoo was not an said he wanted all the wimen to go out of thear at three Oclocke he handed out some cotton at the [illegible] windo in the ofiss and picked out his choisen ones he caled for sirtan pirsons some wold go to the windo and he wold Say you go way I did not call you I hird from good Authaurs that he said thare shoul not go Another bunch of cotton out of theare untill three oclocke that dy report says they carred It out in the knight and hideing of it to make a speulation off of it thay sell It from twelve to fifteene to twenty dolars pr Bunch nothing more at presant

Respectfully yours

Governors' Papers.

C. MARY REED AND OTHERS TO ZEBULON B. VANCE

Little River Alexander County
N. Carolina
May 21st 1863

Mr. Z. B. Vance Gov. of the State of N Carolina we a portion of the citizens and especially the wives of the volunteers feel disposed to lay in a complaint against one certain Wilson Jones who is proprietor of a cotton factory in Sd. County the complaint is that the wives of volunteers are actually in need of thread to make clothing for themselves and children they have applied to mister Jones time and again for thread but all without any relief they cannot get thread from him for confederate notes but says that if they will fetch him bacon or corn which he verry well knows the state has to lay in these articles in to them he will let them have thread whene at the same time he will load waggons from Virginia and the trick that is in is this the waggons Deliver their bacon at Statesville some 25 miles from the factory when at the same time he tells the volunteers wives that he has oblige to have the corn and Bacon to support his factory hands on and we do not believe that it Requires the Bacon and corn of Virginia & N. Carolina to support the hands of one Little Factory provided the like of this is allowed of the wives & children of volunteers must suffer for clothing & we your humble applicants apply to you for protection if it is within your power———those who assign their names to this are a portion of the women who have made application for thread without any relief Yrs truly & they are all the wives of volunteers

Governors' Papers.

---

(2) The Despair of Inflation

The combination of scarcity and a redundant currency drove prices up steadily until a soldier's monthly pay of eleven dollars would scarcely keep him in tobacco. In her charming Diary from Dixie, *Mary Boykin Chesnut includes a witticism current in 1862 that "you take your money to market in the market basket, and bring home what you buy in your pocketbook."*[8] *North Carolina newspapers seldom skipped a day without reporting outrageous prices for the necessities of life. While a few consumers recognized the relationship between high prices and the very nature of Confederate currency, most of them blamed their hardships on heartless speculation and extortion. The following letters represent the outrage at market prices and the conviction that their only cause was extortion. Robert L. Abernethy had been a Methodist minister and a teacher and was now a tax collector (Document A); the writers of Document B were obviously poorly educated. Nevertheless, the writers of both letters saw heartless speculation as the chief cause of their grief.*

A. R. L. ABERNETHY TO Z. B. VANCE

Marion, N.C.
Nov. 4th '/62/
If it is Constitutional, and if your position as Governor of N. Carolina

8. Mary Boykin Chesnut, *A Diary from Dixie*, p. 368.

gives you the power to do so, in the name of God, of suffering humanity, of the cries of widows and orphans, *do* put down the Speculation and extortion in this portion of the State.

Here in Marion, beef is being sold to the poor wives of soldiers who get but $11 per month in the field, at the enormous price of 11 and 12 cents per pound! Leather at $4 per pound! Bacon at 40 & 50 cents per pound; Corn from the heap, at $1.50 per bushel! Salt at near 50 cents per pound! And every thing in proportion.

If this thing is not put down, our Country is *ruined* forever. Many children of the soldiers in the Camps are nearly barefoot and naked without the possibility of getting clothes and shoes.

Here in Marion, Messrs Maroney and Halyburton have a large Tannery, and the tanner is allowed to remain by virture of the Exemption Act, and yet one pound of leather cannot be bought of the concern by private purchase. The leather is put up in lots of 250 sides and sold to speculators at $4.00 & $4.50 per pound! Your correspondent went himself in person to the concern of these gentlemen, and though he laid his case before them, that he had 6 little barefoot children that must have shoes, and offered to give any reasonable price for leather—*just one side*. But the reply was, if we sell to one man privately we must sell to others, and we will not do it.

In the name of the Great God of the universe, what are we to do?

Pardon my presumption in addressing your Excellency, for I could not restrain.

Johnston, *Papers of Zebulon Baird Vance*, 1:304–5.

B.

february The 18th 1863

M Z. vance Govener of NC.

Sir we take the privilege of writing you a fiew lines to inform you of a fiew things that is mooving at this time in the State of N C the time has come that we the common people has to hav bread or blood & we are bound boath men & women to hav it or die in the attempt some of us has bin travling for the last month with the money in our pockets to buy corn & tryed men that had a plenty & has been unable to buy a bushel holding on for a better price we are willing to gave & obligate two Dollars a bushel but no more for the idea is that the slave oner has the plantations & the hands to rais the brad stufs & the comon people is drove of in the ware to fight for the big mans negro & he at home making nearly all the corn that is made & then becaus he has the play in his own fingers he puts the price on his corn so as to take all the solders wages for a fiew bushels & then them that has worked hard & was in living circumstances with perhaps a good little homestid & other thing convenient for there well being perhaps will be credited until the debt will about take there land & every thing they hav & then they will stop all & if not they will hav to Rent there lands of there lords sir we hoos sons brothers & husbands is now fighting for the big mans negros are determd to have bredd out of these barns & that at a price that we can pay or we will slaughter as we go—if this is the way we comon people is to be treated in the confedercy we hope that you & your friends will be as smart as govener Elis & his friends was take us out with out the voice of the people & let us try to maniage & defend our own State we hope sir that you will duly consider the a bove mentioned items & if it is in your power to Remedy the present evils do it speedly it is not our desiar to organise and commence operations for if the precedent is laid it will be unanimous but if ther is not steps taken soon nessesity will drive us into measurs that may prove awful we dont ask meet on fair terms for we can live on bread perhaps it would be better for you to isue your proclamation that no man should sell in the State at more than $2 pr bushel you no best &c if you cant remedy Extosan on the staff of life we will & we as your subjects will make Examples of all who Refuse to open there barn Doors & appoint other men over there farms who per haps will hav better Harts we no that this is unlawful at a common time but we are shut up we cant trade with no body only Just those in the confedersy & they can perish all those that has not and it seems that all harts is turned to gizards—Sir consider this matter over & pleas send us a privat letter of instruction direct it to bryant Swamp post office Bladen county N C & to R.L. as our company will be called Regulators

[no signatures]

Governors' Papers.

---

(3) Desperate Women

At times the combination of scarcity and speculation drove groups of desperate women into acts of open violence. In April 1864, five women were sentenced to five months in jail for raiding a warehouse at the Bladenboro depot and taking seven sacks of grain. The Salisbury raid described in Document A was reported in several newspapers. The day it occurred the owner of the first store raided wrote Governor Vance that a "mob of females" had "cut away a portion of the door" with hatchets while the mayor and some of his commissioners stood by and did nothing.[9] The women's side of such a foray is well described in Document B.

A.

Salisbury, N.C. March 18th [1863]

. . . Salisbury has witnessed to-day one of the gayest and liveliest scenes of the age. About 12 o'clock, a rumor was afloat, that the wives of several soldiers now in the war, intended to make a dash on some flour and other necessaries of life, belonging to certain gentlemen, who the ladies termed "speculators." They alleged they were entirely out of provisions, and unable to give the enormous prices now asked, but were willing to

9. Michael Brown to Z. B. Vance, 18 Mar. 1863, Governors' Papers.

give Government prices. Accordingly, about 2 O'clock they met, some 50 or 75 in number, with axes and hatchets, and proceeded to the depot of the North Carolina Central Road, to impress some there, but were very politely met by the agent, Mr. ———, with the enquiry: "What on earth is the matter?" The excited women said they were in search of "flour," which they had learned had been stored there by a certain speculator. The agent assured them such was not the case. They still insisted on examining the depot, but after a while desisted and made their way up town to the store of one of the oldest and most respected citizens.—They commenced a general attack on his lumber room, in which was stored a large quantity of flour. The old gentleman seeing their determination to have the flour, compromised the matter by saying if they would desist he would give them ten barrels which he readily did.

They then went to the store of a large firm, (one of them a Petersburger,) to impress his flour. They heard he had been speculating, but were sadly mistaken, he only having seven (7) barrels. But he like a good citizen, made them a present of three barrels, and remarked that any soldier's wife could get anything in reason from him. . . .

The word march was given, and onward they went to the Government warehouse, under the superintendence of a gentleman from South Carolina. . . . He very politely opened the door, and gave them every facility to examine the premises. They soon dispersed from there—not finding a thing they could impress.

They then met a gentleman on the street who they had been told, had salt, on which, they said he intended to speculate. He assured them most positively that such was not the case; that it was sent to him to sell. They insisted on having a bag. He . . . said rather than have the salt impressed, he would make them a present of a bag and a twenty dollar Confederate note.

Their cry was still for more, and they proceeded down the street to the store of another . . . merchant, who, I suppose, rather than be bothered gave them a barrel of molasses.

Finally . . . they returned to the depot . . . and again demanded the agent that they be allowed to go in. He still refused, but finally agreed to let two go in and examine the flour, and see if his statement was not correct. A restlessness pervaded the whole body, and but a few moments elapsed before a female voice was heard saying: "Let's go in." The agent remarked:—"Ladies . . . it is useless to attempt it, unless you go in over my dead body." A rush was made, and in they went, and the last I saw of the agent, he was sitting on a log blowing like a March wind. They took ten barrels, and rolled them out and were setting on them, when I left, waiting for a wagon to haul them away. . . .

Salisbury Daily *Carolina Watchman*, 23 Mar. 1863.

B.

> Mcleanesville N c
> Aprile 9th 1863

Gov Vance

I have threatend for some time to write you a letter—a crowd of we

Poor wemen went to Greenesborough yestarday for something to eat as we had not a mouthful meet nor bread in my house what did they do but put us in gail Jim Slone, Linsey Hilleshemer and several others I will not mention—thes are the one that put us to gail in plase of giveing us aney thing to eat and I had to com hom without aneything—I have 6 little children and my husband in the armey and what am I to do Slone wont let we Poor wemen have thread when he has it we know he has evry thing plenty he say he has not got it to spair when we go but just let thes big men go they can git it withou aney trouble. when we go for aney thing they will not hardley notis us Harper Linsey has money for the Poor weman it was put in his handes for the Poor weman I have not got one sent of it yet since my husband has bin gon he has bin gon most 2 years I have went to Linsey for money he told me to go to a nother man and he said . . . he could not do nothing for me—Lindsey would grumble at him for him takeing such a big bil if you dont take thes yankys a way from greenesborough we wemen will write for our husbans to come . . . home and help us we cant stand it the way they are treating us they charge $11.00 Per bunch for their thread and $2.50 for their calico —They threatend to shoot us and drawed their pistols over us that is hard.

Jim Slone sid he would feed we poor weman on dog meet and Roten egges. I tel you if you dont put Slone and Linsey out of offis the Poor weman will perish for the want of something to eat my brother sent home for some shirtes I went to Slone for bunch coten he would not let me have one thread and he had plenty their is bound to be a fammon if I dont git help soon.

if their ant beter better times in greenesborough the waar will end in in that plase The young men has runaway from newburn and come to this plase about to take the country they are speclating evry day their is old Ed. Holt where has a factory on alamance he has maid his Creiges [?] if this war holds on 2 years longer he would own all of allamance county he has cloth and thread and wont let no body have it without wheat or Corn or meet what am I to do I cant git it to eat—three and four men gatherd hold of one woman and took thir armes away from them and led them all up to gail—you have no ide how the men in Greensborough has treated we poor weman we have to pay $3.50 per bushel for goverment corn and half measure and have the exact change or dont git the corn for the meel we dont git nun they seling sugar sugar at $1.50 per pound and black peper $9.00 per pound and say it not half as much as a soldier wife ought to pay and asking $50.00 for a barel of flour so no more

Yours very
Respectfuly
N A N C Y   M A N G U M

Governors' Papers.

(4) Even the Manufacturers

While part of the price spiral was undoubtedly due to profiteering by manufacturers and processors, they themselves were victims of the times. For the first time in North Carolina history, for instance, there was an eager market for all textiles made. But factory owners were forced to sell much of their output to the state for less than it would bring on the market, *and they believed that budgeting and capital planning in the face of rising costs necessitated the high prices they were charging the public. Edwin M. Holt and his son Thomas were prominent cotton manufacturers of Alamance County, and the letter below presents the manufacturers' problems with scarcity and inflation.*

                              Granite Mills
                              Haw River N.C.
                              Sept. 15th. 1863

Capt. W. A. Dowd, A. Q. M
  D Sir

Yours of the 14th. inst to hand. It will afford me pleasure to serve you, as far as I can, but I am *now*, like you caught me before, got a good many promises out. It is almost impossible *now*, for a manufacturer to buy anything for money, Cotton Yarn is *always* required, & I have engagements out for Wood (for Winter use for my operatives), Hay for my stock, & some cotton trades, & some Bacon, which I calculated would carry me through the winter, but if the State requires the goods I will of course come to her assistance. If it was not for the retail trade, I could navigate very well, that is really annoying, for if I sell them all I make, they grumble, because I have not five times as much, if I sell them half I make, they swear I have not sold *any*, so there is no way to satisfy them, & I become almost disgusted with the whole proceedings.

In order to give myself as easy a birth as possible, I would prefer to serve one at the time, for if I undertake to serve you & them at once, they will accuse me of lying &c &c. In order to satisfy the poor ungrateful ones, I would prefer your giving me orders to make yours first, & then work for them. I would therefore thank you to let me know, how much my quota will be, and I will then write you how soon I can fill it, & will get you to give me POSITIVE ORDERS to work for you. I have 4 Spinning Frames, would like you to be as lightly on me as your necessities will permit, in order, to let out as much as possible, to the old women, (for I assure you they are indescribeable) but it makes no difference with me, if you take me for six months, for I never see any peace only when I am running for you. . . .

                              Very Respectfully Yours
                              THOMAS M. HOLT

Civil War Collection, Quartermaster Department Correspondence.

(5) Substitutes

In his article on the "Domestic Economy in the Confederacy"[10] David Dodge commented that its people had to rely so heavily on substitutes "that to this day the word is commonly used by the illiterate people of North Carolina as a synonym for all that is sorry and worthless." Dyes were made from roots, herbs, and bark; buttons, from persimmon seeds. Coffee had been the southerners' favorite beverage and wheat, rye, corn, sweet potatoes, peanuts, dandelion seed, and melon seed were some of the unsatisfactory substitutes for it. Sorghum, or Chinese sugar cane, had been grown since 1857 and was one of the few substitutes that was both satisfactory and abundant. Envelopes were made of wall paper, blackgum roots made fair corks. And the list is endless. Newspapers from time to time carried suggestions for substitutes, and two such suggestions are included below.

OKRA THE BEST SUBSTITUTE FOR COFFEE

Like every other family, perhaps, where the blockade rendered Coffee so scarce . . . my wife began to cast about for a substitute, and we tried . . . Okra seed. Mrs. Cloud had some washed and dried, preparatory for parching. We used about the same quantity by weight or measure, that we had formerly done of coffee. It was carefully parched and the coffee made in the usual way, when we found it almost exactly like coffee in color, very pleasantly tasted and entirely agreeable. All other substitutes were laid aside, and the Okra has been used in my family for the last eighteen months; and for myself, I can say in all candor, prepared as our cook has it done, I should have no preference, at 10 cents per pound between Okra and Coffee. When well made . . . it is delicate and finely flavored, entirely wholesome, of a rich golden color, and in all respects equal to the best Java Coffee, except the Coffee flavor, which may be imparted to it, if preferred, by grinding with the baked Okra seed, ten or twelve grains of baked Coffee, for each meal. . . . The Okra is of the same family of plants with cotton . . . and grows equally well in all latitudes and on all land, where cotton grows. . . . I find it wholesome, nourishing, and perfectly healthy, nor has it any perceptible effects upon the nervous system, through which medium headache is often produce by Coffee, in many debilitated females, especially.

Greensboro *Patriot*, Apr. 30, 1863.

. . . We must fall back upon our vegetable productions for a supply of oil. Linseed oil has been found not to answer for machinery. Oil *can*

---

10. David Dodge, "Domestic Economy," p. 239.

be expressed from cotton-seed but at what expense, in what quantities, or of what quality we hardly know, or we know very indistinctly.

A new article has been spoken of; the castor bean grows, or may be made to grow very luxuriantly in Alabama, Florida, Mississippi and Texas, and probably as far north as this State. It produces a very clear, limpid oil, and, although for obvious reasons it might never be very popular for *table use*, still there is no reason why it would not do very well to work machinery. The experiment is certainly worthy of a trial.

The ground-pea, pea-nut, or gouber pea, furnishes an oil, which, when fresh, is as "sweet as a nut," and is said to be good for lubricating purposes also. We have never had an opportunity to judge of it . . . but have the testimony of others to the fact, that it answers all the purposes of sperm oil. We are pleased to know that some of our energetic citizens have arrangements in progress to go into the making of oil from ground peas, and we trust that they will be enabled to go forward at a very early day. We can hardly doubt that their enterprise will meet a fitting recompense.

Wilmington *Journal,* 21 Oct. 1861.

CHURCH AND SCHOOL

Two North Carolina institutions whose encouraging antebellum development was blunted by the distresses of war were the church and the school. By 1860 the ten leading Protestant denominations had 157,000 members, with 65,000 Baptists, 61,000 Methodists, and 15,000 Presbyterians. Together they constituted a major force in society. Throughout the state numerous denominational colleges and academies provided religious education for ministers and a proper environment for the education of lay men and women.

But not even the churches were exempt from the disorganization and impoverishment of the war years. The Board of Managers of the Baptist State Convention reported in 1862 that they "never have felt such embarrassment. Discouraged by the state of the country, and crippled by their indebtedness, they hardly know where to begin or what to say." Membership in churches and attendance at both churches and conventions were in a state of decline. Except for work with the armies, missionary activity had virtually ended, and it was "painful to the Board to have to state that they have not a single Missionary in their employment."[1] The next year the board reported that the religious needs of the soldiers were so great that rather than divide their small resources they had decided to abandon the department of state missions and devote their full attention to the soldiers. To supervise this work they had appointed N. B. Cobb as superintendent of colportage at a salary of $1,500 a year. The board added that they had been trying to persuade pastors to leave their churches for brief tours as missionaries to the soldiers, but the "strange apathy" of the pastors had defeated this crusade.[2]

What was happening to the Baptists was happening to the other denominations. In addition, the decline in contributions and attendance, plus the erosion of endowments by inflation, prevented repair of church

1. *Proceedings of the Thirty-third Annual Session of the Baptist State Convention of North Carolina, 1862, pp. 10–11.*
2. *Proceedings of the Thirty-fourth Annual Session of the Baptist State Convention of North Carolina, 1863, pp. 18–19, 26.*

property and even drove pastors from their calling. A pall of poverty hung everywhere.

Education fared worse. For nearly a decade before the Civil War North Carolina had been engaged in an educational revival, largely inspired by Superintendent of Public Instruction Calvin Henderson Wiley. Accepting the position in 1853, Wiley brought about an improved efficiency in county school administration, an increase in the number and quality of teachers, better school buildings and libraries, and the organization of the Educational Association of North Carolina. When the Confederacy began the state had approximately 120,000 children enrolled in almost 3,000 common schools. These schools received annually about $100,000 from county taxes and almost twice that amount from the Literary Fund. The average school year was four months and the average teacher salary was $25 a month. In addition the Census of 1860 notes 434 academies and other private schools with over 13,000 pupils. These schools were financed by tuition, offered much better instruction than the common schools, and sometimes operated ten-month terms. The census also listed sixteen colleges and the University of North Carolina with a total of 1,540 students.

But hostilities had hardly begun before educational leaders realized that progress during the war would be impossible and that the very existence of the state's educational institutions was imperiled. Wiley's watchword during the war, therefore, was not improvement but merely "keeping up."

---

(1) Problems of the Presbyterians

On 1 November 1861 the North Carolina Presbyterian Synod meeting in Raleigh condemned "the tyranny and usurpation" of the Lincoln government, seceded from the Presbyterian Church of the United States, and besought God and the North Carolina Presbyterians to support the Confederacy.[3] During the war the Presbyterian churches lost 2,000 communicants in battle, while at home the churches struggled under the debilitating effects of the war as best they could. In its annual "Narra-

tive" describing the state of its Church, the 1863 North Carolina Synod reported that "the year past has been one of multiplied trials and of slight progress." The "occupancy and agitation of the mind of our people by the great events" taking place might partially explain "the spiritual dearth of which our Presbyteries make so sad report. But in addition we may mention as a cause greatly aggravating the evil, the spirit of worldliness, . . . the spirit of speculation, the hastening to be rich, the

---

3. D. I. Craig, *A History of the Development of the Presbyterian Church in North Carolina*, pp. 30–31.

greed of gain—of whose preva-
lence . . . there are overwhelm-
ing evidences in all portions of the
land."[4] *The following report of*
the Fayetteville Presbytery for the
same year gives the local overview.

The Presbytery of Fayetteville met on the morning of the 9th, in the church in Fayetteville, and was opened with a sermon by the Rev. N. T. Bowden from Rom. 8: 32.

The Rev. S. C. Alexander was elected Moderator, and the Rev. N. T. Bowden and Gen. A. D. McLean Temporary Clerks. The attendance both of teaching and of ruling elders was good, considering the condition of the country, and the deliberations of the Presbytery harmonious and pleasant.

The reports from the churches show no very special religious interest. The past ecclesiastical year has been one of much dearth and barren-ness, though considerable accessions were mentioned in several of our churches. Clinton and Ben Salem may perhaps be considered the only churches in which anything like a revival has been enjoyed. It is mani-fest therefore that the hearts of our people have not been upon spiritual and eternal things to the extent that the interests of souls demands of people professing godliness. We have not been obeying the injunction to "seek *first* the kingdom of God and His righteousness," trusting that all other things shall be added unto us. Had this injunction been obeyed in the spirit in which the Master gave it, He would not have left us to report so few accessions to the churches for the past year.

In the matter of contributions, the reports were even more favorable. Notwithstanding the heavy demands upon the people for various objects of benevolence connected with the army, there have generally been lib-eral contributions for the several enterprises of the church.

The report of the Committee on Domestic Missions exhibits little prog-ress in this important work within our borders. There are at present but two missionaries employed within the bounds of the Presbytery; though there are several fields in which laborers might be profitably employed. The scarcity of ministers, however, renders it almost impossible to pro-cure laborers; and it is a question that deserves attention whether, in the more pressing calls for the preaching of the gospel in the army, all the available ministerial resources of the church should not be sent thither. There is great need of preaching at home; but is not the need greater in the army? As will be seen by the address of the chaplains in Gen. Jack-son's corps, which appears in this issue of our paper, the destitution of preaching in the army is far greater than among the people at home. The number of chaplains in the service bears a very small proportion to the whole number of ministers in the Confederacy. This ought not to be. The army is the great field for missionary work.

Resolutions were passed expressing a deep interest in the spiritual condition of the brave men who are fighting our battles and acknowledg-ing our obligations to furnish them, as far as possible, with the preached

4. *North Carolina Presbyterian*, 5 Dec. 1863.

word. It was also urged upon all our ministers, where the way shall not be open to accept of a chaplaincy, to leave their own charges for a short time and visit the camps, &c., for the purpose of preaching the gospel to the soldiers. There ought to be a chaplain to each regiment in the service. This the regulations of the government allow; but the churches in the Confederacy have not by any means yet come up to the measure of their duty by furnishing the men to occupy these places of usefulness. There are few ministers, perhaps, who are serving the church at home, that have more souls under their charge than a chaplain of a regiment has. And then the peculiar dangers and temptations of those in the army, deprived of many of the influences of home and its associations, demand the special care and attention of the christian people of the country. It may therefore safely be assumed that not a few of the pastors of churches would be in the path of duty to leave their flocks and go to preach the gospel in the army. Of course, each pastor must himself, in a great measure, be the judge of whether *he* is one of those who are thus called to this work. But if not called to accept of a chaplaincy, he may still do something in the great work of holding up the Saviour to those who are periling life for our freedom from an earthly tyranny. Pastors can leave their charges for a season, a month or two, and make missionary excursions to the camps, hospitals, &c., preaching to the soldier whenever an opportunity is offered. Thus a large amount of work might be done without disturbing the pastoral relation at home. Such visits of pastors to regiments or hospitals in which are members of their own flock, must be very gratifying to the soldiers, and may be the means of doing much good. It will be seen that, in the Appeal from the Chaplains, published in this paper, this kind of missionary work is recommended to those who are unable to go into the service as chaplains.

Perhaps the most important item of business transacted by the Presbytery during its sittings, related to the Synodical Scheme for the education of the children of deceased soldiers. The members of the Synodical Committee within the bounds of the Presbytery had made dilligent efforts to secure a suitable agent for the collection of funds, &c., for this object; but without success. The brethren to whom application had been made were unable to undertake the work. In this state of the matter, Presbytery resolved to make Church Sessions the agent within their respective bounds. The duty of collecting funds is laid upon them, and also in looking out the proper objects on which to expend them; and each Church Session is to report to the Presbytery the result of their labors— the amount of money collected, the number of children of deceased soldiers within their bounds requiring aid, and the estimated amount necessary to place the children on as favorable a footing in regard to education as though the father had lived. This work can be and ought to be done by the Church Sessions; and if done by them it meets every demand and obviates the necessity of appointing any other agent. Let the Sessions of our churches at once look to the matter, and let no one fail to make the required report to the next regular meeting of the Presbytery.

North Carolina Presbyterian, 18 Apr. 1863.

(2) Colportage

The distribution of religious literature to the soldiers was the churches' one great war effort. Whether motivated by piety or a dearth of free reading material, soldiers soon began requesting religious tracts from home, and the denominations set up procedures to provide such material. Local churches would raise money and channel it to the denomination's superintendent of army colportage. He and his committee would buy Bibles and tracts, and chaplains and civilian volunteers would distribute them to soldiers in camps and hospitals. From 1862 until 1865 the North Carolina Baptists alone contributed $74,000 for such purchases. In the summer of 1861 representatives of "various religious organizations"[5] in Salisbury formed the Rowan Bible Society to buy religious literature for distribution, and soon other communities had similar cooperative programs under way.

Since the supply of this literature from the North was now cut off, the South had to turn to its own presses. In June 1861, the General Tract Agency began operations in Raleigh. Its purpose was to print Bibles and tracts and sell them for distribution to the soldiers. All the tracts were selected and prepared under the joint supervision of four men, the pastors of the Baptist, Episcopal, Methodist, and Presbyterian churches of Raleigh. The operation of the entire system is described in the following letter.

NEW PUBLICATIONS FOR THE SOLDIERS

The General Tract Agency of this city is publishing from 20,000 to 50,-000 copies of each of the following excellent Tracts, approved by all the Pastors here:

"A Mother's Parting Words to her Soldier Boy;" 8 pages, by a Southern lady. "Individual Effort;" 8 pages. "The New Year;" 4 pages. "Lovest Thou Me?" 4 pages. "The French Soldier;" 4 pages. "The Great Gathering;" 4 pages. "Christ In You;" 8 pages, by Rev. C. F. Deems, D.D. "Christ's Gracious Invitations;" 8 pages. "My Spirit Shall Not Always Strive;" 4 pages, by Rev. J. H. Fowles, of S.C. "The Life Preserver;" 4 pages. "Are You Ready?;" 4 pages. "The Precious Blood of Christ, or How a Soldier Was Saved;" 4 pages, and "Why Will Ye Die?" 8 pages, by Rev. A. M. Poindexter, D.D., of Va.

We are striving to supply our whole army with these gospel truths. There is increasing evidence that this means of grace is being blessed of God to the great spiritual good of many of our soldiers. Recently we met at the Railroad Depot in this city, an intelligent soldier of the 3rd South Carolina Regiment. After helping him in the cars we gave him the tract, "Casting Our Burden on the Lord," by Rev. J. M. Atkinson, which

5. Salisbury *Daily Carolina Watchman*, 1 July 1861.

led him to take from his pocket a copy of this tract, given him while in the Hospital, from a package we sent his Regiment, which he stated was made an instrument of God in his conversion.

A pious soldier from this county, now in Virginia, said to me recently, "We have not had a sermon preached in our Regiment in more than three months. The religious reading brought us by the Colporteur is eagerly sought, and productive of great good. Tracts are specially adapted to the camp, and we ought to have a new supply at least every Sunday morning."

A Texan soldier told me that the tract, "Don't Put it Off," (one of the first tracts last June) was the means of leading him to Christ.

One of the 1st North Carolina "Bethel" Regiment says, that "Come to Jesus," which we gave him while encamped here, was blessed to his conversion during the first month he was in Virginia, and that he had committed all of it to memory.

The donation of some one printed these tracts, which have been so greatly blessed. Each dollar given will send out 1,500 pages, which will be carried, through the great kindness of the Express Company, to the soldiers without charge. We can now print 30,000 tracts in a day; and that we may continue this in order to supply the pressing calls for grants, and sell so cheaply, we are mainly dependent on donations to pay for materials and work.

Hymns for the Camp

We shall soon have out an excellent edition of "Hymns for the Camp." It will be convenient for the pocket, containing 150 Hymns, on about 120 pages, and will be neatly bound in paper, boards, and cloth. Wholesale prices are 10, 12½ and 15 cents per copy. Every soldier should have a copy, and by donations we will be enabled to give away a large number of it. We hope to receive liberal order and donations for these publications so greatly needed and sought for by our noble defenders.

Yours truly,

W. J. W. CROWDER,

Raleigh, N.C., Feb., 1862   Agent

Salisbury *Daily Carolina Watchman*, 3 Mar. 1862.

---

(3) The Teacher Shortage

The first problem that the Civil War created for the North Carolina school system was a critical shortage of teachers. Military service of course took many male teachers. Inflation drove others from the profession, for in 1863 the average monthly salary was still twenty-five dollars in paper money while eggs were three dollars a dozen in some areas. Superintendent Wiley had long campaigned for more women in the profession and now saw them as

the solution to the teacher shortage. In one of his reports he stated
"many ladies are compelled, by
the circumstances of the times, to
labor for a living; and there is no
employment better suited to the
female nature, and none in which
ladies can labor more usefully,
than in the business of forming
the hearts and minds of the
young." [6] In a letter in 1862 to the
county examiners Wiley asked

them to persuade qualified women
to take teaching positions, and
both the examiners and the wom-
en accepted this solution. By the
end of the war the percentage of
women teachers had risen from
seven to nearly fifty. The following is an address by the Rev. J. K.
Kirkpatrick, president of Davidson
College, before the young ladies of
Concord Female College urging
some of them to become teachers.

THE DUTY OF FEMALES IN RELATION TO THE FUTURE EDUCATIONAL INTERESTS OF OUR COUNTRY

Let me instance one great interest of society on which the war now rag-
ing has proved especially disastrous. . . . I refer to the education of the
young, particularly in the elementary branches of learning. The extent
to which the schools and . . . education have been interrupted, broken
up, and in many instances utterly destroyed, is a matter of too common
remark to require more than this simple mention. . . .

But what . . . will be our condition when the bloody drama shall
close, though it should be to-morrow? Our children and youth will be
here in full numbers to be instructed, with the arrears of three years'
neglect to be made up. *Who is there to teach them?* Our young men, or
our middle aged men, as to a great extent, in former years? . . . Of
those who may survive to return to us, many were arrested in the midst
of . . . studies . . . by the call to serve their country . . . and it is
scarcely to be hoped that . . . any considerable number of them will
be found willing to resume their course of preparation, or if qualified
already, will be content to engage in an occupation requiring so close
and inactive confinement . . . and offering so inadequate a compensation, either of money or of social position, as that of teaching. . . .

You have, of course, anticipated the conclusion to which these remarks
tend. *Our females must engage in the work of teaching.* . . . There is
no form of business, so to speak, no occupation, to which the educated
woman can have recourse, which is at once so respectable, so certainly
remunerative, so congenial to her tastes, and so suitable to her sex. . . .
So far as the welfare of our children is involved, it would be no loss but
rather the contrary, if their education to a far greater extent . . . were
consigned to females, always provided that they are themselves qualified
for the office by previous acquirements and training. I do not mean the
instruction simply of very young children, and in the most common and
elementary branches, but up almost or quite to the point of preparation

6. "Report of the Superintendent of Common Schools of North Carolina for
the Year 1862," *Public Documents of North Carolina, 1862–'63*, p. 12.

for College. . . . There are doubtless some branches, which as a general thing, can be taught most effectually by males, just as there are others in which females excel. . . . But for that portion of the process of education which comes within the scope of these remarks, females are fully competent, even if we should not say that they are particularly adapted. . . .

If there be any force in these views, there emerges from them a duty of direct, practical import—that of educating our daughters with reference to the office they are to fill—educating them to become teachers. . . . It may not be just such a life as you may prefer for your daughter. . . . You have made your sons an offering on your country's altar. Would you withhold your daughters from a service, noble in itself and befitting their sex, without which their country must be subjected to a yoke more disgraceful and oppressive than that our ruthless enemies would lay upon our necks—the yoke of ignorance and its consequences, vice and degradation. . . .

. . . Our females usually leave school just at the . . . stage of their mental development, when they are about to be prepared to reap the benefits of study and instruction. Teachers know this, lament it and strive against it. But they are powerless to remedy the evil. . . .

In plain words, parents must allow their daughters to remain longer at school. . . . Without such a sacrifice . . . it is impossible for our females to attain that proficiency which will render teaching anything else than a burden or a humiliating failure. This is all the more important, because in addition to the branches of learning . . . , our daughters are expected to devote no inconsiderable portion of their time whilst in school, to what are termed the Ornamental branches. I do not unite in the condemnation which some have pronounced upon these latter. . . . But these embellishments of female education . . . require time and labor for their acquisition, which time and labor must not be abstracted from the solid branches of learning. That . . . would defeat the chief design of education. The woman need not be the less accurately and thoroughly instructed in all the substantial parts of education because she is proficient in the ornamental department, if only time, *time* for both, is allowed; and time, ample time there is, if parents and daughters shall only consent that it be allowed. [Concludes with impassioned call upon young ladies to become teachers.]

J. K. Kirkpatrick, "The Duty of Females in Relation to the Future Educational Interests of Our Country," pp. 85–94.

---

(4) Southern Textbooks for Southern Children

Heretofore southern schools had depended on the North for their   *textbooks. Hostilities ended this supply, and on 9 July 1861 rep-*

resentatives of North Carolina schools and colleges met in Raleigh to discuss obtaining texts suitable for southern minds. The next day a committee reported against reprinting northern texts and recommended the preparation and publication of new books by southerners. The conference then urged the southern people to strive for intellectual independence and suggested that this could be best accomplished by using school-books by southern writers. The next year the president of the State Educational Association re-iterated this plea and denounced northern texts as replete with "covert and insidious attacks upon our social and political institutions."[7] This was a continuing crusade among North Carolina educators, and the following "Address" is representative of many similar statements by educational organizations.

ADDRESS TO PARENTS AND TEACHERS

The undersigned Committee have been appointed by the State Educational Association of North Carolina to prepare an address to Parents and Teachers upon the subject of text-books. . . .

We would urge . . .

First, That *Southern writers are best fitted to prepare Text-books for Southern use.* They are penetrated with the spirit of our institutions, acquainted with our habits, our modes of thought, our social relations &c; hence it is evident that they can so express themselves, that pupils will more readily understand and appreciate lessons in such books, than in those whose writers are destitute of advantages. . . . Take for instance the mass of books which have been in common use for children, when the exercises and illustrations are taken from the harbour, the crowded thoroughfare, the commercial mart and such like scenes with which our children . . . are not familiar, and which are so uninteresting . . . to them. How different the impression, how much happier the effect were those exercises and illustrations taken from the scenes of rural life in country and village, from our fields of corn, our breaths of wheat, our harvest festivals; from the association of farm life and its repose; from the mill, the school house, the quiet church on the hill, the graveyard hard by. . . . But our limits prevent us from developing the idea further.

Another reason . . . is this: That the *present time*, if any, is *the most favorable* for the creation of a home literature, particularly in the department of primary education. We are shut out from the foreign world, and especially from that source on which we have hitherto relied almost exclusively for the supply of Text-books on all the branches of education. If we are ever then to have text-books of our own production, Providence never granted to us a more golden opportunity, and if the support of our people is not withheld, the difficulties which embarrass

7. Marcus C. S. Noble, *A History of the Public Schools of North Carolina,* p. 238.

the speedy manufacture of books—such as the scarcity of paper, printing facilities, &c, will be the more readily met and overcome, and capital will be risked in the enterprise with far less fear of failure. All that is wanted, is the assurance of patriotic and faithful support on the part of those who are truly interested in this whole subject, the teachers, parents and guardians of the youth of our land.

Our *third* . . . reason . . . is a moral one. If we have forever cast off all political association with the people who are now invading our country with fire and blood and remorseless cruelty, who deny to us the right to govern ourselves, to cherish and defend our own institutions, and even *to think for ourselves*—according to conscience and the word of God; then we submit it to the candid judgment of every lover of his country in this trying hour, whether it would not be degrading to us in the extreme to suffer ourselves or our children to depend on them any longer for the means of mental and moral culture? Would it not be, to say the least, inconsistent in us as a people, to use the *reprints* of *their* publications who have, for years past, while we were drinking at their fountains of knowledge, been proclaiming us to the world as an *ignorant, rude* and *barbarous* people? Does it not reflect severely on the intelligent patriotism of our people, as true and as noble as ever breathed on earth, thus to patronize the people that are straining every nerve to crush us beneath the heel of despotic power? How does it present our character for consistency in the eyes of the civilized world to see along side the same bulletin that proclaims a glorious victory over our foe, won at the cost of our most precious blood and the anguish of heart of our mothers, wives and sisters, the advertisement of a reprint of Webster's spelling book or some other successful Yankee speculation? Let us, if possible, correct this thing. . . . It is as easy to print our own books as it is to reprint Northern publications; and honor and patriotism demand that the preference be given to Southern books which in point of excellence, every way, are better adapted for our people than any other. . . .

J. C. MCLEOD,
F. H. JOHNSON, } COM.
WM. M. COLEMAN.

Greensboro *Patriot*, 3 Sept. 1863.

---

(5) Molding Young Minds

The campaign to encourage text-book writing soon bore fruit. By the end of 1862 the Greensboro publishing house of Sterling, Campbell, and Albright was advertising "Our Own Series of School Books." Its "peculiarly Southern" readers were said to contain "useful and interesting information in regard to places and things in the Confederate States," as well as subject matter engen-

dering morality and piety.[8] Other publishing houses advertised in similar fashion. Superintendent Calvin H. Wiley took the responsibility of reviewing all schoolbooks published and recommending to district school authorities all those that met with his approval. Mrs.

Marinda Branson Moore, a Raleigh school teacher, prepared a series of books for Branson and Farrar publishing company of Raleigh. The following excerpts demonstrate how her textbooks were designed to influence impressionable young minds.

NO. 37 — XXXVII
WAR

It makes us sad to hear the booming of cannon in time of war. We think of our dear friends who are in the army, and fear they may be killed.

War is a sad thing, and those who bring it about will have much to answer for.

Some people lay all the blame at the door of the rulers of the nation. In some countries this is true, but in our country it is not so. The people elect their own rulers, and they should not choose bad men. If the rulers in the United States had been good Christian men, the present war would not have come upon us.

The people sent bad men to Congress, and they were not willing to make just laws, but were selfish, and made laws to suit themselves.

The Bible says "When the wicked bear rule the nation mourneth, but when the righteous are in authority, the people rejoice."

People often go wrong, and when trouble comes upon them, they say God sent it.

God has made good laws for man, and if we do right we will be happy; but sin will always bring trouble.

Let every boy learn this lesson, and when he is a man, let him not vote for a bad man to fill an office of trust.—Then the men who wish to be in office will strive to be good, and the nation will be happy.

Marinda Branson Moore, *The Dixie Elementary Spelling Book*, p. 33.

LESSON X
RACES OF MEN

The men who inhabit the globe, are not all alike. Those in Europe and America are mostly white and are called the Caucasian race. This race is civilized, and is far above all the others. They have schools and churches and live in fine style. They also generally have wise and good men for rulers, and a regular form of government. The women are treated with respect and tenderness, and in many cases their wish is law among their male friends.

8. Ibid., pp. 237–38.

2. There is a class of people who inhabit most of Asia which is of a yellow color. They are a quiet, plodding race, but when educated are sensible and shrewd. They have some books, and a regular form of government, but they are heathen; I mean by this that they worship images made of wood and stone. They do not know about Jesus. And yet they pray to those idols much oftener than we christians do to our Savior. This race is called the Mongolion [sic]. . . .

4. The African or negro race is found in Africa. They are slothful and vicious, but possess little cunning. They are very cruel to catch other [sic], and when they have war they sell their prisoners to the white people for slaves. They know nothing of Jesus, and the climate in Africa is so unhealthy that white men can scarcely go there to preach to them. The slaves who are found in America are in much better condition. They are better fed, better clothed, and better instructed than in their native country.

5. These people are descendants of Ham . . . who was cursed because he did not treat his father with respect.—It was told he should serve his brethren forever. That would seem a hard sentence but, it was probably done to show other children how wicked it was to treat their parents so. We can not tell how they came to be black, and have wool on their heads. . . .

LESSON XI
THE UNITED STATES

1. This was once the most prosperous country in the world. Nearly a hundred years ago it belonged to England; but the English made such hard laws that the people said they would not obey them. After a long, bloody war of seven years, they gained their independence; and for many years were prosperous and happy.

2. . . . In a few years, the Northern States finding their climate too cold for the negro to be profitable, sold them to the people living farther South. Then the Northern States passed laws to forbid any person owning slaves in their borders.

3. Then the northern people began to preach, to lecture, and to write about the sin of slavery. . . . And when the territories were settled they were not willing for any of them to become slaveholding. This would soon have made the North much stronger than the South; and many of the men said they would vote for a law to free all the negroes in the country. The Southern men tried to show them how unfair this would be, but still they kept on.

4. In the year 1860 the Abolitionists became strong enough to elect one of their men for President. Abraham Lincoln was a weak man, and the South believed he would allow laws to be made, which would deprive them of their rights. So the Southern States seceded. . . . This so enraged President Lincoln that he declared war, and has exhausted nearly all the strength of the nation, in a vain attempt to whip the South back into the Union. . . . The South only asked to be let alone, and to divide the public property equally. . . .

5. This country possesses many ships, has fine cities and towns, many railroads, steamboats, canals, manufactures, &c. The people are ingenious and enterprising, and are noted for their tact in "driving a bargain." They are refined, and intelligent on all subjects but that of negro slavery, and on this they are mad. . . .

Marinda Branson Moore, *Geographical Reader for the Dixie Children*, pp. 10–14.

(6) Financial Difficulties of the Common Schools

Even with textbooks and teachers the common schools could not continue without money. In the summer of 1861 the sudden increase of military expenses forced the state treasurer to delay appropriating half the dividends of the Literary Fund. This caused a wave of apprehension among educators. A committee of the Raleigh Conference of 1861, fearful that the dividends might be permanently allocated to the military budget, pointed out that all the public funds devoted to education would only keep two regiments in the field for one year. In his address to the legislature on 22 November 1862 Governor Vance assured the public that the state would never rob the children of their schools.

Nevertheless, the delayed appropriation for 1861 spread uncertainty over the school system (Document A), and some districts delayed opening their schools until the dividend was in hand. In addition, some county courts, which had the constitutional right to levy a supplementary school tax, simply decided that their people could not pay both school and war taxes. When this occurred, schools either closed or held a brief session until its state money ran out. Document B written by Mr. McIntyre, a farmer, and Document C written by Mr. Paschall, a county register of deeds, reveal the demoralization caused by such funding problems.

A.

Ashboro, Sept 30/61

C. H. Wiley Esq.
    Dear Sir
    . . . I am applied to daily to know what we are to expect for the schools. I suppose your circular will be forthcoming soon. I should feel at liberty to say it would be the usual amount but for the extraordinary action of the Literary Board in the Spring. That board then felt justified in looking to the general wants of the State and withholding half the amount due to the counties. Whether, after the repeated refusals of the

Genl Assembly to divert the school fund to war purposes, the Board will direct the half which they withheld in the Spring together with the full dividend for the Fall to be paid—or not, I cannot divine, since the former act of the board assumed that they have a discretion on the subject. I have have [sic] never regarded their action withholding one *half* as in any way defensible. They should have paid all or withheld all. No school, I presume was opened upon that pittance. The board had as much right to withhold *all* as *half*. Paying out half did *no* good as to schools. It might have been of some service in the Treasury, on assumed right of the board and Treasurer to apply it to war purposes.

It is certainly very desirable that the action of the board be early known to the public. . . .

Yours very respectfully
JONATHAN WORTH

Calvin H. Wiley Papers.

B.

Lumberton Robeson Cty. N.C.
May 27, 1861

Rev. C. H. Wiley,
　　Dear Sir.
　　I convened the Board of Supts of Common Schools in Robeson Cty last Saturday as you will ascertain from our reply to your Letter of interogation relative to appropriating the common school funds to defraying the expenses of the War. Robeson County is a unit for Secession, and if it was put to a vote I think it would be unanimous and concur in the action of the Board of Supts the Board thinks that Schools would do but very little good during the crisis the Board wants all the money to which the County is entitled from the Literary Fund together with what they raise by taxation in the County applied to the War and to receive credit for it in some way in order that it may appear what disposition they made of it &c, . . . I would like very much to hear your views on the disposition that the Literary Board will make of the School moneys if they are applied to the War. . . . I expect you are troubled with many inquiries of this subject but I am ansious [sic] to hear your views on the Subject.

Respectfully,
D. C. MCINTYRE

Wiley Papers.

C.

Oxford, N.C.
May 22nd 1862

Rev C H Willie
　　My Dear Sir
　　. . . But there is another matter about which I want your advice, in the first place our County Court at May term refused to levy any School

Tax, saying the Schools must Stop until the war is over, this I suppose deprives us of the aid from the Literary fund, twelve months ago last April our board appropriated $100 to each district Supposing we should receive the usual appropriation from the State, this you remember failed in part, and consequently all the districts could not get their $100, but it so turned out that very many of the districts, had no Schools on account of so many male teachers enlisting in the war, all the Schools that were taught, received their $100. and there is still in my hands some 10 or 12 hundred dollars and we have some 405 female teachers who are now teaching in the county but not one male, My plan is to continue these Schools until the money in my hand is exhausted without any reference to previous appropriations (for our Board this Spring made no appropriation of the funds in my hand) this is the matter I wish you to advise me about

That May visit of yours & Mrs Willies to Oxford has not come to pass

Most respectfully yours

L. A. PASCHALL

Wiley Papers, 7:808a.

---

(7) A Deteriorating Common School System

Despite Wiley's plea "let us carry with us our school machinery unimpaired,"[9] the Civil War eroded the common school system. Boards became lax in submitting their reports, and half way through the war Wiley could only estimate from the available figures that there were about 50,000 children attending and that the average term was three months. It was becoming more and more difficult to enlist qualified boards, and the depreciation of the currency was making teaching steadily less attractive. The following letters are typical of the scores from county school board men complaining of the deterioration of their schools.

Oxford N C Mar 20th 1862

Rev C H Willie

My Dear Sir

I have just made up my annual account as chairman, and when you see it you will see the effects of the War upon Common Schools in Granville, in many instances during the past year, our teachers, quit there schools, some soon after they commenced, others at various stages, so that in very many cases, no reports were made either by teacher or Com-

---

9. "Report of the Superintendent of Common Schools of North Carolina for the Year 1862," *Public Documents*, 1862–'63, p. 41.

mittee men, hence so many blanks not filled, not only teachers but Committee men in several instances volunteered, we have not more than 2
or 3 male teachers left, nearly all the schools now being taught are by
females, but very many are not taught at all. I am doing all in my power
to keep the schools in being, but it is a hard task. In several districts in
this County no schools have been taught for three years. I have kept
these districts each year credited with there annual appropriations.
Would it not be best to spend the money in those districts where they are
willing and anxious to keep up schools, in most instances where schools
have not been taught, are those wealthy sections where children are
scarce and generally sent to higher schools. What will become of the
people if this war continues much longer, it looks to me as if the whole
country is going down, down, without a bottom to fall on

We begin to think that promised visit, is slow in its movements we
hope to see you soon

Most truly yours,
L . A . PASCHALL

Wiley Papers.

Salem N.C. May 3, 1863

State Superint.ᵉⁿᵗ of Com. Schools.

Respected Sir.

. . . I learn to my regret, that the active schools of my county have
been but very few during the winter months; & that the spirit for the
successful prosecution of our common school system is lamentably pros-
trate among our people. This may be the natural effect of the war; but I
much fear that a careless superintendence of our school affairs may have
added largely to augment this sad state of affairs. In short, the spirit of
our people is flat on this subject; & the want of good teachers in most of
our districts, has likewise tended to embarras[s] this subject. Near $2000
is due . . . the *various districts*, from which fact I infer, that these districts had no school during the past session. A mighty effort must be
made to counteract the sad effects of this war, and to overcome a careless superintendence. . . . I therefore propose . . . that we fix upon
some day this Fall *for a public* address on the subject, to be delivered in
Salem Church. . . . We have many ladies of our town who are well
qualified for teachers—*you* might prevail on some of them to volunteer
their services for our destitute districts. My object is simply to infuse a
new spirit into this system, & to preserve in order as much as possible
the whole machinery of our great and hopeful system of common
schools . . . & it is only by a thorough re-organization of the system, &
a hopeful interest manifested by liberal donations from separate county
courts that we can ever hope to get general intelligence among the people at large & thus be able to counteract the wiley designs of intrigueing
demagogues. . . .

Yours respectfully
JOSHUA BONER
County Superintendent

Marmaduke S. Robins Papers.

(8) War Comes to the Colleges

Lincoln's call for volunteers to quell the southern rebellion had an explosive impact on North Carolina institutions of higher education. Enrollment dropped precipitately as students volunteered for army service. Young instructors became drillmasters and organized military companies from the remaining students. Meanwhile the presidents bent every effort to keep their schools operating as normally as possible. In July President Kirkpatrick made the following comments on how the first three months of the war had affected Davidson College.

Up to the first of April our students appeared to be diligently pursuing their studies and but slightly affected by the political excitement pervading the country. A few days later, two of them . . . from the State of South Carolina, having previously enrolled their names in a company which was to be formed for the military service of the State were ordered home by their Commanding Officer. . . . Their leaving . . . of course created some excitement among their fellow students. However, there was no open demonstration of a purpose on the part of others to relinquish their studies until . . . the Proclamation of the President of the United States calling for a large army to operate against the seceded states of the South, reached the College. . . .

The excitement became intense and uncontrollable. Some made up their minds at once to enter the army . . . ; some received orders from their parents to come home and join volunteer companies there organizing; some were called home to take the places of older brothers who had volunteered; some were called away to protect widowed mothers in what was supposed to be a time of special danger. . . . The Faculty . . . did not think there was just occasion for such precipitation in leaving the College; yet they could not say to young men who felt impelled to go to the defense of their country . . . that they ought not to do so.

They, however, in addresses to the students and in private conversation, urged the students to be calm, to attend to their regular duties for the time and to await more decisive evidence that their services were actually and instantly needed elsewhere.

. . . We advised the students to form themselves into military companies, and to prepare themselves for service should it be necessary by drilling on the ground, at the same time pursuing their studies.

Some steps were taken toward this; but a large number of these had already committed themselves to companies in other places.

Finding that a large majority of the students had left or would soon leave the College, the President requested a meeting of the Executive Committee to know their views as to the propriety of attempting to continue the exercises or of formally closing them. . . .

The Committee, after much hesitation as to what was best to do, advised that the exercises should be continued unless the number of students should be reduced below eight. In which case they left it to the

Faculty to continue the exercises or not as they might think best. There were only eleven students in regular connection with the College, six of the Sophomore class and five of the Freshman. Those of the Sophomore class remained between two and three weeks longer, when they all withdrew and returned home. Those of the Freshman class remained at their studies about two weeks longer still, when they too left us. For nearly a month past we have not had a student in this place.

It is due to the students to mention that great as was the excitement prevailing among them, there was no violence or disorder. Except that there was a decline in their attention to their studies, as might be expected in their state of feeling, the Faculty found no occasion of complaint against them.

Cornelia R. Shaw, *Davidson College*, pp. 102–4.

(9) Declining Enrollment

Declining enrollment was the critical problem of college campuses. Wake Forest suspended operations in May 1862, when the draft left it only five students. Davidson remained open for the duration, though only ten students matriculated in 1864. President Braxton Craven helped keep Trinity's enrollment at more than forty by organizing a number of students and town people into the "Trinity Guard" for area police duty. The University's enrollment at first averaged about 100 a year, and it was President David L. Swain's letter to Jefferson Davis included below asking for a suspension of the draft of students for the forthcoming year that secured the University a year's grace. The War Department refused a second such request the following spring, and there were about a dozen students enrolled when Sherman's forces entered Chapel Hill.

UNIVERSITY OF
NORTH CAROLINA,
CHAPEL HILL,
OCT. 15, 1863

"To His Excellency, Jefferson Davis, President of the
    Confederate States:
    ". . . At the close of the collegiate year 1859–60 . . . the whole number of students on our catalogue was four hundred and thirty. . . . They were distributed in the four classes as follows: Seniors eighty-four, Juniors one hundred and two, Sophomores one hundred and twenty-five, Freshmen eighty.

"Of the eight young men who received the first distinction in the Senior class, four are in their graves, (soldiers' graves,) and a fifth a wounded prisoner. More than a seventh of these graduates are known to have fallen in battle.

"The Freshman class of eighty members pressed into the service with such impetuosity that but a single individual remained to graduate at the last commencement; and he in the intervening time had entered the army, been discharged on account of impaired health, and was permitted by special favor to rejoin his class.

"The Faculty at that time was composed of fourteen members, no one of whom was liable to conscription. Five of the fourteen were permitted by the trustees to volunteer. One of these has recently returned from long imprisonment in Ohio, with a ruined constitution. A second is a wounded prisoner, now at Baltimore. A third fell at Gettysburg. The remaining two are in active field-service at present.

"The nine gentlemen who now constitute the corps of instructors are, with a single exception, clergymen, or laymen beyond the age of conscription. No one of them has a son of the requisite age who has not entered the service as a volunteer. Five of the eight sons of members of the faculty are now in active service; one fell mortally wounded at Gettysburg, another at South-Mountain. . . .

"A rigid enforcement of the Conscription Act may take from us nine or ten young men with physical constitutions in general better suited to the quiet pursuits of literature and science than to military service. They can make no appreciable addition to the strength of the army; but their withdrawal may very seriously affect our organization, and . . . compel us to close the doors of the oldest University . . . of the Confederacy.

"It can scarcely be necessary to intimate that with a slender endowment and a diminution of more than twenty thousand dollars in the annual receipts for tuition, it is at present very difficult and may soon be impossible to sustain the institution. The exemption of professors from the operation of the Conscript Act is a sufficient indication that the annihilation of the best established colleges in the country was not the purpose of our Congress; and I can but hope . . . that it will never be permitted to produce effects which I am satisfied no one would more deeply implore than yourself.

"I have the honor to be, with the highest consideration, your obedient servant, D. L. SWAIN."

Cornelia P. Spencer, *The Last Ninety Days of the War in North Carolina*, pp. 257–60.

---

(10) Student Life During Wartime

During the war, college students were somewhat more disorganized and undisciplined, provisions became scarce, and curricula made gestures toward military science and tactics. But professors and presidents attempted to keep their institutions as normal as possible and to a large extent succeeded.

William T. Gannaway became president of Trinity College in 1863 and has left the following description of conditions at his college.

When I took charge of Trinity College on the resignation of Dr. Craven, in December, 1863, the civil war was at its height. Men and boys were forced to abandon their pursuits and hasten to the front. Many of our students had already left to join the army. The whole country was in a ferment, society was demoralized, and everything was unsettled and uncertain. . . . The students of the previous session had not been subjected to the usual discipline, and the habits of study had greatly deteriorated; for they, too, were affected by the excitement, the anxieties, and the passions of the war. The fall session of 1863 closed in gloom and uncertainty, without promise or hopeful prospect. But on January 6, 1864, the college opened . . . with a much better patronage than was expected. Girls were admitted to our classes, and our . . . arrangement proved beneficial to both sexes. Fifteen or twenty young ladies occupied my recitation room, and were under my supervision and control. . . . The usual curriculum was still continued, and all of the regular classes were represented. . . . Those were war times, and one professor did as much work then as two or three of our college specialists of the present day. The difficulties to be overcome were anomalous and unprecedented. The country was drained of its supplies to feed the soldiers. . . . Board had ceased to be remunerative and was hard to get within the village. My house was taxed, in that respect, beyond its limits; for, on their arrival, most of the students stopped with me till other arrangements might possibly be made. . . . Some of my boarders paid in kind, some in specie, that had not seen the light for many years. Only six dollars, specie value, was charged per month for board when payment was made *in kind.* . . . A young man, Mr. John B. Yarborough, a crippled soldier . . . paid me for two and one-half months board with seven bushels of wheat and two hundred and fifty pounds of salt, which was brought all the way from the county of Rockingham. . . .

That the college should have survived at all during this stormy and distracted period seems now almost incredible; but with the exception of Dr. Craven the old Faculty retained their places, the regular classification remained intact, and the usual program of college exercises and college methods were carried out for the entire term of 1864. In view of the fact that all able-bodied young men . . . were liable to military service . . . our patronage was remarkably . . . encouraging. The general order was good, the regulations were rarely broken, application to study . . . was satisfactory, and a commendable spirit of improvement pervaded the entire student body. The exactions of the army . . . had left us only one member of the senior class, and he a cripple. . . . He was Mr. E. H. Tapscott, of Virginia. . . .

The fall session of 1864 opened the first week in September. The number of students in attendance was well sustained; the Faculty remained the same, and the organization and general regulations were but slightly changed. . . . Our stock of textbooks had become exhausted, and . . . I . . . canvassed the State, and in that way procured many books from former students and private libraries.

Another serious embarrassment confronted us, and one much more difficult to be overcome—the depreciated money and the scarcity of provisions. Ten per cent. of the products of the country were absorbed by commissaries to feed the army. This government demand . . . so reduced our food resources that I applied to President Davis for a limited exemption from paying the required tithes. Before I received a reply, however, Grant captured Richmond and the Confederacy was rapidly toppling to its fall. General Johnston's army . . . was moving in this direction, and in a few days the advanced division, under General Hardee, arrived at Trinity College, and . . . tents were scattered about among the trees on the north side of the college building. . . . The presence of the soldiers, the excitement of the students, the anxiety and consternation of the people, rendered further college exercises useless, if not impossible. It was determined to close till the storm should pass, peace be made, and civil order once more restored.

William T. Gannaway, "Trinity College in War Times," pp. 324–29.

XV

VICTIMS OF ATTRITION

Three types of persons became particularly unfortunate victims of the war: refugees, Negroes, and families of soldiers. As the war coursed through the South it turned thousands of Confederates into homeless wanderers. Union sympathizers might welcome the approach of enemy forces, but others found life under enemy occupation unthinkable and either fled their homes as Union troops approached or left soon after they had arrived. Often a family had to flee several times, and wherever they stopped they created problems for themselves and others. Friends and relatives who took them in soon found their generosity strained by the overcrowded home life and the rapidly dwindling food supply. The poorer refugees often became problems to the law and even to the military authorities. Confederate home front morale suffered as a consequence.

The Census of 1860 showed North Carolina to have approximately 30,000 free Negroes and 331,000 slaves, the large majority of both being concentrated in the eastern and northern counties. Between 1835 and 1860 most of the state's liberal treatment of its Negroes had vanished, and when war came the increased fear of Negro insurrection provoked even tighter controls. In 1861 the legislature ordered a mandatory death sentence for encouraging discontent among slaves and free Negroes. When the legislature refused to enact other controls, municipalities did so by means of local ordinances. Part of their overall intent was to reduce the number of free Negroes, to prevent them from associating with slaves, and to control them by means of permits, licenses, curfews, and hiring them out for minor infractions of the law. The intent of the city ordinances regarding slaves was to restrict even further their mobility while living and working. The effectiveness of these laws and ordinances is indicated by the fact that government authorities did with all Blacks about whatever they wished and there was no insurrection.

Negro labor prevented the economic collapse of the Confederacy, and both state and nation used it ruthlessly. On 19 December 1862 the legislature authorized the Governor to impress any number of slaves that were needed for work on fortifications and other defense projects. To prevent agriculture from being deprived of too much labor, however, the legislature required that all available free Negroes must be hired before any slaves could be impressed. Needless to say, the former had little choice about whether or not they were for hire. Generally the Confederate authorities obtained laborers by advertising for them or by calls upon the governors for a specific number. If these means proved insufficient, the laws of Congress permitted the impressment of all free Negroes between the ages of eighteen and fifty and of 20,000 slaves when all free Negroes had been taken.

The most restive of these helpless groups consisted of the families of soldiers. Out of a population of approximately 650,000 white inhabitants, North Carolina raised 125,000 soldiers. The resulting labor shortage bore particularly hard on families of enlisted men, whose meager wages even when sent home were far insufficient for wife and children. Real want and even destitution soon settled into hundreds of homes where life had been precarious before the war. In this era charity was not a major interest of the churches, so the responsibility fell to others. At first county governments and local citizen groups administered what charity they could; then the state assumed part of the responsibility. A lack of money, food, and transportation made all these efforts inadequate, but the lot of the soldiers' families would have been far worse had they been left to fend for themselves.

(1) Dislocated Families

Alex MacRae was a wealthy Wilmingtonian with widespread mercantile and blockade-running activities. In January 1863, a force of Union soldiers was at Beaufort to assist in a joint land and naval attack on Wilmington, and MacRae decided to move his family inland. The Washington government, however, decided to attack Charleston, South Carolina, instead, so the MacRaes in their panic became refugees a year too early (Document A).

Refugees who owned property inland and who did not have to depend on the hospitality of friends or relatives seem to have made the transition with comparative ease. But Mrs. Mary R. Anderson of Edenton found refugee life in Hillsborough unbearable. Her cousin Paul Cameron let her use one of his houses there, but Mrs. Anderson found her neighbors "insolent" and "almost insupportable." She complained "We are not as prosperous as we were before the war, but we are still ladies and I trust the fortunes of war will never subject your wife & children to what we have borne from these people."[1]

Those without family connec-

1. Mary R. Anderson to Paul Cameron, 20 Oct. 1862, Cameron Family Papers.

tions were even more miserable. Mary Boykin Chesnut was forced to abandon her South Carolina home at Sherman's approach. Her account of her stay in Lincolnton,

North Carolina, is that of a wealthy sophisticate living in what she considered the most trying circumstances (Document B).

A.

Wilmington N.C. Jany 15th 1863

Dear Don,

I regret exceedingly that the appearent necessity has arisen for sending my folks off—it is very generally believed that we will be attacked here within two weeks—every body that can get away is leaving, & Gen[l] Whiting assures us all that if we postpone the sending of families away until the attack commences it will be too late, as he will then hold all means of communication for the troops, & no one will be permitted to leave—I regret this necessity as I say, not so much that I do not wish to break up my house here, & get Mrs Chambers & the children to a place of safety at once, as on account of the trouble it may put you to—I view the matter however in the light of a dire necessity & therefore do not scruple to place such a burden on you for, I hope, only a short time.

I have spoken a passage for them on the Hart tomorrow (friday), & have told John that you wished me to send him up with them—he consents readily to go—I tell him if you wish to return immediately I will pay his expenses both ways for the care he will have over my folks & effects &—I will send two beds & beadsteads & a few utensils with them for cooking—They cannot carry any provisions & therefore you will have to try & buy them enough to subsist on until I can prepare better for them. Fit them up in your Hotel building the best you can with the appliances they carry & such as you can lend them temporarily say a chair or two & a table.—The Steamer will not carry any more than trunks & a bed or two—I hope however the attack will be delayed long enough for me to send some necessaries up by some ensuing boat—. . . .

I fear my folks will suffer going up tomorrow—as the boat will be crowded to her utmost capacity—All of the berths have been engaged three days ahead—I fortunately secured berths for them, they will probably arrive too late to go up by Saturdays train & will have to lay over at Fayetteville until Monday

Wishing them all comfort & you as little trouble as the case may admit of, I wind up this, I fear, subject—I will send some money with them

Yours truly &c

ALEX MAC RAE JR

MacRae Papers.

B.

FEBRUARY 18th.—Here I am, thank God, settled at the McLean's in a clean, comfortable room . . . and with a grateful heart I stir up my own bright wood fire. I was glad to get away from our landlady's sharp tongue. . . . My bill for four days at that splendid hotel was $240.00, with $25.00 additional for fire. I tried to propitiate the termagent; I was mild, humble, patient, polite. "Do not waste your time! They will never comprehend the height from which we have fallen," suggested Miss Middleton. . . .

Today, dirt has given me a black eye. I have fought a hard battle with that dread antagonist, and it is rather a drawn battle. Ellen has my washing to do, as well as my cooking, so I have elected to do some housework. . . . Ellen tied up her clothes, and with bare feet and legs scrubbed the floor. "He! Misses, this is harder than hoeing corn." I sat on the bedside and watched, after I was too tired to work, but she sent me away. . . . I am very docile now, and I obeyed orders.

On the way I met a cousin, male, elderly, a *ci devant* fire eater . . . extreme in everything. In Columbia he refused to be seen with his son-in-law, who was not in the army. . . . Here he is . . . fleeing before the face of the Yankees; his wife, his children, his Negroes all banked up in one room. One poor Negro woman was taken so the family had to go and camp in the hotel drawing-room, leaving the poor sole to herself and her sister who nurses her, in the sole chamber the landlady would let them have. . . .

FEBRUARY 19th.— . . . The McLeans are kind people. They ask no rent for their rooms, only $20.00 a week for firewood. Twenty dollars! And such dollars, mere waste paper! . . .

MARCH 6th.—Today, a godsend. . . . My larder was empty. A tall mulatto woman walked in with a tray, covered by a huge white serviette. Ellen ushered her in with a flourish. "Mrs. McDonald's maid." She set down the tray upon my bare table and uncovered it with conscious pride. Fowls, ready for roasting; sausages, butter, bread, eggs, preserves. I was dumb with delight. After silent thanks to Heaven, my powers of speech returned, and I exhausted myself in messages of gratitude to Mrs. McDonald. Ellen scolded me afterward. "Missis, you oughtn't to let her see how glad you was. It was a letting of yourself down." . . .

Colonel Fant has turned up. He is a handsome, big Virginian. He is his own man, and he knows the laws and his rights and dares maintain them. The landlady at the Hotel got into one of her tantrums because they wanted eggs in Lent and tried to expel them. He calmly says he won't go, and that he has a right to stay. They are three in the family. They pay $80 a day, with fires extra, in Confederate currency.

They told me a fearful thing. That family who came like the patriarch —man-servants, maid-servants, wife and children—were huddled into one room by the greedy landlady; then their Negro woman was taken sick, and they all had to camp out in the drawing-room while they nursed her with faithful kindness. Now the poor woman is dead and laid out in their one room, and they still camp in the drawing-room. Old Mrs. Graspall makes them pay their $100 a day in Confederate brown paper. . . .

MARCH 21st, 1865. . . . As the train left Lincolnton, and I waved my handkerchief to Mrs. Middleton, Isabella, and my other devoted friends, I could but wonder, will fate throw me again with such kind

. . . friends? The McLeans refused to be paid for their rooms. No plummet can sound the depths of the hospitality and kindness of the North Carolina people.

Mary Boykin Chesnut, *A Diary from Dixie*, pp. 480–507, *passim*.

(2) Municipal Control of Negroes

Though most free Negroes lived in rural areas, some lived in the towns and cities. For the most part their lot was wretched and by 1860 state laws deprived them of much of their freedom of action. Slaves of course had far more legal restrictions upon them. The fol- *lowing Charlotte ordinance reveals the determination of municipalities to tighten even more harshly the restrictions on the free Negroes and in particular to prevent them from associating with hired-out slaves.*

Be it further Ordained by the Commissioners of the Town of Charlotte, That on and immediately after the first day of July, next, and on each succeeding first day of July, thereafter. . . . All Free-Negroes now resident in the Town of Charlotte, or who may hereafter become residents of the same, being of the age of twelve years and upwards shall be required to appear before the Mayor, enroll their names and upon satisfactory evidence of a peaceable character and industrious habits obtain from him a certificate of such enrollment together with a description of their persons characters and trade, or employment; to be signed by the Mayor, countersigned by the Clerk and sealed with the corporate seal of the Town. And if any free person of color liable to such enrollment shall be found without such certificate said free person of color shall be deemed guilty of a misdemeanor and on conviction before the Mayor shall be punished at his discretion by either fine, whipping, imprisonment, or hireing out for a time not exceeding six months for each offence. And for each and every such enrollment and certificate so granted a tax of one dollar shall be collected by the Clerk for the use of the Treasury of the Town.

Be it further Ordained, That no person under any pretence whatever shall hire to his or her slave, or to any slave under his or her control his or her time, or allow them the control of the same under a penalty of forty dollars for each and every offence. And on conviction before the Mayor said slave or slaves shall also be hired out to the highest bidder at public out-cry for the balance of the year, and the proceeds of such hireing shall be for the benefit of the Town.

Be it further Ordained, That no slave shall go at large as a free person exercising his or her discretion in the employment of their time nor shall any slave keep house to him or herself as a free person exercising the like discretion in the employment of his or her time; and in case the owner or person having control of such slave or slaves consent to the same or connive thereat he or she shall be guilty of a misdemeanor and on conviction be fined not exceeding fifty dollars, *Provided* however that any owner or person having control of slaves may permit such slave or slaves to live or keep house upon his or her own lot or land for the purpose of attending to the business of his or her owner or person having such slave in charge.

Charlotte *North Carolina Whig*, 25 June 1861.

---

(3) Impressed Labor

In an effort to avoid discriminating against any section of the state Governor Vance tried to rotate groups of impressed free Negroes and slaves on a two-month service basis. The execution of this plan proved most difficult, and included below are complaints by a free Negro[2] (Document A) and by a slave owner[3] (Document B). Major General W. H. C. Whiting's answer to these complaints was that the promised rotation was not being followed. "It was understood that all would be regularly & promptly relieved by new details.

This has been but rarely done & irregularly when it has been done—"[4] Soon criticism began to reach the Governor's Office about the mistreatment of impressed laborers (Document C), but Whiting waited until early 1865 before making his excuses. He then explained that most laborers reached him badly clothed, that the "want of money & material" prevented him from always outfitting them properly, and that the reports of hardships were "greatly exaggerated."[5]

2. Locklar (Locklear) is a Lumber River Indian name, so possibly the writer was an Indian rather than a free Negro. Under the Constitution of 1835 Indians as well as free Negroes lost most of the attributes of citizenship, and thereafter the dark-skinned, nontribal Indians of the Lumber River Valley were known as "free persons of color." During the Civil War many were conscripted into labor battalions and sent to the coast. Cherokees in the west fared much better. In fact, the Sixty-ninth North Carolina had in it two companies of Cherokee Indians. They were often charged, however, with scalping victims.

3. Francis E. Shober of Salisbury was a lawyer and a planter. Afterward, he served in the United States Congress.

4. W. H. C. Whiting to Z. B. Vance, 21 Mar. 1864, Governors' Papers.

5. Ibid., 4 Jan. 1865.

A.

Laurinburg Richmond Co N.C.
July 28th 1863

His Excellency the Governor

Sir—if your highness will condesend to reply to my feble Note, you will confer a great favor on me, and relieve me of my troubles. My Case is this I am a free man of Color, and has a large family to support, there is a man living near me, who is an Agent of the State Salt workes appointed by Worth, or is said to be, he took all we Colored men last winter to make Salt. he is now after us to make Barrels for the State Salt works. Comes at the dead hours of night and carries us off wherever he thinks proper, gives us one dollar and fifty Cents pr day and we find ourselves. I cannot support my family at that rate and pay the present high prices for provisions, I can support my family very well if I were left at home to work for my neighbors they pay me or sell me provisions at the old price for my labor, this agent says he has the power by law to carry us where he pleases and when he pleases, if that be a law and he is ortherized by law to use that power, I am willing to submit to his Calls, for I am perfectly willing to do for our Country whatever the laws requires of me, but if there be no such law and this Agent taking this power within himself perhaps speculating on the labor of the free Colored men and our families suffering for bread, I am not willing to submit to such, please let me know if this Agent the power to use us as he does

DANIEL, LOCKLAR

He has no such authority
Z B V

Governors' Papers.

B.

Salisbury N.C.
June 12th 1863

His Excellency Z. B. Vance,
My dear Sir—

I have been requested, in behalf of citizens of this County, whose slaves are now said to be at work on fortifications in Wilmington to represent to your Excellency that the term of service for which their slaves were taken expired some two weeks ago, but that they are still held by the military authorities in Wilmington, & are likely to be so held for an indefinite period, unless your Excellency will interpose for their restoration to their owners at once. The harvest is now approaching, & this labor will be needed greatly. One Gentleman told me today, that he has promised to cut wheat for several widows & wives of soldiers in his neighborhood, but that he will be unable to comply, unless his slaves are returned, as he will have barely enough hands to attend to his own crop. These instances are common all over the county. I think that the military authorities are acting in bad faith with regard to these negroes, &

that their conduct in this respect will have the effect of destroying the confidence of the slave owners, & prevent a ready compliance hereafter with these [torn] for slave labor upon public works.

A Gentleman, who was sent down to Wilmington last week, for the purpose of bringing back the negroes from this County, has returned home without them, & he was told by the officer who had them in charge, that they were not yet ready to deliver them up, & from his tone, this Gentleman infers that they intend to retain them indefinitely. He says also that these negroes are not employed on fortifications, but are doing odd jobs about Wilmington such as cleaning up the public streets &c.

I therefore would beg your Excellency, in behalf of our people, to interpose for the immediate return of these slaves to their homes.

I remain yours very truly
F. E. SHOBER

[On reverse] I have peremptorily ordered the negroes to be returned by harvest, and Gen. Whiting has promised to comply—Z B V

Governor's Papers.

C.

Engineer Department
Wier's Point Battery
Roanoke Island, Sept. 19th 1861

To his Excy
  Gov. Clarke
    Dear Sir:
      Not knowing under whose immediate jurisdiction the payment & clothing of the Negro laborers upon the Coast defenses of North Carolina may come I address you[r] Excy. directly, hoping it is in your power to correct a condition of affairs, among the needy & ragged Negroes, that demands prompt action.

Many of the Negro laborers engaged upon the defensive works at this point—all I believe of whom are free—were secured many months since and have worked at Beacon Island, Oregon Inlet & now here without having received either salary or clothing. A miserable squalid set, they traverse the leads, with their wheelbarrows, without a sufficient amount of dirty rags upon their persons to prevent indecent exposure. With scarcely an extra shirt &, I believe, entirely without blankets, these hands were taken during & before May last & led to believe their days of occupation, upon the coast defenses, would be but few—hence nearly all came unprepared for so long a term & entirely unprovided, even if they had been able to have rendered themselves comfortable. The alacrity with which these poor creatures work, & the sadness of their appearance, has weighed upon me like a night-mare, since I took charge of the defense of this place, & now induces me to urge your Excy. to have them clothed at once & their wages paid, if only in part. Many of them I would have sent home, despite of the pressing necessity for their aid, but for their nakedness and want of money. I would respectfully suggest that after these sufferers have been clothed & paid that they be allowed a respite, which can only—with justice to the progress of the constructions for the defense of Albemarle Sound—be done by sending others in their place.

With the belief that the good people of Albemarle Sound may ere the close of the month sleep with a sense of entire security

I am Your Excy's
Most Obt. Servt.
CHAS. H. DIMMOCK
Capt. Engrs.

Governors' Papers.

---

(4) "Running the Negroes"

As Union forces began occupying parts of the coastal area, many of the more daring slaves fled into enemy lines. By early 1862 so much of the coast was occupied that a mass seizure of slaves by Union soldiers and local "Buffaloes" seemed imminent. Planters then began considering moving their slaves inland where presumably they would be free from capture until the enemy was driven from the state. One wealthy planter wrote that "not fewer than two thousand negroes have been brought from the counties of Washington & Tyrrel[l] within the last ten days."[6] Slaves were generally reluctant to be moved, partly because they saw their chance of freedom vanishing and also because they were being forced to leave friends and even families. When rumors of such removal occurred in a particular district there was often wholesale flight of slaves.

The Pettigrew family was one of the wealthiest in eastern North Carolina. The letters below reveal their plans to move their slaves inland and their difficulty in using them profitably once the safe interior had been reached.

Thursday—
Hillsboro. Feb 26th 1862

My dearest Charles.

. . . *None* of the servants have given me the slightest trouble. I have heard from J. Collins the stampede of the negroes before your letter came. My dear Charles I was infinitely shaken & disappointed. I never dreamed of ours doing so, tho' not surprised at William's. George said that if you *cld* have left with them *immediately* he believed to a man they *wld* have come with you, but that the whole thing originated at Magnolia he thought & spread among them like a panic. I have not hinted it to a servant but am sure they will hear it, for that precious Barney is coming with some horses I believe. By the way he is cordially disliked here. I

---

6. William S. Pettigrew to Charles L. Pettigrew, 14 Oct. 1862, Pettigrew Family Papers.

heard Mr C. say "pity he had not been shot." & Mrs C. can't bear him, he behaved very badly here last summer. I told Armstrong of the stampede—she was horrified said she had never heard such a word from any one at home, but knew as far back as Mr W. ordering tops for his wagons, that his people had said they *wld* not go with their master. Truth dear Charles it does not impress me thinking of it as such a strange thing, it was not like violent resistance to your authority, but dislike to leaving their wives & children. The wonder is it *shld* have been so universal, did Tom leave? If you had had the luck to be the first as Mr Collins was, you *wld* have had no trouble. G. C. of course heard from William Penny disadvantageous *accts* of our side, for instance that Gilbert had said "he had no intention of going with his master"—all of *wch* may or may not be true to enhance their own merit. Jackson reported those he saw at Tarboro, on his way from Miss Slade's, as very discontented, the men who left their wives, some of whom were expecting to be sick. He told Armstrong or some of the servants. To test the contrition the fugitives expressed, I think you must have felt tempted to pack off some of the young ones immediately. Mr Cameron told me he had obtained work on the R.R. for 45 of the C's negroes at $65 a year & had written to an army officer to get some 30 of the hands off. Between our selves Mr Collins does business so slowly, that it worries the other *dreadfully* & he does not hesitate to show it. I have felt for George more than once, he was not to blame at all.

Your own wife
C A R O L I N E [Pettigrew]

Pettigrew Family Papers.

Hillsboro N.C. Jany 23ᵈ 1863

My own dearest wife.

I have now been in Hillsboro some days the guest of Mrs Cameron. I wrote you last from Greensboro, and would have written you soon from this place, but paper is so scarce that I was unwilling to ask the Camerons for even a sheet. I got this one from them, however. It must seem strange that I do not come to Cherry Hill, but I am closely watching the events as they occur, and must come to some conclusion as to the proper course to pursue before the time to plant a crop. I think that the hope of making something above support at Cherry Hill is not to be entertained. If I move fifty negroes to Cherry Hill, there would not be room for them to work on the low ground, and I should regret exceedingly to cut down the hills for they would not make corn, and the times do not justify a cotton crop. I have a farm of good lands offered to me on the N.C. Rail Road very advantageously situated and within two miles of the depot. I think the place will cost me 25 thousand dollars. I am most unwilling to involve myself any more than I am already; and am therefore most reluctant to purchase. If the price of corn and wheat were to keep up, the place would pay for itself in one year, but that is the great question, and I am awaiting here to come to some conclusion. . . . You may well ask me why I should not be willing for the negroes to remain on the road. In the first place they are dreadfully crowded and if summer finds them in this state I am sure there will be great death among them. They are not allowed a moments leisure to rest, neither men nor women. They were allowed a holiday off only on Christmas day. The contractors charge me with every days sickness they have, and I think contrary to our agreement. It is often a great struggle that Mr Mert can get the allowance for the laborers and the women & children. I am charged $3 a bushel for every bushel of meal they eat. In fine the net profit from all those people I have on the road is only 470$ for two months, which will scarcely cloth and pay the taxes for the year. Now there is certainly a mismanagement in the management of the road, or as much as it is in demand labor would pay better on the road. Now the objection to the purchase of the farm of which I speak is, that lands will be exceedingly low after the close of the war, and when I offered this place for sale I could not get half price, and think it would add rather than decrease my troubles. We are passing through a dreadful ordeal, and I trust in the blessings of a good Providence in his protecting care over you and our dear children, and enable us to bring them up as we hope to be able to do. . . . There have been a great many deaths among the negroes on the rail road. Dr Fishman of N.C has lost 40 men, and many more are sick. By the way I forgot to mention that Mr West sent to me to go to my camp as soon as possible, upon my arrival he said to me that he had found out the company contractors intended to establish a hospital and bring all the sick on the road for miles to that place; you may well wonder that I was greatly displeased, for it would cause me to lose many of my people and I had better give Wilkes the entire care of my negroes than allow such a thing to be done. Among other faults I find, I let Wilkes have my mules to work, if he would keep them in good order. They can scarcely drag one leg after the other, indeed, are nearly starved to death, he feeds them on half the corn they are accustomed to have at home. . . . Now as to bringing any number of the negroes to Cherry Hill, I must keep the men where I can get some income, for there will be a heavy war tax to foot up, and I would have to pay about 10$ apiece per fare, for even the children, and as much to bring them back. Carrying 50 negroes would amount to $500 and as much of course to bring them back when the war closes. So you see the trouble I am in.

> Always your truly devoted and
> loving husband
> CHARLES [L. Pettigrew]

Pettigrew Family Papers.

---

(5) The Fear of Slave Insurrection

The comprehensiveness of the laws and ordinances controlling	*the action of slaves forced them to be even more discreet during*

the war. Whites generally over-
looked minor infractions of the
law by slaves but gave swift and
severe punishment for anything
resembling insurrection. Consequently while the slaves undoubtedly anticipated the coming of
freedom they had little choice but
to wait for it. They became openly
defiant only after gaining the shelter of Union armies.

Nevertheless, white fear of insurrection steadily increased. Efforts had been made in the General Assembly in 1862 and again
in 1864 to enact even stricter laws
against inciting slave insurrection, and proponents of the bills

cited rumor after rumor of insurrection plots in their home counties. But the laws already on the
statute books could hardly have
been strengthened and the majority of the legislators decided
that no new ones were necessary.
The decision was the correct one
because, as evidenced by the letter
below from a prominent merchant, local action could be swift
and merciless upon nothing but a
rumor. No record has been found
that such a slave conspiracy existed in Bladen County, but the
records show that the authorities
assumed the rumor to be true and
took the action as described.

Prospect Hall P. O. Bladen Cty.
N.C.
12th Decr. 1864

To his Excellency
  Z. B. Vance, Governor N.C.
    Raleigh N.C.

Governor

I presume ere this, you have heard
all the particulars, from parties on the spot, but as it is possible you may
not have been so informed, I feel it my duty to avail myself of this the
earliest opportunity to inform you of the discovery of a well planned,
formidable, & most diabolical scheme of Insurrection among the Negroes, of this section of the State, extending from Troy, in Montgomery
County to Society Hill in So Carolina, how far it extends on either side of
the line between these points is not known. Their courier was arrested on
his way into Robeson County, his confessions led to the arrest of some
forty or fifty others on the above line, a list of one hundred & ten names
were found. The county is aroused & every one on the alert, & parties are
now out in search of as many of the culprits as can be found, but the
country is very deficient in men to arrest & convey them to a safe prison.
The negroes all tell the same story, that there are some white men (deserters) concerned. That they were regularly organized by the election
of a Chief, Captains, Lieutenants, couriers & C. rules & regulations were
adopted for their government & action, one of their rules was that all
Negroes who refused to participate were to be murdered, & about Christmas the general Massacree was to commence of all white persons, regardless of age, sex or condition, except such as they might choose &
select for wives or concubines, One of the Negroes was hung in Richmond County on friday last, & some four or five others were to be hung
to day, some forty others would be sent to prison for safety & trial, but

there is no jail in Robeson, or this county & there are no spare men to send them by, it is considered unsafe to keep or to send them away, consequently I think it more than probable the whole of them will be hung by the enraged populace without the form or sanction of the Civil Law. . . .

Our Country (this region particularly) is so thoroughly drained of white males from 13 years old upwards, that it is impossible to sustain a patrol, or any police regulations whatever, there is hardly any government of Negroes at all, the few old men & women who own Negroes tell them what to do & that is all, they have no power whatever, to enforce any order, & you know what the result of such a state of things must lead to, & you know further, enough of the Negro character to know, *"that he will exist in no community in any other Capacity than as Slave or Master."* In connection with this subject, I beg leave to suggest, most respectfully to your Excellency, The propriety of instituting, or organizing some systematic plan of preserving, under practicable restrictions & limitations, a sufficient number of men, uniformly scattered over the country, to help make provisions for the people & for the families of those who are in the army & to serve in some degree as a protection to their homes & families, if it is not done, I fear that it will be difficult to keep our soldiers in the field, & desertions in the army will increase. . . .

Your friend & Obt Servt

H. [ENRY] NUTT

Governors' Papers.

---

(6) The Slaves' Perspective

One former slave wrote that when the war began "there were stories of fights and freedom. The news went from plantation to plantation and while the slaves acted natural and some even more polite than usual, they prayed for freedom."[7] But Negroes who lived in Confederate North Carolina left no extended description of how the war affected their everyday life. During the 1930s workers in the Federal Writers' project interviewed over 2,000 former slaves, and these autobiographical accounts constitute the Slave Narrative Collection, a tremendously valuable source for historians. Most of those interviewed made no distinction between antebellum and Civil War times; but a few of them, mainly men and women who were quite young at the time and whose memories of slave life could only have been of the 1860s have left us tantalizing glimpses of how the war affected the slaves. Two excerpts from the narratives have been included, little girls' recollections of plantation life and of the most remembered of all Civil War events— the "coming of the Yankees."

---

7. Norman R. Yetman, ed., *Life Under the "Peculiar Institution,"* p. 17.

FANNY CANNADY
FORMER SLAVE 79 YEARS OLD

"I don' 'member much 'bout de sojers an' de fightin' in de war kaze I wuzn' much more den six years ole at de surrender, but I do 'member how Marse Jordan Moss shot Leonard Allen, one of his slaves. I ain't never forgot dat.

My mammy an' pappy, Silo an' Fanny Moss belonged to Marse Jordan an' Mis' Sally Moss. Dey had 'bout three hundred niggahs an' mos' of dem worked in de cotton fields.

Marse Jordan wuz hard on his niggahs. He worked dem over time an' didn' give dem enough to eat. Dey didn' have good clothes neither an' dey shoes wuz made out of wood. He had 'bout a dozen niggahs dat didn' do nothin' else but make wooden shoes for de slaves. De chillun didn' have no shoes a tall; dey went barefooted in de snow an' ice same as 'twuz summer time. I never had no shoes on my feets 'twell I wuz pas' ten years ole, an' dat wuz after de Yankees done set us free.

I wuz skeered of Marse Jordan, an' all of de grown niggahs wuz too 'cept Leonard an' Burrus Allen. Dem niggahs wuzn' skeered of nothin'. . . . Leonard wuz er big black buck niggah; he wuz de bigges niggah I ever seed, an' Burrus wuz near 'bout as big, an' 'spized Marse Jordan wus'n pizen. . . .

Marse Jordan's two sons went to de war; dey went all dressed up in dey fightin' clothes. Young Marse Jordan wuz jus' like Mis' Sally but Marse Gregory wuz like Marse Jordan, even to de bully way he walk. Young Marse Jordan never come back from de war, but 'twould take more den er bullet to kill Marse Gregory; he too mean to die anyhow kaze de debil didn' want him an' de Lord wouldn' have him.

One day Marse Gregory come hom on er furlo'. He think he look pretty wid his sword clankin' an' his boots shinin'. He wuz er colonel, lootenent er somethin'. He wuz struttin' 'roun' de yard showin' off, when Leonard Allen say under his breath, 'Look at dat God damn sojer. He fightin' to keep us niggahs from bein' free.'

Bout dat time Marse Jordan come up. He look at Leonard an' say: 'What yo' mumblin' 'bout?'

Dat big Leonard wuzn' skeered. He say, I say, 'Look at dat God damn sojer. He fightin' to keep us niggahs from bein' free.'

Marse Jordan's face . . . turned so red dat de blood near 'bout bust out. He turned to Pappy an' tole him to go an' bring him dis shot gun. When Pappy come back Mis' Sally come wid him. . . . She run up to Marse Jordan an' caught his arm. Ole Marse flung her off an' took de gun from Pappy. He leveled it on Leonard an' tole him to pull his shirt open. Leonard opened his shirt an' stood dare . . . sneerin' at Old Marse.

Den Mis' Sally run up again an' stood 'tween dat gun an' Leonard.

Ole Marse yell to pappy an' tole him to take dat woman out of de way, but nobody ain't moved to touch Mis' Sally. Den Old Marse let down de gun. He reached over an' slapped Mis' Sally down, den picked up de gun an' shot er hole in Leonard's ches' big as yo' fis'. Den he took up Mis' Sally an' toted her in de house. . . .

Slave Narrative Collection, 11:160–62.

AUNT LUCY'S LOVE STORY

An interview with Lucy Ann Dunn, 90 years old, 220 Cannon Street, Raleigh, N.C.

"My pappy, Dempsey, my mammy, Rachel an' my brothers an' sisters an' me all belonged ter Marse Peterson Dunn of Neuse. . . .

"My mammy wus de cook, an' fur back as I 'members almost, I wus a house girl. I fanned flies offen de table an' done a heap of little things fer Mis' Betsy, Marse Peterson's wife. My pappy worked on de farm, which wus boun' ter have been a big plantation wid two hundert an' more niggers ter work hit.

"I 'members when word come dat war was declared, how Mis' Betsy cried an' prayed an' how Marse Peter quarreled an' walked de floor cussin' de Yankees.

"De war comes on jist de same an' some of de men slaves wus sent ter Roanoke ter hep buil' de fort. Yes man, de war comes ter de great houses an' ter de slave cabins jist alike.

"De great house wus large an' white washed, wid green blinds an' de slave cabins wus made of slabs wid plank floors. We had plenty ter eat an' enough ter wear an' we wus happy. We had our fun an' we had our troubles, lak little whuppin's, when we warn't good, but dat warn't often.

"Atter so long a time de rich folkses tried to hire, or make de po' white trash go in dere places, but some of dem won't go. Dey am treated so bad dat some of dem cides ter be Ku Kluxes an' dey goes ter de woods ter live. When we starts ter take up de aigs er starts from de spring house wid de butter an' milk dey grabs us an' takes de food fer dereselbes.

"Dis goes on fer a long time an' finally one day in de spring I sets on de porch an' hears a roar. I wus 'sponsible fer de goslins dem days so I sez ter de missus, "I reckin dat I better git in de goslins case I hear hit a-thunderin'.

"Dat ain't no thunder, nigger, dat am de cannon', she sez.

"What cannon', I axes?"

"Why de cannon what dey am fightin' wid', she sez.

"Well dat ebenin' I is out gittin' up de goslins when I hears music, I looks up de road an' sees flags, an' 'bout dat time de Yankees am dar a-killin' as dey goes. Dey kills de geese, de ducks, de chickens, pigs an' ever'thing. Dey goes ter de house an' dey takes all of de meat, de meal, an' ever'thing dey can git dere paws on.

"When dey goes ter de kitchen whar mammy am cookin' she cuss dem out an' run dem outen her kitchen. Dey shore am a rough lot.

"I aint never fergot how Mis' Betsy cried when de news of de surrender come. She aint said nothin' but Marse Peter he makes a speech sayin' dat he aint had ter sell none of us, dat he aint whupped none of us bad, dat nobody has ever run away from him yet. Den he tells us dat all who want to can stay right on fer wages. . . ."

Slave Narrative Collection, 11:279–81.

---

(7) County Aid to Soldiers' Families

For the first two years of the war the only state aid to distressed families of soldiers was a guarantee that unpaid bounties due to deceased soldiers would reach their families. But in many counties the courts of pleas and quarter sessions, which set county financial policy, began quite early extending charity to soldiers' families. The letter below describes, if the writer's figures can be accepted, the generosity of the Chatham County Court.

Pittsboro N C Oct 15th 1863

His Excy
    Gov Z. B. Vance
        Dear Sir,
            I have just received your letter enclosing that of Antoniette Williams which you refer to the relief Committee for information—As I am chairman of that Committee and pay out all the money, it gives me pleasure (not in the way of boasting) to answer it so as to inform you how nobly this County has acted and continues to act, and as far as I can learn far exceeds any County in the State in providing for the Soldiers Families. At the commensement of the war our County Court appropriated $40.000 and since that amount has been expended I have been instructed to provide for the families regardless of the amount required. In order that all might be taken care of the Court appointed 3 Committee men in each Capt district to ascertain who were in want & required assistance and to see that they were provided for—I have no doubt but that it will cost the County this year $100.000 as I am now feeding some of the families at an expense of $75 per month and none less than $25 & there are over three hundred Adults & 1200 children—I am daily in receipt of such letters as A. Williams and upon investigation find that there is no truth in them and that they complain without any cause and I think that when I see the Committee in the Haywood District, I will learn that A. Williams is not to be believed *or* that the Committee are satisfied she is not in want.

I remain very Respt
Your Obt Servt
HENRY A. LONDON [8]

Governors' Papers.

8. Merchant of Pittsboro and secretary-treasurer of the Cape Fear and Deep River Navigation Company.

(8) State Charity

*In some areas charity was inade-
quate or nonexistent, and it was
not long before the governor's
office was receiving heart-rending
appeals for help. One Davidson
County mother wrote "i ame a
pore woman with a pasel of little
children and i wil have to starve
or go naked me and my little children ef my husband is kept way
from home much longer. . . ."*[9]
*On 12 December 1862 the legisla-
ture appropriated $500,000 and
authorized the governor to appoint
agents to buy provisions and sell
them at cost to county courts for*

*distribution to the poor and to
needy soldiers' families, with any
excess to be sold to army commissary agents. The following February it appropriated $1 million and
ordered the justices of the peace
of each county to select and bond
a commissioner to use the money
for the support of indigent wives
and families of soldiers. Complaints about the operation of the
system were numerous (Document A), but the county commissioners seemed to believe that they
were doing well with what was
available to them (Document B).*

A.

Hillsdale N.C
Apr. the 3 rd /64

Sir I write you a feiw lines to inform you how we are treated about something to eat truly hopeing you will have things changed from what they
are now I will inform you what I am alowed per month I am only alowed
$10.00 for my self and one child a woman with two childrens only
alowed $13.00 per month to get meat and bread with grain is from
$20.00 to $30.00 per bushel bacon from $3. to $5.00 per pound and we
cant get it for the money the men that has it to sell wont have the money
for it and there is aplenty both meat and bread and molases in the
country for us all to have plenty but those men that has it wont let the
soldiers familys have it they send one load of privisian to the factory
after another to get spun cotton and the soldiers familys may suffer
while their men are in the army fighting for them and what they have
my husband and father has been in the survis over two years Ma is left
with three children and is only alowed $13.00 per month and you well
know that wont half support her the way evry thing is selling I know
some men that has plenty of molases and wont sell them for any thing
but grain and that is what soldiers familys has not got I dont know how
they can expect the N° Cᵃ soldiers to fight and their familys treated as
they are. I never have tried to discourage my husband any at all—I try
to encourage him all I can I am willing to work for every thing to eat I

9. Lydia A. Bolton to Z. B. Vance, 5 Nov. 1862, Johnston, *Papers of Zebulon B. Vance,* 1:308.

can but I cant live with my work and what I get from Mr A Reid I sent to
him for something to eat yesterday and he sent me word his orders was
not to let any of us have any thing untill May court and I have not had
any thing at all in over a month and I am very unhealthy not able to do
much work and I dont know what I will do and many others that is left
in my situation unless you will have this matter attended to in a short
time I beg you to have things arranged better for if you dont the soldiers
will get disheartened and come home and I dont want them to have to
come home without an honerable peace and ef they will find me plenty
to eat my husband will fight through this war if he is spaired to live before he will quit and come home but you think yourself of this matter if
you was in the army and was to hear your wife and children was suffiring
and could not get anything to eat I think you would be very much tempted to start home and you knew there was plenty for them and they was
not allowed have it pleas fix this as soon as you can I hope you will send
and press this provisions from those men that has it for if you dont I am
afraid the women will have it to do and I dont want to press any thing if
I can help it they have got spun cotton out our reach it is $80.00 per
bunch in Greensborough that will take nearly eight month wages that a
soldier gets to get one bunch cotton I will close this by saying pleas provide for us

yours truly
S U S A N   C   W O O L K E R   (?)

Governors' Papers.

B .

May 18th 1863

Govenor Vance,
Dear Sir. I received a letter from you a few days past, calling my attention to the case of Mrs. H. A. Allen, you say she writes that she is in great
distress. I have been acting as com. for this Dist., for the last 15 months,
and in the time, I have visited in person nearly every needy family once
in every 3 months. I am happy to be able to inform you that up to the
present that there has been but little if any suffering at all, the most
trouble that I have had, is with cases that are not needy—Some sell their
provisions & then apply to me for help.—Not being authorized by the
county, I refuse in all such cases. Mrs Allen lives in one mile of me, I
am well acquainted with her case. A few days before she wrote you I
furnished her with 15 or 20 lbs of good bacon & about $15.00 in cash to
buy corn. She was offered at $3.00 per bu. & bot 2 bu, & refused to buy
more because she said she was not out, I learn from the miller that she
had a grist ground last Thursday So you may see from this, she is not
quite so bad off as one might suppose. She has herd of some women
writing to you & getting help & no doubt thats the main cause of her
letter. We are not going to let soldiers wives suffer as long as it can be

helped, but some cant be satisfied. The more we do the more dissatisfied some will bee. I have sons in the service and am well prepared to simpathise with soldiers & soldiers wives. As you are not personally acquainted with me I would refer you to Sam. Philips Esq of Chapel Hill, or Sam Young of Raleigh.

Yours very truly
J . ATWATER

Governors' Papers.

XVI

LIFE GOES ON AT HOME

As well as they could, those at home strove to keep the family's affairs operating as usual. This proved an almost impossible task for the thousands of rural yeoman families. Most of these humble people lived in badly furnished houses, owned only a small amount of arable land, were lucky to have even one slave, and desperately needed their men at home. Few men of the small farmer class were exempt from military service, children and older men were of limited use, and even husbands who deserted could only occasionally come out of hiding and help with the chores. The woman now ran the home. The majority of their families probably had enough food and clothing for basic survival, but the cost of everything made life grim. These people could ill afford coffee, cane sugar, fresh meat, new clothing, and dozens of other simple needs. Tools and implements wore out and could not be replaced, livestock dwindled for a variety of reasons, speculators preyed on them, and the war in general seemed most inglorious.

The letters of these proud, capable, and often badly educated women to their husbands in service lacked the subtleties of polite exchange and simply related what was happening at home. They expressed fear of hunger and cold, worries of sickness, thoughts on the weather and crops, comments on neighbors and relatives, tragedies in the community, and ordinary occurrences that meant so much to their men in distant places. The best collection of such letters now in print is "The Correspondence of David Olando McRaven and Amanda Nantz McRaven, 1864–1865" in Volume XXVI of the *North Carolina Historical Review*. The following letters (Documents A, B, and C) are from wives of slightly more humble circumstances than Amanda McRaven. They can only suggest the loneliness and hardships of these patient women.

The war created different problems for the wealthier families. When their men entered service they could do so as officers, and if they wished they could generally secure an exemption. Scarcity to such people meant the absence of luxuries, their financial problem was not lack of money but how best to invest it, their labor problem was not the absence of slaves but how best to use them. New demands of course accrued to the women, but their patriotism sustained them and many served outside the home: group sewing, teaching, nursing, entertaining soldiers, and whatever else was needed of them. The problems of men at home were those of management and production, with the happy assurance that as they prospered so did the Confederacy.

The members of the Lenoir family of Caldwell County had extensive landholdings and were stockholders in cotton mills at Patterson. Rufus T. Lenoir was excused from army service for medical reasons, but the production of his lands was of great benefit to the Confederacy. Two of his brothers—Walter W. and Thomas L.—served under Stonewall Jackson, and the former lost a leg in combat. The letters below (Documents D, E, and F) give some indication of the ways in which the war affected the planter class.

A.

October The 19 1862

Dear husbin

I take the opportunity this eavning to rite A few lines to you I am not well I was very sick last sunday and monday and Tena has bin very bad with the sore throat tho he is better now tho his throat is sweld mitelen yet I heard to day that you was very sick it trubles me almost to deth if it was so that I culd get A bout you mout look for me thare if you get very bad and have to go to the hosptle I want you to tri you very best to get A furlo and come home and if you cant get A long by your self rite to me and I will tri to get some one to come after you I went down to see John Canner yester day and he sed if William Flynt haden to come after him he wouldden to got to come A toll He looks very bad he doant look like he would be able to go back this winter nat terry is at home on A sick furlo he past here last weak he looks ver bad he went to dockter bitting and dock tery is ded I heard that Rubin Burrough got home to day I made sertin I would get A letter from you yester day all I want now is to see you come home I haven got no wheat soad yet I have had alford to hall out the manur and A hard bargin to get him and have to pay A dollar a day it looks like culd get him when every I wanted him at that prise I pute up the hogs last weak but hant got no corn up yet to fead them they have had another battle at ole allen flynts latela old nancy got slitela wounded . . . I have never have left the house A lone since you left. . . .

your affectionate
M A ZIMMERMAN

J. C. Zimmerman Papers.

B.

This December 30 [1863]

Dear husban I take my pen in hand to drop you A few lins to let you know that I am well at this time an the chrildren is well an I hope that these few lins may reach an find you the Same. I recived A letter from you yesterday morning rote the 15 of December an was glad to here from you an here that you ware well an I recived one hundred dollars in it of Confedrate. an I war glad to get it for I am in det for provision an it will take it all excepting five or ten dollars. I bought A hog from mr charles tetterton wade 100 an 25 pound I had to give him fifty dollars for him Dear James I have Sent you tow letters that I have had no answer from. I rite to you every chance I have it is A bad chance for me to get A letter to you for there is not much passing that I know of an when there is I never know of it until it is too late. I have not had no letter from you before sence Acquitch [?] Woolard come in

Dear James the time is A geting very Strict about here if the time Should come that I cant rite to you you must not think hard of me. I intend to rite to you as long as I can. I have got A little meet an bred now an have one big hog an A Shoat to kill an that will not last me long but it will [be] all I shall get. if it was not like it is an I did have the rite sort of mony I could fare very well. it is A bad chance for me for your wages is So low an every thing So high I dont See how I can live here much longer. I dont get no help now I did get 25 dollars about the last of August an that was not half A nuf but I under Stand there is no more to come. Dear husban you rote me about the chrildrens haveing Shoos. they have had Shoos all along untill now but uncle Dick Daniel has promist to make the two girls Shoos. an Caleb Cleat was to make Charles Shoos but he has broke his arm an if I cant get John to make them I dont know how I Shall get them. . . .

[CAROLINE S. ALLIGOOD]

William Slade Papers.

C.

At Home July 8th 1864

My Dear Husband

Yours of the 10th came to hand last saturday. you can image my feelings pretty much I suppose as you have lately experienced the same that I have, that is not got a letter in so long a time, I felt so good that everything went right with me I do not think any person could have made me mad for two or three days if they had of spit in my face. it is now just dark supper is over the children asleep and I have seated myself to write to my "dear old boy" a pleasant task when Minnie is not up to torment me, need I say how much more pleasant it would be to have him here with me, if you would come riding or walking up I would give you some nice light bread, butter, and milk, for supper, and then invite you to sleep with me, do you suppose you would take the invitation as an insult? if you did I would ask your pardon and invite you as politely as I could to take a bed up stairs.

I believe I have nothing of much importance to write, I will therefore in the first place endeavor to answer your questions as near as I can. I will take them as they come so that I will be certain to answer all. Fannie likes to go to school tolerably well is learning pretty well, Mrs Mc-

Loud is the teacher, Dee is still at home, speculating I recon, as that is generally the case these days when a man is at home, he and Henrietta were here wednesday. . . . the wheat and rye is not very good I will have it cut monday if nothing prevents, the oats is no account, Trim is cutting them and feeding them to the horses. we have the new ground and the old field by it, the piece at the gate that was sowed in wheat, Sallies wheat patch two patches next to Fords and a little patch across the branch where flax was sowed and the patch Arter had last year in corn. I think I will have a clover patch by next year, as to your timothy it is about like Batey's clover I think all the seed you put there has come up we will try and save the seed, and maybe we will get it thick enough in a year or two. there is about a half of an apple crop not many peaches. my horses are fatter than any of my neighbors work horses, Trim is a very good hand to manage horses. Bob Slagle does what little blacksmithing I have done we have not had much done. I like my darkies better I believe, than I did at first, I have found out that Trim can cut and make his own clothes and that suits me very well, he can cut a pair of pants out of less cloth than any body I ever saw cut. I have plenty of lettuce but the moles worked on the onions until they will be of no size. we have beans and potatoes to eat now, will have plenty if we can have rain occasionally I think if the season is suitable I will have a good crop of irish potatoes, but no sweet potatoes I planted two bushels but between the chickens and dry weather they will do no good. I have a pretty good crop of cane and some peas. we still have old rye for coffee. The cows look pretty well the white heifer is a nice thing the pasture is tolerably good will be better now we have had some rain. we got a right smart of milk and make some butter and upon the whole I recon we have about as much to eat as most any person else, if we get no scarces we have no need to grumble. . . .

> Believe me as every your own
> MARY [BELL]

Alfred W. Bell Papers.

D.

Raleigh, August 11th 1862

My dear sister,

It would gratify you not a little I am sure to know how great a pleasure your letter gave me. I am glad you liked the book—I have 2 others by the same author, "The words of Jesus," & "memories of Bethany"— they are a rich spiritual feast. I handed your donation to Br. Crowder that very evening at our weekly prayer meeting—our patriotic meeting as Br. Long calls it—as it is to unite in praying for the country & for our gallant soldiers. Br. C. said it came in excellent time, & was appropriated immediately—it would do you good to hear him sometimes give an account of his work at the camps & hospitals in & near Raleigh. he always seems greatly encouraged—believes he sees the hand of Providence oftentimes when he has been out of papers & other material & has obtained an unexpected supply—I think him "a man full of faith & the Holy Ghost."

Your account of the wayside hospital was especially interesting—we certainly have needed something of the kind here, tho' we have soom good Samaritans in the neighborhood of the depot who have I believe done all in their power to supply the place of such an establishment—Br. John Palmer's kind wife & others have taken seven or eight at a time kept them as long as they chose to stay & nursed them most kindly. But sometimes we would hear there were soldiers there detained without food &c. my sister C. would send off dinner as soon as possible. Have you seen the article on this subject in the last Ch. Intelligencer? also in the last Rgster. We have a Confederate Hospital here, & the physician in charge sends their ambulance wagons every day when the sick are expected to the depot to bring them to the hospital to spend the night or stay as long as necessary. If you were here we could find plenty for your active spirit to do, which I am sure would be congenial work.

We have 3 soldiers aid societies in Raleigh attached to the different churches which have done a great amount of work, but not so much now because it is difficult to get material & it is so high also—we had to pay 40 cts. per yard for the last bolt of unbleached homespun we bought. Lately we have been sending a box of fruit & vegetables once in 2 weeks to the hospitals in Richmond. Sister Eliza's time is so occupied with her large school that she gives her aid in money—she has now nearly sixty pupils which I fear is wearing her out this very hot weather—I go to assist her every morning but not in the afternoon. . . .

[LOUISA HILL]

Lenoir Family Papers.

E.

The Dan Mar. 6th 1863

Dear Brother [W. W. Lenoir]

I wrote to you last week but have forgotten what about, except that I told you what I would like to have some of those fruit trees at Mike Hart's next year but that I had more for this spring than I could take care of—

I would especially like to have some of the basket willows this spring —I also advised you to try to get some cloth, thread, & leather to bring with you & asked you to get more thread & cloth for me & said that I would contrive some way to get it hauled after a while—I could sometimes get work for such articles, when folks won't look at money—

Well Poston & Trull have moved at last—They vacated on the 3[d], last Tuesday, & Andy moved up the same—I have been up several times lately, & find every thing *outen fix*—

Poston has had nothing resembling a stable this winter, & the crib was so near rotten that it had to be repaired—I went to Gaddy's a few days ago to examine his corn, & found from the smell that it was rotting, & sent the wagon & hauled it away the next day—had it shucked and measured it yesterday evening—only 18 bu. sound corn & 15 bu. unsound—as the sound corn seemed to be damp I had it piled in one corner of your cabin—& the other in the smoke house for the oxen

When I was taken sick I sent Mr. Hartgrove up to tell your tenants to crib your corn in the shuck until I called for it, & Gaddy told me several times that nothing was interrupting his but the squirrels——— John Trull and Jesse Anderson think that you have about 100 bushels at each of their houses, but I don't think there is so much at Anderson's—I hope you will have plenty and some to spare—Poston's folks made scarcely any grain of any kind—He supposed that your part would be 10 bu. which he promised to pay for—D. L. Trull sowed nearly all of his part in small grain & made a failure as he generally does—He sowed a good deal of oats, & nearly every body failed in the oats crop. He paid about two bu. corn rent, 14 bu. rye, & the wheat is not threshed. Suppose there will be 5 or 6 bu.

Jesse Anderson & Gaddy expect to go to the war soon, & Tom Crawford, & I don't know what I am to do with those places—

John Trull is all the tenant you have that has done well—If Poston is not called off I hope he [will] do better this year he is a little over forty years old—but I don't know where he is to get bread & meat for his family this summer.

I have about 200 bu. corn less than I usually have at this season of the year, & will have to stunt my poor stock some, but I intend to make it do me—I am much troubled by people who wish to get smith work done, & labor is so scarce here that I wish to shut up my shop except on rainy days—I notified John & Jake to make you some plows &c more than a month ago but they have not done half the work for you which you need. . . .

[THOMAS LENOIR]

Lenoir Family Papers.

F.

Friday 24 April 1863

Dear Rufus

I was at Elkin yesterday & got a few sheets of paper that I can write on & I will write to you, altho' I hardly expect you will get it before this day week.—In the first place I am glad I can tell you that we are all tolerable well; and the friends at Elkin are also tolerable well; brother R. was complaining some with head ache but was about.—Richard was off at the South & would not be home before tomorrow.—They are greatly rushed there for cotton & cloth Such a mess as they have there daily & such pulling & hauling & growling grumbling & even cursing you hardly ever heard—its impossible to supply half that go for yarn & cloth & its a scuffle who shall have it—The Co. are abused at round rates, & threatened with mobs & with burning &c because they cannot after running night & day supply all that come for yarn & cloth; They stand it better

than I could do, I am sure The factory land (12 acres) with the pastures
&c is assessed at 80.000$ only!!! Great inducement to try & supply any
body with yarn & cloth at 50 pr cent less than the other factories is it
not? Brother R⁵. lands were put at 22.000 at least 6 or 7.000 too much
in proportion to the other lands in the County He is a great deal put out
at the way they have imposed on him & the Co. & speaks of going to
Dobson on Monday to complain, but thinks it useless, as it was the work
of a Clicque at Dobson. I was one of the County board of appraisers &
must go to Town on that business on Monday I suppose, I think we got
a tolerable uniform valuation on the land & negroes in this County,
though I hear of some complaints; which we must try to satisfy. I am
not done planting yet, it will take us till Tuesday or Wednesday to finish,
the rain has stoped us some.—I have broken all of my land twice & I
think it is in rather better condition for a crop than usual, though some
of it is cloddy.—My small grain looks tolerable now & if nothing happens
to spoil it bids fair to make a good crop; I am putting in a little more
corn than I have done before; I shall plant but little tobac[c]o & that
upon a poor piece of new ground, which would not bring more than 5⁰⁰
bu corn to the acre & would not tend that but I have no more land for
corn & my force can hardly cultivate that much in tobac[c]o. My stock
is doing pretty well I think, I have 3 young mules, all very good ones.
. . . I met with Calvin Jones at McReston's on Monday & he wanted to
know if I would take Confᵈ. money on the note I got of the estate on
Thoˢ. Jones & others—I told him for property I had to sell or for any I
had sold since the war began, I received that money & expected none
other, that the price of property was in keeping with the money but I
received that note in lieu of that much money which was then equal or
nearly so to gold & silver & that in justice to myself & family I did not
think I ought to take Confᵈ. money for it—He seemed to get angry &
said *I* ought not to refuse it still I asked him why? He said because *I* was
able & did not owe any thing & it was my pvt Government money & *I*
ought to take it—I asked him if it was not his govᵗ. too, no it is not I
abhor it, I detest it &c—a good deal more was said by us both about ce-
session &c he went out & up to Cowles & made a great blow about it, I
heard next day he & Cowles carried me high & I would not be surprised
if it is sent to the Standard for publication.— . . .

You must write soon & more frequently; we must keep up our spirits.
. . . Our good President says our prospects and Condition is better now
than it ever has been before & he is an honest man & tells the truth I
dare say. . . .

Affectionately yours,

J. G. MAYER

Lenoir Family Papers.

XVII

STATE RIGHTS AND STATE PRIDE

Secession apologists had argued that the writers of the Constitution of 1787 had precisely divided the powers of government between the states and the nation, and that each was sovereign in its own sphere. They maintained that they had supported the Union as long as the Constitution had been interpreted in the spirit of Jefferson and Madison; but that sacred compact had become so distorted by interpretations beneficial to the North and injurious to the South that the latter had been forced to exercise the ultimate state right—secession. The Confederate Constitution incorporated a few safeguards to prevent future misinterpretations, but radical alteration seemed unnecessary for presumably the South would never again be threatened by aggressive nationalism.

But paradoxically the only president of the Confederacy was one of its strongest nationalists. Jefferson Davis had used state rights arguments and rhetoric throughout his political career but probably had never fully believed in them. Now that he was Confederate president he found them impractical. He was convinced that the disparity of resources between the contestants made centralism vital to Confederate survival. For this reason he was quite willing to establish as powerful a central government as was needed. Neither the rights of a state nor of its citizens should be allowed to endanger the war effort.

Until the Conscription Act of April 1862, the extent of the Confederacy's authority in North Carolina was not seriously argued, for the moderate war measures of the first year posed no threat to state authority or individual freedom. For the most part North Carolina's grievances stemmed from the neglect of its defenses. Typical of Governor Clark's many letters to the War Department was his plea "I cannot refrain from referring you again to the urgent necessity . . . for more arms and munitions . . . for the . . . defense of the coast."[1] The North Carolina

---

1. H. T. Clark to J. P. Benjamin, 25 Sept. 1861, *Official Records*, Ser. 1, 4: 658.

delegation to Congress asked that the state "be erected into a separate and distinct military department."[2]

But beginning with conscription and continuing until the end of the war the Richmond government made increasing demands upon the people of North Carolina. Even then Governor Clark let the newspaper press, particularly W. W. Holden's *Standard*, handle doctrinaire disputation with the president and the War Department. But when Vance became governor he showed little hesitancy in embroiling himself in heated controversy with the Confederacy over the rights of his constituents or the jurisdiction of his state. Was he fearful that the principles of Jefferson and Madison were once again endangered?

One interpretation, now in general disrepute, of Vance's motives is that he was willing to sacrifice the Confederacy rather than abandon state rights. Another, voiced twenty years later by Vance himself, was that he was merely trying to uphold the dictum that personal liberty could be preserved during war. "No man within the jurisdiction of the State of North Carolina was denied the privilege of the writ of *habeas corpus*, the right of trial by jury, or the equal protection of the laws, as provided by our constitution and the bill of rights."[3] This sounded good in 1886, but it is only part of the truth, for many of Vance's controversies with the Confederacy did not concern individual rights. While Vance was undoubtedly genuinely concerned with state and personal rights, he was also a loyal Confederate and the supreme politician.

The fairest evaluation of Vance's apparent hostility to the Confederacy is to assume that much of it was a deliberately contrived political ploy. There is no evidence in his public or private papers that his loyalty to the Confederacy ever waned. But this same Confederacy was steadily imposing on his constituents a series of measures that, however necessary, sapped both their spirit and their sustenance. Exploiting this discontent was a wing of the Conservative party that was openly hostile to the Davis administration and then to the Confederacy itself. To keep the loyal element of the Conservative party in power Vance had to make himself the apparent champion of his state. To do this he magnified his genuine concern for personal and state rights into a series of strident confrontations with the Confederacy. Undoubtedly he believed that there were some war measures that the state could accept compliantly and others which it could not. The task of striking the proper balance was the most difficult of his administration.

Other self-appointed guardians of state rights and state pride exercised different judgment. For them there could be no compromise between state rights and Confederate needs—if the one were threatened the other must give way. And this doctrinaire inflexibility caused them to bristle at any suggestion by outsiders that their position was impractical. Within the state their loudest voice was that of William W. Holden,

2. W. T. Dortch et al. to G. W. Randolph, 27 Sept. 1862, ibid., 51, Pt. 2: 627.

3. Dowd, *Life of Zebulon B. Vance*, p. 453.

speaking through the columns of his Raleigh *Standard* with increasing crescendo from early 1862 until the collapse of the Confederacy. In Richmond more than half the state's delegation to the Second Congress was almost as extreme.

The following material illustrates the reaction of North Carolina to real or imagined insult, mistreatment, or neglect by the Richmond government. Together they demonstrate the strongest concern for state rights and state pride that existed in the Confederacy.

---

(1) Impolitic Confederate Appointments

Many North Carolinians soon came to the conclusion that far too many out-of-staters held responsible positions within the state. Senator William T. Dortch objected to the appointment of a Virginian as "controlling Quartermaster for the State" and demanded his replacement by a North Carolinian, "not as a concession to the unsound but as an act of justice to the true people of the State."[4] *Governor Vance complained about the appointment of a Marylander as medical director at Raleigh and of a South Carolinian to command the Salisbury prison; but in the letter below he took particular offense at Thomas P. August of Virginia being made commandant of conscripts for North Carolina. Secretary of War Seddon answered that August would be replaced, but expressed his regret "that such susceptibility prevails in North Carolina, when it has not been displayed in other States where similar appointments have been made of officers not native."*[5]

Raleigh, January 26, 1863

HON. JAMES A. SEDDON,
     Secretary of War, Richmond, Va.:
     SIR: I had the honor to complain to His Excellency the President and your immediate predecessor, Mr. Randolph, in regard to the manner of enforcing the conscript act in this State. . . . I am compelled again . . . to complain of the appointment of Colonel August as commandant of conscripts for North Carolina, who has recently assumed command here. Merely alluding to the obvious impropriety and bad policy of wounding the sensibilities of our people by the appointment of a citizen of another State to execute a law both harsh and odious, I wish to say, sir, in all candor, that it smacks of discourtesy toward our people, to say the least of it. Having furnished as many (if not more) troops for the

4. W. T. Dortch to J. P. Benjamin, 18 Aug. 1863, John C. Pickett Papers.
     5. J. A. Seddon to T. S. Ashe and Others, 23 Feb. 1863, *Official Records*, Ser. 4, 2:409.

service of the Confederacy as any other State, and being, as I was assured by the President, far ahead of all others in the number raised under the conscript law, the people of this State have justly felt mortified in seeing those troops commanded by citizens of other States, to the exclusion of the claims of their own. This feeling is increased and strengthened into a very general indignation when it is thus officially announced that North Carolina has no man in her borders fit to command her own conscripts, though scores of her noblest sons and best officers are now at home with mutilated limbs and shattered constitutions. Without the slightest prejudice against either Colonel August or the State from which he comes, I protest against his appointment as both unjust and impolitic. Having submitted in silence to the many—very many—acts of the Administration heretofore so well calculated to wound that pride which North Carolina is so pardonable for entertaining, it is my duty to inform you that if persisted in the appointment of strangers to all the positions in this State and over her troops will cause a feeling throughout her whole borders which is my great desire to avoid. . . .

Z. B. VANCE

Official Records, Ser. 4, 2:375.

(2) The Rights of Conscripts

In an effort to make the first conscription law as palatable as possible, Congress ordered that conscripts raised under the act, if they wished, must be assigned to companies from their own state in the Confederate service. Occasionally an officer would ignore the men's preferences and place them in units whose numbers had been decimated in combat. When Vance voiced his protest below, President Davis gracefully ignored the superfluous rhetoric, complimented him for "the cordial manner in which you have sustained every proposition connected with the public defense," and promised to attend to the matter of the disappointed soldiers at once.[6]

Raleigh, October 25, 1862

His Excellency President DAVIS:

MY DEAR SIR: When in Richmond I had the honor to call your attention, in the presence of Mr. Randolph, to the subject of allowing the conscripts the privilege of selecting the regiments to which they should go. I understood you and the Secretary both to assent to it willingly. A few days after my return home, therefore, I was much surprised and grieved to find an order coming from the Secretary to Major Mallett to

6. Jefferson Davis to Z. B. Vance, 1 Nov. 1862, ibid., p. 154.

disregard an order to this effect from Brigadier-General Martin and to place all of them in certain brigades under General French. . . .

Last week about 100 men were brought into camp from one county alone, from a region somewhat lukewarm, who had been got to come cheerfully under the solemn promises made them by my enrolling officer that they should be allowed to join any regiment they desired. . . . General Martin said they might yet have their choice . . . and wrote to General French, begging his consent to the arrangement. He refused, of course, and . . . the men were stopped at Petersburg and "distributed equally" to certain regiments, as quartermaster's stores or any other chattel property, alleging that by not coming in sooner they had forfeited all claims to consideration.

Of the shortsightedness and inhumanity of this harsh course toward our people I shall offer no comment. . . . I wish not only to ask that a more liberal policy be adopted, but to make it the occasion of informing you also of a few things of a political nature which you ought to know.

The people of this State have ever been eminently conservative and jealous of their political rights. . . . Prior to Lincoln's proclamation the election for delegates to our proposed convention exhibited a popular majority . . . against secession. . . . The late elections . . . show conclusively that the original advocates of secession no longer hold the ear of our people. Without the warm and ardent support of the old Union men North Carolina could not . . . have been brought to the support of the seceding States, and without that same influence constantly . . . given the present status could not be maintained forty-eight hours. . . .

The corollary to be deducted is briefly this: That the opinions and advice of the old Union leaders must be heeded . . . or the worst consequences may ensue. . . . I believe, sir, most sincerely that the conscript law could not have been executed by a man of different antecedents . . . and now, with all the popularity with which I came into office, it will be exceedingly difficult for me to execute it under your recent call. . . . If . . . West Point generals, who know much less of human nature than I do of military science, are to ride roughshod over the people, drag them from their homes, and assign them . . . to strange regiments and strange commanders, without regard to their wishes or feelings, I shall be compelled to decline undertaking a task which must certainly fail.

These conscripts . . . comprise a number of the best men in their communities, whom indispensable business, large and helpless families, property, and distress in a thousand shapes have combined to keep them at home until the last moment. In spite of all the softening I could give to the law, and all the appeals . . . to their patriotism, much discontent has grown up, and now the waters of insubordination begin to surge. . . . Many openly declare that they want not another conscript to leave the State until provision is made for her own defense; others say it will not leave labor sufficiently to support the women and children, and therefore it must not be executed. Thousands are flying from our eastern counties . . . to the center and west to devour the very short crops and increase the prospect of starvation. . . . You see the difficulties which beset me. But through them all I have endeavored and shall endeavor to hold my course straightforward for the common good. It is disheartening, however, to find that I am thwarted in so small a matter as this, which is yet a great one to the conscript.

I . . . should also be pleased to know what our sister States are doing in support of the conscript law, as a very general impression prevails that this State is doing vastly more than its share. . . .

Z. B. VANCE

Official Records, Ser. 4, 2:146–47.

---

(3) The Honor of the State Judiciary

Despite the adroitness with which Vance handled the conflicts over military service between the War Department and the North Carolina judiciary,[7] he firmly upheld the state Supreme Court's authority when challenged from Richmond. Nor would he ignore derogatory comments against it. In mid-1863 Secretary Seddon sent Vance a letter from General R. E. Lee reporting a "fearful increase" in desertion of North Carolina soldiers from Lee's army. Seddon asked Vance's help in stopping desertion and then added undiplomatically that "a full remedy can, however, only be found in the removal of the cause. . . ." He then blamed Chief Justice Pearson for most of the desertions and asked Vance to "restrain the too ready interposition of the judicial authority in these questions of military obligation. . . ."[8] Vance retorted hotly in the following letter.

Raleigh, May 25, 1863

HON. J. A. SEDDON,
Secretary of War, Richmond, Va.:

SIR: . . . I regret, sir, that you should have deemed it necessary to adopt as an explanation of the cause for so much desertion—an idea which has its origin solely in political prejudice—that "too ready interposition of the judicial authority in these questions of military obligation," and the false constructions given to the decisions of our judges in the army. That such impressions do prevail in the army I make no doubt. You are not the first authority I have had for that fact; but why it should exist and how it was first made I am unable to determine, except upon the ground that there exists among our neighbors, and even among some of our own citizens, "a too ready" disposition to believe evil of the State.

7. See pages 150–54 for a discussion of this matter.

8. J. A. Seddon to Z. B. Vance, 23 May 1863, *Official Records*, Ser. 1, 51, Pt. 2:714.

When it is known that North Carolina is the only State in the Confederacy which employs her militia in the arrest of conscripts and deserters; that she has better executed the conscript law; has fuller regiments in the field than any other, and that at the two last great battles on the Rappahannock . . . she furnished over one-half of the killed and wounded, it seems strange, passing strange, that an impression should prevail that desertion would receive official countenance and protection in her borders.

The decisions of our judges have been published in all the papers of our State, and any perversion of their meaning must be designed and willful. Neither have our judges been "too ready" to offer them. Heavy penalties . . . are annexed to the refusal of a judge to grant the writ of habeas corpus, and an upright judge must deliver the law as he conceives it to be, whether it should happen to comport with the received notions of the military authorities or not. . . . Whilst, therefore, it is my intention to make every possible effort to sustain the common cause, it is my firm determination to sustain the judicial authorities of the land, the rights and privileges of the citizens to the utmost of my power. By the action of Congress no appeal lies from the supreme court of a State to that of the Confederate States, and the decisions of the supreme court of North Carolina when formally rendered will be binding upon all parties. I also regret to see that the impression will be made by these letters of yours and General Lee's that desertion is greater among the North Carolina troops than those of her sister States, which I have every reason to believe is not true. . . . Excuse me, sir, for writing in this strain; I feel that our exertions are scarcely appreciated properly, and I can but speak plainly when I approach the subject.

> Very respectfully, your obedient servant,
> Z. B. VANCE

Official Records, Ser. 1, 51, Pt. 2:715–16.

(4) Fear of Despotism

As early as 1862 the Confederacy, in its efforts to counterbalance the North's superiority in men and material, had been forced to inaugurate programs which to extreme state righters smacked of military despotism. The first of these was conscription, and when Congress enacted the law of 16 April 1862 a prominently placed letter to the editor of the Raleigh Standard *warned "*LET THE PEOPLE BEWARE! . . . *that we are rapidly tending to military despotism."*[9] *As the vigor of Confederate legislation intensified,*

9. Raleigh *Standard*, 19 Apr. 1862.

such warnings became shriller. Augustus S. Merrimon, later United States senator, wrote in 1864 that there was "wide spread alarm among the people . . . growing out of the constant exercise of high and questionable powers on the part of Congress and the President."[10] On 28 May 1864 the General Assembly adopted the following resolution, indicating that the fear of despotism was not limited to only a few alarmists.

RESOLUTIONS CONCERNING CERTAIN ACTS OF THE LATE CONGRESS OF THE CONFEDERATE STATES

Resolved, That while the people of North-Carolina have ever been and still are anxious to strengthen the administration of the Confederate government in every legitimate way, and to promote the success of the common cause in order that we may have a speedy and honorable peace, they view with deep concern and alarm every infraction of the Constitution by the Congress of the Confederate States, and this General Assembly doth, in their name, protest against such infractions as of pernicious example and fatal tendency.

Resolved, That the act of the late Congress, entitled "An act to suspend the privilege of the writ of *habeas corpus* in certain cases," violates the fundamental maxim of republican government which requires a separation of the departments of power, clothes the Executive with judicial functions which Congress cannot constitutionally confer even on the judiciary itself, and sets at naught the most emphatic and solemn guarantees of the Constitution.

Resolved, That this General Assembly, representing the people of North Carolina, doth not consent to the sacrifice of the vital principles of free government in a war carried on solely to secure and perpetuate them, and doth declare that "no conditions of public danger," present or prospective, probable or possible, can render the liberties of the people incompatible with the public safety.

Resolved, That the act of the same Congress, entitled "An act to organize forces to serve during the war," declaring all white men, residents of the Confederate States, between the ages of seventeen and fifty, to be in the military service, embracing in its provisions every State officer in all the departments, executive, legislative and judicial, and subjecting all the industrial pursuits of the country to military supervision and control, reduces the State government to mere provincial administrations, dependent on the grace and favor of Congress and the Executive, is destructive of state sovereignty, and imports an assertion of the power on the part of Congress to convert the Confederate government into a consolidated military despotism.

Resolved, That this General Assembly doth therefore request our Senators and Representatives in Congress to use their best endeavors to procure a repeal of the first mentioned act, and such modifications of the

10. A. S. Merrimon to Z. B. Vance, 22 Feb. 1864, Governors' Papers.

second as shall secure the rights and preserve the integrity of the States of the Confederacy. . . .

Public Laws of North Carolina Passed by the General Assembly at the Adjourned Session of 1864, pp. 23–25.

---

(5) In Defense of State Loyalty

North Carolina's stream of controversies with the Confederate government soon won for her considerable notoriety, but at first her loyalty was not seriously questioned. State rights was still a precious symbol in the South and few regarded her leaders' demands and protestations as more than an overzealous protection of her citizens' best interests. Eventually, however, some of the nation's levelest minds began to suspect that North Carolina was rife with treason. Radical state righters retorted that loyalty to the Confederacy had not diminished loyalty to their state, and they reacted sharply to both real and imagined insults. On 30 January 1863 the members of the General Assembly passed a resolution protesting the "slanderous reports" upon the state's loyalty and denounced them as "utterly false in letter and in spirit. . . ."[11]

The North Carolina delegation to the Second Congress reflected this attitude. On the floor of the House, Representative Josiah Turner, lawyer and planter of Orange County, rose to denounce a report of the Conscription Bureau which seemed to impugn his state's honor (Document A); the entire delegation had an interview with President Davis to protest the Confederacy's mistreatment of the state, and Senator Edwin G. Reade wrote Governor Vance a long account of the interview (Document B). Reade, a Roxboro attorney, had been appointed to the Senate to serve the last month of George Davis's term. While senator, he opposed virtually all the war measures of the Davis administration.

A.

Mr. Turner, of North Carolina, offered the following:

. . . *Resolved*, That General Preston is in error as to the number of conscripts furnished by the State of North Carolina, as well as in the number of his so called *quasi* volunteers.

Mr. Turner said General Preston's figures were incorrect, and he did violence to all rules of conjecture and good guessing, in which he freely

---

11. *Public Laws of North Carolina Passed . . . at the Adjourned Session of 1862–'63*, pp. 80–81.

indulges in his report, so far as North Carolina was concerned. Nor was this the first paper from his office that reflected upon the State of North Carolina, doing her, by his figures and statements, gross injustice. . . . General Preston attempts to draw invidious distinction between the States of Virginia and South Carolina on the one side, and Georgia and North Carolina on the other. His report says: "In Virginia and South Carolina there has never been exhibited the slightest opposition to the conscript law. In North Carolina and Georgia there was popular and constituted resistance." Mr. Turner said that neither the conscript law nor any other law of Congress had been resisted in North Carolina. Her people were renowned wherever they are known for their dignified obedience and cheerful submission to all just law, and even to unjust law, while they are in force. . . .

Mr. Turner said that General Preston was a gentleman fond of books and reading, and he would suggest that he relieve and refresh himself from the labours of his office by a little useful reading; and he would call his attention to the history of this war, and the reports of General Lee, "Stonewall" Jackson, D. H. Hill, Longstreet, A. P. Hill, and other hero generals, who had led North Carolina conscripts to battle. . . . He would find more frequent and honourable mention made of North Carolina soldiers than of any other State; and . . . upon the great battle fields of Virginia, North Carolina had left more dead and wounded . . . than Virginia and South Carolina combined.

Mr. Turner said that General Hill, in his official report, says that his division alone at Malvern Hill fought the whole Yankee army unaided by a single Confederate arm. His division was composed almost entirely of North Carolina and Georgia troops. . . . In the seven days fighting around Richmond North Carolina lost twice as many men as did South Carolina and Virginia. She lost more in the . . . battles of Fredericksburg than did those two States. In the Maryland expedition, at Boonsboro and Sharpsburg, she also lost more men that [sic] either of those States. . . .

Mr. Turner said he had made this comparison . . . because General Preston had drawn a distinction, in his report, . . . prejudicial and injurious to North Carolina. He did not mean to reflect on Virginia or South Carolina, but his purpose was to defend his own State. . . . She had shed more blood and left more dead upon the battle field than any other State, and he would not sit quietly by and see her delinquencies held up to the gaze of her sister States and the world by those who have shown as much delinquency and much less heroism.

"Proceedings of the Second Confederate Congress," 52:428–30.

B.

Richmond Feby 10th /64

My dear Sir:

On the next day but one after my arrival here, the N.C. delegation were summoned to meet the President. He opened the conference by reading to us a very long letter from somebody in Raleigh of "considerable intelligence" whose name he withheld, giving a bad account of the state of things in N.C. & advising the suspension of the writ of *habeas corpus* & that prompt & vigorous measures should be taken to "over awe & silence" the people. He also read us some scribbling upon the margin of a newspaper, anonimous even to him, of the same character. These two were all that he exhibited. . . . I characterized the letter as mischievous—doing the writer no credit & the state gross injustice—that if that letter were published in the state & Known to be the basis of any unfavorable action against the state that . . . there would be 100 000 majority to rise up against it,—That her people were sensitive & spirited & could be easily controled by Gov. Vance Gov. Graham & others who had their confidence, but if attempted to be over awed or silenced by force, N.C. would be bloodiest field of the South. I told Mr. President that N.C. had the right to expect that he would form his estimate of her from what was said & done by her constituted authorities & not from partizan letter writers & anonimous scribblers who were always malicious & seldom truthful. At this he flared up a little & said "Well but Mr. Reade we had better understand what it is that you censure so strongly in this letter." I answered that the whole of it was mischievous, that it advised that N.C. should be "over awed & silenced" He said I had mistaken the letter. He turned to the letter & there was the language. He said "Well, but he only means the leaders" I told him the writer did not so qualify it, but if he did it was all the same. I told him it advised that he should be made military dictator. He said "There you are mistaken again" I asked "does not the letter advise the suspension of the writ of *habeas corpus*?" He said, "Yes." "Well does not that clothe you with dictatorial powers?" He replied "Well if it does, it does not show that I would abuse the power" I told him I had not intimated that he would, but that the people of N.C. were unwilling to trust any body with the power. We were both getting up our pluck, & Mr Smith told me afterwards that there would probably have been a scene, but that my manner was so entirely respectful as to afford no excuse. The interview lasted I suppose some two hours & I have given you a very poor account of it. Mr. Smith sustained me fully in what I said of the loyalty of our people & he instanced the ease with which you stopt the meetings last summer. Mr Gaither also properly defended the state. When about leaving we all formed a sort of long circle with Mr Davis at one end of it, I extended my hand & walked up towards him & said with emphasis "Mr President, trust North Carolina & *let her alone.*" He grasped my hand & said "I earnestly hope that your strong faith in your state may be realized." . . .

The interview was not confidential but you will see from the nature of it that it was not intended for the crowd.

I have been a little tedious in detailing but I thought that in that way I would give you the best idea of things here.

I have been informed that it was charged that, from my remarks in the Senate, I was in favour of a Convention. That could only be inferred from the part that I did not *denounce* it. But to have denounced the movement as disloyal would have been inconsistent with my proposition that the dissatisfaction in N.C. *did not mean disloyalty.* . . .

Very truly yours

E. G. READE

Governors' Papers.

---

(6) In Defense of the Peace Agitators

The sharpest criticism by outsiders of North Carolina's loyalty came when it became clear that the state was a center of the peace movement. Though some of its adherents desired reconstruction with the Union, the large majority probably believed that negotiations with the Lincoln administration had a good chance of obtaining southern independence. This had been a central issue in several district races during the congressional elections of 1863, and a number of so-called peace men had been elected. Congress had hardly assembled when the Richmond Examiner *carried an insulting editorial beginning " 'The eyes of the Universe' are fixed upon those members of Congress from North Carolina, returned as Peacemen or Conservatives."*[12] *Representatives James M. and James T. Leach of Randolph and Johnston counties, respectively, were both named on this infamous list and both rose to defend their own and their state's honor. Both had been elected in protest against the war measures of the Davis administration, and both supported little of its program during the Second Congress.*

Proceedings in the Confederate House of Representatives,
May 4, 1864

Mr. Leach said he did not stand upon the platform attributed to him, "that this war had lasted long enough." . . . He supposed the rumour that he stood on a peace platform of this kind had come up to the editor from the clamour raised in North Carolina on one political question and another; he did not deny but that there had been some clamour; but it was the clamour for equal rights, and not the clamour for a degrading peace. Because of these internal dissensions, the position of North Carolina has been persistently misrepresented and stubbornly misunderstood. He (Mr. Leach) knew enough of his own State to warrant the presumption and assertion that all the villification and abuse heaped upon the

12. "Proceedings of the Second Confederate Congress," 51:16.

head of the old North State came from her own recreant sons—the press and the men who denounce Governor Vance as a peace man. He (Mr. Leach) was for peace on the basis of the independence of the Confederate States of America, and that as soon as possible; he believed that was the sentiment of his constituents, and nothing short of it. . . .

During the political canvass which gave him a seat in this House, though elected by Conservatives, he had heard of no expression of sentiment looking to reconstruction. Yet it goes forth that the State is filled with treason, traitors and deserters. He believed, as for deserters, there were fewer from his State than any other. . . .

Mr. J. T. Leach, of North Carolina, . . . said he agreed with every word his colleague had said in vindication of himself—For himself (J. T.) he would say he was a peace man, but he was not a submissionist. . . . He did not believe that it was an evidence of disloyalty to try to negotiate peace. If it is, then there had been a great deal of disloyalty manifested. A great many wars have been terminated by negotiation that would never have been terminated by fighting. Look at the Revolutionary War. How was it ended? By negotiation. There was the war of 1812. How was that ended? By negotiation, wasn't it? . . . He did not deny but there was some disloyalty in North Carolina . . . but it was disloyalty to bad laws and bad legislation, and not disloyalty to the Confederate Government. There would continue to be this sort of disloyalty in North Carolina until North Carolina had even-handed justice done her. . . .

Mr Staples of Virginia, (interrupting)—Mr. Speaker, I ask the privilege of being allowed to ask the gentleman a question. He says he is for peace. I would inquire what kind of peace would he accept if the terms were other than those of independence?

Mr. J. T. Leach—I am for peace upon the terms of independence. If we cannot get that—if that is impossible—I would accept any other peace that could be obtained short of subjugation. That's what I would do.

Mr. Miles, of South Carolina (*sotto voce*)—Peace short of extermination! That's what it means.

Mr. Barksdale, of Mississippi—Umph!

Mr. James M. Leach, of North Carolina, (to reporters)—Put my name down hereafter in full. I don't want to be confounded. I'm not that Leach (pointing to J. T.) but another Leach.

The Speaker called the States for the report of business.

"Proceedings of the Second Confederate Congress," 51:16–19.

---

(7) Confederate Interference with State Blockade-Running

North Carolina's ability to keep her troops in the field had depended to a large degree on the success of her blockade-runners. By far the most important of these was the state-owned Advance, *and it* had proved so successful in bringing goods from Europe that the state sold half interest in it and bought a quarter interest in two other steamers, the Don *and the* Hansa. *Meanwhile the Confederate War Department was having enormous difficulties in supplying the soldiers from the other states. In the fall of 1863 it ordered all ship owners to rent the Confederacy one-third of their cargo space. Vance, however, believed that the fact that the three vessels were partly state-owned should exempt them from the cargo space ruling. He protested so forcefully that Secretary of War Seddon reluctantly replied "I shall give orders to meet your wishes. . . ."*[13]

But on 6 February 1864 Congress ordered all vessels owned entirely or in part by private individuals to carry half their cargo on Confederate account. The infuriated governor now questioned of the War Department was it "possible that such an unblushing outrage is intended" and vowed to "fire the ship[s] before I will agree to it."[14] *In a more subdued fashion Vance presented his case to the president in the letter below and eventually wrung from the government on a technicality the tentative exemption of the Ad-vance, but not the* Don *or the* Hansa, *from the requirements.*

Raleigh, March 17, 1864

HIS EXCELLENCY JEFFERSON DAVIS:

SIR: I beg your attention to a matter of great importance to this State and the entire Confederacy. I allude to the business of blockade running. I learn that the new regulations upon foreign commerce are to be imposed as rigidly upon the ships of this State as upon those of private individuals, and I beg leave most respectfully, but earnestly, to enter my protest against such action and to state some of the many and obvious reasons which induce me to persist in the trade which this State has so successfully established.

The right of the State to engage in the exportation of its own productions and the importation of articles needed for the welfare of its soldiers and people is too plainly recognized to require discussion. I presume it was less to establish a right new to the States than to recognize and affirm the policy and utility of the enterprises that the law "imposing regulations upon foreign commerce" declared "that nothing in this act shall be construed to prohibit the Confederate States, or any of them, from exporting any of the articles herein enumerated on their own account." I learn, therefore, it is conceded in conformity with the letter of the law that a ship owned wholly by the State may sail unmolested by the claims of the Confederate Government. Under these regulations, which it is asserted, as I believe, in derogation from this spirit of the law as well as of the rights of the States, independent of the law of Congress, that ships owned jointly by the State and individuals, and though sailed under contract with the State and with the whole benefit which the individual can

13. J. A. Seddon to Z. B. Vance, 14 Jan. 1864, *Official Records*, Ser. 4, 3: 28–29.

14. Z. B. Vance to J. A. Seddon, 8 Mar. 1864, ibid., Ser. 1, 51, Pt. 2:828.

afford to surrender already conceded, must suffer the imposition of the "regulations" as to the individual share and be made to surrender more than as much more to the Confederate States. In the experience and practice of North Carolina it has been found that convenience, economy, and success have been best attained by inducing individuals with their ships and capital to conduct the enterprise of exporting and importing on joint account. If the Confederate Government seizes the shares of individuals in the ships thus indicated . . . , it not only destroys the means and power for performing these contracts, but by indirection prohibits the State from exporting on her own account and in the way most convenient and advantageous to her. . . . In these cases . . . North Carolina, having by well-considered contracts secured herself an adequate benefit and advantage, . . . is warranted in asserting an interest in the whole voyage . . . of exportation as well as importation "on her own account." Seeing nothing in the law requiring the State to surrender these contracts or to suffer them to be interfered with by these "regulations," is there anything in policy or the public interest to induce the abandonment of her enterprise? . . .

Now that the Confederate Government has no ships, [and] little money abroad . . . it is more than ever necessary for this State to continue to relieve her troops and people by persisting in her own enterprises. . . . I only desire to be allowed to adhere to a system long since entered into, without interference by these "regulations" or otherwise, which has given so much success and done so much good. It is said that one scheme is at variance or in competition with the Confederate one and destroys its chance of success; so in like manner, it appears to me, the scheme of the "regulations" offers an opportunity and alternative in the thirteenth section for individuals to buy the cotton bonds, now at near 50 per cent. of depreciation, and to export the cotton paid on them at about half the "regulation" price, without benefit to the Government in the outward voyage and without importation of needed goods in return; much more out of harmony with the general system sought to be established by the "regulations" than the separate traffic of North Carolina and infinitely less useful. . . . I beg leave in this connection to ask you to cause your Quartermaster-General to institute a comparison both as to quality and price of the articles furnished the Confederate Government by this State and those furnished by speculators and contractors. . . . I deem it hardly necessary to add that the "regulations" if persisted in will destroy the trade absolutely, except it may be under the tenth section alluded to. . . . The vessels in which North Carolina is interested cannot and will not operate under those terms. Money would be lost on each trip, and of course the State cannot incur losses for the benefit of the whole which are not to be shared by the whole. . . . Earnestly hoping that . . . I shall hear from you soon, as my ships are idle at the wharf, I beg to assure you of the great respect, &c., of

Your obedient servant,

Z. B. VANCE

Official Records, Ser. 1, 51, Pt. 2:837–39.

(8) An Impasse Is Reached

The running dispute between North Carolina and the Confederacy over the limits of national authority reached its peak early in 1864 when Vance exploded with a letter questioning the right of Congress to suspend the writ of habeas corpus, and then continued with an emotional defense of North Carolina's loyalty in the face of constant provocation (Document A). On 29 February President Davis denied at length these charges in Vance's letter and challenged Vance to support them, which he did in his letter of 9 March (Document B). On 31 March Davis indignantly denied some of the charges and affirmed that he was ignorant of the circumstances of the others. Nevertheless he asked that the correspondence be concluded for it "had so far infringed on the proprieties of official intercourse," was "so unpleasant" and "so unprofitable" that it would be fruitless to continue it.[15]

A.
Raleigh, February 9, 1864

His Excellency JEFFERSON DAVIS:

MY DEAR SIR: . . . I hear with deep regret that a bill is certainly expected to pass the Congress suspending the writ of habeas corpus throughout the Confederacy, and that certain arrests will immediately be made in North Carolina. . . . If the bill referred to . . . be strictly within the limits of the Constitution, I imagine the people of this State will submit to it. . . . If it be adjudged, on the contrary, to be in violation of that instrument . . . it will be resisted. Should it become law soon I earnestly advise you to be chary of exercising the powers with which it will invest you. . . . I am . . . convinced that you believe it to be the only way to secure North Carolina in the performance of her obligations to her confederates. The misfortune of this belief is yours; the shame will light upon those unworthy sons who have thus sought to stab their mother because she cast them off. If our citizens are left untouched by the arm of military violence I do not despair of an appeal to the reason and patriotism of the people at the ballot box. Hundreds of good and true men, now acting with and possessing the confidence of the party called Conservatives, are at work against the dangerous movement for a convention, and whilst civil law remains intact will work zealously and with heart. . . . I do not fear to trust the issue now to these potent weapons in the hands of such men as will wield them next summer; I do fear to trust bayonets and dungeons.

I endeavored soon after my accession to the Chief Magistracy . . . to make you aware of both the fact of disaffection in this State and the cause of it. . . . The truth is . . . that the great body of our people have been suspected by their Government . . . and . . . this con-

15. Jefferson Davis to Z. B. Vance, 31 Mar. 1864, ibid., pp. 844–46.

sciousness . . . of being suspected has been greatly strengthened by what seemed to be a studied exclusion of the anti-secessionists from all the more important offices of the Government—even from those promotions in the army which many of them had won with their blood. Was this suspicion just? . . . [W]here and when have our people failed you in battle or withheld either their blood or their vast resources? To what exaction have they not submitted? What draft upon their patriotism have they dishonored? Conscription, ruthless and unrelenting, has only been exceeded in the severity of its execution by the impressment of property, frequently intrusted to men unprincipled . . . and filled to overflowing with . . . petty meanness. . . . The files of my office are filled up with the unavailing complaints of outraged citizens to whom redress is impossible. Yet they have submitted . . . , though the noise of their natural murmurs is set down to disloyalty. . . . I make no threat. I desire only . . . to speak those words . . . which may . . . best subserve the cause of my suffering country. Those words I now believe to be . . . to refrain from exercising the extraordinary powers about to be given you by the Congress, at least until the last hope of moral influences being sufficient is extinct.

Though you expressed a fear in your last letter that my continued efforts to conciliate were injudicious, I cannot yet see just cause for abandoning them. . . .

Z. B. VANCE

Official Records, Ser. 1, 51, Pt. 2:818–19.

B.

Raleigh, March 9, 1864

His Excellency JEFFERSON DAVIS,
    Richmond, Va.:
SIR: Your letter of the 29th ultimo has been received. Several portions of it were read with anything but pleasure, as it was very far from my intention . . . to raise any issue of a disagreeable and unprofitable character with you. . . .

You object seriously to that part of my letter which alleges that there seemed to have been a studied exclusion of all once termed anti-secessionists from office in this State, even from promotions in the army.
. . .

I desire to call your attention to the fact that out of some twenty-five or thirty generals appointed from North Carolina only three were anti-secessionists. . . . Now, does it not seem strange, when it is remembered that two-thirds of the people of this State were opposed to secession until Lincoln's proclamation, that God should have endowed the remaining one-third with all the military talents. . . . Branch, Clingman, Scales, Ransom, and Gordon—all politicians—are promoted at once. What representative of the old Unionists was thought fit to receive similar favors? Colonel McRae . . . was the senior colonel of his brigade.

On the first vacancy a junior officer from another State was put over him. He was a Douglas Democrat. Colonel Garrett, his successor, was an old Union Whig previous to the war; had fought for three years, and was covered with wounds. . . . Lieutenant-Colonel Johnston, a secessionist, was put over him. Colonel McElroy . . . who had fought his glorious regiment from 1,200 down to 150 men . . . and who was, I learn, recommended by General Pender for promotion, was superseded by Colonel Scales, a secessionist. I . . . only wonder at the passing strangeness of . . . nature in so partially and arbitrarily distributing the military capacity of the country. As to the allegation that the great body of the people of North Carolina have been "suspected" by their Government, which you deny . . . I deem the facts just alluded to . . . sufficient proof. But proof of this, direct and positive, was given in the refusal to reappoint R. P. Dick, esq., district attorney under the late United States Government, for the avowed reason that he "was slow to leave the old Government." . . .

In reference to my remarks about the outrages of the military upon the citizens, you . . . assert that no complaint has been made to you of such a character without redress being granted when possible. . . . I have sent up to the Secretary of War's office many complaints of wrong and outrage and, to my knowledge, no case whatever has been redressed. Others . . . , after going through the circumlocution of military reference for several weeks, perhaps months, are finally "respectfully returned to Governor Vance for his information," that is to say, the matter stopped in the acceptance of the story of the accused party as a full exculpation. . . . Some time last year a company of cavalry went into Tyrrell County . . . and stole . . . a lot of horses from owners who actually had them in the plow. The poor farmers . . . employed a neighbor by the name of Lewis to go to Richmond to get the horses back or pay for them. Lewis was paid for the horses by a lodgement in Castle Thunder upon the accusation by the men who had the horses.

In the winter of 1862–63 a squad of cavalry were sent into Cherokee County, N.C., by Colonel Lee, of Atlanta, Ga. They seized a number of old citizens beyond the age of conscription . . . chained them together like galley slaves, and drove them before their horses 120 miles to Atlanta. Then they were thrown into prison and told that they could volunteer in the army or remain in prison during the war. Upon my earnest remonstrance they were finally liberated. Was that wrong redressed? Was anybody punished for that outrage? The Fifty-sixth North Carolina Troops was lately sent to Wilkes County to arrest deserters. . . . Whole districts were . . . robbed and the inhabitants reduced to the verge of starvation. Cattle and horses were seized from loyal men, carried into the neighboring counties, sold, and the money divided. . . . [Secretary of War] Seddon . . . says he can do nothing in the matter except to withhold the salaries of the officers, if they can be convicted of permitting it. . . . I know these things in a greater or less degree are inseparable from a state of war, and that it is utterly impossible for you to prevent them or to adequately redress them. But they do add to the discontents in North Carolina, and kindly efforts to redress would cause these poor people to love their Government and support its laws far more than the terrors of the suspension of the writ of habeas corpus and a display of force. To impress you with this was the object aimed at in my letter of the 9th ultimo. . . .

Very respectfully, your obedient servant,

Z. B. VANCE

Official Records, Ser. 1, 51, Pt. 2:830–33.

XVIII

THE PEACE MOVEMENT

As early as the victory at First Bull Run a few optimistic Confederates suggested that the United States was ready to consider peace negotiations based on southern independence, but almost everyone considered the suggestion premature and preferred first to prove their invincibility in battle. By the fall of 1862 some felt that this point had been made and that the Confederacy should seek to avoid a ruinous military stalemate. They also argued that peace proposals would divide the North politically and hamper the passage of war measures by the northern Congress. A few Confederate congressmen made desultory gestures in this direction, but the majority agreed with the president that the move was still inappropriate.

Within the next year, however, peace became one of the critical issues in the Confederacy. The prospect of an early victory had vanished and even defeat now seemed possible. Conscription, impressment, suspension of the writ of habeas corpus, the embargo, and varied other war measures were testing people's loyalty to the utmost; inflation, loneliness, and battle casualties were eroding their physical endurance. Whether it was the Confederacy's place to suggest peace negotiations was becoming in the eyes of many far less important than the possibility that the offer might be accepted. For his part, Jefferson Davis was convinced that Abraham Lincoln had been sufficiently advised that the Confederacy wanted only its independence and that any further suggestion of negotiations would be interpreted in the North as a sign of southern weakness.

But must a Confederate offer of peace come only from the president? Certainly as chief executive he was constitutionally empowered to conduct the nation's foreign affairs, but was his inaction final? Some peace advocates suggested that the Senate under its treaty-making power could order the president to take action; others wanted Congress to appoint its own commissioners, who would take the first embarrassing steps and then turn the negotiations over to the president; others suggested that a sovereign state could pave the way for presidential action; and still others believed that a single state could negotiate peace terms with the

United States and then refer them to the Richmond government for acceptance or rejection, the state to follow its own judgment in case of Confederate rejection.

North Carolina was unquestionably the leader of the Confederate peace movement. It began formally on 15 March 1862 when a meeting near Asheboro raised a white flag and prayed for peace. For the next few months peace advocates held back, stalled by successive victories at the front. But after Antietam and Lee's withdrawal from Maryland, William W. Holden began prophesying in his Raleigh *North Carolina Standard* that the Confederacy had little chance of independence. Somewhat later Holden devised a new gambit, that unless peace came quickly the military despotism into which the Davis administration was evolving would be complete and North Carolinians would be in far worse condition than before secession. By the summer of 1863 the leaders of the peace movement knew that they had widespread support. Holden believed that four-fifths of the people actually desired reconstruction with the United States. Jonathan Worth was one of these and wrote that "the masses, and many of the best and most intelligent citizens sympathize with the *Standard*." He did not credit Holden, however, with originating the movement, stating that the *Standard* was "merely the escape valve through which the repressed strain escapes."[1] It was then that Holden launched his major attack.

The peace forces held "spontaneous" rallies all over the state in which they both condemned the despotism of the Davis administration and urged it to begin peace negotiations on honorable terms. Holden then proposed that both ends could best be accomplished by means of a state convention. The Vance wing of the Conservative party considered the convention call a poorly disguised move toward unconditional reconstruction and refused to countenance any separate state action. In early 1864 the Vance–Holden gubernatorial race centered on the convention call, and Vance's overwhelming victory indicated that the majority of North Carolinians were discontent but not disaffected. The General Assembly then formally recognized that the president and the Confederate Senate "are the only legitimate agents for entering into negotiations for peace with the enemy," and requested them after the next "signal success of our arms" to make "an official offer of peace on the basis of independence and nationality. . . ."[2]

When the General Assembly met in January 1865, the House defeated a reconstructionist resolution by a vote of fifty-nine to forty. In the Senate John Pool proposed that North Carolina appoint its own peace commissioners and was supported by a beautifully phrased speech by R. P. Dick arguing that it was "not possible . . . that this war of a ruptured brotherhood can ever be settled by arms. . . ."[3] It, too, was defeated and the movement was now in the hands of the president and Congress.

1. Jonathan Worth to John M. Worth, 9 Aug. 1863, Hamilton, *Correspondence of Jonathan Worth*, 1:253.
2. *Public Laws of North Carolina Passed . . . at the Adjourned Session of 1864*, pp. 20–21.
3. Raleigh *Standard*, 18 Jan. 1865.

Davis eventually made a weak effort to secure a promise of independence for the Confederacy, but had no success. While some privately still worked for "reunion on the best terms we can get,"[4] most people resigned themselves to continued battle.

---

(1) The Peace Movement Takes Shape

During the summer of 1863 the Raleigh Standard *reported over one hundred peace meetings taking place in every part of the state. A horrified official wrote of them that "the most treasonable language was uttered, and Union flags raised."[5] The reports claimed that these meetings were spontaneous, but obviously Holden and his lieutenants masterminded them, for the resolutions adopted at the meetings were amazingly similar and were crammed with phrases lifted directly from* Standard *editorials. The following is a typical account of such a meeting. It includes the usual set of grievances against "Confederate despotism" and makes the same meaningless peace proposals. These resolutions probably expressed not treason but rather a genuine yearning that in some way a negotiated peace based on Confederate independence was possible.*

PUBLIC MEETING IN WAKE COUNTY

At a meeting of the people of Little River district, Wake County, held at Rosenburg on the 24th July, on motion of B. T. Strickland, Dr. G. M. Cooley was called to the chair, and Harrington Daniel was appointed Secretary. On motion, B. T. Strickland, A. R. Horton, and H. Daniel were appointed a committee to report resolutions. The committee soon after reported the following resolutions through their chairman, which were unanimously adopted:

WHEREAS, The time has arrived when people of North-Carolina should watch their own rights and interests with a jealous eye; and WHEREAS we, a portion of the people, have thought proper to meet together to express our views in relation to the policy pursued towards this State by the Confederate government, and to take a position in defence of our liberties . . . against kings abroad or tyrants at home. Therefore—

Resolved, That the course of the administration at Richmond towards North-Carolina has been any thing but fair. While she has put more men in the field than any other State according to population, and while her

---

4. Jonathan Worth to J. J. Jackson, 22 Mar. 1865, Hamilton, *Correspondence of Jonathan Worth*, 1:373.

5. J. C. McRae to Peter Mallett, 21 Aug. 1863, *Official Records*, Ser. 1, 29, Pt. 2:660.

sons have every where fought and charged the enemy with unsurpassed courage, she receives but little credit for valor or patriotism, and has fewer Generals than any other State to command her troops. Our people have long complained of this injustice, but thus far their complaints have been disregarded.

Resolved, That North-Carolina has men as well qualified to examine and enrol[l] her conscripts as can be sent here from the City of Richmond; and the course pursued in this respect towards the State is an insult to the intelligence of her people.

Resolved, That we utterly abhor the appointment of one Bradford as chief Tithingman from Virginia for North-Carolina . . . and we demand his removal.

Resolved, That the President having called upon the Governor of the State for more troops, we deem the call unjust until other States have furnished their quota. . . .

Resolved, That it is a great crime . . . to conceal the truth from the people. From the beginning of this war until the present the enemy has gained slowly but surely upon us, and but for the extraordinary courage of our troops, their flag would long since have floated from all our capitols.

Resolved, That we favor a proposition of peace to the enemy upon such terms as will guarantee to us all our rights upon an equality with the North; and if such a proposition should be made to and rejected by them, we would be willing to die to the last man upon the battle-field in defence of those rights and that equality. We feel that it is time to consult reason and common sense, and to discard prejudice and passion. The people must look and act upon things as they are.

Resolved, That peace cannot be reached merely by fighting. This, we think, is now apparent to all. The birth of a nation is a great event, and so is the decay and death of a nation. Unless Providence should smile upon us—and we see no indication that He will—the war will go on until one side or the other shall conquer.

Raleigh *Standard*, 5 Aug. 1863.

---

(2) Reactions to the Peace Meetings

Reactions to the peace meetings of 1863 depended on each individual's opinion of what might come from attempted negotiations. The editors of the state generally believed that honorable peace terms from the Lincoln government were impossible and that the North Carolina agitators were actually plotting reconstruction on northern terms (Document A). Private citizens who accepted this point of view were deeply shocked at what the suggestion of such discussion implied (Document B). Undoubtedly a large number of those who supported the peace meetings had allowed themselves

to be convinced that honorable
terms could be obtained. But
many humble men, who may very
well have originally been enthu-

siastic Confederates, were now
convinced that any terms were
better than continued war (Document C).

A. "AN HONORABLE PEACE"

Who, in the Confederate States, from President Davis to the most humble citizen, does not pray that peace may again smile upon our once
happy land? We presume there are none. And an HONORABLE
PEACE is what all do or should desire. The gentlemen who in their
public meetings declare for peace most generally qualify the term by
prefixing the word *honorable*; but as this phraseology admits of am-
biguity, we are inclined to believe that our enemies construe the resolutions as implying a desire for reconstruction of the Union,—that those
North Carolinians who so resolve for peace, are anxious to become the
slaves of Yankee task-masters, and wish to give over their possessions
and property to the brigands now devastating our country.—But we
know the men who in the assemblies before mentioned declare a wish
for peace, mean it upon no such terms as indicated above. Recreant to
their interests, indeed, would they be if they desired peace upon terms
of submission to yankee tyranny, and yet if intended for a directly opposite effect, no course could be pursued better calculated to lead us to
subjugation and ruin, than that which a designing and crafty politician
is holding up to the people at this time, and to whose delusive and dangerous doctrines and teachings too many, we fear, are favorably listening.

As we have said on more than one occasion, we believe the larger
number of those who compose the "peace meetings" are honest and sincere in their deliberations, yet the slightest reflection should convince
them that never were patriots committing a more serious blunder—an
error, which if persisted in, will entail upon themselves and all Southerners miseries and hardships such as have never before befallen a people
worthy of being freemen.

Every "peace meeting" held in the State is only one more invitation
for the barbarous foe to invest our own beloved section, in which event
all its inhabitants will fare alike. The lives and property of one class or
party will be no more safe than that of another; and he who was most
clamorous for "peace"—whose fatal song courted the presence of the
enemy—will suffer by his ravages and despoilations precisely the same
as he whose breast is now bared to the vandals on Virginia soil. These
are truths, and, we deem it our duty to warn the people of the impending
danger, and to caution them in regard to adopting random resolutions,
the great instigator of which would betray his country and inveigle his
innocent dupes in untold miseries for a less price than was demanded by
his prototype, Judias [sic] Iscariot, for the performance of a similar
service.

Greensboro *Patriot*, 10 Sept. 1863.

B .

Near Orange C.H. Va-
August 14th 1863

D[r] John M[c]Iver.

My Dear Sir. It is with great pleasure I acknowledge the receipt of yours 7 inst. . . . I had before heard that my name had been proposed as a candidate. . . . I hope *no one* will vote for me who entertains the idea that I do or ever expect to favor reconstruction under any conseavable circumstances whatsoever. If those at home, who favor reunion, knew half as much about the Yankees as I do, they would blush to think of such a thing. How people at home can act as they do is strange indeed. You have no idea my dear sir what deep mortification we N Carolinians of this army feel at the course of our people at home. It is the talk day & night, not with a few, but with not less than *40 NC Regt* in this army—They say we have been enduring unbounded hardships, for more than two years, we have denied ourselves all comfort & pleasure, we have shed our best blood, we have whipt the degraded foe on *every battle field*. N.C. Troops have the name where ever they go of fighting with unsurpassed gallantry. . . . Notwithstanding, (they say) we have made all this sacrifice & have been so wonderfully successful, some of our own people at home, for whom we have endured so much, are at last about to turn against us, and aid our enemies to do, what they acknowledge they are unable to do.—*subjugate us*. Oh, it is discouraging, it is mortifying, it is a shame, a burning shame. If we are to be subjugated, our own people will do it, it is simply impossible for the yankees to do it. Were it not for this party at home, . . . I have no idea that the yankee army could be induced to come on this side of the Potomac again, as it is, they will no doubt take new courage and fight us more desperately than ever on Va. soil. . . .

Yours Truly
J A S . D . M C I V E R [6]

John McIver Papers.

C .

"Hill Country," N.Ca.
Jan. 1st, 1864

His Excellency, Z. B. Vance, Dear Sir

. . . After three years of fearful conflict the end of our pursuit, seems to be no nearer achieved. I wish to say to you, what I believe to be the sentiments of four fifths of the *freemen* of this Confederacy—We want this war stoped, we will take peace on *any terms* that are *honorable*. We would prefer our independence, if that were possible, but let us prefer *reconstruction* infinitely to *subjugation*. This never was a war of the majority: with all its horrors, it has been forced upon the people contrary to their will and wishes, and it is now perpetuated by the minority

6. A first lieutenant in the 26th North Carolina Regiment, from Moore County.

against the will of the majority. To prove this, you have only to look at the recent elections, especially that of our own old State and at the desertions from the army, and at the numbers who have gone and are still going from this "Hill Country" to the Federal Army. These things prove to a demonstration, that the hearts of the people are not, and never have been in this accursed war. . . . Our country is now almost depopulated; our men up to 50 years are now, all in the field, . . . and our precious children down to 16. . . . Want in a thousand forms, if not actual starvation, is now staring us in the face. I know more than twenty families within a few miles . . . who are now in a most destitute, not to say suffering condition, most of them are scantily clad and many of them are the families of soldiers, who are now doing battle for their country, others are the widows and orphans of those who have fallen on the field or died from disease. . . . If you could see the suffering that I see, and knowd by observation the destitution of the many thousands in our land, I know your heart would be touched, as it has never been touched before. As a candid man I tell you my Dear Sir, unless there is something done for our suffering people, and that speedily, our condition will be awful— beyond endurance. . . . What we most want and need is *peace, blessed peace.* . . . I am a Southern man by birth, in interest and in feeling, and would rejoice with you in our complete and triumphant success, but is it possible! . . . We claim brilliant victories every where, but the Yankees have their heel on three fourths of our country. We have . . . never yet been able to repossess ourselves of a single important position they have occupied. . . . Will we ever be stronger in the future than we were in the past? . . . Was our foe ever more determined than at the present time? Is it reasonable to suppose that he will abandon the contest. . . . Sir, . . . everything is against us, I fear the God who rules the destinies of nations is against us. Let us then sue for *peace* before the heel of the oppressor is upon our necks for ever. I know our troops have displayed a valor the world has . . . never surpassed, but the greatest heroism can not achieve impossibilities. . . . Do not sit me down as one of the *croakers* and *timid ones.* I am a silent, but anxious looker on upon this fearful and unequal contest, and but breath[e] the *sentiments* of *thousands,* could they only find *utterance.* Let us make one honest effort to stay the offusion of blood and restore *peace* to our bleeding and distracted count[r]y, and if we fail, we can but meet the worst. . . .

AN OLD FRIEND

Governors' Papers.

---

(3) The Attack on the *Standard*

The strongest response to the peace agitation came from the army. On 12 August a great contingent of North Carolina troops held a convention at the Orange County courthouse and denounced

the peace movement as a dangerous folly. *Loyal newspapers carried over thirty accounts of "spontaneous" meetings in army camps
that did likewise. On 9 September
a group of Georgia soldiers in the
command of General Henry L.
Benning, abetted by a few North
Carolina soldiers, broke into the
Standard office, scattered its type,
and frightened Holden out of his
wits. Vance hurried down (some
said that he sauntered) and prob-*

*ably saved the office from total
ruin, but a few hours later a group
of Holden's supporters reduced
the loyalist* State Journal *to ruin.
Vance placed the blame entirely
on Benning and the Georgians.
The following letters show the un-
repentant nature of the Georgia
soldiers, Vance's appeal to the
president for future protection,
and Benning's interpretation of
the affair.*

RALEIGH, Sept. 9, 1863

MR. HOLDEN — SIR: . . .

From what I learn, considerable injury has been done your office. I
hope this will be a warning to you and all others not to pursue a course
calculated to encourage the enemy either by words or acts. The motives
of this party were patriotic. They believe you to be opposed to our cause,
and desire to betray us into the hands of the enemies of our peace, our
property, and our independence.

I am, very respectfully,

E. M. SEAGO,
Lt. Col. 20th Geo. Reg.

TELEGRAPH

RALEIGH, Sept. 10, 1863

President Davis, Richmond:

A Georgia regiment of Benning's brigade entered this City last night,
at 10 o'clock, and destroyed the office of the *Standard* newspaper. This
morning a mob of citizens destroyed the office of the State *Journal*, in
retaliation.

Please order, immediately, that troops passing through here shall not
enter the City. If this is not done, the most frightful consequences may
ensue.

Respectfully,

Z. B. VANCE

HEADQUARTERS,
BENNING'S BRIGADE,
Near Chattanooga, Sept. 28, 1863

Sir: — . . . I arrived at Raleigh with a part of the brigade at the beginning of night, and immediately busied myself in procuring transportation for the troops in this direction. Having arranged this in an hour
or two, I returned to the depot where the troops were, lay down with my

head on a cross tie and slept till eleven o'clock, when the train to carry the troops forward came in from Goldsboro. I then put them aboard the cars. Whilst engaged in that work I heard, for the first time, of the outrage on the printing office. It was then too late for me to do any thing preventive or remedial. I had not had a suspicion that any such outrage was contemplated. . . . And, as far as I could learn, no officer of the brigade was engaged in the affair.—As to Maj. Shepherd . . . the imputation of complicity is in an especial manner unfounded and unjust. He was conspicuous in the suppression of the outbreak. When it commenced he was at a hotel awaiting his supper, and was found there by Gov. Vance. He immediately accompanied Gov. Vance to the place, and aided him to stop the work of destruction. It was he who, after Gov. Vance's address, ordered the troops off, and they, without a word, obeyed him. . . .

The true explanation of the affair I take to be this: when my brigade arrived at Weldon, we found there a party of North Carolinians, commanded by a Lieutenant, who informed me that he was ordered to the vicinity of Salisbury . . . to arrest some deserters, and urged me to let his party go along with my brigade. . . . I told him that he might do so. Accordingly he and his party took the tops of the cars, and went with my brigade through Raleigh. After we left Raleigh, this party freely avowed themselves the authors of the deed, and claimed credit for it. They said they led some of my men into it with them . . . but I think not many, and these merely unorganized individuals, each acting for and by himself. These things I learned from officers and men who heard the talk of the North Carolinians on the train after it left Raleigh. . . .

Very respectfully, your ob't serv't,
HENRY L. BENNING,
Brigadier General

To S. Cooper, Adj't and Insp. General, Richmond, Va.

Raleigh *Standard*, 28 Oct. 1863.

---

(4) The Demand for a State Convention

Holden had originally expected that Vance would ally his forces with the peace movement in an effort to wring concessions for North Carolina from Richmond. But actually, despite his quarrels with President Davis, Vance was becoming the leader of the loyal elements in the state, leaving only the true malcontents to support Holden. In July Davis suggested that he and Vance take "joint or separate action" against the subversive press.[7] Vance indignantly denied that neither the Standard *nor the peace meetings were recon-*

7. Jefferson Davis to Z. B. Vance, 24 July 1863, *Official Records*, Ser. 1, 51, Pt. 2:739.

structionist and insisted that they only criticized certain Confederate policies, not the Confederacy itself. He advised Davis that "it would be impolitic in the very highest degree to interfere with [Holden] or his paper."[8] At the end of 1863, however, Vance felt compelled to seek Davis's help against the peace agitation, admitting that "after a careful consideration of all the sources of discontent in North Carolina, I have concluded that it will be perhaps impossible to remove it except by making some efforts at negotiation with the enemy."[9] Davis, as intractable as ever, replied that he had already made "three distinct efforts to communicate with the authorities at Washington" and that all had been "invariably unsuccessful." Lincoln would only consider peace based on reconstruction and emancipation, and any further Confederate pleas for negotiation would only subject the Confederacy "to indignity without the slightest chance of being listened to. . . ."[10]

It was against this background that Holden initiated a demand for a state convention. By 1864 he had become convinced that peace negotiations could only be begun by separate state action. Through the *Standard* columns he argued "we believe that if the war should be continued twelve months longer negro slavery will be utterly . . . destroyed. . . . Its sudden destruction would involve the whole social structure in ruin." Meanwhile the Richmond government would have "blotted out" the rights of the states and individuals. He then proposed a state convention. Holden denied advocating a convention to take North Carolina from the Confederacy. He explained that its value would be "to protect the rights of the State against the common government, and to aid that government in obtaining an honorable peace."[11] To give Holden the benefit of all doubt, he may actually have thought that separate state negotiations might in some way lead to formal negotiations between Davis and Lincoln. The following explanation to his readers is as close as he ever approached to explaining his expectations.

A DIALOGUE

Destructive.—I understand, Sir, that you are in favor of a Convention to take the State out of the Confederacy.

Conservative.—I am in favor of a Convention, but not for that purpose. I believe that in union there is strength, and I should not be for secession until every other remedy had failed.

Destructive.—What, then, do you want with a Convention? What good can it do?

8. Z. B. Vance to Jefferson Davis, 26 July 1863, ibid., p. 740.
9. Z. B. Vance to Jefferson Davis, 30 Dec. 1863, ibid., p. 807.
10. Jefferson Davis to Z. B. Vance, 8 Jan. 1864, ibid., pp. 808–10.
11. Raleigh *Standard*, 20, 27 Jan. 1864.

Conservative.—I want it mainly for the purpose of taking steps to obtain peace. We have been fighting nearly three years. We are growing weaker . . . and if we keep on fighting and losing, or keep on fighting and gaining nothing, the time may come when we shall have to lie down and take such terms as the enemy may impose upon us. I am, therefore, for negotiating and fighting at the same time, and would do so with the other States, if they would hold Conventions as I hope our State will, and I would also join the common government in negotiating.

Destructive.—How would you do that? The common government alone has the right to negotiate.

Conservative.—Admit it, but then the States in Convention are sovereign, and could withdraw or modify that power; and besides, under our Constitution any three States can call a Convention of all the States. Such a Convention would certainly have the power to treat or do any thing else; but if that should not be done, any one State could demand terms for her co States and herself, and insist that the federal government should treat with her through the Confederate government, she submitting the terms offered and received to the latter. . . .

Destructive.— . . . But what sort of peace do you expect?

Conservative.—The very best we could get. I want separation and independence. We could have got better terms twelve months ago than we can now, . . . I fear it would be hard work now to save slavery on any terms. We went to war on account of slavery in the Territories, and we are now in danger of losing it in the States.

Destructive.—Is that all you want a Convention for?

Conservative.—No. The Confederate government, which is the agent of the States, has recently shown a disposition to absorb and use the whole power of the country. The States . . . are becoming mere blanks in the system. This alarms me. I want a body clothed with sovereign powers constantly in existence, to protect the State against the encroachments of its own agent, as well as to aid that agent in all constitutional ways against the common enemy. Independence without liberty would not be worth having. . . .

Destructive.—But what would you do with the army while you were holding Conventions and negotiating?

Conservative.—Keep it up, and fight on,—fight and talk peace at the same time. Whip the enemy one day, and offer to treat with him the next. . . . In this way we would increase the clamor for peace at the North, and thus add moral strength to our cause.

Destructive.—All that *sounds* very well, but I believe in fighting to the last. . . . I am tired of this peace talk and tired of submissionists.

Conservative.—Yes, and that *sounds* very well too; but if I mistake not, my friend, you volunteered and backed out without firing a gun, and rumor says that you have made a snug fortune since the war began. . . . If the tide of invasion is never rolled back until *you* help do it, it will roll on and roll over us. . . .

Raleigh *Standard*, 3 Feb. 1864.

(5) Vance Responds to the Convention Call

*In a letter about the peace agita-
tion to his old mentor, President
David L. Swain of the University
of North Carolina, Vance admitted
that "there is something to be said
on both sides." Possibly reunion
was inevitable. Though horrified at
the thought, he conceded that
"liberty and independence can only
be gathered of blood and misery
. . . and our people will not pay
this price."[12] Vance had already
determined that he would not let
Holden bring dishonor upon the
state, so now he daringly decided
to challenge Holden in a hotbed of
discontent. On 21 February the
"Johnny Reb" band from Salem
began playing before the Wilkesboro courthouse, almost two thousand people assembled, and Vance
spoke. In a sometimes serious,
sometimes humorous, rambling
address he divided his time between explaining what he was doing to counter the numerous unpopular Confederate policies and
speaking against the proposed
convention. The long Wilkesboro
speech, delivered later on several
other occasions, is included below
in a severely edited version.*

FELLOW-CITIZENS, LADIES AND GENTLEMEN:—I do not
know how it is possible for me to make myself heard by this large audi-
ence, unless I adopt the plan of the one armed soldier who could not hug
his sweetheart all the way around, and so was forced to chalk the distance he could reach on one side, and then turn and hug as far on the
other. . . . I shall endeavor to justify both the public interest you display and the compliment you bestow, by to day doing something which
is very rare in a politician—by telling the truth. . . .

In consequence of . . . continued suffering which experience had
not prepared the people to endure with the fortitude possessed by some
nations who have been nurtured to the shock of arms, a certain discontent has pervaded and a funeral gloom hung over the community, en-
gendering, if we credit a wide rumor, throughout the State, a notion that
we must have a Convention—that we must secede from the Southern
Confederacy; that we must repudiate the whole thing and go back and
do our first work over again. . . .

Secession was tried after it had been considered for a period of forty
years, and the whole country understood it as completely as an abstrac-
tion could be understood. . . . Our destines . . . have now been cast
in another government; and although, as you all know, I regretted to go
out of the former government . . . I never expected, and do not now
expect to see it resurrected. . . . The government we selected is ours,
as much so as are our own children. The spirit of patriotism is akin to
the love of our offspring which God has implanted in us—the highest,
holiest sentiment of humanity. . . .

Now what is it you desire above all other present earthly good?
(Voices—"peace," "peace," "we all want peace.") I know you do. Every-

12. 2 Jan. 1864, Zebulon B. Vance Papers.

body wants peace. Peace, blessed peace! Why, the man who does not desire peace is unworthy [of] existence.—Peace. It is one of the highest and holiest attributes of Deity, so much so, that our blessed Saviour Jesus Christ, was called the Prince of Peace. . . . I suppose, as reasonable men, you are willing to take the best plan to obtain this consummation so devoutly wished. Which is the best plan?

A Convention is proposed by some. . . . Suppose you call a Convention without any design that it shall put the State out of the Confederacy. . . . You elect your delegates, and the first thing they do on taking their seats is to swear . . . to support the Constitution of the Confederacy. . . . What does that Constitution say? . . . "The President shall have power by and with the advice and consent of the Senate, to make treaties, provided two-thirds of the Senate concur." . . . If you do not intend to instruct your delegates to take your State out of the Confederacy . . . your Convention assembled can do nothing more towards realizing the end in view than your Legislature or your Governor can accomplish. It can't turn a wheel.

Well, suppose you . . . instruct your delegates to take the State out of the Confederacy, because when it is out it is relieved from the obligation of the Constitution and rests upon a separate and independent basis. . . . [W]hat would Uncle Abraham say to it—that old gentleman whose personal pulchritude has been the subject of so much remark? . . . He would put his thumb up to his nose and make certain gyrations and evolutions with his finger, and say: "Waul ole North Carolina, I'm tarnation glad ter see yer come outer Jeff Davis' little consarn, I swow; but yer don't mean to say yer ain't in the Union agin, and under the pertection of the best government the world ever saw? Bin fitin' yer too long to let you sneak out that way." . . . Old Abraham is fighting us not because we are a part of the Southern Confederacy, but because we are in rebellion to the old Union; and so long as we refuse obedience to him he would continue to fight us. . . .

Suppose, as the last alternative for obtaining peace, your Convention should take the State out of the Confederacy and put it into the arms of Lincoln. Just as soon as you entered into the old Union . . . just so soon would you have imposed your share of the debt, taxes, burthens of the United States . . . the Federal agent comes to you demanding "greenbacks" and gold to assist in carrying on the war. Instead of getting your sons back to the plow and fireside, they would be drafted . . . to fight alongside of his negro troops in exterminating the white men, women and children of the South. Is there anything very desirable about a peace such as that? . . . I think I can assure you today . . . that any step of this kind will only involve you in a deeper and bloodier war. . . .

What would become of the currency should you abandon the cause of the Southern Confederacy. . . . Widows, soldiers' families and orphan children have no other kind. . . . What would become of the gallant soldiers who have been maimed and mutilated in the service. . . . The reply would be "You infamous rebel, have you the impudence to ask support from a government you have been fighting to destroy? No. You will get no pension. . . ."

But suppose . . . we would see what terms we could get from the United States. What does the enemy offer you? . . . Old Abe has perjured himself and he wishes to put you in the same category of villainy. —Not only must you swear to endorse his infamous document . . . but you must also take an oath to support all the acts of Congress . . . abolishing slavery, confiscating your property . . . and publicly executing your glorious Chieftains, and every officer from a Colonel up to Gen. Lee. . . .

What is to become of your negroes? . . . They are all to be turned loose upon us if we consent to the only terms Mr. Lincoln offers us. . . . I will only cite you one case of which there are hundreds of illustrations all pointing to the same dreadful result. In . . . Beaufort, South Carolina . . . the land has been recently laid off . . . and put up for sale. —I read the account of the sales . . . in the Philadelphia Inquirer. The correspondent says:

"The sale commenced on Tuesday and . . . the colored men are the principal buyers. . . . It is said by some that Beaufort is destined to become a second Jamaica. . . . This will certainly change the complexion of that once delightful inland watering place. . . ."

Your lands confiscated and sold to your own slaves! . . . I tell you my fellow-citizens, if we could consent to this thing we would deserve the fate of dogs. . . . Is there any man so lost to reason as to imagine the only possible way to save his negroes is to make terms of peace . . . and place them under the care and protection of Mr. Lincoln? . . .

I tell you now candidly, there is no more possibility of reconstructing the old Union and reinstating things as they were four years ago, than exists for you to gather up the scattered bones of your sons who have fallen in this struggle . . . reclothe them with flesh, fill their veins with the blood they have so generously shed, and their lungs with the same breath with which they breathed out their last prayer for their country's triumph and independence. (Immense applause.)

The old Union was . . . a moral Union. The cement of confidence was what held it together so long. . . . It has gone forever. . . . There never can be peace . . until the North and South are independent and distinct nations. There might be a temporary peace . . . but . . . insurrection after insurrection, revolution upon revolution, war after war would burst upon the country . . . victims would be demanded and blood flow in torrents, compared to which a drop would have at first won independence and permanent peace. The only way to obtain continued peace—and I want no other—is to fight it out *now*. . . .

Fellow citizens, we do not know what we can do until we try. There never was a war . . . that has been, in my opinion, so badly managed; but we have, notwithstanding, accomplished wonders. . . . Instead of being whipped by an invading army . . . we have whipped in [sic] invading army in four-fifths of our engagements. . . . I have no more doubt now about the establishment of the independence of the Southern Confederacy than I have of my existence, provided we remain true to the cause we have solemnly undertaken to support. . . .

Raleigh *Daily Conservative*, 16 Apr. 1864.

(6) Peace Hopes Vanish

On 12 January 1865 the administration forces in Congress barely defeated a House resolution requesting President Davis to seek informal peace discussions with the Lincoln government. Finally persuaded that he must alter his tactics, Davis appointed three notable southerners to confer with Lincoln and Secretary of State William H. Seward at Hampton Roads, Virginia. He destroyed their bargaining power, however, by instructing them to negotiate on the basis of independence and they could only return empty-handed. One last wave of determination now swept through the remains of the Confederacy. On 14 February Vance issued his longest and most emotional proclamation, describing the horrors of submission and vowing that victory in the field was still possible. Newspapers added their voices, and the ever loyal State Journal carried the following typical analysis.

THE PEACE BUBBLE BURST

As we announced on Sunday morning, Peace our [sic] Commissioners have returned from Fortress Monroe to Richmond. They reached that city on Saturday night.

Behold the result! By Lincoln and Seward they were informed, substantially, that peace could only be attained by UNCONDITIONAL SURRENDER to the . . . United States, and that the slavery question had been disposed of by the *Yankee Congress having adopted amendments to the constitution abolishing slavery in the United States!*

Those of our readers who have any respect for our opinion or judgment will have been prepared for this result. Indeed we are happy in thinking that the great majority of the people throughout the Confederacy will have been prepared. . . .

When our Commissioners were appointed, we felt it was done in deference to the peace sentiment of the country and to show that our Government was willing to make an honest effort to prevent the further shedding of blood. But we said we had no hope of peace resulting, unless there was an outside pressure on Lincoln which he could not disregard. As between the South and the North . . . there could be no peace. The South was fighting for independence and there was no alternative left but death. The North, on the other hand, demanded the unconditional surrender of the South, with all its horrors, and had resolved upon the total abolition of slavery. . . . We said the North knew our terms and we theirs, and that it did not need the appointment of commissioners on either side to learn this. . . .

But good must surely result from this attempt on the part of our Government. It *must* result in making the people of the South a unit. When all see, as they now must, that not only is the institution of slavery arrogantly abolished, but that the confiscation of every other species of property will be enforced—that by the decrees of the vile foe, they are to become landless, houseless, homeless, the slaves of their slaves and the bondmen of their foes—one universal cry for Liberty or Death will echo through the land. That must now become the stern battle cry; and when men understand its true meaning and fully realize its great import, new hope will invigorate each heart, and with it will come the truthful evidence of the inexhaustable power of the South to achieve *unconditional independence*. Would to God we could make every man in the Confederacy feel, as we do, that there is no doubt in the ultimate triumph of our cause—that we could make them believe, as we do, that in men and means, guided and employed in the right spirit, the South is yet a giant power. We ask our readers to believe us when we tell them there is no cause for despondency. Let all now be thoroughly united, and above all let us fully realize the condition to which we shall all be reduced in the event of our subjugation—a condition to which we never can be degraded if we be true to ourselves and to each other. Wake up, then. We now know the worst, let us meet the foe defiantly and firmly and trust in God for the final, glorious issue.

Raleigh *State Journal*, 7 Feb. 1865.

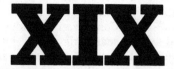

WARTIME POLITICS

Secession and the exhilaration of war preparations gave the North Carolina Confederate party—composed mainly of former Democrats and a few secessionist Whigs—firm command of state affairs during the early war months. Considering themselves largely responsible for the creation of the new nation, throughout the war they supported the Davis administration as far as conscience would permit, often deferring their state rights convictions to the centralism radiating from Richmond. They never fully accepted the professions of loyalty to the Confederacy that their political opponents, the Conservatives, constantly reiterated.

The Conservative party had originally consisted mainly of old Whigs and Unionists. After failing to block a secession movement which they blamed on northern abolitionists and southern fools they avowed themselves to be completely loyal Confederates and expected to be treated as such. They differed from the Confederate party in that they refused to countenance war measures that threatened the rights of individuals or states. Conservatives spoke of their opponents as "Destructives," not as a criticism of their former secessionism but of their apparent willingness to accept a military despotism for the sake of victory.

The year 1861 ended with only a few bubbles of discord disturbing the surface of the new found political harmony. Some disgruntled Conservatives complained of being denied the honors of office, and one of them wrote "I have not *seen* it as you have, but I know well enough the proscriptive, unscrupulous & corrupt policy of the dominant party, of which you speak."[1] They were probably partly right, but as yet grounds for genuine political division had not developed, as evidenced by the uncontroversial nature of the congressional elections that took place in the fall.

But politics soon reverted to normal, reborn out of the war measures

1. Edwin G. Reade to William A. Graham, 2 July 1861, Joseph G. de R. Hamilton and Max R. Williams, eds., *The Papers of William A. Graham*, 5: 281.

of the Confederate government. Holden could now rant to attentive ears that the old "Ultras" were "utterly incompetent," were motivated by "impulse and passion" rather than reason, and unless checked would permit a "military despotism."[2] The Conservative leaders then formally organized their party and began searching for a gubernatorial candidate. After failing to persuade William A. Graham to run, they decided upon young Zebulon B. Vance, former Whig congressman and Unionist and at that time colonel of the 26th North Carolina Regiment. The Confederate party had already nominated William Johnston of Mecklenburg, an early secessionist Whig known for his business and administrative abilities.

The eleven newspapers supporting Johnston attacked Vance for his youth, his lack of administrative experience, his constant joking, and his association with Holden; the ten Conservative papers had nothing against Johnston except his secessionism, but they directed their arrows at the Confederacy through him and his party. Vance's majority of 52,833 to 20,174 was more a vote against unpopular war measures than for Vance himself.

Elections to the Second Confederate Congress were scheduled for November 1863, but campaigning began almost a year in advance. Now not even Confederate party candidates expressed total support for the Davis administration, but they argued that excessive criticism would only demoralize the people and that victory must be won on the battlefield. Conservatives attacked all war measures which seemed to violate either state or individual rights, and as these measures now affected almost everyone the Conservatives seemed basically anti-Confederate. Conservatives were divided among themselves over whether to pressure the Confederate government into seeking peace negotiations with the Lincoln government, but they managed to delay an open break until after the elections. The outcome of the elections was a stinging rebuke to the "Precipitators." In a delegation of ten representatives, only Rufus R. Bridgers had favored secession, and in the First Congress he had allied with the anti-Davis faction. All except Bridgers and Burgess S. Gaither were peace candidates to some degree, and almost half the delegation were "Holdenites."

Spurred by his successes, Holden next determined to contest Vance's reelection if Vance opposed a call for a state convention. Vance realized that now his strategy of "fight with the Yankees and fuss with the Confederacy" might be inadequate to keep people confident in him and loyal to the Confederacy. He saw the convention demand as a first step toward reconstruction and wrote to Edward J. Hale, respected editor of the Conservative Fayetteville *Observer*, "the convention question is to be my test. . . ."[3] Two days later he wrote William A. Graham "I can not of course favor such a thing for any existing cause. I will see the Conservative party blown into a thousand atoms and Holden and his under strappers

2. Raleigh *Standard*, 24 May 1862.
3. Z. B. Vance to E. J. Hale, 30 Dec. 1863, E. J. Hale Papers.

in hell . . . before I will consent to a course which I think will bring dishonor and ruin upon both State & Confederacy! Is Holden the leader of the Conservative party? If so I don't belong to it." [4]

While Holden drummed through the *Standard* his vague arguments for a convention, Vance tried to persuade President Davis to take some peace step. Davis not only refused but compounded Vance's problems by having Congress once again suspend the right of habeas corpus. Under these circumstances Vance opened his campaign with his Wilkesboro speech and followed it with a series of speaking tours that left the Holdenites almost helpless. He wooed Conservatives by condemning the suspension of habeas corpus and the other unpopular Confederate policies; at the same time he promised that victory in battle was possible and that subjugation was too dreadful to contemplate. Of the seven planks in his platform, four appealed to Conservatives and three to the moribund Confederate party. Holden, with the help of only three other newspapers, charged Vance with venality, waste, corruption, secessionism, and vulgarity, but to no avail. The election results vindicated both Vance's honor and his middle-of-the-road strategy. He won the soldier vote by a margin of 13,209 to 1,824. His total majority was 57,873 to 14,432.

(1) A Moratorium on Politics

At first Confederates tried desperately to avoid the old partyism that had so divided them under the United States. The first test occurred during the elections for representatives to the First Congress under the permanent constitution, and to a considerable degree traditional politicking was absent. Candidates generally refused to campaign on the grounds of army duty or of the times being inappropriate. Instead, they placed "cards" in newspapers, vowing loyalty to the Confederacy and promising a "vigorous prosecution of the war." William N. H. Smith of Murfreesboro represented the First District in every Confederate Congress. He had opposed disunion until Lincoln's call for volunteers, but then demanded secession. Later he became a leading critic of the Davis administration. The announcement of his candidacy for reelection (Document A) in September 1861 expresses his genuine sympathy for the Confederacy at this time. W. W. Holden was one of the few who complained openly of what many Conservatives felt privately, that their loyalty was unfairly suspect (Document B).

4. Z. B. Vance to William A. Graham, 1 Jan. 1863 [1864], Z. B. Vance Papers. Vance's misdating of this letter resulted in its being omitted by the editors of the Graham Papers.

A. TO THE VOTERS OF THE FIRST CONGRESSIONAL
DISTRICT, COMPOSED OF THE COUNTIES OF
TYRRELL, WASHINGTON, MARTIN, BERTIE,
NORTHAMPTON, HERTFORD, GATES, PERQUIMANS,
CHOWAN, PASQUOTANK, CAMDEN AND CURRITUCK:

The permanent Constitution for the government of the Confederate States supersedes the present Provisional Government in February next. Preparatory to organization under it, elections are appointed by law to be held for members of . . . the permanent Congress, from the several districts into which the State is divided, on the first Wednesday of November preceding.

There are no movements in progress of which I am advised, indicating a disposition to resort to the instrumentality of Conventions for the purpose of making nominations for the . . . office. Those agencies, however appropriate or even necessary, during the heated party strifes of the past, to secure concert of popular opinion and action, seem to have disappeared before the generous and patriotic impulses which the presence of a common danger has inspired.

The day of election is near at hand, and I do not consider that I am over-stepping the proprieties of my position, in announcing myself a candidate to represent the district in the first permanent Congress of the Confederate States.

Unwilling to revive controversies calculated only to distract the entire harmony of sentiment and feeling which now prevails, in maintaining with undivided strength and loyal hearts, the action of the State in separating from the old and entering into the new Confederacy, for the security of her constitutional rights and the defence of the imperilled liberties of her people, I avail myself of this mode of communicating with you, and shall content myself with declaring my purpose to yield a cordial support in public and private station, to such measures of war and finance as promise to make the impending struggle on our part, vigorous, short and decisive. To this end, mutual confidence and a zealous cooperation unimpaired by former differences of opinion, alone are wanting.

W. N. H. SMITH

Murfreesboro, N.C. Sept. 24, 1861

Raleigh *Standard*, 2 Oct. 1861.

B. PARTY! PARTY!!

Why is it that in the midst of a bloody war waged for the very existence of the State . . . that many of our best and wisest men are rigidly and constantly excluded from the councils of the State and nation, and by our State authorities from the public service?

Mr. Branch and Mr. Davis and others—men surfeited with office, it seems are very proper persons to be sent to confer with the Confederate government at Richmond, or to fill other important positions—pet-men, sometimes filling two or more offices of trust and profit at the same time, but the State, now in imminent hazard, stands in no need of the services of such men as Ruffin or Badger, Brown or Graham, Reid or Morehead . . . and a host of others! Indeed the tried men of the State—men whose ability, wise fore-caste and great prudence, have secured them the confidence of the people, like the above named . . . are put under the ban, to give place to others—*faster* men we suppose, mere politicians or rampant original secessionists of far less weight—who are to sit in the high scale of the synagogue. . . .

What is the reason for all this? We will tell you, fellow-citizens. *It is party*! Party! when war is upon us, and when our brave men of all parties and all positions are suffering and dying for their country. Yes, the depraved oracle of the destructives in this city, clamors for the spoils— must have *all* the fat offices for the original secessionists—indeed yawns and growls like a dog with a sore head, if the original Yancey men, the *democratic secessionists don't get them all*. Yes, the men who were un- willing to break up the old government until every effort was made to restore and preserve it—those who in February and April preferred peace to war, but who rose in their might as one man to resist the first indications of coercion and tyranny, as promulgated in Lincoln's procla- mation, they are the men who may pay their money to support the war and shoulder their muskets to drive the invader from our soil, but as a general rule, there are no offices for *them*. And forsooth, if *we* dare com- plain of the corrupting, damaging course of the destructives, because of its manifest injustice and impolicy during the war, we are charged with personal or partizan venom.

The *principle* upon which this miserable policy is based, is rotten to the core—when put in action, it is damaging to the peace and the har- mony and the efficiency of the State in this war; and this is the sole ground of our complaint. . . . We contend that North Carolina at this juncture, needs her purest, wisest, ablest, most reliable men, no matter what their politics are or have been. We want the office to fit the man and the man to fit the office—let him have been a whig or democrat, a Union man or a secessionist, we care not a groat. But when we see orig- inal secessionists planning and scheming and plotting to fill every office, military or civil, with original Yancey men, we are alarmed for the safety and perpetuity of the new government, and for the prosperity and suc- cess of the South in this war. And why, not because we doubt the per- sonal integrity of all of them.—Certainly not. But because their action is based upon a principle which is destructive to the perpetuity of Con- stitutions, and law, and order, and a permanent government. . . .

Let us say to those who thus carry on, the day is coming when the people will take vengeance for all this.

Raleigh *Standard*, 25 Sept. 1861.

---

(2) The Vance–Johnston Race of 1862

In the early spring of 1862 part of the old Democratic press began suggesting a nonpartisan convention which would nominate a governor and pledge its support to the Confederacy. Their nominee was William Johnston and they hoped that he would be elected by acclamation. W. W. Holden was the chief spoiler of this ruse. Largely at his instigation a mass meeting was held on 21 May in Raleigh at which the Conservative party was formally organized, its principles expounded, and its candidate offered to the electorate. Holden later wrote in his Memoirs *that after William A. Graham had refused to run "I then determined to fix on Z. B. Vance for Governor."*[5] *At first, then, Vance could rightly be considered Holden's "creation." Document A describes this culmination of Holden's long and able planning. Vance became so popular that soon he, rather than Holden, dominated the Conservative party. After Johnston's defeat the Confederate party dwindled so rapidly that its members complained of "proscription" much as the Conservatives had done in 1861 (Document B).*

A. MASS MEETING IN WAKE

According to previous notice, a portion of the people of Wake County, irrespective of party, met in the Court House in Raleigh, on Saturday, the 31st ult. . . .

Mr. Holden explained the object of the meeting to be to express a preference for a candidate for Governor . . . and on his motion a committee of seven . . . was appointed to draft resolutions for the action of the meeting. . . . The committee . . . reported, through their Chairman, Mr. Holden, the following resolutions:

WHEREAS, The people of North Carolina will be called upon, on the first Thursday in August next, to elect a Governor and members of the General Assembly; and it is highly important that . . . better men [be] placed in office than those . . . now in office: Therefore,

Resolved, That the partyism, favoritism, inefficiency and misrule which have marked the administration of public affairs . . . since the commencement of the present war, deserve the stern and unqualified rebuke of the people; and that a change in this respect is indispensable to the preservation of the credit and character of the State. . . .

Resolved, That our Constitutions, both State and Confederate, should never be violated on any pretense whatsoever, but should be sacredly observed by all whose duty it is to enact, expound, and enforce the laws. . . .

Resolved, That it is the duty of the legislative and executive departments to retrench and reform, as far as practicable, in the administra-

---

5. W. W. Holden, *Memoirs of W. W. Holden*, p. 19.

tion of the government. . . . All useless offices should be abolished, and no more money should be expended than is absolutely required to carry on the government, and to enable the State to contribute her due proportion of men and means to the common defence.

Resolved, That the military power should always be subordinate to the civil power, whether in war or in peace; and that martial law should never be declared, nor the writ of *habeas corpus* suspended, except when indispensable to the preservation of civil society or of the State itself. . . .

Resolved, That we recommend to our fellow-citizens, for the office of Governor, the patriot, soldier, and statesman, Col. Z. B. Vance, of the County of Buncombe; that we regard him as eminently qualified for the place, and we trust he will consent to be a candidate. . . .

Raleigh *Standard,* 4 June 1862.

B. THE ANTI-SECESSIONISTS

The great point in dispute between the North and the South, is the right of the latter to secede. . . . In only one State of the Confederacy exists an organized party opposed to secession, and . . . that state is North Carolina.

A majority of her Legislature has adopted as a political test of office, that a secessionist is unworthy of confidence, and has actually turned out able and efficient men, avowedly upon that ground. These factionists did not stop here, they have deliberately violated the law and the Constitution in declaring vacant two important offices—those of Adjutant and Attorney Generals—in order to fill them . . . with men suspected of disaffection to the Confederate States. . . .

Another proof . . . that the Conservative party is . . . inimical to Southern independence, is the fact that they are deliberately adopting a mode of raising State troops, which will inevitably lead to a conflict with the Confederate Government. They propose to take them from that class of citizens whose ages bring them under the Conscript law, which will provoke a disastrous contest with the officers appointed to enroll the conscripts, thus nullifying an act of Congress, and violating their oaths "to support the Constitution of the Confederate States." . . . It was proposed by the friends of Southern States Rights, who are in a minority, to take them from the exempts of the conscript law, and thus bring into the service . . . magistrates under 45, able-bodied, rich men who have procured substitutes; and feather-bed officers of the militia, and the balance from those under 18 and over 45. This was rejected with scorn. It was then proposed to take the conscripts "with consent of the President." This was also rejected! clearly developing that the . . . object was to force the President to some measures in support of the Confederate Law, which would place him and his administration in an odious light before the people of North Carolina.

But . . . by nullifying the Conscript law and detaining conscripts on State duty . . . , no more reinforcements can reach the army now in face of the enemy. We tell the gallant, illclad and benumbed soldiers who may read this . . . , that if he now returned to his native State; the fact of his being a secessionist would . . . close against him every office of profit and honor, from Constable to Governor! such is the tyrannical proscription of the disaffected faction. To have sprung to arms, or even denounced the act of the tyrant Lincoln, when he threatened invasion, *is a crime that disqualifies* from holding office, even the warrior veteran who shed his blood, to shield the homes and families of the cravens who now rule the State. Conservatism means to stay at home, and therefore, their proscription does not extend to the military officers. Soldiers . . . , remember these things on your return. . . . Soldiers, you are sacrificed that able-bodied magistrates, skulking militia officers, and rich men, who have purchased substitutes, may remain in their comfortable homes. . . .

Raleigh *State Journal,* 24 Dec. 1862.

---

(3) The Congressional Elections of 1863

The Eighth District congressional election in the fall of 1863 demonstrates the startling change that had occurred in the state's political climate. In 1861 the district had sent William Lander, former secessionist and Democrat of Lincolnton, to Richmond where he had been one of the administration's strongest supporters. Lander sought reelection in 1863. In a published statement (Document A) he defended his voting record and then carried his message to the people in a series of addresses. Lander's opponent was Dr. James G. Ramsay, physician of Rowan County, who had supported the Constitutional Union party in 1860 and had been steadfastly Unionist until Lincoln's call for volunteers. Ramsay openly sought Holden's support, published his position (Document B) in the local newspapers, and campaigned actively against everything that Lander represented. He crushed Lander, and in Congress he voted so consistently against the administration and in favor of state and individual rights that his loyalty was suspected.

A. TO THE VOTERS OF THE EIGHTH CONGRESSIONAL DISTRICT OF NORTH CAROLINA

I respectfully announce myself to you as a candidate for re-election.
By your kind partiality I have the honor of a seat in the First Congress

of the Confederate States. From the time of my election the Confederacy has been engaged in a stupendous war for the purpose of driving back the ruthless invaders of its soil, and establishing the peace and independence to which it is so justly entitled. Overtures having been repeatedly made by our Government to terminate hostilities and settle the existing difficulties by negotiation and honorable adjustment, and these overtures having been as often indignantly rejected, no alternative remained to us but to drive back the invaders and conquer a peace by force of arms.

While in Congress, therefore, as your representative, I used every exertion in my power to strengthen and increase the army, to give proper assistance and encouragement to the Executive, and to prevent, as far as possible, those disastrous collisions between the civil and the military authorities which are so apt to occur and so difficult to adjust in time of war.

I voted for both Conscription acts, not because I desired to force the Southern citizen from his home and family to the camp and battle-field, but because I considered them indespensable to the independence of the country. . . .

I voted against the Exemption acts, not because I was opposed to all exemptions, but because I considered those acts wrong in principle, dangerous in policy, and unjust in many of their discriminations.

I voted for the Funding bill, because I thought it necessary to diminish the volume of the currency and thereby to give more healthy action to the finances of the country.

I voted for the Tax bill of the House, which was rejected by the Senate; but, before the conference bill, which is the present Tax law, came up for action in the House, I was called away by affliction in my family. . . .

In fine, I voted for every measure which I thought would give strength to our army, vigor to the Government, and confidence to the country.

Should you endorse my course as your representative by re-election to Congress, I shall be guided by the same principles and policy which my record indicates . . . ; and, although I desire peace as ardently as any one, and shall use every honorable means to obtain it, yet I will consent to no adjustment which does not bring with it the independence of the Confederate States. . . .

Our cause is just. Our trust is in God. Our destiny, I firmly believe, is to be victorious in this struggle. . . . Let us be united in our efforts and the whole world combined cannot enslave us.

> I am, very respectfully,
> Your obedient servant,
> W. LANDER

Linconton, N.C., }
    August 27, 1863 }

Salisbury *Daily Carolina Watchman,* 31 Aug. 1863.

B. TO THE FREEMEN OF THE EIGHTH CONGRESSIONAL DISTRICT, COMPOSED OF THE COUNTIES OF ROWAN, CABARRUS, UNION, MECKLENBURG, GASTON, LINCOLN, CATAWBA AND CLEVELAND.

FELLOW-CITIZENS:—Having . . . acceded to the wisdom of my friends, to become a candidate for Congress, I . . . take this method of publishing a synopsis of my views, on the most prominent subjects of public interest.

I was ardently attached to the Union . . . until . . . the famous proclamation of Abraham Lincoln, left no alternative . . . but to take up arms . . . for the defence of our common rights. . . . I regard a vigorous prosecution of a defensive war as the best avenue to national independence, and an honorable peace.

A christian people, however, should not be too sensitive on the subject of honor, when principle is not involved; and a brave people should carry the olive branch of peace in one hand and the sword in the other. And, inasmuch, as Mr. Lincoln has recently announced that "any peace compromise shall not be rejected," if proposed by any of those controlling the army, I think it advisable that the President should instruct those having this power to open negotiations for peace. . . . When our armies are victorious, as they now are, propositions of peace, on the basis of our national independence, may be made and received, with the least prejudice to our interests and honor. . . . Entertaining the opinion that the . . . Conscript laws . . . [were] of doubtful constitutionality and expediency, I could not have voted for them, if I had been in Congress. But I do not propose their repeal, and advise a prompt and cheerful acquiescence in their requirements. . . . Should the war continue much longer, it will be necessary to modify, if not entirely abolish the Exemption acts.

Neither the Tithe, the Funding, nor the Impressment laws are necessary . . . in any other sense than as the result of improvident legislation. The "tax in kind" . . . should be modified as to operate more particularly on those products not necessary to the support of animal life upon the farm. . . . Let the currency be placed upon a secure footing and the Tithe laws will be no longer necessary.

If the Impressment law is not repealed, it will be necessary to provide, with more certainty, that the provision of the Constitution which declares, that "private property shall not be taken for public use without just compensation," shall not be violated. . . .

The power of Congress to suspend . . . the Writ of *Habeas Corpus* is limited, but I cannot agree to its exercise. . . . Much less would I clothe the President with this power. The personal liberty of the people should not be in the keeping of any one man, however pure or exalted. . . . There are those . . . who desire a strong government—who advocate the closing of our Legislative halls and Courts of Justice—the overriding of all other laws by Military law—the concentration of the whole force of the people in the hands of a military Chief . . . in a word, they want a Dictator, and would obtain a Military despotism.

Whether in or out of Congress, such views shall receive no aid or comfort from me. . . . Let the laws, Civil and Military, be enforced within their respective spheres, and their majesty vindicated against all offenders, whether of citizens or soldiers. . . .

The rights of the States should be guarded with untiring vigilance, while the powers delegated to the Confederate government should be duly observed. Hence I demand for . . . North Carolina, full faith, credit and respect; and regarding her soldiers, in the field equally brave and patriotic with any in the world; and her people, at home, both patriotic and competent, I insist that they be appointed to fill the offices within the State.

The Administration of the Government shall receive from me, if elected, all proper and due assistance, and I shall not fail to urge all needed reforms, and hold the administration up to the condemnation of the people should it, in my opinion, deserve it. To the Army, I shall give every constitutional encouragement, comfort and succor—to the people every possible protection . . . ; and I shall use all lawful and honorable efforts to bring about the . . . heavenly blessings of peace with independence.

Most Respectfully,
J A M E S G. R A M S A Y

Oct. 16, 1863

Salisbury *Daily Carolina Watchman*, 19 Oct. 1863.

(4) The Vance–Holden Race of 1864

In the gubernatorial election of 1864 the devotion of Holden's followers deceived many about the extent of his support. One of Kemp P. Battle's correspondents wrote "some children came to me begging bread the other day, & I heard afterwards that their father, had lately sent money to get 'The Standard'—to read—We read of Indians in Peru who will chew coco & starve in a delirium of delight." He added that Holden's best campaign gambit was to portray Vance as the candidate of the "Destructives." [6] *Holden did at-* *tempt this ploy and, as one of Vance's worried supporters wrote, was prophesying that Vance's support of the Confederacy "will ruin the Country, & produce anarchy despotism, & confusion & utter ruin."* [7] *But Holden was never able to portray himself as demonstrably more concerned with the state's welfare than Vance, nor was he able to clarify what a convention might accomplish (Document A). The Vance press easily pointed out the inconsistencies of Holden's peace crusade and asked all moderates to support the "True*

6. Charles Phillips to K. P. Battle, 22 June 1864, Battle Family Papers.
7. James M. Leach to Z. B. Vance, 5 Mar. 1864, Governors' Letter Books.

Conservative Platform" (Document B). The Confederate party did not bother to put up a candidate. The Wilmington Journal *stated that both Vance and Holden were "riding the same* hobby-horse, *but have only quarrelled at*

last because more than one wanted to ride in front. . . ." It chose to support Vance only because he was "in the main patriotic and true to the cause in which the Confederacy is engaged." [8]

A. THE APPROACHING ELECTION

We appeal to our friends to be at the election ground early in the day, and to work for the true Conservatives and against the Destructives and their associates, until sunset, with the utmost determination and zeal. The issue is *War* or *Peace*, and *Liberty* against *Despotism*. Gov. Vance and his supporters are not only in favor of the war going on, and on, and on, and not only opposed to negotiations for peace unless they can be brought about in *their* way, which is the way pointed out by President Davis; but they are *Davis* men—endorsers of his administration, and *with* him in every essential particular. To vote for Gov. Vance is to endorse President Davis, and at the same time to encourage the continuance of the war with all its horrors, with no earnest or determined efforts to stop it by negotiations.

We are known to be in favor of peace, and also to be in favor of civil liberty and the rights of our State. We do not fear to trust the people with their own affairs, whether in Convention or otherwise; and we would regard any treaty of peace that might be made as honorable, which, after having been submitted to the people at the ballot-box, should receive their approval. If rejected by them, it would be dishonorable. The people of North-Carolina will never agree to any peace that is not honorable. One of the best plans thus far presented . . . will be found in the resolutions introduced in the last House of Representatives by the Hon. J. T. Leach, of the 3d District from this State. . . . Gov. Vance is *opposed* to the peace plan contained in these resolutions, as is conclusively proved by his speeches and the course of his subsidized organs.

Remember that Gov. Vance is the Destructive candidate for Governor; that the Destructives expect to use him for their own purposes, and thus destroy the Conservative party; that if elected by their aid he will be bound to carry out their views; that if elected it will be understood that the war is to go on until *the South subjugates* the North, or the North subjugates the South; and that if defeated, *a great moral influence will at once go out in favor of negotiations and an honorable peace.* Mark the fact . . . that the Destructives are his most active supporters. "A man is known by the company he keeps." . . . Let every true Conservative *work* to prevent this result. . . .

Raleigh *Standard*, 13 July 1864.

8. Wilmington *Journal*, 19 June 1864.

B. THE TWO PLATFORMS

No one can deny that there exists two separate and distinct political platforms in this State at the present time. . . .

The designing demagogue and tricky politician is ever engaged in the suppression of truth and reality, employing his time in . . . lighting up treacherous fires by which to deceive and ensnare, but which false lights invariably . . . lead to his dismay and confusion. And the efforts of Mr. Holden to dodge the real issue and raise questions of merit between himself and Gov. Vance is plainly manifest in his solemn, dumb silence. . . .

At the close of 1863 he wanted another State Convention, and doubtless would have been glad to have been a member of the proposed Convention to give us another dose of his famous Secession Bitters, the great panacea for endangered rights and privileges; and now in 1864 he desires a separate State Convention, without informing the people what good it could effect. . . .

But when he attempts to palm off upon the people of North Carolina the doctrine that he has always been with Georgia and her leading men, and now stands alongside with them his record proves the contrary. And the record of Georgia and her leaders deny his principles. . . . Vice-President Stephens . . . says: "I know nothing of the politics of North Carolina—nothing of the position of her leading men." And speaking of habeas corpus: "You can invoke its repeal and ask the Government officials and the people in the meantime to let the question of constitutionality be submitted to the courts, and both sides to abide by the decision." And the Linton Stephens resolutions, passed . . . by the Georgia Legislature . . . resolve that . . .

"Our Government immediately after signal successes of our arms, and . . . when none can impute its actions to alarm . . . shall make to our enemy an *official* offer for peace," &c.

And then the last resolution:

"We renew our pledges of the resources and power of this State to the prosecution of this war . . . until peace is obtained upon just and honorable terms, and until the independence and NATIONALITY of the Confederate States is established. . . ."

Does Mr. Holden occupy the ground as indicated in the above extracts? He will not deny that he is causing to be printed the speech of Mr. Stephens to be used as a campaign document; but has he since December last, occupied this platform—the platform and principles of which Governor Vance is pioneer? . . . Mr. Holden entirely ignores Nationality.—He merely desires to lead the people into more perplexing difficulties. . . .

We hope to hear no more of Mr. Holden's "platform." Let us contrast his with that of Gov. Vance and the true conservative party:

THE TRUE CONSERVATIVE PLATFORM. —

The supremacy of the civil over military law.

A speedy repeal of the act suspending the writ of *habeas corpus.*

A quiet submission to all laws, whether good or bad, while they remain upon our statute books.

No reconstruction, or submission, but perpetual independence.

An unbroken front to the common enemy; but timely and repeated negotiations for peace by the proper authorities.

No separate State action through a Convention; no counter revolution; no combined resistance to the government.

Opposition to despotism in every form. . . .

Such are the features of the platform of our noble Governor, around which truth and virtue will cluster, and triumphant victory will plant her banner.

Greensboro *Patriot*, 28 Apr. 1864.

SHERMAN IN NORTH CAROLINA

In January 1865, General William Tecumseh Sherman's 60,000 veterans began crossing the Savannah River for their march through the Carolinas. Sherman's plan of campaign called for a march directly on Columbia, South Carolina, and then to Goldsboro, North Carolina, by way of Fayetteville on the Cape Fear. Goldsboro was important to Sherman because it was connected to the Carolina coast by two railroads running respectively from Morehead City (via New Bern) and Wilmington.

Between Savannah and Goldsboro the general planned, however, to destroy all rail lines in his path and live off the land. This would not only provide the army with food and forage but also give it considerable mobility. At the same time Sherman's plan of total war called for the devastation of the heart of the two Carolinas. Factories and public property were to be burned. Furthermore, since Sherman considered all of the people of the South technically as enemies of the Union, he planned to use his military forces against the civilian population as well as the troops opposing him. He believed this phase of his total war concept would demoralize not only the noncombatants at home but also the men under arms.

By 3 March Sherman's army had reached Cheraw, its last stop in South Carolina. Here the general learned that Joseph E. Johnston had replaced P. G. T. Beauregard as commander of the Confederate forces in the Carolinas. He now correctly surmised that his able opponent would unite his various small bands, which were scattered from Mississippi to the Carolinas, and at a place of his own choosing strike one of the Union columns on the move.

Five days later Sherman had his entire army on North Carolina soil in the vicinity of Laurel Hill Presbyterian Church (in present-day Scotland County). The most formidable obstacle ahead was the treacherous water of the Lumber River and its adjacent swamps. "It was the damnest marching I ever saw," remarked Sherman.[1] "Such a wild scene of splash-

---

1. William W. Calkins, *The History of the One Hundred and Fourth Regiment of Illinois Volunteer Infantry*, p. 294.

ing and yelling and swearing and braying has rarely greeted mortal eyes and ears" wrote an Ohioan.[2] After dark the men and animals moved in the eerie light of thousands of torches and blazing pine forests. Seldom did the soldiers pass up an opportunity to fire the trees, for the burning rosin and tar created an unbelievable spectacle of flame and smoke.

That Sherman would eventually arrive in North Carolina had been anticipated since he began his march in January, but when the state line was finally crossed, many North Carolinians surrendered themselves to a wave of despondency. "Sherman's army is in nine miles of Fayett-ville. . . ." wrote a schoolgirl from Louisburg. "We are greatly alarmed. What will we do . . . ?"[3] Possessions were hidden in an effort to save them. But for Carolinians outside the direct line of Sherman's march the primary concerns were not those of personal safety and protection of property. In Charlotte attention focused on the large number of refugees overrunning the city. A lady wrote her son: "There is the greatest crowd of refugees from South Carolina passing into Charlotte, we are impor-tuned everyday to take Boarders. . . . I feel sorry for them but still I can't love my neighbors better than myself and I really have as much as I can do now. . . . Tis reported here . . . that Sherman has taken Columbia. What on earth do the people mean by making no resistance and the South Carolinians who made all the fuss are swiftest on foot."[4]

On 10 March at Monroe's Cross-Roads below Fayetteville, the Union cavalry, under Judson Kilpatrick, was surprised and driven back by Wade Hampton and Joe Wheeler.[5] But Kilpatrick eventually regained control of his camp which opened the way for the Union occupation of Fayetteville on the eleventh.

Here Sherman crossed the Cape Fear and turned east toward Golds-boro. At the same time the general became careless in the management of his army. He placed little importance on the Confederate delaying action at Averasboro on 16 March, and three days later he allowed his Fourteenth Corps to become isolated. It was almost crushed by Joseph E. Johnston at Bentonville, a small town west of Goldsboro. The battle, the largest fought on North Carolina soil, lasted through the twenty-first and resulted in a Union victory. Still the first day belonged to Joe John-ston's small army of 21,000 effectives. By the afternoon of the twentieth, however, Sherman had 60,000 men on the field.

At Goldsboro the forces of Generals Alfred Terry and Jacob D. Cox of John M. Schofield's command awaited Sherman. They had marched up from the coast. Sherman now hoped to join forces with Grant in Virginia for the final push against Lee. The commanding general was unwilling, nevertheless, to delay his move at Petersburg until the troops from Golds-

---

2. Wilbur F. Henman, *The Story of the Sherman Brigade*, p. 918.

3. Pauline H. Brooks, "Extracts from School Girl's Journal During the Six-ties."

4. Letter of Mrs. R. Burwell to "Edward," 16 Feb. 1865, Burwell Papers.

5. Hampton commanded the cavalry opposing Sherman. Wheeler actually outranked Hampton but was his junior in service.

boro could arrive. Thus Sherman on 10 April put his army in motion for Raleigh. Johnston, who had been at Smithfield since the Battle of Bentonville, fell back rapidly in the same direction.

During the night of the eleventh Sherman learned of Lee's surrender at Appomattox, and the next evening peace commissioners from Raleigh arrived in camp. By this time the capital city had been evacuated by Confederate troops, and Johnston had reported to President Davis in Greensboro. Here the general was authorized to contact Sherman concerning a suspension of hostilities. This led to a meeting on 17 and 18 April between Johnston and Sherman at the James Bennett farmhouse[6] a short distance west of Durham.

When the generous surrender terms granted to Johnston by Sherman were turned down by Washington, the two officers met again at the same farmhouse. This time, 26 April, Sherman granted and Johnston accepted terms similar to those Lee had received at Appomattox. Except for the stacking of arms at Greensboro the war was over in North Carolina.

---

(1) Pioneer Corps

General Sherman knew the success of his campaign depended to a large extent on the efficiency of the Pioneer Corps whose job it was to build and repair roads and bridges. The corps performed a remarkable feat in maintaining the roads through the swampy and sandy areas of the Carolinas. The pioneers made extensive use of the corduroy process whereby logs were laid transversely across the muddiest part of a roadway to give it foundation.

The New Bern North Carolina Times, 25 April 1865, carried a Union soldier's interesting description of how difficult it was to corduroy a road.

The road was imprecated a great deal which did no good; then it was corduroyed, which did a great deal of good for a time, but after the passage of a score or two of heavy laden wagons, the corduroying sank into a muddy chasm, and [a] new layer of rails and trees had to be put down on the muddy surface through which the first had disappeared. It is detestable work felling trees and trimming them of limbs and boughs among those boggy pines, after working knee-deep in the oozy soil. After the trees are shaped they have to be dragged through morass to the pool or mud pits where they are needed and then laid down. . . . At times,

6. Recent research has revealed that the owner of the house spelled his name "Bennitt" not "Bennett." Nevertheless, most accounts refer to the farmhouse as belonging to James Bennett.

as a wagon goes bumping over the road, a log flies up on end, one end piercing through the bottom of the wagon, the other sinking deep down in the mud by force of the sudden jolt. The wagon thus becomes transfixed. The driver sits in his saddle and swears. If the army in Flanders were as profane as our teamsters, then the atmosphere of Flanders must have assumed a certain hue at times. While the drivers utter their horrid and needless imprecations, the soldiers more philosophical, get under the wagon, cut the upright log, bid the teamster pull up and repair the road for the next customers.

New Bern *North Carolina Times*, 25 Apr. 1865.

---

(2) "Bummers"

Since Sherman planned to cut himself off completely from his base in Savannah, he could expect no government supplies until he reached the Cape Fear River in North Carolina. Thus his army had "to forage liberally on the country during the march."[7] Very strict orders were issued regulating the foraging parties, but there was a wide discrepancy between the orders and the actions of some of the men who conducted themselves more as mounted robbers than as disciplined soldiers. They operated not under the supervision of an officer but on their own. Much of the pillage and wanton destruction of property in the Carolinas was the work of these raiders known primarily as "bummers." The plantation of J. M. Rose near Fayetteville was wrecked by Sherman's undisciplined foragers (Document A). Lieutenant Charles Booth of the Twenty-second Wisconsin deplored such conduct by the "bummers," but thought their foraging activities necessary to the success of the campaign (Document B).

A.

The Federal soldiers searched my house from garret to cellar, and plundered it of everything portable; took all my provisions, emptied the pantries of all stores, and did not leave me a mouthful of any kind of supplies for one meal's victuals. They took all my clothing, even the hat off my head, and the shoes and pants from my person; took most of my wife's and children's clothing, all of our bedding; destroyed my furniture, and robbed all my negroes. At leaving they set fire to my fences, out-houses, and dwelling, which fortunately, I was able to extinguish.

7. William T. Sherman, *Memoirs of General W. T. Sherman*, 2:175–76.

The remains of a dozen slaughtered cattle were left in my yard. (Nine dwellings were burned to the ground in this neighborhood. Four gentlemen . . . were hung up by the neck till nearly dead, to force them to tell where valuables were hidden. One was shot in his own house, and died soon after.) The yard and lot were searched, and all my money, and that of several companies which I represent, was found and taken. All my stocks and bonds were likewise carried off. My wagon, and garden, and lot implements were all burned in my yard. The property taken from another family—the jewelry, plate, money, etc.—was estimated to be worth not less than twenty-five thousand dollars.

Spencer, *The Last Ninety Days of the War in North Carolina*, pp. 67–68.

B.

But I must not close without telling you half—how our boys have marched without shoes or hats—how we have been without soap for three weeks, and obliged to cook over pitch pine fires—how with "giant great hearts" they have waded through sloughs of despondency, and have finally secured rest, food and raiment. But I must tell you a little about a class in our army (and no inconsiderable portion of General Sherman's army do they compose) called "bummers." Imagine a fellow with a gun and accoutrements, with a plug hat, captured militia plume in it, a citizen's saddle, with a bed quilt or table cloth, upon an animal whose ears are the larger part of the whole. Let us take an inventory of his stock as he rides into camp at night. Poor fellow he had rode upon that knock-kneed, shave tail, rail fence mule over 30 miles, had fought the brush and mud, and passed-through untold dangers, and all for his load, which consists of, first, a bundle of fodder for his mule; second, three hams, a sack of meal, a peck of potatoes, third a fresh bed quilt, the old mother's coffeepot, a jug of vinegar, and a bed cord. You call him an old, steady bummer. I'll give you one more picture. Here comes a squad of eighteen or nineteen, no two alike. Look at the chickens, geese, beehives; see that little fellow with a huge hog strapped upon his nag's back. There rides the commander, a Lieutenant, completely happy for the day had been a good one, and his detail has got enough for a day's good supply for his regiment.

These "Bummers" were detailed for foragers, and upon them the army depended for subsistence for be it known that we started with a very small stock of supplies and our campaign was lengthened after starting from our base (Savannah), consequently the "Bummers" were the life of the army. Many outrages were committed by them. . . . [enough] to make a soldier blush with undignation. Every effort that could be made was made to check the demoralization of the foragers; but the occupation tended to demoralization, and "the army must be fed, and Bummers must feed us."

G. S. Bradley, *Star Corps: or, Notes of an Army Chaplain During Sherman's Famous March to the Sea*, pp. 274–76.

(3) Engagement at Monroe's Cross-Roads, March 1865

On 10 March 1865, at Monroe's Cross-Roads near Fayetteville, Sherman's cavalry under Judson Kilpatrick was surprised and temporarily routed by Wade Hampton's horsemen. To make his escape on the morning of the attack Kilpatrick had to spring from the warm bed of a lovely lady who had been his traveling companion for three weeks. A Confederate cavalryman in on the attack could hardly believe his eyes when a young woman in night dress appeared in the doorway of Kilpat-

rick's headquarters.

The Union cavalrymen eventually regained control of the camp, but infantrymen in blue were soon contemptuously calling the affair Kilpatrick's shirttail skedaddle. E. L. Wells, a member of Hampton's command thought the morning call on General Kilpatrick "not without brilliancy in conception and romantic dash in execution, and its results failed of being decisive simply from the vast disproportion of numbers."[8]

In a moment the cavalrymen were dashing with a magnificent Confederate yell through Kilpatrick's camp. All there were buried in the profound slumber of supposed security. The sleepy camp guards and a few cooks busied about camp-fires attempted no resistance, and the troopers, thus rudely awakened, rubbed their eyes and peered out from under their canvas flies in droll bewilderment at the row. It was very good fun at first. . . . Presently they began to rally in knots, and then the hand-to-hand skirmishing became pretty brisk, as compliments were being exchanged at close quarters. It was especially lively near a little house which loomed up through the mist and around which were tied many horses. . . .

Just then there bolted from the door a sorry-looking figure in his shirt and drawers. The fugitive made no fight, but cutting loose and springing astride a horse "tarried not on the order of his going," but sped for safety through the fog and powder-smoke as fast as a militiaman. No one stopped him, thinking it not worth while in presence of such abundance of better-seeming game. Only one man recognized in the humble runaway the quondam bumptious Major-General and future politician, and he gave chase . . . [But] unhappily his horse fell on the wet, slippery ground, and he had the mortification of seeing General Kilpatrick disappear.

And now in wild alarm there emerged from the house, whose weatherboards were fast being perforated by chance bullets, a strange apparition, one quite out of place in such wild scenes a forlorn, forsaken damsel—one who was "neither maid, wife, nor widow," and who was

8. E. L. Wells, "A Morning Call on General Kilpatrick," p. 129.

"attached" to headquarters. She looked for a moment disconsolately at her carriage, which was close at hand, as if with the vague idea in her dazed head that it was high time for her to be leaving, and then stood still in mute despair as it broke upon her that it could not move without horses. Seeing that she was in imminent danger from stray shots that were flying about, a cavalryman dismounted and conducted the poor thing, in all courtesy, to a drainage-ditch, within which she crouched in safety as if it had been a rifle-pit. It was noticed, however, that, in spite of the risk thus incurred, she persisted in lifting her head from time to time and peered above the ditch to see what was going on, thus showing, as some one said, that female curiosity is stronger even than love of life. . . .

It was not long before the entire camp was in our possession, those who had not fled to the cover of the infantry or sought refuge in a swamp hard by having been slain or captured. . . . It only remained to hold what had been gained, but that was the difficulty. . . .

Most of our men were dismounted and thrown forward as infantry to hold the ground until the captured horses, artillery and wagons could be removed or destroyed. . . . At length portions of the scattered Federal cavalry began to take heart and rally under the wing of their infantry, and it became necessary for our command to withdraw before the pressure of the latter. We carried away many hundred prisoners (nearly as many as the entire attacking force) and numbers of horses, among them three of Kilpatrick's private mounts . . . [a] gallant black . . . a pie-bald, and a bay. When we had retired it was practicable for that General to return to his headquarters, which he had left in the rather abrupt manner that I have attempted to describe. . . .

Some weeks afterwards, when Johnston's army had been disbanded, I passed over the ground of this fight, as I was making my way southward by night. I reached the house which had been Kilpatrick's headquarters at a late hour, and a more dismal, unearthly scene than I beheld it would be difficult to imagine. The dwelling was entirely deserted. Perhaps its owner driven forth . . . to make room for the Woman of the Ditch. . . . At all events it was unoccupied by any living thing; the windows were without sashes, the front door broken from its hinges, and all fences and out buildings had disappeared. Near the dilapidated piazza, to the railing of which several horses had been tied on the morning when the corps was stampeded, were some carcasses, and at a few paces distant, where many horses had been fastened to a fence, there were numerous skeletons of the poor brutes. . . . The . . . remains [of the slain cavalrymen] had been interred, but rain and wind, assisted probably by animals, had in many instances partially removed from them the earth, so that the fleshless faces peered up at one, and bony hands stretched forth as if to beckon. The effect was heightened by the faint moonlight. It was an uncanny place, and the least superstitious would have been likely to have experienced some strange feelings there. . . .

E. L. Wells, "A Morning Call on General Kilpatrick," pp. 123–30.

(4) Refugee Train

Sherman especially wanted to reach Fayetteville in order that he could retake the arsenal located there. At the outbreak of the war the Confederates had taken over the United States arsenal in the city and for four years this valuable government property had served the South. It is not surprising, therefore, that the city suffered a great deal as a result of the Union occupancy. Besides the destruction of numerous public buildings, including the arsenal, there was considerable plundering of private property.

While at Fayetteville Sherman also took the opportunity to clear his columns of the vast crowd of white refugees and Negroes that followed his army. He called these followers "twenty to thirty-thousand useless mouthes."[9] Fenwick Y. Hedley, a member of Sherman's staff, in his book Marching Through Georgia *gives a colorful description of this refugee train as it departed for Wilmington.*

The white refugees and freedmen traveled together in the column, and made a comical procession. They had the worst possible horses and mules, and every kind of vehicle, while their costuming was something beyond description. Here was a cumbersome, old-fashioned family carriage, very dilapidated, yet bearing traces of gilt and filagree, suggesting that it had been a very stylish affair fifty years before. On the driver's seat was perched an aged patriarch in coarse plantation breeches, with sky-blue, brass-buttoned coat very much out of repair and his gray grizzled wool topped off with an old fashioned silk hat. By his side rode mater-familias, wearing a scoop-shovel bonnet resplendent with faded ribbons and flowers of every color of the rainbow; a silk or satin dress of great antiquity, and coarse brogans on her feet. The top of the carriage was loaded with featherbed, two or three skillets, and other "plunder." From the glassless windows of the clumsy vehicle peered half a score of pickaninnies of all sizes, their eyes big with wonder. Elsewhere in the column a pair of "coons" rode in a light spring wagon, one urging the decrepit horse to keep up with the procession, while the other picked a banjo, and made serious attempts to sing a plantation song, which was almost invariably of semi-religious character. Those who traveled on foot, men and women, of all colors from light mulatto to coal black, loaded down with bedding, clothing and provisions, were legion. Occasionally a wagon was occupied by white refugees, who, being unionist, had been despoiled by the Confederates. These were sad and hopeless. The colored people, on the contrary, were invariably gay hearted, regarding their exodus as a pleasure trip, and evidently strong in the faith of their lot on "gittin to freedom," was to be one of bliss.

Fenwick Y. Hedley, *Marching Through Georgia: Pen-Pictures of Every-*

9. *Official Records*, Ser. 1, 47, Pt. 2:803.

day Life in General Sherman's Army from the Beginning of the Atlanta
Campaign Until the Close of the War, pp. 402–5.*

---

(5) Battle of Averasboro, March 1865

The Battle of Averasboro, 16 March 1865, was fought in a section of Harnett County called Smithville, so named after a prominent family of Smiths living in that rural neighborhood. After the engagement Janie Smith, a seventeen- *year-old in the Farquhard Smith home, wrote her friend Janie Robeson a lengthy and bitter letter giving her impressions of the Union soldiers and her reaction to the sight and sound of battle.*

Where Home used to be,
Apr. 12th 1865

Your precious letter, My dear Janie, was received night before last, and the pleasure it afforded me, and indeed the whole family, I leave for you to imagine, for it baffles words to express my thankfulness when I hear that my friends are left with the necessities of life, and unpoluted by the touch of Sherman's Hell-hounds, my experience since we parted has been indeed sad, but I am so blessed when I think of the other friends in Smithville that I forget my own troubles. Our own army came first and enjoyed the cream of the country and left but little for the enemy. We had a most delightful time while our troops were camped around. They arrived here on the first of March and were camping around and passing for nearly a week. Feeding the hungry and nursing the sick and looking occupied the day, and at night company would come in and sit until bedtime.

I found our officers gallant and gentlemanly and the privates no less so. The former of course, we saw more of, but such an army of patriots fighting for their hearthstones is not to be conquered by such fiends incarnate as fill the ranks of Sherman's army. . . . Now our recources increase every year and while I confess that the desertion in our army is awful, I am sanguine as to the final issue to the war.

Gen. Wheeler took tea here about two o'clock during the night after the battle closed, and about four o'clock the Yankees came charging, yelling and howling. I stood on the piazza and saw the charge made, but as calm as I am now, though I was all prepared for the rascals, our soldiers having given us a detailed account of their habits. The pailing did not hinder them at all. They just knocked down all such like mad cattle. Right into the house, breaking open bureau drawers of all kinds faster than I could unlock. They cursed us for having hid everything and made bold threats if certain things were not brought to light, but all to no effect. . . .

Mr. Sherman, I think is pursuing the wrong policy to accomplish his designs. The negroes are bitterly prejudiced to his minions. They were treated, if possible, worse than the white folks, all their provisions taken and their clothes destroyed and some carried off.

They left no living thing in Smithville but the people. One old hen played sick and thus saved her neck, but lost all of her children. The Yankees would run all over the yard to catch the little things to squeeze to death.

Every nook and corner of the premises was searched and the things they didn't use were burned or torn into strings. No house except the blacksmith shop was burned, but into the flames they threw every tool, plow, etc., that was on the place. The house was so crowded all day that we could scarcely move and of all the horrible smelling things in the world the Yankees beat. The battle field does not compare with them in point of stench. I don't believe they have been washed since they were born. . . . General [H. W.] Slocum with two other hyenas of his rank, rode up with his body-guard and introduced themselves with great pomp, but I never noticed them at all. Whenever they would poke out their dirty paws to shake my hand, I'd give the haughtiest nod I could put on and ask what they came for. I had heard that the officers would protect ladies, but it is not so. . . . If I ever see a Yankeewoman, I intend to whip her and take the clothes off of her very back. We would have been better prepared for the thieves but had to spend the day before our troops left in a ravine as the battle was fought so near the house, so we lost a whole day hiding. I can't help laughing, though the recollection is so painful when I think of that day. Imagine us all and Uncle John's family trudging through the rain and mud down to a ravine near the river, each one with a shawl, blanket and basket of provisions. The battle commenced on the 15th of March at Uncle John's. The family were ordered from home, stayed in the trenches all day when late in the evening they came to us, wet, muddy and hungry. Their house was penetrated by a great many shells and balls, but was not burned and the Yankees used it for a hospital, they spared it, but everything was taken and the furniture destroyed. The girls did not have a change of clothing. The Yanks drove us from two lines of fortifications that day, but with heavy loss, while ours was light. That night we fell back to the cross roads, if you remember where that is, about one sixth of a mile from here, there our men became desperate and at daylight on the sixteenth the firing was terrific. The infirmary was here and oh it makes me shudder when I think of the awful sights I witnessed that morning. Ambulance after ambulance drove up with our wounded.

One half of the house was prepared for the soldiers, but owing to the close proximity of the enemy they only sent in the sick, but every barn and out house was filled and under every shed and tree the tables were carried for amputating the limbs. I just felt like my heart would break when I would see our brave men rushing into battle and then coming back so mangled.

The scene beggars description, the blood lay in puddles in the grove, the groans of the dying and the complaints of those undergoing amputation was horrible. The painful impression has seared my very heart. I can never forget it. We were kept busy making and rolling bandages and sending nourishment to the sick and wounded until orders came to leave home. Then was my trial, leaving our poor suffering soldiers when I could have been relieving them some. As we passed the wounded going to the woods they would beseech us not to go. "Ladies, don't leave your home, we won't let the enemy fire upon you," but orders from headquarters must be obeyed and to the woods we went. I never expected to see the dear old homestead again, but thank heaven, I am living comfortably in it again.

It was about nine o'clock when the courrier came with orders. The firing continued incessantly up and down the lines all day, when about five in the evening the enemy flanked our right, where we were sent for protection, and the firing was right over us. We could hear the commands and groans and shrieks of the wounded.

A line of battle was formed in front of us, and we knew that was certain death to us should we be unsuccessful in repelling the charge. Lou and I started out to do the same thing, when one of the vedetts saw my white flag (my handkerchief on a pole) and came to us. I accosted him, "Are you one of our men or a Yankee,?" "I am a Reb, mam." "Can't you go and report to the commanding officer and tell him that the hillside is lined with women and children he sent here for protection, and that the line of battle over there will destroy us?" "I'll do all I can for you" was the gallant reply and in a short time we were ordered home. . . .

You inquired after Cam I believe the excitement cured her. She is better now than she has been for years.

Their house is ruined with the blood of the Yankee wounded. Only two rooms left, Aunt Mary's and the little one joining. . . . Every piece of bed furniture, etc. is gone. The scamps left our piano, used Aunt Mary's for an amputation table.

The Yanks left fifty of our wounded at Uncle John's whom we have been busy nursing. All that were able have gone to their homes, and the others except four, are dead. The poor things were left there suffering and hungry with only one doctor. I felt my poverty keenly when I went down there and couldn't even give them a piece of bread. But, however, Pa had the scattering corn picked up and ground, which we divided with them, and as soon as the Country around learned their condition, delicases of all kinds were sent in. I can dress amputated limbs now and do most anything in the way of nursing the wounded soldiers. We have had nurses and surgeons from Raleigh for a week or two. I am really attached to the patients of the hospital and feel so sad and lonely now that so many have left and died. My favorite, a little black eyed boy with the whitest brow and thick curles falling on it, died last Sunday, but the Lord has taken him to a better land. He was the only son of his widowed mother. I have his ring and a lock of his hair to send her as soon as I can get an opportunity. It is so bad to receive the dying messages and token for the loved ones at home. It grieves me to see them buried without coffins, but it is impossible to get them now. I have two graves in my charge to keep flowers on, the little boy just mentioned and Lieutenant Laborde, the son of Dr. Laborde of Columbia College. The latter had passed through the fight untouched, and while sitting on the fence of our avenue resting and making friends with his captain whom he had challenged, a stray ball pierced his head. His with three other Confederate graves are the only ones near the house. But the yard and garden at Uncle John's, the cottage and Aunt Mary's are used for Yankee grave yards, and they are buried so shallow that the places are extremely offensive. The Yankees stayed here for only one day, a few for a day or two would come. We had a romantic time feeding the Confederate captain they brought here, hiding the bread from the rogues.

We had to walk about three miles going to the hospital at first to avoid the Yankee pickets. Our soldiers were there suffering and we were determined to help them. . . .

I am not afraid of perishing though the prospects for it are very bright. When our army invades the North I want them to carry the torch in one hand and the sword in the other. I want desolation carried to the heart of their country, the widows and orphans left naked and starving just as ours were left. I know you will think this a very unbecoming sentiment, but I believe it is our only policy now.

They took a special delight in burying the stinking carcases at everybody's door. . . . All nature is gay and beautiful, but every Southern breeze is loaded with a terrible scent from the battlefield, which renders my home very disagreeable at times.

Janie Smith to Janie Robeson, 12 Apr. 1865, United Daughters of Confederacy Papers.

---

(6) Battle of Bentonville, March 1865

At Bentonville 19–21 March 1865, the total Confederate command under Joseph E. Johnston numbered only 21,000 infantry, artillery, and cavalry. Yet within this skeleton force was an abnormally large number of seasoned officers. Present on the field of battle were two full generals as well as a score of lieutenant and major generals. In no engagement of the Civil War were so few men led in battle by so many veteran officers of high rank. With regiments scarcely larger than companies and battle flags close together, the Confederate offensive on the nineteenth was, to one young soldier, a gallant but painful sight (Document A).

Among Johnston's effectives at Bentonville were three regiments of North Carolina Junior Reserves —the Seventieth, Seventy-first, and Seventy-second. The youths were seventeen and eighteen years of age. Also on the field were 4,000 veterans of the Army of Tennessee, the sad remnants of a once proud fighting force. Young Wal-

ter Clark of the Seventieth North
Carolina was pleased to write his
mother after the battle that the
junior brigade had been complimented for its performance by
General Hoke (Document B). At

the same time an officer of the
Army of Tennessee proudly noted
in his journal the "quick recuperation" of the westerners "from the
disaster at Nashville"[10] the previous December (Document C).

A.

On 16 March the battle of Averasboro was fought and the next morning
we moved forward to meet Sherman. The night of the 18th we camped
in the woods beyond the stream which runs through Bentonville. The
next day, 19 March, was a bright Sunday morning. Hoke's Division lined
the road and at right angles to us was the Army of the West [Army of
Tennessee]. The enemy were in the angle. In the afternoon we saw the
Western army at right angles to us as it charged and took two successive
lines of breastworks, capturing the enemy's artillery. Several officers led
the charge on horseback across an open field in full view, with colors
flying and line of battle in such perfect order as to be able to distinguish
the several field officers in proper place and followed by a battery which
dashed at full gallop, wheeled, unlimbered and opened fire. It looked like
a picture and at our distance was truly beautiful. It was gallantly done,
but it was a painful sight to see how close their battle flags were together, regiments being scarcely larger than companies and a division
not much larger than a regiment should be. In the meantime Hoke's division was sharply engaged with a corps which was trying to turn our
flank. The enemy's large force enabled him to do this and next morning
Hoke's Division was thrown back and formed a new line of battle facing
nearly due east, whereas the day before we had been facing southwest.

Walter Clark, ed., *Histories of the Several Regiments and Battalions
from North Carolina in the Great War 1861–1865*, 4:20–21.

B.

Camp 4 miles North of Smithfield,
Mar. 27th 1865

Our Brigade was engaged in the battles of the 19th, 20th and 21st at
Bentonville. The Main fight was on Sunday (19th) when we attacked
two Corps of Sherman's Army before the rest had come up and drove the
Yanks two miles. On Monday they were reinforced and were the attacking party. They attempted to swing round our left (of which our Division

10. Otto Eisenschiml and Ralph Newman, *The American Iliad*, p. 665.
Only a remnant of the Army of Tennessee survived the defeat at Nashville,
15–16 December 1864.

formed the extreme left). They were well repulsed. On Tuesday they attempted to swing still farther round to the left and had got nearly thro' when [B. F.] Cheatham's Corps which had just arrived on the field of battle met and drove them back taking some prisoners. Tuesday night we fell back beyond the creek. Wednesday we fell back to the Neuse and Thursday to our present Camp 7 miles north of Neuse on Louisburg Road. During the battles & the retreat I had no means to write and since then I have been too sick from the exposure—it was raining nearly all the time—I incurred during them. Since we have been in Camp I have been confined to bed until to-day.

The Enemy at Bentonville were badly off for Provisions. His troops had positively nothing but parched corn. As to his animals that his Q. M. accounted were so fat when we captured some Artillery the horses were actually too poor to pull the pieces off. We captured about three hundred mules and horses all in same condition. Our teams are in better order than I ever saw them I think.

I commanded the Skirmish line of our Brigade on Monday. It was in a good wood for skirmishing with little or no undergrowth. We had a regular Indian fight of it behind trees. They charged my line twice but were both times driven back. That night the whole skirmish line kept up an almost continuous firing as they expected our Army to leave. That together with the scamps trying to creep up on us in the dark kept us up all night.

I suppose Neverson told you that my shirts suited me exactly. They are very pretty and have been much admired.

My Box came just in the nick of time and was I think the best you ever sent me. At least it seemed so while it lasted. I can't imagine where you got so many eggs. Not one of them was broken. I intended to have written you a long letter about the box shirts etc but we have been moving so constantly and the wagons and generally been at the rear—besides no way to send letters—that I haven't had a chance. . . .

Gen. Hoke complimented our Brigade very highly. Our loss 40 or 50.
. . .

A. L. Brooks and Hugh T. Lefler, eds., *The Papers of Walter Clark*, pp. 136–37.

C.

March 16, 1865, General J. E. Johnston took command yesterday of the Army of the South.

March 17. Conducted General Johnston to our headquarters found him surprisingly social. He endeavors to conceal his greatness rather than to impress you with it. I expressed to him the joy of the Army of Tennessee manifested on hearing of his restoration to command.[11] He

11. Johnston had been removed from command of the Army of Tennessee during the Atlanta Campaign of the summer of 1864. He was reassigned to command on 23 February 1865.

said that he was equally gratified to be with them as they were at his coming, but he feared it "too late to make it the same army."

March 19. Both armies commenced the march. Three miles beyond Bentonville, at Cole's farm, we met and skirmished heavily for a short time. Armies went into position—Bragg commanded left wing, [A. R.] Stewart the center, and [W. J.] Hardee the right. At one o'clock the enemy charged [H. D.] Clayton's division and was repulsed handsomely. General Johnston now ordered an advance. The hour for attack agreed upon was fifteen minutes to three o'clock. With a Rebel shout we drove the enemy nearly a mile and routed them for two lines of breastworks, capturing eight pieces of artillery and 417 prisoners. The excitement of the occasion and the many ravines we had to cross broke our line to such an extent that we halted and re-formed. While doing this, the enemy rallied, reinforced and charged repeatedly upon our lines until nightfall but with no effect. The brunt of this battle was on the Army of Tennessee, and the more praise should be accorded them for their quick recuperation from the disaster at Nashville. "Old Joe" drove back Sherman's disciplined veterans with a demoralized army of not exceeding 12,000 men. In consequence of a flank movement to our left, we were ordered to retire.

March 27. We saw a squad of forty Yanks. From their brazen looks, they consider us virtually whipped and our complete overthrow only a question of time. Numbers may subdue but cannot conquer.

April 4. I witnessed today the saddest spectacle of my life, the review of the skeleton Army of Tennessee. But one year ago replete with men, it now filed by with tattered garments, barefooted and with ranks so depleted that each color was supported by only thirty or forty men. The march of the remnant was so slow—colors tattered and torn with bullets —that it looked like a funeral procession. Oh, it is beginning to look dark in the east, gloomy in the west and almost like a lost hope when we reflect on the review of today!

Otto Eisenschiml and Ralph Newman, *The American Iliad*, pp. 664–65.

---

(7) Goldsboro Review

Sherman's army as it marched through eastern North Carolina presented a comical picture. The men, their faces begrimed from the smoke of burning pine forests, had drawn no quartermaster stores in three months. Therefore their uniforms were either in shreds or long since replaced by civilian attire. On the other hand, these veterans were robustly healthy. The Carolina countryside had provided them with a bountiful supply of rations. Some of the men trudged along in company with pets while others tended the large number of sheep, cattle, and hogs that were distinctive of this fighting force.

Near Goldsboro Sherman held a review for Generals A. H. Terry,

J. D. Cox, and J. M. Schofield who *city. An Indiana soldier recorded*
had been awaiting him at this rail *the ususual parade in his diary.*

Two or three days later General Sherman took his station by the road-
side, and we passed in review as we approached Goldsboro. We marched
in platoons, and I doubt if at any time the troops of the rebel army were
more ragged than we. Probably one man in a dozen had a full suit of
clothes, but even this suit was patched or full of holes. . . . Many were
bareheaded or had a handkerchief tied around their head. Many had on
hats they had found in the houses along the line of march, an old worn
out affair in every instance—tall crushed silk hats, some revolutionary
styles, many without tops, caps so holely that the hair was sticking out,
brimless hats, brimless caps, hats mostly brim. Many men had no coats
or wore buttonless blouses, and being without shirts their naked chests
protruded. Many a coat had no sleeves, or one only, the sleeves having
been used to patch the seat or knees of the trousers. . . . Generally both
legs of the trousers were off nearly to the knees, though now and then a
man more fortunate had only one leg exposed. Socks had disappeared
weeks before, and many a shoeless patriot . . . kept step with a half-
shod comrade. But the men who had cut off the tails of their dress coats
"to stop a hole to keep the wind away," though bronzed and weather-
beaten, marched by General Sherman with heads up. . . .

Samuel Merrill, *The Seventieth Indiana Volunteer Infantry in the War
of Rebellion*, pp. 260–61.

---

(8) News of Lee's Surrender

The news that Lee had surren- *dore Upson quite a celebration*
dered to Grant at Appomattox *took place in the camp of the First*
brought rampant joy to Sherman's *Division of the Fifteenth Corps.*
men. According to Sergeant Theo-

April 12, 1865

We have recd word that Lee and his Army have surrendered to General
Grant. Our boys hardly believed it at first, but it is sure now as we have
an order to that effect. Just as we were starting from Goldsboro I [Ser-
geant Theodore Upson] was ordered by Colonel Johnson to go to General
[C. R.] Woods HD Quarters and take charge of his HD Quarter guards.
. . .

We had a great blow out at HD Quarters last night. I was just josting
[posting] my guards when Gen Woods came out saying "Dismiss the
guards, Sergeant, and come into my tent." I thought he was crazy or

something, so asked for what reason. Said he, "Don't you know Lee has surrendered? No man shall stand guard at my Quarters tonight. Bring all the guard here."

I went and got all the guards and marched them up in front of the General's tent. By that time officers were coming from every direction. I paraded the guard. Gen Woods said, "Have them stack arms and bring two of them into my tent."

He had a great big bowl setting on a camp table. Evrybody was helping themselfs out of it. The general handed me a tin cup. "Help yourself," said he. I dipped in, took a little drink, handed it to the other boys. Then a Darky came with a tin pail full of what I suppose was punch. We took it out to the rest of the guards who stood in line behind the stack of guns. Gen Woods came out, made a little speech telling us Richmond was ours, that Lee and his Army had surrendered, that it was the end of the War and that we should celebrate as we had never done before. I think most of our boys did celebrate but I was pretty careful. I never had drank much liquor, and I did not know what it would do to me.

After a while a Band came. They played once or twice, drank some, played some more, then drank some more of that never ending supply of punch, then they played again but did not keep very good time. Some of them could not wait till they got through with a tune till they had to pledge Grant and his gallant Army, also Lee and his grand fighters. Some of them seemed to think perhaps that was going a little too far but it passed. The Band finally got so they were trying to play two or three tunes at once. Officers from all the Regiments in our Brigade were there and some from others. Col Johnson came over from our Regt after a while. He saw me, took me by the arm and brought me to General Woods, introduced me by a flattering speech. General Woods shook my hand and said he would promote me, that I could consider myself a Lieut. After a little more talk from Colonel Johonson [Johnson] he made me a Captain, and I might have got higher than that if the General had not noticed the Band was not playing. Going out to see about it, he found the members seated on the ground or anything else they could find, several on the big brass drum. Then he realized that they were tired, very tired, and he would relieve them. He got the big drum, other officers took the various horns and started on a tour through the camps—every fellow blowing his horn to suit himself and the jolly old General pounding the bass drum for all it was worth. Of course we all followed and some sang, or tried to sing, but when "Johnny Comes Marching Home Again" and "John Browns Body" or "Hail Columbia" and the "Star Spangled Banner" are all sung together they get mixed so I don't think the singing was a grand success from an artistic stand point at least. But it answered the purpose and let out a lot of pent up exhuberant feeling that had to have an outlet.

Away along in the wee small hours the parade broke up and a day or two later the General addressed me as Sergeant same as ever. But one thing is sure: Lee had surrendered and Richmon[d] is ours.

Oscar O. Winther, ed., *With Sherman to the Sea*, pp. 164–66.

(9) Surrender Terms

Although General William Tecumseh Sherman felt that the South should suffer for its role in bringing on the war, he held out to his enemies the sincere promise of a helping hand if they would lay down their arms. In his surrender negotiations with General Joseph E. Johnston at the James Bennett home near Durham on 17 and 18 April 1865, he lived up to the promise. The terms agreed upon restored to the South a large measure of its antebellum status quo. But Sherman, neither politician nor lawyer, was unaware of the full political and legal implications of his concessions. Consequently he was greatly surprised when Grant arrived in Raleigh on the twenty-fourth with the news that Washington had rejected the agreement. Earlier Sherman had sent the general a copy of the surrender terms.

Hdqrs. Military Division of the
Mississippi
In the Field, Raleigh N.C.,
April 18, 1865

Lieut. Gen U.S. Grant or
Major General Halleck
    Washington, D.C.
    General: I inclose herewith a copy of an agreement made this day between General Joseph E. Johnston and myself, which, if approved by the President of the United States, will produce peace from the Potomac and the Rio Grande. . . . You will observe that it is an absolute submission of the enemy to the lawful authority of the United States, and disperses his armies absolutely, and the point to which I attach most importance is that the dispersion and disbandment of these armies is done in such a manner as to prevent their breaking up into guerrilla bands. . . . Both Generals Johnston and [J. C.] Breckinridge[12] admitted that slavery was dead, and I could not insist on embracing it in such a paper, because it can be made with the States in detail. I know that all the men of substance South, sincerely want peace, and I do not believe they will resort to war again during this century. I have no doubt that they will in the future be perfectly subordinate to the laws of the United States. . . . I would like to be able to begin the march north by May 1. I urge on the part of the President speedy action, as it is important to get the Confederate armies to their homes as well as our own.
    I am, with great respect, your obedient servant,
                        W. T. SHERMAN
                        Major-General, Commanding

    12. At this time Breckenridge was Confederate Secretary of War and was traveling with President Davis. He attended the meeting at the Bennett home on the eighteenth.

Memorandum or basis of agreement made this 18th day of April, A . D . 1865, near Durham's Station, in the State of North Carolina, by and between General Joseph E. Johnston commanding the Confederate army and Maj. Gen. William T. Sherman commanding the army of the United States in North Carolina, both present.

First. The contending armies now in the field to maintain the status quo until notice is given by the commanding general of any one to its opponent, and reasonable time, say forty-eight hours, allowed.

Second. The Confederate armies now in existence to be disbanded and conducted to their several State capitals, there to deposit their arms and public property in the State arsenal, and each officer and man to execute and file an agreement to cease from acts of war and to abide the action of both State and Federal authority. The number of arms and munitions of war to be reported to the Chief of Ordnance at Washington City, subject to the future action of the Congress of the United States, and in the meantime to be used solely to maintain peace and order within the borders of the States, respectively.

Third. The recognition by the Executive of the United States of the several State governments on their officers and legislatures taking the oaths prescribed by the Constitution of the United States, and where conflicting State governments have resulted from the war the legitimacy of all shall be submitted to the Supreme Court of the United States.

Fourth. The re-establishment of all the Federal courts in the several States, with powers as defined by the Constitution and laws of Congress.

Fifth. The people and inhabitants of all the States to be guaranteed so far as the Executive can, their political rights and franchises, as well as their rights of person and property, as defined by the Constitution of the United States and of the States, respectively.

Sixth. The Executive authority of the Government of the United States not to disturb any of the people by reason of the late war so long as they live in peace and quiet, abstain from acts of armed hostility, and obey the laws in existence at the place of their residence.

Seventh. In general terms, the war to cease, a general amnesty, so far as the Executive of the United States can command, on condition of the disbandment of the Confederate armies, the distribution of the arms, and the resumption of peaceful pursuits by the officers and men hitherto composing said armies.

Not being fully empowered by our respective principals to fulfill these terms, we individually and officially pledge ourselves to promptly obtain the necessary authority and to carry out the above programme.

> W . T . SHERMAN ,
> Major-General, Comdg. Army
> United States in North Carolina
> J . E . JOHNSTON ,
> General, Commanding C.S. Army
> in North Carolina

Official Records, Ser. 1, 47, Pt. 3:243–44.

(10) Vance's Proclamation

Governor Vance departed Raleigh for Hillsborough the night before Sherman's victorious troops entered the capital city. From Hillsborough the governor proceeded to Greensboro where he boarded a train for Charlotte and his last interview with President Davis. But Vance was back in Greensboro when he learned of Johnston's second meeting with Sherman, 26 April, and the new surrender terms.[13] Realizing that further resistance would be futile the governor announced the collapse of the Confederacy to the people of North Carolina.

At Greensboro, where dispirited soldiers crowded the streets and the "excitement of war and fear" showed on every face, Vance viewed firsthand the chaos accompanying the collapse of the Confederacy: "Horses and horsemen were dashing through the mud from street to street. The drum and fife and bugle were heard . . . and the nightly camp-fires blazed.

. . . The rumbling of passing cannon, the neighing of frightened horses, the jingling of spurs and clashing of sabres, the shrill whistle of . . . engine, the tramp of the soldiery, the movement of the wagons . . . the rushing to and fro of citizens and soldiers, the insubordination of desperate men . . . all presented a scene and sound . . . never before witnessed or heard in . . . this inland town."[14]

From Greensboro the governor went to his home in Statesville where on 13 May he was arrested by Union authorities. In the meantime Johnston's army at Greensboro had been paroled, the men having been urged by their commander "to observe faithfully the terms of pacification agreed upon, and to discharge the obligation of good and peaceful citizens at your homes as well as you have performed the duties of thorough soldiers in the field."[15]

State of North Carolina
Executive Department,
Greensborough, April 28th, 1865
By The Governor of North Carolina
A PROCLAMATION

Whereas, by the recent surrender of the principal armies of the Confederate States, further resistance to the forces of the United States has become vain, and would result in a useless waste of blood; and whereas all the natural disorders, attendant upon the disbanding of large armies are upon us, and the country is filled with numerous bands of citizens and soldiers disposed to do violence to persons and property:

Now, therefore, I, ZEBULON B. VANCE, Governor of the State

13. See above, p. 323.
14. Greensboro *Patriot*, 3 Mar. 1866.
15. Joseph E. Johnston, *Narrative of Military Operations*, pp. 418–19.

of North Carolina, in the sincere hope of averting some of the many evils which threaten us, do issue this my Proclamation, commanding all such persons to abstain from any and all acts of lawlessness, to avoid assembling together in crowds in all towns and cities, or doing any thing whatsoever calculated to cause excitement; and earnestly appealing to all good citizens who are now at home to remain there, and to all soldiers of this State to retire quietly to their homes, and exert themselves in preserving order. Should it become necessary for the protection of citizens, I also appeal to the good and true soldiers of North Carolina, whether they have been surrendered and paroled or otherwise, to unite themselves together in sufficient numbers in the various counties of the State, under the superintendence of the civil magistrates thereof, to arrest or slay any bodies of lawless and unauthorized men who may be committing depredations upon the persons or property of peaceable citizens, assuring them that it will be no violation of their parole to do so. And I would assure my fellow-citizens generally that, under God, I will do all that may be in my power to settle the government of the State, to restore the civil authority in her borders and to further the great ends of peace, domestic tranquility and the general welfare of the people. Without their aid I am powerless to do anything.

Z. B. VANCE

Proclamation by the Governor of North Carolina, 28 Apr. 1865, Governors' Papers.

BIBLIOGRAPHY

MANUSCRIPT COLLECTIONS

Atlanta, Ga.
    Georgia Department of Archives and History
        S. J. Richardson Papers
Chapel Hill, N.C.
    North Carolina Collection
        Samuel A. Ashe. "End of the North Carolina Navy."
            Unpublished typescript.
        Pauline H. Brooks. "Extracts from School Girl's Journal During the
            Sixties." Unpublished reminiscences of Confederate veterans.
    Southern Historical Collection
        J. L. Bailey Papers
        Battle Family Papers
        Harriet Ellis Bradshaw Papers. "General Stoneman's Raid on Salis-
            bury, North Carolina." Unpublished reminiscence.
        Burwell Papers
        Cameron Family Papers
        Elizabeth Collier Papers
        Charles Carroll Gray Papers
        Lenoir Family Papers
        Mangum Papers
        George F. Mordecai Papers
        Pettigrew Family Papers
        Marmaduke S. Robins Papers
        David Schenck Journal
        Williamson Whitehead Papers
Durham, N.C.
    Duke University, Manuscript Department, William R. Perkins Library
        Alfred W. Bell Papers
        Lawrence O'Bryan Branch Papers
        John McIver Papers
        Hugh MacRae Papers

William Slade Papers
J. C. Zimmerman Papers
Philadelphia, Pa.
Free Library of Philadelphia
H. L. Carson Papers
Raleigh, N.C.
North Carolina State Archives
C. P. Bolles Papers
Civil War Collection
Governors' Letter Books
Governors' Papers
William A. Graham Papers
Edward J. Hale Papers
W. L. de Rosset Papers
Janie Smith letter, United Daughters of Confederacy Papers
Julia Ward Stickley Papers
Zebulon B. Vance Papers
John D. Whitford Papers
Calvin H. Wiley Papers
Washington, D.C.
Library of Congress
John C. Pickett Papers
Winston-Salem, N.C.
Wake Forest University
Slave Narrative Collection, microfilm copy
Moravian Archives
Memorabilia of the Congregation at Salem

OFFICIAL DOCUMENTS

Atlas to Accompany the Official Records of the Union and Confederate Armies. 2 vols. Washington: Government Printing Office, 1891–95.

Journal of the Convention of the People of North Carolina, Held on the 20th Day of May, A.D., 1861.

Journal of the House of Commons of North Carolina, Session of 1860–'61.

Matthews, James M., ed. *Public Laws of the Confederate States of America.*

———. *Statutes at Large of the Provisional Government of the Confederate States of America.*

North Carolina Supreme Court Reports.

Official Records of the Union and Confederate Navies in the War of the Rebellion. 30 vols. Washington: Government Printing Office, 1894–1922.

Ordinances and Resolutions Passed by the State Convention of North Carolina, 1861–1862.

Public Documents of North Carolina, 1861–1865.

Public Laws of the State of North Carolina Passed by the General Assembly, 1861–1865.

Report of the Joint Committee on the Conduct of the War of the Rebellion at the Second Session Thirty-Eighth Congress Red River Expedition, Fort Fisher Expedition, Heavy Ordnance. Washington: Government Printing Office, 1865.

U.S. *War Department, 39th Congress, 1st. Session, House of Representatives, Document No. 98.*

War of the Rebellion: A Compilation of the Official Records of the Union and Confederate Armies. 70 vols. and index. Washington: Government Printing Office, 1880–1901.

NEWSPAPERS

Charlotte *North Carolina Whig,* 1861–1965.
Charlotte *Western Democrat,* 1861–65.
Elizabeth City *Economist,* 1900.
Fayetteville *Observer,* 1861–65.
Greensboro *Patriot,* 1861–66.
Milledgeville (Ga.) *Southern Recorder,* 1864.
Milton *Chronicle,* 1861–65.
New Bern *North Carolina Times,* 1865.
New York (N.Y.) *Times,* 1861.
North Carolina Presbyterian, 1861–63.
Raleigh *Daily Conservative,* 1861–65.
Raleigh *Progress,* 1863.
Raleigh *Standard,* 1861–65.
Raleigh *State Journal,* 1862–65.
Salisbury *Daily Carolina Watchman,* 1861–65.
Wilmington *Journal,* 1861–65.

OTHER PRIMARY SOURCES

Allen, George H. *Forty-six Months with the Fourth Rhode Island Volunteers in the War of 1861–1865.* Providence: J. A. and R. A. Reid, 1887.

Bradley, G. S. *The Star Corps: or, Notes of an Army Chaplain During Sherman's Famous March to the Sea.* Milwaukee: Jarmain and Brightman, 1865.

Brooks, A. L., and Lefler, Hugh T., eds. *The Papers of Walter Clark.* Chapel Hill: The University of North Carolina Press, 1948.

Brown, Louis A. "The Correspondence of David Olando McRaven and Amanda Nantz McRaven." *North Carolina Historical Review* 26 (January 1949): 41–98.

Browne, Junius H. *Four Years in Secessia: Adventures within and Beyond the Union Lines.* Hartford: O. D. Case and Co., 1865.

Burkhead, L. S. "History of the Difficulties of the Pastorate of the Front

Street Methodist Church, Wilmington, N.C." *Trinity College Historical Society Papers* 8 (1908–09): 35–118.

Butler, Benjamin F. *Butler's Book.* Boston: A. M. Thayer, 1892.

Calkins, William W. *The History of the One Hundred and Fourth Regiment of Illinois Volunteer Infantry. War of the Great Rebellion 1862–1865.* Chicago: Donahue and Henneberry, 1895.

Chesnut, Mary Boykin. *A Diary from Dixie.* Edited by Ben Ames Williams. Boston: Houghton Mifflin Co., 1961.

Clark, Walter, ed. *Histories of the Several Regiments and Battalions from North Carolina in the Great War 1861–'65.* 5 vols. Goldsboro: Nash Brothers, 1901.

Cushing, William B. "Destruction of the 'Albemarle'." *The Century Illustrated Monthly Magazine* 36 (1888): 432–39.

Dodge, David. "The Cave-Dwellers of the Confederacy." *Atlantic Monthly* 68 (1891): 514–21.

Eisenschiml, Otto, and Newman, Ralph. *The American Iliad. The Epic Story of the Civil War as Narrated by Eyewitnesses and Contemporaries.* Indianapolis: The Bobbs-Merrill Co., 1947.

Ganaway, William T. "Trinity College in War Times." *The Trinity Archive* 6 (May 1893): 324–29.

Gorgas, Josiah. "Notes on the Ordnance Department of the Confederate Government." *Southern Historical Society Papers* 12 (1884): 67–94.

Hamilton, Joseph G. de Roulhac, ed. *The Correspondence of Jonathan Worth.* 2 vols. Raleigh: Edwards and Broughton, 1909.

——, ed. *The Papers of Randolph Abbott Shotwell.* 2 vols. Raleigh: North Carolina Historical Commission, 1929.

——, ed. *The Papers of Thomas Ruffin.* 4 vols. Raleigh: North Carolina Historical Commission, 1918–20.

—— and Max R. Williams, eds. *The Papers of William Alexander Graham.* 6 vols. in progress. Raleigh: North Carolina Historical Commission, 1957–.

Hedley, Fenwick Y. *Marching Through Georgia: Pen-Pictures of Everyday Life in General Sherman's Army from the Beginning of the Atlanta Campaign Until the Close of the War.* Chicago: M. A. Donahue and Co., 1884.

Henman, Wilbur F. *The Story of the Sherman Brigade.* Privately Printed, 1897.

Holden, W. W. *Memoirs of W. W. Holden.* Edited by William K. Boyd. Durham: The Seeman Printery, 1911.

James, Horace. *Annual Report of the Superintendent of Negro Affairs in North Carolina, 1864.* Boston: W. F. Brown & Co., 1865.

Johns, John. "Wilmington During the Blockade." *Harper's New Monthly Magazine* 33 (1886): 497–503.

Johnston, Frontis W., ed. *The Papers of Zebulon Baird Vance.* Raleigh: State Department of Archives and History, 1963.

Johnston, Joseph E. *Narrative of Military Operations, Directed, During the Late War Between the States by Joseph E. Johnston, General CSA.* New York: D. Appleton and Co., 1874.

Kirkpatrick, J. K. "The Duty of Females in Relation to the Future Educational Interests of Our Country." *North Carolina Journal of Education* 7 (July 1864): 85–94.

Lamb, William. "Fort Fisher," *Southern Historical Society Papers* 21 (1893): 257–90.

Merrill, Samuel. *The Seventieth Indiana Volunteer Infantry in The War of Rebellion*. Indianapolis: The Bobbs-Merrill Co., 1900.

Moore, Frank, ed. *The Rebellion Record: A Diary of American Events, with Documents, Narratives, Illustrative Incidents, Etc.* 12 vols. New York: G. P. Putnam & D. Van Nostrand, 1863–68.

Moore, Marinda Branson. *The Dixie Elementary Spelling Book*. Raleigh: Branson & Farrar, 1864.

———. *Geographical Reader for the Dixie Children*. Raleigh: Branson & Farrar, 1863.

Paris, John. *A Sermon: Preached Before Brig.-Gen. Hoke's Brigade at Kinston, N.C. on the 28th of February, 1864*. Greensboro: A. W. Ingold & Co., 1864.

Porter, David D. *Naval History of the Civil War*. New York: Sherman Publishing Co., 1886.

Proceedings of the Baptist State Convention of North Carolina, 1862–1863.

"Proceedings of the Second Confederate Congress." *Southern Historical Society Papers* 51 [n.s. 13] (1938).

Proceedings of the Thirteenth Annual Meeting of the Stockholders of the North Carolina Railroad Company, Held at Hillsboro, July 10th & 11th, 1862.

Scharf, J. T. *History of the Confederate States Navy from Its Organization to the Surrender of the Last Vessel*. New York: Rogers & Sherwood, 1887.

Sherman, William T. *Memoirs of General W. T. Sherman*. 2 vols. New York: D. Appleton and Co., 1875.

Spencer, Cornelia P. *The Last Ninety Days of the War in North Carolina*. New York: Watchman Publishing Co., 1866.

"Story of the Powder-Boat." *Galaxy* 9 (1870): 77–88.

Taylor, Thomas E. *Running the Blockade*. London: John Murray, 1896.

Tolbert, Noble J., ed. *The Papers of John Willis Ellis*. 2 vols. Raleigh: State Department of Archives and History, 1964.

Welles, Gideon. *Diary of Gideon Welles, Secretary of the Navy Under Lincoln and Johnson*. 3 vols. Edited by John T. Moore, Jr. New York: Houghton-Mifflin Co., 1911.

Wells, E. L. "A Morning Call on General Kilpatrick." *Southern Historical Society Papers* 12 (1884): 123–30.

Wilkinson, John. *The Narrative of a Blockade Runner*. New York: Sheldon and Co., 1877.

Winther, Oscar O., ed. *With Sherman to the Sea. The Civil War Letters, Diaries and Reminiscences of Theodore F. Upson*. Baton Rouge: Louisiana State University Press, 1943.

Yetman, Norman R., ed. *Life Under the "Peculiar Institution."* New York: Holt, Rinehart and Winston, 1970.

SECONDARY SOURCES

Bardolph, Richard. "Inconstant Rebels: Desertion of North Carolina Troops in the Civil War." *North Carolina Historical Review* 41 (1964): 163–89.

Black, Robert C. *The Railroads of the Confederacy*. Chapel Hill: The University of North Carolina Press, 1952.

Connor, Robert D. W. *North Carolina: Rebuilding an Ancient Commonwealth, 1584–1925*. 4 vols. Chicago and New York: The American Historical Society, Inc., 1929.

Craig, D. I. *A History of the Development of the Presbyterian Church in North Carolina*. Richmond, Va.: Whittet & Shepperson, 1907.

Dodge, David. "Domestic Economy in the Confederacy." *Atlantic Monthly* 58 (August 1886): 229–42.

Dowd, Clement. *Life of Zebulon B. Vance*. Charlotte: Observer Publishing and Printing House, 1897.

Hamilton, Joseph G. de R. "Heroes of America." *Publications of the Southern Historical Association* 11 (January 1907): 10–19.

———. "The North Carolina Courts and the Confederacy." *North Carolina Historical Review* 4 (October 1927): 366–403.

Henman, Wilbur F. *The Story of the Sherman Brigade*. Privately Printed, 1897.

Hill, Daniel Harvey. *A History of North Carolina in the War Between the States*. 2 vols. Raleigh: Edwards and Broughton, 1926.

Hyde, Mrs. Charles R. "The Women of the Confederacy." *Confederate Veteran* 32 (January 1924): 23.

King, Henry T. *Sketches of Pitt County, A Brief History of the County, 1704–1910*. Raleigh: Edwards and Broughton, 1911.

Lefler, Hugh T. and Newsome, Albert R. *North Carolina, The History of a Southern State*. Chapel Hill: The University of North Carolina Press, 1963.

Lonn, Ella. *Desertion During the Civil War*. New York: Century Co., 1928.

———. *Salt as a Factor in the Confederacy*. University, Ala.: University of Alabama Press, 1965.

Lowrey, Laurence T. *Northern Opinion of Approaching Secession*. Northampton, Mass.: Department of History of Smith College, 1918.

McPherson, Edward, comp. *The Political History of the United States of America, During the Great Rebellion from November 6, 1860, to July 4, 1864*. Washington: Government Printing Office, 1865.

Massey, Mary Elizabeth. "The Confederate Refugees in North Carolina." *North Carolina Historical Review* 40 (April 1963): 158–82.

———. *Ersatz in the Confederacy*. Baton Rouge: Louisiana State University Press, 1952.

Mitchell, Memory F. *Legal Aspects of Conscription and Exemption in North Carolina, 1861–1865*. Chapel Hill: The University of North Carolina Press, 1965.

Nelson, B. H. "Some Aspects of Negro Life in North Carolina during the

Civil War." *North Carolina Historical Review* 25 (April 1948): 143–66.

Noble, Marcus C. S. *A History of the Public Schools of North Carolina*. Chapel Hill: The University of North Carolina Press, 1930.

Raper, Horace W. "William W. Holden and the Peace Movement in North Carolina." *North Carolina Historical Review* 31 (October 1954): 493–516.

Shaw, Cornelia R. *Davidson College*. New York: Fleming H. Revell Press, 1923.

Sitterson, Joseph Carlyle. *The Secession Movement in North Carolina*. Chapel Hill: The University of North Carolina Press, 1939.

Sprunt, James. *Chronicles of the Cape Fear River, 1660–1916*. Raleigh: Edwards and Broughton, 1916.

Stick, David. *The Outer Banks of North Carolina, 1584–1958*. Chapel Hill: The University of North Carolina Press, 1958.

Tatum, Georgia Lee. *Disloyalty in the Confederacy*. Chapel Hill: The University of North Carolina Press, 1934.

Thomas, Emory M. *The Confederacy as a Revolutionary Experience*. Englewood Cliffs, N.J.: Prentice-Hall, Inc., 1971.

Vandiver, Frank E. *Their Tattered Flags*. New York: Harper & Row, 1970.

Webb, Elizabeth Yates. "Cotton Manufacturing and State Regulation in North Carolina, 1861–'65." *North Carolina Historical Review* 9 (April 1932): 117–37.

Wood, J. E., ed. *Year Book Pasquotank Historical Society*. 2 vols. Elizabeth City: Historical Society, 1956.

Yates, Richard E. *The Confederacy and Zeb Vance*. Tuscaloosa: University of Alabama Press, 1958.

———. "Governor Vance and the End of the War in North Carolina." *North Carolina Historical Review* 18 (October 1941): 315–38.

———. "Governor Vance and the Peace Movement." *North Carolina Historical Review* 17 (January and April 1940): 1–25, 89–113.

INDEX

WITHDRAWN

DATE DUE

7-8-92			
NOV 20 '96			

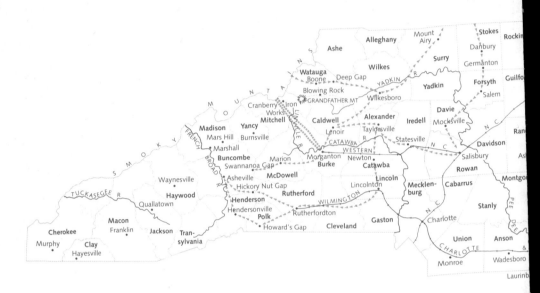

Stokes
Mount
Airy
Alleghany
Rockin
Ashe
Danbury
Wilkes
Surry
Germanton
Watauga
Boone
Deep Gap
Forsyth
Guilfo
Blowing Rock
Wilkesboro
Yadkin
YADKIN
Cranberry
Iron
Works
GRANDFATHER MT
Salem
Madison
Yancy
Mitchell
Caldwell
Alexander
Iredell
Davie
Mars Hill
Burnsville
Lenoir
Taylorsville
Mocksville
Marshall
CATAWBA
Statesville
Ran
WESTERN
Davidson
Buncombe
Marion
Morganton
Newton
N C
Swannanoa Gap
Burke
Catawba
Salisbury
As
Waynesville
Asheville
McDowell
Rowan
Haywood
Hickory Nut Gap
Lincoln
Montgo
Quallatown
Rutherford
Lincolnton
Mecklen-
burg
Cabarrus
Henderson
WILMINGTON
N C
Hendersonville
Stanly
Macon
Polk
Rutherfordton
Franklin
Jackson
Tran-
Howard's Gap
Cleveland
Gaston
Cherokee
sylvania
Charlotte
Murphy
Clay
Union
Anson
Hayesville
CHARLOTTE
&
Monroe
Wadesboro
Laurinb

TUCKASEGEE R
FRENCH BROAD R
SMOKY MOUNTAINS
PEE DEE